POWER & RESPONSIBILITY

BRUCE JONES, CARLOS PASCUAL,
and STEPHEN JOHN STEDMAN

POWER & RESPONSIBILITY

BUILDING INTERNATIONAL ORDER IN AN ERA OF TRANSNATIONAL THREATS

BROOKINGS INSTITUTION PRESS
Washington, D.C.

Library of Congress Cataloging in Publication data
Jones, Bruce D.
    Power and responsibility : building international order in an era of transnational
threats / Bruce Jones, Carlos Pascual, and Stephen John Stedman.
        p.   cm.
    Includes bibliographical references and index.
    Summary: "Makes the case for forming new international partnerships and revitaliz-
ing instruments of cooperation to address global challenges that post-WWII multilateral security systems cannot. Establishes a new conceptual foundation for international
security: 'responsible sovereignty,' which entails obligations and duties and attitudinal
changes toward other states as well one's own"—Provided by publisher.
    ISBN 978-0-8157-4706-2 (cloth : alk. paper)
    1. Security, International. 2. Sovereignty. I. Pascual, Carlos. II. Stedman, Stephen
John. III. Title.
    JZ5588.J66 2009
    355'.033—dc22   2008050917

1 3 5 7 9 8 6 4 2

The paper used in this publication meets minimum requirements of the American
National Standard for Information Sciences—Permanence of Paper for Printed
Library Materials: ANSI Z39.48-1992.

Typeset in Sabon with Ocean display

Composition by Pete Lindeman
Arlington, Virginia

Printed by R. R. Donnelley
Harrisonburg, Virginia

For Elizabeth
For my parents, Carlos and Gladys
For Corinne, Zoé, and Luc

One cannot rise to be in many ways the leading community in the civilized world without being involved in its problems, without being convulsed by its agonies and inspired by its causes. If this has been proved in the past, as it has been, it will become indisputable in the future. The people of the United States cannot escape world responsibility.

WINSTON CHURCHILL

This idea that the UN was and should be different from its members and could assume responsibility without power has been a curiously persistent one.

DEAN ACHESON

With great power comes great responsibility.

STAN LEE

CONTENTS

FOREWORD

JAVIER SOLANA

THE AIM OF THE Managing Global Insecurity project is to launch a reform effort of the global security system in 2009. That task is both ambitious and urgent.

It is clear that globalization remains the dominant trend shaping our world. It has offered millions a chance to live better lives. But globalization has also unleashed forces that governments can neither stop nor control on their own. The list of problems is by now familiar. The "dark side" of globalization requires us to address climate change, nonproliferation, state failure, energy security, and financial instability. In recent years, all these problems have become more urgent and complex. But our capacity to address them has not kept pace.

The question that lies at the heart of this project is this: how do we organize our globalized world? This is a world where problems are mostly global in nature, but where resources and legitimacy are mostly held at the national level. And how do you do that in a world where power is shifting in fundamental ways—both within political systems and between them?

The MGI project is an attempt to find answers. This book assesses the performance of the existing multilateral framework. It analyses the causes of past successes and failures—and draws lessons for the future.

It makes a strong case for how the concept of responsible sovereignty can help us to form much-needed bargains on the pressing global problems of our time.

The book lays out a broad but practical vision. It examines the characteristics of each specific threat and what needs to happen at the global and regional levels to address the challenges presented. It calls our attention to the critical role that states can and should play, but also to the contribution that the private sector, NGOs, and others can make.

It does not shy away from tough problems, for instance, on how we must bring the rising powers into positions at the top table of global politics, through an expanded G-8 and in the UN Security Council. It does so by underlining the twin imperatives for global governance: effectiveness and legitimacy.

It is important that the recommendations here came out of consultations on virtually every continent, and above all with Europe and the rising powers. That kind of dialogue is essential if we are to forge a shared understanding of both the nature of the major problems and the best solutions.

The case for deep reform of the current international system is clear. Today, this must start with the international financial institutions, led by the Group of 20 (G-20). But we need to go further and extend the process to also cover climate change and critical security issues.

The MGI project, through this book and through the Plan for Action published in November 2008, shows us the way forward. The time to act on it is now.

JAVIER SOLANA
Secretary General, Council of the European Union
High Representative for the Common Foreign and Security Policy

FOREWORD

BRENT SCOWCROFT

FOR ALMOST TWO DECADES American foreign policy has been trying to steer us to safety in uncharted waters. Globalization has eroded national borders everywhere and brought new transnational challenges to the fore: weak states, global warming, emerging deadly infectious diseases, and the possibility of catastrophic terrorism. Our security and prosperity depend on robust cooperation with others around the globe.

It is more than troubling that the United States still lacks a forward-looking vision of our role in this new world, and of how best to further the interests of the American people. Since 9/11, fear has been our compass. We have lost touch with America's core ideal: the belief that we can make ourselves, and the rest of the world, better.

It is not just the United States that is foundering. The international institutions that we helped create after World War II need new capacity and direction. At the same time, new divisions in international politics, based on poverty and global inequality, make it impossible for the United States and its traditional allies, Europe and Japan, to dictate reform. Decisionmaking in international organizations needs to reflect changes in international power, especially the importance of rising powers such as China, India, and Brazil.

American leadership is still essential to produce order in these chaotic times, but its exercise must reflect an interdependent world. Consultation, persuasion, and pragmatism need to replace unilateralism and hubris. With the election of a new president, we have an opportunity to break out of the political environment of fear and suspicion.

Based on their extensive international consultations, Bruce Jones, Carlos Pascual, and Stephen Stedman argue that large parts of the world still hope for the United States to exercise enlightened leadership. They show how dedicated efforts can help find cooperative solutions to climate change, nuclear proliferation, biological threats, civil war and regional conflict, terrorism, and poverty and economic instability. By insisting that sovereignty be exercised responsibly, they put human dignity, moral authority, and optimism at the core of international order and American diplomacy. By insisting that power be exercised responsibly, they adapt realism to an interdependent world. The vision, ideas, and solutions they put forward in this book have the potential to redeem American foreign policy.

BRENT SCOWCROFT
President, Scowcroft Group
Former U.S. National Security Adviser

PREFACE

IN ITS OPENING YEARS, the twenty-first century has distinguished itself as an era of paradox. Globalization has created unprecedented opportunities to better the lives of people around the world. The ability to access global markets for capital, technology, and labor has allowed the private sector to amass wealth unfathomable fifty years ago. It has raised incomes for millions of people in emerging economies such as China, India, and Brazil. Indeed, for China, integration into the global economy has driven the most remarkable story of national progress in human history: 500 million people have been raised out of poverty in just thirty years.

Yet the forces of globalization that have stitched the world together can also tear it apart. As seen in the fall 2008 financial crisis, economic turbulence in one country can undermine economic growth half a world away. The spread of nuclear technology and know-how means the most lethal weapons are within the reach of terrorists. The same technologies that speed the transfer of information and capital around the world are used by international criminals for illicit gain. Investments in energy subsidies in one part of the world can contribute to skyrocketing food prices that drive hunger and social unrest in scores of countries. The ease and frequency of international air travel hasten the spread of emerging deadly infectious disease.

The net result of globalization is profound interdependence. Our prosperity and security depend greatly on the actions—or inaction—of people and governments all over the world. But U.S. foreign policy has yet to come to grips with this simple truth.

In an interdependent world, if you need the cooperation of those outside your borders to ensure your own national security, you had better listen to them. They may not get a vote in your elections, but they have an unprecedented impact on whether your foreign policy succeeds or not, indeed even on whether you have the financing needed to bail out failing banks and industries in turbulent times. This insight is fundamental to why we wrote this book as part of the Managing Global Insecurity project, and how we wrote it.

Bruce Jones and Stephen Stedman worked for UN Secretary General Kofi Annan in 2003–05 on the most sweeping effort to transform the United Nations and the larger global security system since 1945. We saw up close the weaknesses and strengths of international cooperation to address security and prosperity. We gained a pretty good sense of what works and what doesn't, and where, in American parlance, the bodies are buried.

We also learned a secret about American foreign policy. Every day Washington, D.C., uses international institutions to help protect the American people. We saw that U.S policymakers are genuinely frustrated at the performance of those institutions and want them to be more effective and efficient. And finally, we saw a yawning gap between what American policymakers want and the vision and capacity to translate this into action.

On issue after issue, whether working on nonproliferation, dealing with regional conflicts, alleviating poverty, or preventing deadly disease, we saw potential gains from cooperation left at the bargaining table. Not all of this was the fault of how Washington engaged the process, but a good portion of it was. Too often the United States did not pay attention to the priorities, fears, and aspirations of others.

In formulating proposals for UN reform, Stedman and Jones traveled to every continent. We engaged in discussions about what people, governments, and NGOs thought were the biggest threats to international security. We learned a simple, but invaluable lesson: depending on one's region, power, and level of prosperity, one sees a world of very different threats.

An example makes the point. When we traveled to Africa to discuss threats to security, and engaged African diplomats around the world, they never once brought up the threat of catastrophic terrorism. They wanted to talk about poverty and deadly disease, especially malaria and HIV/AIDS. And why not, when tens of millions of people have died, more than ten million children are orphans, and those living in some African countries face a life expectancy reduced by more than forty years because of HIV/AIDS?

The three of us first met during the negotiations for the World Summit in 2005. Stedman was special adviser to Kofi Annan, responsible for working with governments to adopt the secretary general's recommendations for UN transformation, and Jones was his deputy, tasked especially to assist the negotiations over a new Peacebuilding Commission and Peacebuilding Support Office at the UN. For much of that time Carlos Pascual was the American interlocutor on these issues as the coordinator for reconstruction and stabilization at the U.S. Department of State. Pascual brought a perspective grounded in the frustrations of developing and implementing American policy at a time when the world was changing radically, yet the instruments and approaches to American policy-making had not.

Working in the National Security Council in the late 1990s on the former Soviet Union, Pascual recognized early the new challenges to effective American policy. American interests seemed best served by Russia, Ukraine, and the other former Soviet states adopting Western notions of democracy and market economics. Attempts were made to bring nations into Western clubs—with Russia it was the G-8, with others the World Trade Organization. But American visions were not necessarily theirs. America could not dictate outcomes for others.

Limitations in the use of American power became poignant after 9/11. Serving in Ukraine as American ambassador, Pascual could see the emerging split between the United States and Europe. The dark side of globalization had struck against the United States. Americans were poised to retaliate. Europeans looked on in sympathy and with anxiety. But the United States and Europe never reached consensus on a global response to transnational terrorism.

By 2004 when Secretary Powell tasked Pascual to start an interagency office at the State Department on reconstruction and stabilization after conflict, American rhetoric had changed. The U.S. National Security Strategy declared that weak states threatened the United States more than aggressive ones. Yet rhetoric still had not translated into a willingness to invest in the international institutions needed to succeed in statecraft.

When Pascual, Stedman, and Jones met on plans for a new UN Peacebuilding Commission, the congruity of experience at the UN and in Washington became striking. Global challenges had become the rhetoric of international policy. It was not accompanied, however, by the political investment to change policy or build capacity. Suggestions to more than tweak the status quo were rejected as extravagance.

The three of us left our last postings feeling the same way: that the institutions we had worked for could, and had to, do better at achieving results. We decided from the start to try a different approach to thinking about American foreign policy, one that better reflected a globalized, interconnected world. We believed that now was a historic opportunity for a convergence of American interests and the resolution of global problems. And believing that a successful American policy is one that must resonate in capitals around the world, we wanted to craft recommendations that could win bipartisan support within the United States, while also winning support internationally.

We set ourselves a tall order. It is much easier to prescribe American foreign policy if you don't take the rest of the world into account. (And vice versa for that matter: global discussions about what American policy should be are much more elegant if they don't take into account American interests and needs!) We benefited from two extraordinary advisory groups that guided us—one American and bipartisan, one international. Both were composed of experienced leaders who have thought hard about how the world is changing and how national policy and international institutions need to be transformed. We brought these groups together for meetings in Washington, D.C., New York City, Ditchley Park in the U.K., Singapore, and Berlin. Advisory group members arranged for consultations with government officials, foreign policy elites, and NGOs in European cities, Delhi, Beijing, Tokyo, Doha, Mexico City, at the UN, and with African representatives in Washington and New York. In the United States, we met with congressional and administration officials as well as foreign policy advisers to the U.S. presidential campaigns. Both in the United States and internationally, groups of leading experts reviewed our threat-specific analysis and proposals, and leading foreign policy scholars reviewed our manuscript as a whole.

For eighteen months we created a simultaneous dialogue—American and global—about today's threats, the changing nature of security, what kind of international order is needed to make the world more peaceful, the meaning of sovereignty, and America's role in the world. Working issues both domestically and internationally made this venture much more difficult than if we had kept this an American conversation. But our global conversations convinced us that in 2009, a new American president should put forward a bold vision of international cooperation that will resonate around the world, a vision based on states exercising their sovereignty responsibly and cooperating to address threats that defy borders and pose grave challenges to our planet—from nuclear proliferation, civil war and failed states, and climate change to terrorism, infectious disease, and global poverty.

This book is the second of two products from the project. The first, an action plan, was launched in November 2008 and is available at www.brookings.edu/reports/2008/11_action_plan_mgi.aspx. Based on the analysis here, the plan suggests a set of concrete policies for the Obama administration and other governments around the world to adopt in 2009 and 2010 in order to bolster international cooperation against transnational threats. Put into action, these policies would begin to build the international order that we describe in these pages.

We launched our action plan days after the first-ever meeting of G-20 leaders. Called by President Bush in response to the 2008 financial crisis, the G-20 set out an agenda for coordinating policy and beginning deep reform of the international financial institutions. The group's actions mirrored a central argument of this book: that political cooperation between the major powers, including through an expanded G-8, is the critical first step toward forging common strategy and revitalizing international institutions, both necessary for managing transnational threats.

The G-20 meeting was called after the financial crisis had wiped out two trillion dollars from global stock markets, and after years of stalled efforts to improve the oversight functions of the International Monetary Fund. Such a delayed reaction to the eroding arrangements for nuclear nonproliferation would lead to catastrophic consequences, and the world could not tolerate such a delay in building up our defenses against infectious disease before the first deliberate release of a deadly biological pathogen. When it comes to climate change and our security we cannot afford to wait before investing in the concepts, tools, and institutions of a more robust international order. We hope our book stimulates debate and action toward that goal.

ACKNOWLEDGMENTS

WE COULD NOT HAVE undertaken this ambitious agenda without the concerted support of a Managing Global Insecurity (MGI) project network that we built both domestically and internationally. The hub of this network is made up of our U.S. and international Advisory Group members. For the time they took from exceedingly busy schedules to contribute to our endeavors, we thank Madeleine Albright, Richard Armitage, Sandy Berger, Howard Berman, Chip Blacker, Sylvia Mathews Burwell, Fernando Henrique Cardoso, Chester Crocker, Lawrence Eagleburger, Jan Eliasson, Ashraf Ghani, Jeremy Greenstock, Rima Hunaidi, Anwar Ibrahim, Wolfgang Ischinger, Igor Ivanov, Wu Jianmin, Kishore Mahbubani, Lalit Mansingh, Vincent Maphai, Paul Martin, Ayo Obe, Sadako Ogata, William Perry, Thomas Pickering, John Podesta, Salim Salim, Brent Scowcroft, Abraham Sofaer, Javier Solana, Strobe Talbott, Timothy Wirth, and James Wolfensohn.

We are particularly indebted to Strobe Talbott and Javier Solana for their leadership on the project and the tenacity and energy they have shown us in tackling the complexities of revitalizing global governance.

Organizations and individuals providing financial and in-kind support for MGI have also formed an integral part of the MGI network and made our work possible. We thank the Ford Foundation, the William and Flora Hewlett Foundation, the John D. and Catherine T. MacArthur Foundation, the Rockefeller Brothers Fund, and the UN Foundation. MGI also received funding and in-kind support to facilitate global consultations from the Bertelsmann Stiftung, the Ditchley Foundation, the Ministry of Foreign Affairs of Finland, the Royal Ministry of Foreign Affairs of Norway, the Lee Kuan Yew School of Public Policy, and several individual donors. In addition to the many members of our MGI Advisory Group who participated in MGI events, we thank Martti Ahtisaari, Francis Deng, Kemal Dervis, Mohamed ElBaradei, Joschka Fisher, Chuck Hagel, Ban Ki-Moon, Rajenda Pachauri, George Soros, and Frank-Walter Steinmeier for giving their time to join us in workshops and public events. It would be impossible to name all the participants in our meetings and everyone who commented on some of our materials, and we thank them again for their understanding and generosity.

In writing this book we had the benefit of drawing from a series of case studies from leading regional and subject experts who evaluated the performance of international regimes in the hardest cases. Jon B. Alterman, Sarjoh Bah, Daniel Benjamin, Robert Carlin, Alex Evans, Ann Florini, Ashraf Ghani, Richard Gowan, John Wilson Lewis, Peter M. Lewis, Khalid Mustafa Medani, George Perkovich, Steven Pifer, Kenneth Pollack, Pavel Podvig, Bruce Riedel, Eric Rosand, Barnett R. Rubin, Scott Sagan, Adam Townsend, and Christine Wing provided a rich substantive base for our recommendations.

We appreciate the time and energy of officials and former officials in the United States and around the world who contributed to our agenda. Officials from foreign affairs agencies including many foreign ministers, political directors, policy planning staff, national security advisers, ambassadors, and deputy chiefs of mission of Australia, Brazil, China, Colombia, Czech Republic, Finland, France, Germany, India, Italy, Japan, Mexico, New Zealand, Norway, South Africa, Spain, and the United Kingdom all contributed time to us. We thank numerous diplomatic missions, especially in Washington and New York, which hosted meetings, lunches, and dinners to facilitate our consultations. In the United States, we received feedback and counsel from officials in the U.S. Congress, National Security Council, the Department of State and of Defense, and the intelligence services.

We are grateful to our manuscript readers, some who read the whole book and others individual chapters. They raised the right questions, contributed extensive expertise, and provided a fresh take on many of our recommendations and approaches: Ken Bernard, Chip Blacker, Colin Bradford, Tarun Chhabra, Larry Diamond, Lynn Eden, Jonathan Elkind, Ann Florini, Shepard Forman, Jim Goldgeier, Michael O'Hanlon, Homi Kharas, Johannes Linn, Michael McFaul, Lex Rieffel, Peter A. Singer, Anne-Marie Slaughter, Abe Sofaer, Strobe Talbott, and Achilles Zaluar. We extend a big thanks to Dick and Faith Morningstar for providing their house for a writing retreat.

MGI has also benefited from partnerships, dialogue, and joint events with numerous organizations in the United States and around the world including the European Council on Foreign Relations; Munich Conference on Security Policy; Center for European Reform; Salzburg Global Seminar; Finnish Institute of International Affairs; European Union Institute for Security Studies; Danish Institute for International Affairs; Japan Institute for International Affairs; China Foreign Affairs University; Brookings-Tsinghua Center at Tsinghua University (Beijing); Centre for Global Studies (India); U.S.-Islamic World Forum (Doha); Lowy Institute for International Policy (Australia); National Defense Advisory Board (India); Institute of Peace and Conflict Studies (India); Institute for Public Policy Research (U.K.); Center on the U.S. and Europe and Saban Center at Brookings; Conflict Prevention Program and Program on Global Governance, Council on Foreign Relations; Aspen Institute; Center for International Governance Innovation (Canada); and the United States Institute of Peace.

We are indebted to those who helpfully prodded and cajoled us to finish this book. We express our sincere gratitude to the staff at the Brookings Institution Press for their patience and flexibility, including Bob Faherty, Janet Walker, Chris Kelaher, and our tireless copyeditors, Rene Howard and Eileen Hughes. We also benefited from early editing by Steve Strasser.

We are especially indebted to MGI's core research team and staff— Holly Benner, Jessie Duncan, and Kathy Wyporek at the Brookings Institution; Catherine Bellamy and Richard Gowan at New York University's Center on International Cooperation; and Kate Chadwick at Stanford University's Center for International Security and Cooperation. We also thank Sara Batmanglich, Alexa Van Brunt, Miriam Estrin, Paul Flach, Andrew Hart, Nick Marwell, Adam Pienciak, Michele Shapiro, Aiza Siddiqi, and Devorah West for their research and event support. We are also indebted to the Foreign Policy Studies administration, finance, and communications staff at Brookings for their contributions to ensure the success of the project, including Adrienne Anzanello, Charlotte Baldwin, Julia Cates, Gail Chalef, and Peggy Knudson.

Finally, we want to thank our loved ones for putting up with extended absences and the general grumpiness that accompanies writing a book.

It is customary to say that despite the impressive amount and exceptional quality of advice we received during the writing of the book, we alone are responsible for errors, misstatements, and bad sentences. This time, however, it is the fault of the other coauthors.

POWER

ONE

SOVEREIGNTY'S LAST BEST CHANCE

WHEN IT COMES TO THREATS to global security, there has been no shortage of wake-up calls. Transnational criminals illegally traffic sophisticated nuclear technology to unstable regimes in the most conflict-prone regions of the world. Terrorist groups that seek to inflict mass casualties are found with training materials on using biological weapons. Sea levels rise, droughts last longer and longer, and storms are more frequent. Skyrocketing energy prices lead to astronomical rises in food costs, prompting riots and warnings of food emergencies in poor countries. Economic turbulence and insecurity drain savings and jobs in large parts of the world. Deadly viruses cross borders, continents, and species.

This is the world of transnational threats, where the actions—or inaction—of people and governments anywhere in the world can harm others thousands of miles away. It is a world where national security is interdependent with global security and where sovereign states acting alone are incapable of protecting their citizens. It is a world for which we are woefully unprepared.

It is also a world in which American leadership has been shallow and sometimes misguided, but is greatly needed. It is a world where major and rising powers must agree to cooperate through strong international institutions and embrace new standards of responsibility for all states, so that their peoples can be safe and prosper. This book proposes how.

THE INTERDEPENDENCE OF NATIONAL
SECURITY AND GLOBAL SECURITY

A profound but underappreciated truth about globalization is the extent to which national security and international security have become inseparably linked. This is true even in the most powerful countries. In the United States, for example, most Americans would agree on a short list of threats to their national security: transnational terrorism, proliferation of nuclear weapons, a pandemic of a new deadly disease, global warming, and economic instability and crisis. What stands out is that these threats can affect every country's security.

Nor do the threats that preoccupy other parts of the world stand in isolation. Poverty, civil wars, and regional conflicts are all connected to what threatens the United States. Transnational terrorism uses ungovernable spaces for sanctuary and to gather recruits, capital, and weapons, and it uses a narrative of grievance stoked by protracted civil and regional conflicts. Climate change exacerbates competition for land and water and places greater burdens on the poor. Poverty not only increases the risks of civil war and state failure but also precipitates the emergence of deadly infectious diseases.

The interconnectedness of these threats and their cumulative effect pose grave dangers to the ability of states to protect their sovereignty. For many states the domestic burdens of poverty, civil war, disease, and environmental degradation point in one direction: toward partnerships and agreements with international institutions. Entering agreements or accepting assistance does not weaken sovereignty; it preserves it.[1] Even stronger states, to preserve sovereignty, must enter into agreements to counter transnational threats such as deadly infectious disease and nuclear proliferation that cannot be overcome in the absence of sustained international cooperation.

U.S. foreign policy has yet to come to grips with the implications of security interdependence. Especially in the last seven years, Washington has elevated one threat—transnational terrorism—above global warming, poverty, deadly disease, and other dangers, neglecting to notice that terrorism is the least salient threat to many states and that most of these threats affect each other. The United States has not seen the wisdom of placing threats to its security in a global framework. And that neglect has cost it much in the way of international cooperation. The reality of a world of interconnected and transnational threats is a simple one: you have to cooperate with others to get them to cooperate with you.

THE POST–COLD WAR INTERNATIONAL VOID

Writing in 2008, we are seventeen years into the post–cold war era and seven years into the post–9/11 era, and some pundits now advocate the need for a "post-post–9/11 foreign policy," without much indication of what that might be. All of which is to say that we live in a foreign policy void, bereft of vision. We understand that the world has changed, but our institutions, policies, and leaders have not fully comprehended how profound that change has been.

Our international institutions to promote cooperation for peace and prosperity were all designed in a different era of different threats and different power relations. This does not mean they are obsolete. Some have shown remarkable resiliency, while others have adapted in rather ad hoc fashion to changing realities. It is better that we have them than not, but they are inadequate to produce the capacity and collective action to address predictably today's new threats. Similarly, new international norms have emerged, but these have been of the "what should be done" as opposed to the "what will be done" variety. As a result, international order is now frayed; we have commitments without compliance and resolutions without resolve. We lack predictability and confidence in international responses to today's challenges.

International order requires a source of power, and since the Second World War, the United States has been that source. The United States led in the creation of international security and financial institutions, and when those institutions work effectively, they help meet America's security interests as well as those of its friends and allies, and indeed those of all but the most recalcitrant states.

For much of the second half of the twentieth century, key allies of the United States and many of their citizens regarded the United States as a vital provider of international order. That belief has vanished. Fewer people around the world accept or trust American power—or regard it as legitimate. International public opinion polls over the last several years show that many people believe that U.S. foreign policy has made the world a more dangerous place since 2001.[2]

The 2003 invasion of Iraq casts a long shadow on America's standing in the world and its relations with friends and competitors alike. But it would be wrong to trace all of America's difficulties to the decision to go to war or its conduct of the war. Rather, America's standing in the world today reflects a fifteen-year failure to create the rules and institutions of international order.

When the Soviet Union collapsed, American military strength was unrivaled. Democracy and liberal capitalism, the ideological alternatives to communism, were triumphant. America's economic wealth and power were ascendant. Both U.S. presidents since 1992, William J. Clinton and George W. Bush, had historical opportunities to reinvigorate international cooperation and put in place new international institutions, rules, and understandings appropriate for today's world.

The end of the cold war was a moment akin to the end of other great-power wars, a time ripe for making sweeping international changes to refashion international order. The Clinton administration in the 1990s understandably believed that the U.S. challenge at hand was to incorporate Russia and Central and Eastern Europe into a democratic community—and beyond that to fashion post–cold war diplomacy into a driver of global peace and prosperity. They expanded NATO and sought to anchor Russia, and later in the 1990s, China, into international financial institutions. They worked hard to address the effects of the Soviet breakup on nuclear proliferation, instituting new programs to deal with loose nukes, working with new governments in Ukraine, Belarus, and Kazakhstan to give up nuclear missiles on their territory.

Beyond the challenge of cold war reconstruction, there was the need to bring cohesion to an increasingly diverse world, characterized by more actors that could disrupt, fewer actors that could control, and greater opportunity in global markets, yet greater risk in the movement of pollution, disease, and weapons across borders. The Clinton administration concluded international negotiations on a comprehensive nuclear test ban treaty, global warming, an international criminal court, and a new World Trade Organization.

But the Clinton administration, by its own admission, never formulated a global vision of order, and it was largely silent on how the rest of the world would fit into a peaceful, democratic community.[3] Like many other governments, it dimly understood that the challenge of international order was changing dramatically. In a remarkably prescient article published in 1992, James Goldgeier and Michael McFaul described a world that was rapidly splitting in two: a largely peaceful democratic and liberal core, where Kant triumphed over Hobbes, and a violent periphery of weak, fragile states, corrupt and feeble markets, and ideologies hostile to liberal ideas.[4] Analysts like Robert Kaplan and John Steinbruner observed that if the security issues of the periphery could not be contained, they would corrode the order and predictability necessary for prosperity and peace.[5]

Despite its larger support for international institutions and partnerships, the Clinton administration frequently derided the one international institution with operational responsibility for failed states: the United Nations. The Clinton administration blamed the organization for failure in Somalia, which entrenched anti-UN sentiment in Congress, and in the immediate aftermath of the Somalia debacle, it supported the withdrawal of peacekeepers during the genocide in Rwanda. In Iraq, the administration's early cooperation with the United Nations Special Commission (UNSCOM) deteriorated into what one analyst described as "creeping unilateralism," in which the Clinton administration took upon itself the right to decide how UN Security Council resolutions would be implemented.[6] It was the Clinton administration, in 1998, that declared regime change as the U.S. goal in Iraq.[7]

The U.S. failure to strengthen the United Nations and address the security issues of the periphery—poverty, weak states, civil war, and regional instability—made the world a more dangerous place over the last fifteen years. And those security issues erupted on September 11, 2001, when terrorists based in one of the world's poorest, most violence-torn regions carried out the most deadly attack on U.S. territory in history.

The 9/11 attacks changed American views about security. The Bush administration began to understand that failed states and ungoverned space in the international system were resources for transnational terrorism and organized crime. But whereas 9/11 changed threat assessments, it powerfully reinforced the administration's unilateral tendencies.

It is easy to forget the outpouring of international empathy, concern, and friendship for the United States after the September attacks, and the many offers of assistance. The battle against transnational terrorism, shared with China, India, and Europe, presaged the possibility of extensive cooperation among these powers. American policy and leadership at that moment could have transformed international order.

Instead, all the goodwill became a second wasted opportunity. The United States shut out its NATO allies from Afghanistan in the fall of 2001, only to realize by the summer of 2002 that it needed them. Instead of focusing on defeating al Qaeda and its Taliban supporters in Afghanistan, the Bush administration declared a global war on terror—with no boundaries and no finite end—that alienated allies and potential collaborators in the Arab world and beyond. Its willful, driven pursuit of war in Iraq poisoned international cooperation.[8] Coupled with a new national security doctrine that embraced preventive war, along with casual references to forcible regime change as its preferred method of dealing with rogue states, the United States set itself up as self-appointed sheriff and judge of the international system.

The global war on terror squandered one of the United States' great assets: its reputation for protecting and promoting human rights and the rule of law. Guantánamo, Abu Ghraib, torture, and rendition destroyed U.S. credibility on human rights in large parts of the world, especially in Muslim-populated countries.

Like the end of the cold war, 9/11 was a potentially transformative moment. Leaders could have rebuilt international cooperation to last deep into the twenty-first century. Unlike President Clinton, who strove toward a stronger international order, but did not have the vision and strategy to reach it, President Bush did not even try.

Historically it has taken war or crisis to bring about a fundamental transformation of international order. The failure to seize the opportunities afforded by the end of the cold war and 9/11 creates a much more difficult challenge: to use the urgency of looming existential security challenges to prompt global action before their worst consequences are felt.

RESPONSIBLE SOVEREIGNTY

Rebuilding international order will require focusing on specific institutions for addressing specific threats—and making them effective. But as a prerequisite it also requires a vision, a foundational principle that gives a moral value to order and brings coherence to expectations about how states should act across multiple issue areas. Such a principle must appeal to diverse populations in every region of the world, win the support of key states, and resonate with America's self-image.

We believe that responsible sovereignty, or the injunction that sovereignty entails obligations and duties to one's own citizens and to other sovereign states, is such a principle. Responsible sovereignty differs from the traditional interpretation of sovereignty (sometimes called *Westphalian sovereignty*) as noninterference in the internal affairs of states. As initially articulated by African statesman and scholar Francis Deng in the 1990s, responsible sovereignty meant "that national governments are duty bound to ensure minimum standards of security and social welfare for their citizens and be accountable both to the national body public and the international community."[9]

In this book we refine and extend the concept and apply it to diverse transnational threats to formulate solutions. We argue that responsible sovereignty requires all states to be accountable for their actions that have impacts beyond their borders, and makes such reciprocity a core principle in restoring international order and for providing for the welfare of one's own citizens. In a world of interdependent security, states cannot exercise their responsibility to their own citizens without also exercising it in concert with other states. Responsible sovereignty also implies a positive obligation on the part of powerful states to provide weaker states with the capacity to exercise their sovereignty responsibly—a "responsibility to build."

Why an order based on responsible sovereignty? We emphasize *sovereignty* because states are still the primary units of the international system. As much as globalization has diminished the power of states, and as much as sovereignty has been used as a shield to protect governments from accountability for their behavior, it is hard to think of any major international problem that can be addressed without responsible, capable states. States create incentives and disincentives for social and economic actors, from nongovernmental organizations (NGOs) to businesses, within their borders. And we know from example the horrific consequences for citizens of states that fail. Sovereignty also reaffirms states as the central decisionmakers in international cooperation. As a former head of state told us, "International cooperation depends first and foremost on decisions taken by governments to cooperate."

Sovereignty's moral justification over the centuries is that it helps to produce international order—the regular, patterned behavior of states that reduces violence, ensures that commitments are kept, and enforces stable property rights.[10] Sovereignty, the external recognition of governmental authority over a territory, provides the legal autonomy of governments to choose the international agreements they will enter into and the policies they will pursue to protect and provide for their citizens.

Traditional sovereignty, and its emphasis on noninterference in domestic affairs, developed as a norm because in a world of vastly unequal powers and never-ending interventions in the affairs of other states, it was the best generator of order, reciprocity, and predictability among states. It also protected weaker states from the predation of stronger states. Sovereignty had its costs, but its benefit was international order.

We emphasize *responsibility* because in a transnational world, traditional sovereignty has failed to produce order and in important cases has actually undermined it. When he first introduced the concept of sovereignty as responsibility in 1993,[11] Deng felt that traditional sovereignty had failed his continent. Waves of humanitarian emergencies in the 1980s and early 1990s met indifference among some African states as millions of their citizens died. Traditional sovereignty posed a constraint on international access to the victims of famine and civil war.

Deng's work focused on the gap between the juridical sovereignty of Africa's postcolonial states, based on external recognition, and the empirical sovereignty of those states: the legitimate monopoly over the use of coercion, the ability to extract resources and use them for development, the provision of security to citizens, and the promotion of their human dignity. Too many states in Africa, according to Deng, hid behind juridical sovereignty to mask their failures in achieving empirical sovereignty. The result was civil wars that spilled over borders, producing regional insecurity. In short, disorder within states became disorder across states. For Deng, when states manifestly failed to provide for the basic survival needs of their population, powerful, capable states had an obligation to help the victims.

Deng's work was pathbreaking in two ways. First, it transformed expectations about sovereignty and the obligations of states in Africa. As late as 1990, one scholar, Robert Jackson, asserted that the international regime of quasi-states—the name he gave to the tens of juridical, but ineffective, states—was unlikely to change because of a powerful taboo that operates "silently as a form of self-censorship by virtually all agents and representatives of states and international organizations and adds decisive normative sanction to the traditional reluctance of diplomats to engage in public criticism of each other's domestic affairs."[12] Deng's work breached that taboo. Prominent African leaders like Olusegun Obasanjo and Salim Salim took up the concept in the 1990s and pursued a Conference on Security, Stability, and Development Cooperation in Africa (CSSDCA), inspired by the Helsinki process in Europe in the 1970s. The vision and ideas negotiated in the CSSDCA helped shape the far-sighted charter of the African Union and its Peace and Security Council, adopted in 2002.[13]

Second, Deng's work helped redefine sovereignty away from then-current interpretations based on strict noninterference in the domestic affairs of states. His emphasis on the responsibility of others to protect the citizens of failed states was picked up in 2001 by an international panel led by Gareth Evans and Mahmoud Sahnoun. That panel coined the term "responsibility to protect"—the injunction that although states have primary responsibility for protecting their citizens from genocide, ethnic cleansing, and mass atrocities, the international community has a responsibility to intervene if a state is unable or unwilling to do so.[14] In 2004, a group of eminent individuals, the High-Level Panel on Threats, Challenges, and Change, supported the principle.[15] In 2005, the African Group at the United Nations, led by Rwanda and South Africa, fought a tough battle to win General Assembly endorsement of the principle.

The universal endorsement of the responsibility to protect by all UN member states was, in some ways, the clearest evidence of a sea change in the understanding of sovereignty. This shift has taken place in a remarkably short amount of time. As recently as 1999, then Secretary General Kofi Annan addressed the General Assembly and spoke of the need for acceptance of humanitarian intervention to address genocide and ethnic cleansing, only to be sharply criticized by many members of the G-77 developing countries and the Nonaligned Movement. Merely six years later, the General Assembly accepted that sovereignty was not sacrosanct, that it imposed positive obligations on states in their treatment of their own citizens and in their response to genocide and crimes against humanity.

The moment brought the United Nations closer to shifts in understanding of sovereignty emerging in different regions of the world, enshrined in the constitutive acts of regional organizations such as the African Union, the Organization of American States, and the European Union. That moment also brought the General Assembly's interpretation of sovereignty closer to UN practice since the end of the cold war. During the cold war, the United Nations and regional organizations seldom sought to prevent or mediate civil violence within states. Failing states insisted that diplomacy aimed at managing internal violence violated their sovereignty and degraded their legitimacy by treating the state and rebels as equals. Now, when civil wars break out, it is normal and expected that outsiders attempt to mediate an end to violence.

Similarly, during the cold war UN peacekeepers were mostly used in interstate disputes. It was barely conceivable that states would deign to admit neutral international soldiers to their territory during civil war. Today, the overwhelming bulk of peacekeepers are deployed to resolve internal violence. Such interventions are justified not only because they save lives; they are carried out to create states that are *capable* of exercising their sovereignty. The result has been a 40 percent reduction in civil wars between 1993 and 2005, one of the most dramatic declines in numbers of civil wars in the past 200 years.[16]

The challenges to traditional sovereignty have grown more acute since the end of the cold war. In many parts of the world, the state is weak and overwhelmed by a host of transnational threats. Technological and economic developments have further eroded the ability of states to control borders and populations. The interdependence of national and international security further requires the interpretation of sovereignty we propose here. For example, to protect its citizens against the ravages of climate change, a state must exercise its sovereignty to enter into cooperative agreements with other states to constrain carbon emissions.

An emphasis on responsible sovereignty helps address a problem pointed out by many scholars of international cooperation: In a world of self-interested states, who is concerned with the medium to long term?[17] How does one create what those scholars refer to as "the shadow of the future," the sense that our interactions will continue long into the future and require consideration in what we do now?[18] Responsible sovereignty introduces medium- to long-term considerations into calculations of narrow state interest and places issues of trust and reputation at center stage.

By putting responsible sovereignty at the heart of international order, we seek to calibrate the content of sovereignty with the challenges of order in a radically different international environment. In some ways this is nothing new: sovereignty's content has varied throughout history, and its rules for recognition and intervention have changed over time.[19] Traditionally, renegotiation of sovereignty has been the purview of great powers, which at times of seismic shifts in global politics perceive new threats to the stability of the international system and attempt to alter sovereignty to meet those new threats. The challenge in today's globalized world is to open up the process beyond a few great powers.

Such a renegotiation is long overdue. The last global attempt to define the content of sovereignty was the creation of the United Nations in 1945. Its creators enshrined nonintervention. Simultaneously, they affirmed self-determination for nations going through decolonization, and they introduced universal human rights to guide the internal practice of sovereignty. The irony is that these rules, thought to be complementary in the UN Charter, have been anything but. On one hand, many people look to the United Nations as an embodiment of an international commitment to universal rights, which can be seen as eroding sovereignty. On the other hand, the United Nations has been a strong defender of the sovereignty of deadly states. Still, a consensus is growing: global security will decrease unless a way can be found to encourage more responsibility in the internal and external policies of states.

What we propose here is on one level deeply conservative: we seek to strengthen and enhance sovereignty, not eliminate it, as a linchpin of international order. On another level, what we propose here is transformative: it insists that in the twenty-first century, sovereignty can be preserved only through its responsible exercise. Maximalist interpretations of sovereignty—states can do as they damned well please—will endanger the essence of sovereignty: the freedom to decide on how best to protect one's citizens and promote their well-being and dignity. State failure will be more frequent in the face of climate-induced hardship and conflict, pandemics of infectious disease, and assaults by nonstate actors. Pursued to its natural end, maximalist sovereignty will gradually and inevitably constrict the freedom of states, even the strongest and richest, to determine their own policies.

WHO DEFINES RESPONSIBILITY?

A vision of international order based on responsible sovereignty will prompt predictable criticisms from all sides. International audiences will assert that this is an American attempt to circumscribe traditional sovereignty, that it is about the powerful dictating standards of behavior for small, weak states, and that it will be a one-sided determination of what it means to be responsible. Americans will want to know if others will dictate what it means for the United States to be responsible, whether the order we suggest will respect American institutions and ideals, whether it will provide greater security and prosperity than a world in which the United States maintains maximum freedom of action—and indeed whether the United States will somehow be constrained in its ability to protect itself.

The compelling answer to these concerns is that the rules of this new order must be negotiated, not imposed. Gone are the days when the largest powers could simply dictate the rules of international engagement; and the idea that international institutions can impose rules on states is a myth, not a reality.

Throughout this book we apply the principle of responsible sovereignty to key global issues—nuclear disarmament and nonproliferation, counterterrorism, global warming, biological security, peacekeeping and peacebuilding, and economic prosperity—but always derive those standards of responsibility from existing international treaties, conventions, and forums to which the United States and others have agreed. Where we encounter new international challenges that demand new commitments, we suggest directions for extending responsibility, but insist that its content must be negotiated.

Sovereign states must remain the fundamental unit of a viable international system. Yet each state must recognize that the only way to protect those within its borders is to take responsibility for national actions that have impacts beyond borders. In effect, we must recognize today's reality: we *do* affect one another, and by reaching agreement on how we *should* affect one another, we stand in the best position to protect ourselves and create an environment that fosters security for all.

Some will argue that democracy, not responsible sovereignty, should be the bedrock of international order. As we make clear in the book, democracy and human rights have a central role in an international system based on responsible sovereignty. Most fundamentally, these values are enshrined in the Universal Declaration of Human Rights, a founding document of the United Nations. Moreover, responsible sovereignty emphasizes the obligations of states toward their citizens, and by making human dignity a core value to be promoted, it has the promise of creating a world in which individuals can reach their human potential, and, in the words of the UN Charter, live their lives "in larger freedom."

A foreign policy driven by responsible sovereignty, however, departs from a foreign policy driven by democracy promotion in two respects. The first is that it acknowledges that nondemocracies influence international order as much as democracies. Democratic states need the cooperation of, and must engage, nondemocratic states, whether it be to halt global warming, stop an outbreak of deadly infectious disease, or prevent catastrophic terrorism. Exclusion is not the answer. The second, as we elaborate further in chapter 9, is that a foreign policy driven by responsible sovereignty insists that democracy must be achieved from within and cannot be imposed. This does not preclude democracy promotion, but it does insist that it is done with prudence and a better understanding of the limits of what outsiders can accomplish.

THE ARGUMENT

International order in an age of transnational threats requires power in the service of responsibility. Major powers must be convinced to exercise their sovereignty responsibly, and weak states must become capable of exercising their sovereignty responsibly. Building this order depends on four prerequisites: effective international leadership by the United States; institutionalized cooperation between the United States and the major and rising powers; negotiated understandings of the applicability of responsible sovereignty to different issues; and effective institutions that provide legitimacy, mobilize resources, and coordinate multiple actors toward common goals.

Part I of the book, the opening three chapters, addresses the role of power in creating an international order based on responsible sovereignty. In chapter 2 we make a case for why an order based on responsible sovereignty is in the interest of the United States and other powers.

The United States needs strong international institutions to combat threats to its citizenry, including climate change, nuclear proliferation, deadly infectious disease, and catastrophic terrorism. It needs strong partners to wield influence with actors such as North Korea and Iran, and to share the burden of complex challenges. It is in America's self-interest to act now while its influence is strong, to model leadership for the twenty-first century based on the premise of partnership and recognition of interdependence.

Internationally, policymakers must recognize that there is no prospect for international order in the next twenty years that does not rely on U.S. power and leadership. The United States has the world's largest economy, the strongest military, and the broadest alliances. The world needs the United States to use its leadership and resources for the resolution of transnational threats. If the United States blocks international solutions on issues such as climate change, nuclear security, and financial stability, sustainable global outcomes are unachievable. The United States has veto power across key international institutions; without its acquiescence, major reforms are unattainable.

In chapter 3 we introduce the single most important innovation for the order we propose: an institution to foster dynamic, cooperative interaction among the United States, other major powers, and the rising powers—who together must lead in forging effective solutions to transnational threats. To this end we call for the creation of a G-16—the smallest (and therefore most efficient) number of states that includes all the major and rising powers and key regional states.[20] This would not be an expansion of the G-8, but a new body that will build consensus among the leading powers on transnational threats and challenges; forge networks between policymakers in these states and key international institutions; and prenegotiate agreements before seeking broader international endorsement and legitimation of them. In addition to elaborating on the functions and design of the G-16, we examine the central role the United Nations plays in peace and security, and we describe how to strengthen its core functions, widen its scope on transnational threats, and revitalize its management. We highlight the role that regional organizations can play in strengthening international order and indicate how they can be bolstered, or where they do not currently exist, how they can be created.

In part II of the book, chapters 4 through 9, we show how responsible sovereignty and the support of the United States and other powers can make a tangible difference in coping with transnational threats. Three threats to U.S. and global security pose existential danger and if their worst case is realized will threaten species, societies, and the planet's ecosystem: climate change, proliferation and use of nuclear weapons, and abuse of new discoveries in biotechnology. At the same time that these existential threats mount, civil and regional conflicts fester, states languish in poverty, and terrorism spreads. Two of these threats—civil and regional conflict, and terrorism—can become vectors for the existential threats of proliferation and use of nuclear and biological weapons. Poverty increases the risk of civil war, regional conflict, and deadly infectious disease, and robs states of the capacity to act in the face of transnational threats. Severe economic crises and instability create an environment that hinders states from seeking cooperative solutions to transnational threats. Because of interdependence, global security is only as strong as the weakest link, and international order depends on effective states with the capacity to exercise their sovereignty responsibly against all these threats.

These chapters illustrate how responsible sovereignty can be a foundational principle for international cooperation against transnational threats; they also identify the institutional arrangements to best align actors and capabilities to fit the problem. The United Nations, for example, should have a leadership role in coordinating postconflict peacekeeping or meeting emergency humanitarian needs.

In other areas the UN will not lead but will offer a platform to scrutinize commitments and performance (for example, on poverty eradication), or create a forum to negotiate international agreements (for example, climate change), or contribute operationally to building state capacity (for example, training in the rule of law). Similarly, roles will vary for other global, regional, and national actors and for the private sector and NGOs.

This is not multilateralism à la carte. Institutional alignment on given problems must be predictable in order to promote stability. Predictability comes from agreed standards of responsible sovereignty and from investment in institutions so that they deliver.

In part III of the book we discuss what an international order based on responsibility can deliver. Global leaders must have confidence that a twenty-first-century international security system will produce better outcomes on the crises at the top of their national security agendas. Otherwise they will not invest the necessary resources and political energy to cultivate global partnerships and effective international institutions.

In chapter 10 we show how an international order based on responsible sovereignty can help in the hardest case, the broader Middle East. The Middle East is the most unstable region in the world and a vortex of transnational threats and interlocking crises from Palestine to Afghanistan. Unless crisis response in the region is galvanized through U.S. leadership and robust cooperation with the major and rising powers, regional stability, global energy supplies, and key security arrangements such as the Nuclear Non-Proliferation Treaty (NPT) are threatened.

The United States is neither solely responsible for nor solely capable of managing or resolving the several interlocking crises in the broader Middle East. Many states point to the U.S. role in stoking regional instability, civil war within Iraq, rising anti-Western sentiment, and volatility of international energy markets. Each member of the G-16 and much of the world, though, share an overriding interest in a stable Middle East. All will be worse off if crises in the Middle East escalate, if terrorism spreads further, if energy prices swing out of control, if Iraq falls into permanent chaos, or if tensions between the Arab/Muslim world and the West fester or escalate. The complexity of the challenge will require a truly international response.

In chapter 11 we weigh alternatives to the international order that we prescribe. Current global trends—rising tensions among major powers, the worst economic crisis since the Great Depression, and escalation of conflicts in the broader Middle East—demonstrate the perils of a world tipping toward entropy. Although such trends make it more difficult to forge cooperative solutions to global problems, they also demonstrate why cooperative solutions are urgently needed. Some may agree that today's status quo is untenable, but they propose that international order is best pursued through multilateralism a la carte or through a "Concert or League of Democracies."

When carefully scrutinized, however, neither alternative would perform credibly. International order cannot be built in ad hoc configurations on an issue-by-issue basis; the interconnections among transnational threats require policy solutions that when addressing the problem at hand, do not exacerbate other problems or make them more intractable. Moreover, solutions to today's transnational threats require the contribution and consent of the new rising powers. Multilateralism a la carte ignores the festering resentment of these powers, who are becoming more intransigent in specific issue negotiations because they have not been accorded voice and influence in the larger international architecture.

Nor is greater cooperation among democracies an antidote for today's global problems. Democracies alone will not provide the international cooperation essential for addressing transnational threats. Ensuring security, enhancing prosperity, stopping deadly infectious disease, and solving global warming require cooperating with nondemocracies. Climate change or financial instability cannot be tackled without China. Nuclear nonproliferation and disarmament, and energy security, cannot be furthered without Russia.

The key challenge for global cooperation is to find a way to bring old and new sources of power to bear on the transnational threats of the twenty-first century. An institution that helps the sixteen major and rising powers to reach common ground on shared threats has a far greater chance of producing effective results than an institution that strives to unify the interests and strategies of 60 to 100 democracies, only to find that cooperative solutions still depend on powers that are not at the table.

CONCLUSION

The twenty-first century will be defined by security threats unconstrained by borders—threats from climate change, nuclear proliferation, and terrorism to conflict, poverty, disease, and economic instability. The greatest test of global leadership will be building partnerships and institutions for cooperation that can meet the challenge. Although all states have a stake in solutions, responsibility for a peaceful and prosperous world will fall disproportionately to the major and rising powers. The United States most of all must provide leadership in an era of transnational threats.

In this book we put forward a vision of international order built on responsible sovereignty. In weighing this order, we encourage readers to take a cold, hard assessment of where we are now and to judge whether we are gaining the security and prosperity we need through existing international institutions and a policy of maintaining maximum freedom of action by the United States.

We also urge readers to compare this order against realistic alternatives. A long streak of idealism, in the United States and elsewhere, tends to weigh the value of international cooperation against a vision of perfect order. Today's version of that perfect order is a world where the United States can protect itself by dealing only with like-minded democratic countries, who will agree with U.S. policies.

In such comparisons cooperation always loses, for it seems too slow and too episodic. It requires patience as others participate in decision-making and demand to have their say and be heard. It is frustrating because it involves compromises. But in a world where your security and prosperity depend on the actions of others, cooperation is the only game in town.

In the United States, history offers a valuable lesson about the risks of perfectionism, which led to a turn inward in the 1920s and 1930s. As Franklin D. Roosevelt warned the public in 1945,

> Perfectionism, no less than isolationism or imperialism or power politics, may obstruct the paths to international peace. Let us not forget that the retreat to isolationism a quarter of a century ago was started not by a direct attack against international cooperation but against the alleged imperfections of the peace. In our disillusionment after the last war we preferred international anarchy to international cooperation with nations which did not see and think exactly as we did. We gave up the hope of gradually achieving a better peace because we had not the courage to fulfill our responsibilities in an admittedly imperfect world.[21]

Today's world is still imperfect. In the next chapter we argue why it is in the interests of the powerful to find the courage to fulfill new responsibilities and build an international order for an age of transnational threats.

TWO

INTERESTS AND ORDER

THE UNITED STATES AND
THE MAJOR AND RISING POWERS

AN INTERNATIONAL ORDER based on responsible sovereignty must be in the interest of those actors who have the power to build it. Softhearted appeals to the common good are insufficient. The primary question is whether the resulting order provides the vision, institutions, and tools to enable major and rising powers to address the large and complex agenda of transnational crises and challenges before them.

The summer of 2008, when we concluded this book, hardly seemed a propitious time for a vision of international order based on responsible sovereignty. The combination of the Russian invasion of Georgia, the failure of the UN Security Council to address Robert Mugabe's thuggery in Zimbabwe, and China's assertiveness in Tibet before the Olympic Games all seemed to portend a new era of political competition between the West and the rising powers. In July the collapse of the Doha Round of trade talks signaled a worrying inability of the major and rising powers to balance their economic interests. By the end of the summer, it seemed more likely that Russia would be ejected from the G-8 than China included in it.

It is tempting to dismiss the tensions of 2008 as solely a legacy of the unpopularity of the George W. Bush presidency or as fallout from Iraq. Certainly, the credibility of President Bush in decrying Russia's invasion of Georgia was diminished internationally by the still open wounds from the U.S. invasion of Iraq. Condoleezza Rice's repeated assertion that in the post–cold war era the use of force to annex territory was simply not an option was met with raised eyebrows even by the many states that opposed Russia's invasion of Georgia. Similarly, the U.S. and U.K. inability to move South Africa toward a more assertive stance on Zimbabwe reflected in part a decline in the international credibility of the West's message on democracy, again a function of the long shadow of Iraq.

More fundamentally, however, the summer of 2008 revealed the urgent need in U.S. foreign policy for a realistic assessment of the structure and nature of power in a transitional era. Respected foreign policy analysts now openly discuss the relative decline of U.S. power and the rise of new powers, including China, India, and Brazil.[1] Some go so far as to argue that we have entered an age of nonpolarity: the United States' unipolar moment has ended and no recognizable power structure has emerged to take its place.[2]

Power itself is more diffuse than at any time in the last several hundred years. The ability of governments to get what they want varies by issue. In some cases, businesses, foundations, and civil society organizations wield greater influence than governments. Power is soft as well as hard, and culture, values, and diplomacy often matter more than the number of infantry divisions under a state's command. Even in the realm of hard power, the United States possesses more military might than ever in its history, yet it cannot dictate outcomes in relatively poor states such as Iraq and Afghanistan. Greater lethal capacity is falling into the hands of small, renegade, nonstate actors that do not respond to the traditional incentives and disincentives used to influence states.

It seems self-evident that the United States wields less power relative to the rest of the world than it did twenty years ago. The United States brought some of its decline on itself through a combination of overweening ambition abroad and underinvestment at home. The country's relative decline is also a function of the economic rise of India, China, and Brazil. By 2050, those three dynamic economies and Russia are projected to produce 40 percent of global output, twice the amount of the United States and equal to that of the members of the original Group of Seven (the so-called leading industrial nations), combined.[3]

Nonetheless, the United States still exerts disproportionate power on the global stage. By any metric of military power, the United States still dwarfs its nearest rivals. By the Pentagon's own analysis, not for twenty years could the Chinese military be a competitor of the United States.[4] As others point out, that could occur only if China diverts substantial resources away from poverty eradication, social service provision, pollution reduction, and other demands of its population.[5] Russia can compete with the United States for influence on its periphery, but its nuclear deterrent is degraded, its diplomacy and reputation severely diminished, and its global power gone for good. Brazil, South Africa, Mexico and the rest of the rising economies collectively do not come close to the global impact of the U.S. economy. And although Europe is quick to point out that its market share is equal to that of the United States, the fact remains that Europe has yet to translate that economic position into diplomatic clout, let alone military capacity.

Yet each of the rising powers has *blocking power*. That is true of some of the rising powers on global issues, such as China on climate change, Brazil on food supply, and India on trade. Within their regions, the rising powers can stop initiatives that harm their interests and they can be indispensable to any crisis management effort. They have enormous sway in the regional blocs within international institutions and can veto initiatives that they oppose or on which they have not been consulted. While the individual and collective blocking capacity of the rising powers is not as broad as that of the United States, it is an everyday concern for international diplomacy and global order.

A world in which many countries have blocking power is a formula for paralysis, not action, in the face of transnational threats. That is, of course, unless the traditional and rising powers have enough shared interests to create a more effective international order. Leaders in China, India, Brazil, and South Africa recognize that their economic growth relies on a strong and resilient international trade and finance system. Europe is the world's most rule-based society, yet erosion of a rule-based international system means that Europe is taking on commitments, such as on carbon emissions and foreign aid, with increasingly marginal impact. Japan has a vital interest in a stable transition in security arrangements in Asia and around the world. To continue to develop its oil and gas reserves, Russia will need international technology and sufficient trust from its partners to invest in and secure transnational pipelines. None of the traditional or rising powers profits from the unchecked proliferation of nuclear weapons or the spread of global terrorism.

Moreover, as we demonstrate in part II, on some issues, such as global public health and peacekeeping, there has been good cooperation among the traditional and rising powers. There certainly has been no evidence of a new authoritarian bloc rising to challenge the United States. Russia's invasion of Georgia prompted a swift, negative reaction from China, and their bilateral relations have cooled noticeably. It was telling that China's reaction to the subprime lending crisis in the United States was to call for greater international cooperation in the banking and financial industries.

From a geopolitical perspective, the shifting balance of international power demands a reordering of the international system—and for all parties, the sooner the better.

THE CASE FOR A NEW RULE-BASED INTERNATIONAL ORDER

A new U.S. foreign policy must face seven discomforting facts about the world. Taken together, these facts should shake any complacent assumptions about U.S. power and make a strong case for the United States to build an international order on the principle of responsible sovereignty:

In a world of new, transnational dangers, the United States cannot defend itself unilaterally against the array of threats that it faces. Take, for example, the threat of catastrophic terrorism, a nightmare that has haunted policymakers in Washington during both the William J. Clinton and George W. Bush administrations. Scientists estimate that terrorists could construct a nuclear bomb with only the amount of highly enriched uranium (HEU) that would fit into six one-liter bottles. Given the amount of contraband that crosses U.S. borders daily, terrorists who could acquire that amount of HEU have a good chance of bringing it into the United States. Scientists further confirm that a small group of terrorists with comprehensive knowledge and excellent engineering skills could create an improvised nuclear weapon. A robust defense against this threat involves layers of international cooperation:

—cleaning up existing stocks of fissile materials around the world to reduce the likelihood of acquisition by terrorists

—strengthening the worldwide nonproliferation regime to reduce the desire of states to enrich their own fissile materials

—working to stop state sponsors of terrorism

—acquiring foreign intelligence about possible terrorist suspects

—strengthening the ability of states around the world to regulate the movement of dangerous people and materials across their borders

—cutting off terrorists' access to funding.

These measures, as important as they are, in some ways just scratch the surface of the problem. They do not even begin to address the spread of extremist ideas or the conditions that are conducive to recruitment of new members of terrorist organizations. But they all require robust, sustained cooperation from other states.

Likewise, U.S. biological security is only as good as global biological security. The United States is at risk from new infectious diseases and a global influenza pandemic. It must be vigilant against potential bioterrorism, a threat that will grow exponentially along with progress in biotechnology. As with catastrophic terrorism, there is no unilateral defense against transnational biological threats. In a world of 830 million annual international air passengers, in which the incubation times of most infectious diseases are longer than most international flights; in which, on average, two new deadly infectious diseases emerge each year; in which scientists predict a recurrence of an influenza pandemic with 100 percent certainty; and in which tens of thousands of small biotechnology laboratories around the world are or will be capable of manipulating genes to create devastating new pathogens, the United States cannot defend itself without constant, vigorous international cooperation.

In 2007 President Bush belatedly acknowledged that global warming is a threat to U.S. security, indeed to the viability of the planet. But it is a threat that defies any solution pursued by the United States alone. Every unit of carbon in the atmosphere contributes equally to global warming, whether it originates in Detroit or Beijing. Moreover, the impact of global warming will be shared in the form of drought, catastrophic weather events, human migration, and conflicts that go beyond what we see in Darfur. If the United States, arguably the biggest driver of historical climate change, does not lead in policy and technological development to counteract the threat, the newest big emitters—China and India—will be loath to make similar commitments and everyone will lose.

If the United States is to secure sustained, energetic international cooperation to address the major threats to its own security, it must cooperate with other states to address the threats that plague them. In a world where dangers know no borders, U.S. security depends on the help of others. How is the United States to obtain their help? How will others get the cooperation that they need from the United States? We believe that these questions must be answered through refashioning and revitalizing the concept of collective security.

Collective security is an old idea, premised on a shared perception of threats and a commitment to mutual defense—if one state is attacked, all other states will respond. This idea lies at the heart of the United Nations. In 1945, states created the United Nations to respond to the common threat of state aggression and to address the underpinnings of that threat: economic insecurity, beggar-thy-neighbor trading policies, ultranationalism, and human rights violations.

Several problems now bedevil the concept's relevance. Today international aggression is but one of many threats, and in fact it may not be the most salient threat to many states, including the United States. Moreover, different states face different threats, a complexity that challenges the formation of a shared perception of threats. If those two problems can be overcome, a third arises in translating vision to action—states must overcome collective action problems, such as free riding, and respond effectively to threats not only to themselves but also to others.

To update perceptions of "shared threats," the UN High-Level Panel on Threats, Challenges, and Change, appointed by former UN Secretary General Kofi Annan in 2003, posed a simple question to governments and civil society organizations alike, in every part of the globe: "What are the most salient threats to your security?" Depending on power, privilege, and region, respondents articulated very different threats—poverty and disease in Africa, economic crisis and lack of confidence in democracy in Latin America, catastrophic terrorism in the United States, and so on.

Any global security system must take these differing views into account. But how? Do we rank various threats? Do we simply say that some threats might be economic or social but that they are not threats to security? Do we acknowledge a world with differential threats and seek to accommodate that diversity? We believe, as did the High-Level Panel, that acknowledging diversity creates a more viable pathway to collaboration. We also adopt the panel's definition of "security threats" as "any event or process that leads to large-scale death or lessening of life chances and undermines states as the basic unit of the international system."[6] We see such security threats in climate change and energy insecurity, in the spread of nuclear weapons, in the prospect of deadly infectious disease and potential harmful use of biotechnology, in terrorism, in war and conflict, and in poverty and economic instability.

The diverse threats on this list all defy unilateral solutions, and they probably are more interconnected than many governments and citizens acknowledge: what threatens humans in faraway countries and regions also threatens us. Even if one does not believe that these threats are interconnected (and for some threats, the empirical jury is still out), states should still cooperate to address what threatens others in order to gain cooperation against what threatens them. This is as true for the United States as it is for the smallest, most vulnerable states.

In an interdependent world, military power alone is overrated, and it can be counterproductive in gaining the essential cooperation necessary for U.S. security. The United States' unparalleled military strength has yielded few discernible diplomatic gains. If power is about guns and rockets—cutting-edge technology married to lethal capacity—and the ability to send soldiers and weapons anywhere in the world in the shortest amount of time, the United States is unequaled. By almost any measure, the United States has the strongest and most mobile military the world has ever seen. The Bush administration's fiscal year 2009 budget request included $515 billion for the Department of Defense's core budget, before factoring in the supplemental costs of waging war in Iraq and Afghanistan.[7] All other members of the North Atlantic Treaty Organization (NATO) combined spend only $202.1 billion annually. Estimates for China's yearly defense budget range between $45 billion and $139 billion.[8] Russia spends around $60 billion on defense annually.[9]

Military power has not, however, allowed the United States to achieve its objectives unilaterally in Iraq or Afghanistan. It alone could not stop Iran and North Korea from their pursuit of nuclear weapons. The Middle East is further from stability than at any time in recent memory. The so-called "global war on terror" has led to greater numbers of terrorists.

And despite its military might and perhaps because of it, the United States is distrusted as a nation as never before. Since 2002, its image has declined in most Muslim countries in the Middle East and Asia, and it continues to decline even among many of our oldest allies. In a January 2007 BBC World Service poll of more than 26,000 people in twenty-five different countries, one in two respondents said that the United States was playing a mainly negative role in the world.[10] From 2000 to 2007, polls indicate that the percentage of citizens in England holding a favorable view of the United States declined from 83 to 51 percent. In Germany the decline was from 78 to 30 percent; in Indonesia, from 75 to 29 percent; and in Turkey, from 52 to 9 percent.[11]

Global distrust of U.S. leadership is reflected in increased disapproval of the cornerstones of U.S. foreign policy. Those polled in a Pew Research Center survey in forty-seven nations not only favored withdrawal of U.S. troops from Iraq but also expressed opposition to U.S. and NATO operations in Afghanistan.[12] In addition, global support for the U.S.-led war on terrorism declined even more in 2007, with majorities or pluralities in most countries surveyed saying that they disliked U.S. ideas about democracy. The United States is also the nation most often blamed for harming the world's environment.[13] Even some of the closest U.S. alliances—with Japan, Australia, and NATO—have frayed in recent years, and they will need attention at both the elite and public level.

Military might has lulled many Americans into believing that the United States can tackle most problems without international help, that we can have "allies without alliances," and that we should eschew international treaties and institutions because they are, in the assertion of key Bush administration officials, weapons of asymmetrical warfare that the rest of the world uses to constrain the United States.[14] At some point, however, a lightbulb will switch on, and U.S. leaders will realize that in today's world, punitive power alone does not and cannot solve the most pressing problems facing the United States.

International institutions are much more important to U.S. security goals than policymakers admit or the public realizes. The United Nations is the international institution that many U.S. foreign policy elites love to hate. But at a time when its reputation in the United States has fallen to an all-time low, the United Nations is more important to the United States than ever. A slim majority of Americans polled do not support the organization, but that number is at its lowest in the organization's sixty-two-year history.[15] Only one-third of the American people believe that the United Nations is effective.[16] Both Democratic and Republican foreign policy elites hastily write off the organization and its potential contribution to international peace.

Yet even with its flaws, the United Nations has played a major role in tackling collective security threats, and by doing so it has furthered U.S. security interests around the globe—especially in the broader Middle East, the most dangerous region in the world. Since 9/11, the United Nations has proven helpful in a number of crises:

—In Afghanistan, the United Nations mediated the Bonn process, which established the framework under which President Hamid Karzai was able to create a government that unified disparate anti-Taliban factions. In addition, the United Nations played an instrumental role in helping to produce the constitution and a popular consultative process to legitimize it, organized the national elections, and subsequently shepherded political negotiations through two of the UN's best mediators, Lakhdar Brahimi and Jean Arnault.

—In Iraq, the United Nations carried out the 2005 national elections. At the request of the Bush administration, Brahimi garnered the support of Grand Ayatollah Sayyed Ali al-Sistani and brokered an agreement for an interim government in 2004 when the Bush administration was unable to do so. Brahimi, again at the request of the Bush administration, quietly met with various insurgents to persuade them to join political negotiations.

—In Iran, the International Atomic Energy Agency (IAEA) has been at the forefront in demanding transparency and providing information about Iran's nuclear program. UN Security Council sanctions have been the principal means for sustaining pressure on Iran's leaders. That pressure has two goals: to constrain Iran's uranium enrichment capacity, and to create a diplomatic coalition that will prevent Iran from developing nuclear weapons.

—In North Korea, UN Security Council sanctions in October 2006 created pressure on the government and opened the prospect for the new agreement reached in the 2007 Six-Party Talks.[17] As of mid-2008, North Korea had halted its plutonium production program, although the complete denuclearization of the Korean Peninsula is far from certain.

—In Lebanon, the United Nations is responsible for implementing Security Council Resolution 1559, which led Syria to withdraw from the country. The United Nations is in charge of the special inquiry into the assassination of Rafiq Hariri, the former prime minister of Lebanon. In 2006, the United Nations deployed 15,000 peacekeepers to secure the border with Israel and to provide a face-saving means for Israel and Hezbollah to end what would otherwise have been a long, drawn-out war.

—In Sudan, the United Nations has placed more than 12,000 peacekeepers to implement the North-South peace agreement, mediated in part by Senator John Danforth (R-Mo.) and strongly supported by the Bush administration. In Darfur, Kofi Annan and current UN Secretary General Ban Ki-moon have been vocal proponents of a robust mission to stop the killings and atrocities, and the United Nations is deploying a joint peacekeeping operation with the African Union.

—In Liberia, a country with important cultural and historical ties to the United States, the United Nations deployed 17,000 peacekeepers and carried out new elections that brought Ellen Johnson-Sirleaf, the first woman elected head of state in Africa, to the presidency.

—In Haiti, the United Nations has more than 6,000 peacekeepers and is once again trying to bring some stability to the troubled island, which is just off the U.S. shore.

International institutions besides the United Nations also have helped the United States meet important goals. Alongside the UN political mission in Afghanistan, NATO is fielding 40,000 troops to combat a resurgent Taliban and protect the nascent government. The IAEA has provided vital information about nuclear proliferation threats. At the Organization for Economic Cooperation and Development (OECD), the Financial Action Task Force has been a vital tool for blocking financing of terrorist groups. The World Health Organization (WHO) was pivotal in arresting the severe acute respiratory syndrome (SARS) epidemic and is a frontline actor against avian flu, which has the potential to become a deadly pandemic.

So how is it that the American public does not know all this? The short answer in current U.S. politics is Iraq. In 2003, the Bush administration cast the United Nations as feckless and irrelevant because the Security Council did not authorize the administration's bid to invade Iraq to prevent Saddam Hussein's use of weapons of mass destruction, which allegedly were hidden from world view. Few administration officials have gone back to acknowledge that Iraq had no weapons of mass destruction, that the UN inspection regime was successful, and that the UN Security Council was right in its decision. If the United States had abided by the Security Council's decision, it would have saved itself and others from the war in Iraq and the new terrorist networks that have since emerged in that country. Despite all this, the image of UN failure has stuck with the public.

The long answer is rooted in the failure of the Clinton and George W. Bush administrations to create a vision for international order in a transnational world and to explain how and why the United Nations plays an important role. For the past twenty years, that lack of vision and clarity has enabled a concerted attack by right-wing conservatives and the media, stoked occasionally by several U.S. ambassadors to the United Nations who were less concerned with reforming the institution than with scoring points at its expense. Pundits constantly harp on examples of the UN's headline-making failures and seldom look beyond them to recognize that the organization is a tool that furthers U.S. interests daily.

At a time when the United States makes daily use of international institutions to help meet its security needs, those institutions need to be strengthened or reinvented and new ones created. Solutions to key security problems in diverse regions of the world—including nuclear proliferation in Iran and North Korea and instability in Lebanon, Sudan, Afghanistan, Congo, and Haiti—all depend fundamentally on international institutions, whether for legitimacy, influence, or resources, such as peacekeeping forces. Yet these institutions face serious limitations. For example, the UN's peacekeeping capacity is stretched to the breaking point, and NATO's peacekeeping machinery, as shown by its performance in Afghanistan, has serious flaws. Neither organization has an effective mechanism for deploying civilians to undertake vital law enforcement, legal, or governance support operations. The UN's preventive diplomacy and mediation capacities are slender, and its peacebuilding entities are far too numerous and marred by incoherent strategies and lack of coordination among departments and agencies. Enforcement of UN Security Council resolutions, which depends on unity among permanent members of the council, is haphazard. As a decisionmaking body, the United Nations is often paralyzed by the need to find consensus on issues, or it is imprisoned by lowest-common-denominator positions.

The problems facing these institutions have two dimensions, and both must be addressed. One is substantive—today's threats to international peace and security are transnational and therefore demand greater cooperation among states and new arrangements that include the private sector. The second is political—the United Nations and other global institutions still reflect the distribution of power that existed after World War II. Some key UN member states have grown frustrated because of their perceived inability to influence its decisions. Japan, the second-biggest financial contributor to the UN budget, pays more UN dues than China, France, Russia, and the United Kingdom, all permanent members of the Security Council, *combined*. The three most dynamic economies in the world are Brazil, India, and China, yet only one of the three is on the UN Security Council and none participates in the G-8. If they are to be convinced to invest in revitalizing the tools of cooperation, powerful member states must have the confidence that their interests will be advanced by doing so.

Although the limitations of the United Nations are apparent, neither regional nor coalition-based arrangements have yet shown that they alone can handle the scale and complexity of sustained, major security challenges without wider international engagement—as demonstrated by NATO's struggles in Afghanistan, the European Union's laborious deployments in Congo and the Central African Republic, the inaction of the Association of Southeast Asian Nations (ASEAN) on Myanmar, or the African Union's limited capacity in Sudan and the Horn of Africa.

At a time when the United States needs stronger international institutions, its policies since 9/11 have prompted many countries to resist reforms that would strengthen these institutions. In 2005, the Bush administration reversed course, deciding that it had a stake in a reformed United Nations after all and engaging on a host of key issues under negotiation for the 2005 World Summit. Of course, the fact that John Bolton, the man chosen to show U.S. support for reform, was an unabashed critic of the organization did little to establish U.S. bona fides in the reform process. Nonetheless, some goals that had U.S. backing were advanced. But many of those goals have languished, and commitments made to create new institutions, such as a peacebuilding commission, or to uphold new norms, such as the responsibility to protect citizens from mass atrocities, have been diluted in implementation. That watering down of commitments reflects the willingness of many countries, including some traditional allies, to undermine strengthening of the United Nations because they believe that reform is a means for the United States to pursue a unilateral agenda under a multilateral cloak.

In this, as in so many other U.S. interactions with the rest of the world over the last five years, Iraq casts a long shadow. The Bush administration had proclaimed early on that its national security goal was to preserve U.S. primacy long into the twenty-first century. After it presented false and misleading intelligence to the Security Council and went to war in Iraq without a council resolution, the United States, in the words of one U.S. diplomat whom we interviewed, "lost the benefit of the doubt." Even when the United States contributes to international organizations—for example, by paying 26 percent of the cost of the largest buildup of UN peacekeeping forces in history—or when it helps tackle problems elsewhere in the world, such as fighting AIDS in Africa, it is met with skepticism.

Confronted with the overwhelming punitive power of the United States, few states are willing to confront Washington or to try to counterbalance its power through their own actions and alliances. But at the same time, few countries have been willing to join the U.S. bandwagon, and when they have done so, it has been in the spirit of taming the beast to curb its most dangerous tendencies. In the United Kingdom, for example, this strategy proved bankrupt—it largely failed to constrain U.S. foreign policy and it has proven unpopular with many British citizens and civil servants. It also exacted a large political cost from the leader most closely aligned with the Bush administration—former prime minister Tony Blair.

Many countries do not want to throw in their lot with the rather unsavory group of available counterbalancers (such as Iran, Venezuela, and Syria), nor do they wish to fall in line with U.S. policies and initiatives. Those countries, then, are tempted to pursue "soft balancing." Using such a strategy, they deny the legitimacy and legality of U.S. policies, and they undermine attempts by the United States to obtain cooperation on its terms. Many countries prefer to use the United Nations as a great global encounter session, where they can vent freely about U.S. perfidies, rather than as a great problem-solver—especially if it solves the problems of the United States.

If the United States is to obtain cooperation in strengthening international institutions, it must see those institutions as more than tools of U.S. foreign policy to be used or abandoned as best suits short-term U.S. political interests. Of course, international institutions are useful tools of U.S. foreign policy and therefore should be strengthened. No nation is so naïve that it does not recognize that the United States and all other countries act most fundamentally to advance their own interests.

But focusing on instrumentality alone has two shortcomings. First, a better toolbox does not constitute a comprehensive vision of order. Without a shared vision—which we have proposed should be rooted in responsible sovereignty—there is little to guide the nature of the institutions and relationships needed to promote global security and prosperity. Second, the United States cannot win the confidence of others to invest in building international order if the world distrusts U.S. intentions or questions its commitment. Outside the United States, there is a deep desire to see a U.S. commitment to a rule-based international system, a pledge to abide by those rules, and consistent support of international institutions. To put it bluntly, even friendly governments reject American instrumental use of institutions—using them when they suit U.S. interests, ignoring them (and rhetorically trashing them) when they do not.

U.S. global leadership would be enhanced by a commitment to institutions beyond their value as tools. As a powerful state in the global system, the United States has a great stake in promoting international order, which can serve to legitimize power, assure weaker states that stronger states are not predatory, and marry power to principle to convince states to follow its leadership instead of seeking to counterbalance it. But such order must be constructed and validated, and the cooperation required to maintain it must have a longer shelf life than whatever is convenient in the short term for any great power.

Leadership of the international system is based on example and reputation. In a rule-based international order in which the exercise of power is seen as legitimate, the most powerful state cannot be episodic in its compliance with the rules. In a world in which the United States benefits from having others live up to their commitments and restrain themselves, the United States, too, must live up to its commitments. This issue will long be at the heart of U.S. relations with rising powers such as India, Brazil, and South Africa. It will determine whether U.S. relations with

China will be marked by conflict or competition. Will China and India have a stake in international order, rules, and institutions or will they ignore them, at the future peril of the United States?

U.S. diplomatic history gives us important examples of the exercise of restraint. Presidents Franklin D. Roosevelt and Harry S. Truman understood well the importance of the willingness of the United States to bind its unilateral power. As Truman said in his speech at the final plenary session of the UN conference in San Francisco in 1945, "We all have to recognize—no matter how great our strength—that we must deny ourselves the license to do always as we please."[18] In international trade, the United States has agreed to bind itself to decisions of the World Trade Organization. The WTO and, before that, the General Agreement on Tariffs and Trade are examples of powerful states understanding the catastrophic risks of selfish trading policies and creating institutions that restrain freedom of action. The U.S. economy has benefited hugely from such agreements.

THE OTHER SIDE OF THE COIN:
THE NECESSITY OF U.S. LEADERSHIP

Just as the United States must rediscover its interest in creating international order, other countries need to acknowledge the importance of U.S. leadership. Consider, for example, the following points:

The major and rising powers benefit from a strong United States. Leaders in China, India, and the emerging economies recognize that their economic growth relies on a stable international trade and finance system. Most of them have requested and received help in addressing public health emergencies. None of them wants to see a wave of nuclear proliferation. All depend on advances in science and technology. In sum, they all benefit from the economic openness and global public goods that a strong United States provides.[19]

Without financial support from the United States, international organizations that provide essential international services such as public health protection; trade, travel, and security oversight; development assistance; refugee management; and human rights monitoring could not function. The United States is the largest overall financial contributor to the United Nations, supplying more than one-quarter of its regular and peacekeeping budget and up to half of the voluntary budgets of well-regarded international agencies. The United States even funds one-third of the budget of the Comprehensive Test Ban Treaty Organization, although it has not ratified the treaty.

The United States also creates other kinds of public goods that are not measured by financial contributions. For example, the United States is still the prime driver of advances in scientific knowledge and technological innovations, from which the rest of the world benefits.[20]

With respect to international security, international governments still recognize the merits of U.S. power and leadership. The U.S. military secures international trade routes, protecting allies and competitors alike from the closing of vital sea routes (such as the Strait of Malacca and the Strait of Hormuz) and from the disruption that would result if oil could not be shipped around the world.[21] Should the United States retreat from this role, the global economic consequences would be profound.

In Afghanistan, even after the United States spurned NATO's support in late 2001, its rapid military success against the Taliban generated cooperation from Russia, China, Pakistan, and Iran. Despite years of unpopular U.S. policies, U.S. engagement has been the critical variable in multiparty negotiations to contain Iran's and North Korea's nuclear ambitions. Indeed, these two cases exemplify the irony and confusion present in much contemporary discussion of the "multilateral" or "unilateral" nature of U.S. foreign policy. Major powers and key allies complained about the U.S. refusal to engage in direct bilateral talks with both Iran and North Korea. And although the United States emphasized the sticks of sanctions and the threat (stated or implied) of the use of force, international diplomats contended that for both countries the big carrot was a direct and positive bilateral relationship with the United States.

Even in the Middle East, where U.S. policy has reached astonishing levels of unpopularity, the region's states ultimately recognize that there is no substitute for U.S. engagement in the search for a solution to the Israeli-Palestinian conflict or to the other border and power disputes that plague the region.

There is no prospect for international stability and prosperity in the next twenty years that does not rest on U.S. power and leadership. The United States has the world's largest economy and strongest military. It is not the only financial hub, but it is an essential one. On a per capita basis, it exceeds any other major power in the consumption of fossil fuels. The world needs the United States to use its resources positively in helping to resolve transnational threats. If the United States blocks international solutions to climate change, nuclear security, and financial instability, better and sustainable global outcomes cannot be achieved.

Transitions in world power take place over decades. There is little guarantee that the world in fifty years will look anything like what a linear forecast might predict. Few scholars foresaw the end of the cold war and bipolarity. And in the 1980s, many international relations scholars believed that Japan, not China, would someday overtake the United States as the world's hegemon.

If there is to be international cooperation against transnational threats and if we are to revamp international institutions to make them more effective, there is no credible alternative to U.S. leadership. At least for the next twenty years and perhaps beyond, no other actor will have any comparable level of power to forge global alliances, shape international action, provide security guarantees, or mobilize collective action.

The U.S. experience with unilateralism should be a salutary warning against similar temptations for new rising powers. Important voices within the rising powers revel in the overreaching of the United States and believe that its era is coming to a close, to be superseded by a new power distribution in which they are on top. They look forward to the day when their countries can act free of international restraint, just as the United States has done increasingly since the end of the cold war.

If anything, the experience of the last fifteen years should be sobering for any aspiring global hegemon. The early years of the twenty-first century have demonstrated that, exercised individually, military power is an ineffective means of eliminating threats; that unfettered power brings with it hubris, temptation, and overreaching; and that in a world of transnational threats and interdependent security, national security and sovereignty can be protected only through international cooperation.

The costs of delaying the revitalization of international cooperation will increase over time; it is best to engage now. The gold standard for international cooperation should be prevention. With regard to transnational threats, that means taking effective action before a catastrophic terrorist attack involving nuclear or biological weapons occurs; before a devastating influenza virus kills millions; before a security breach leads to malicious abuse of cutting-edge biotechnology; and before a cascade of countries obtains nuclear arms and one of them breaches the nuclear taboo.

On climate change the question of time is both acute and determinative. As we explain in chapter 4, the world's economies continue to make investments in infrastructure that will determine energy use, transportation modes, and manufacturing methods for the next three decades. If those investment patterns do not change so that greenhouse gas emissions peak by 2015, we will create a catastrophic environmental reality for 2050 that will change irrevocably the nature of life as we know it, bringing floods, hunger, disease, and conflict to different parts of the world.

The longer it takes to build robust international partnerships to address our problems, the more difficult they will be to solve. And we cannot assume that if one of these threats does materialize, international cooperation will be easier in the aftermath. If a nuclear bomb is used in an act of terrorism, key states might react unilaterally, strongly rejecting international institutions as feckless and undependable. In the event of an influenza pandemic, countries may recognize the need for cooperation at a time that the resources needed to take effective action are woefully inadequate.

Other countries must ask themselves the question that we put to the U.S. public at the end of chapter 1. Will our security and prosperity best be ensured through revitalized international cooperation that rests on strengthened institutions and norms or through the status quo? Those who believe that they, as rising powers, will face a more advantageous order in twenty years must ask themselves how, during that time, they will shield themselves from today's transnational threats. And what if the international balance of power is as tenuous and opaque in twenty years as it seems now? Why would a state assume that as its power rises, that trajectory will continue forever, with no sharp discontinuity, decline, or stagnation?

The United States will not be tied down like Gulliver; it will commit itself to international norms and institutions only if it is convinced that they serve its interests. The United States remains a pivotal actor whose behavior can make or break efforts at effective international cooperation. In recent years, U.S. policymakers have viewed international rules and laws as attempts by Lilliputian states to bind the American Gulliver and have rejected international institutions and laws indiscriminately. And indeed, some countries have looked at such institutions and laws as a way to constrain the United States against its will. All such attempts have failed, regardless of whether the administration has been Republican or Democratic; U.S. policymakers, like policymakers everywhere, are very good at understanding when others are attempting to trap them into arrangements that they do not believe serve their interests.

A different literary allusion offers a better metaphor for rekindling U.S. commitment to international rules: Ulysses and the sirens. To resist the siren song of unilateral power, U.S. policymakers must rediscover their long-term interest in tying U.S. power to the mast of international order. Given the nation's overwhelming military power, the temptations of unilateralism are great and constant. Those temptations, however, often lead to self-defeating traps, and the unilateral exercise of power engenders resentment and resistance. After World War II, the United States understood that to legitimize its great power, it was necessary and in its self-interest to voluntarily restrain itself.

For those governments that seek to embed U.S. power in international institutions, the lesson is obvious. They must convince U.S. leaders and the U.S. public that their interests will be served by more effective institutions and norms. The experience of the Iraq war and the costs of unilateral action begin to make the case. In the end, however, the argument must show how other countries will reciprocate U.S. investment in international order and themselves contribute to cooperative efforts that will stanch nuclear proliferation, address global warming, stop terrorism, and prevent outbreaks of new deadly infectious diseases. The best argument will be one that promises and produces results.

The road to a more effective international system that gives non-Americans a stronger voice still runs through Washington. As we have seen, today's international institutions and organizations do not reflect the major changes that have taken place in the structure of international power. For countries that are not permanent members of the UN Security Council, such as India, Japan, and Brazil, that is a source of immense frustration and resentment, while an economic juggernaut like China is irritated by being left out of the G-8. Moreover, as global financial power shifts toward Asia, it is self-defeating to not have that shift reflected in the governance and mandate of the international financial institutions (IFIs). Redefining the roles of the International Monetary Fund (IMF) and the World Bank to monitor, guide, and provide incentives for investment in the world's financial system becomes all that much harder. Asia's ascendance and impact on the world economy must be taken into account. Lack of representation of Asian countries not only offends their national pride, it deprives them of opportunities to make contributions to international order that are commensurate with their power and influence, and that is a global loss.

No major overhaul of the international order is possible unless the United States takes a leading role. The key is to convince U.S. leaders that decisionmaking within international institutions must reflect major changes in international power. India, Japan, Brazil, China, and South Africa, for example, can make enormous contributions to real solutions for global problems.

With a greater voice and influence in the international order comes greater responsibility. In a trenchant analysis of U.S. relations with what they call the pivotal powers (India, China, Europe, Russia, and Japan), Nina Hachigian and Mona Sutphen note that although they all "want a seat at the table, it is unclear how much they are willing to pay for the privilege."[22] That is a critical question for the viability of international order in the twenty-first century, but it also is a critical question for the United States as it contemplates broader participation in major international bodies—participation that it fears will dilute its own influence.

For many countries, international institutions are about voice and legitimacy. For the United States, they are primarily about getting results. Those stances need not be in tension, but it is an open question whether greater participation in global governance will lead to more effective solutions to key global problems. The policies, contributions, and actions of rising states like India, China, Brazil, and South Africa will answer that question. Moreover, their rise in prominence and visibility in international institutions will command greater public and international scrutiny. Free riding becomes more difficult when you are driving the bus.

FROM DISCOMFORTING FACTS TO UNCOMFORTABLE DECISIONS

The United States and the major and rising powers would all benefit from a revitalized international order. We believe that responsible sovereignty is a foundational principle for such an order and that it can guide the creation of issue-specific norms and institutions that will solve global problems. But before the construction process can begin, some hard, uncomfortable decisions must be made.

The United States will need to lead in creating a greater institutional voice in international security for the rising powers. Europe will resist many institutional changes at the United Nations and in the IFIs because all viable options involve diluting its voice. Europe's seats on the UN Security Council are disproportionate to its global wealth, population, and power. Europe's position at the helm of the IMF does not reflect changing global financial balances. Japan will not want to bring China into an expanded G-8 unless China supports a Japanese seat on the UN Security Council. Russia will not welcome diluting its role in a G-8 that it just recently joined. To break out of the current stalemate in governance and achieve better solutions, the United States must lead, even if it is not used to sharing power and influence on the world stage. The United States will need to reorganize the conduct of its foreign policy and pay greater attention to the rising powers in Asia, Africa, and Latin America that have new clout in international affairs.

For those who stand to benefit from a stronger voice and greater influence in global affairs, uncomfortable decisions will be required by this discomforting fact: the best way to convince the United States to create an order to which it is prepared to bind itself and to press for greater participation in global decisionmaking is to show that the United States will benefit in return.

After President Obama takes office in 2009, there will be a radical disjunction between the crises that will require his attention and the pent-up demand from allies and rising powers for a greater say in international institutions. Whatever aspirations the new administration has to revitalize international security arrangements or to build the foundation for a lasting international order based on the principle of responsible sovereignty, it will have to deal with a series of immediate crises that it will inherit on day one. Afghanistan and Iran will demand sustained attention. Slower-burning political crises in Lebanon, Syria, and Pakistan have the potential to heat up. Iraq and the U.S. military presence there will continue to pose difficult choices for international and domestic policy. Fundamentally tied to that issue is the often-ignored question of whether a diplomatic surge can lead to a political settlement that supports the gradual handover of responsibilities to the Iraqi government.

In any discussion between the United States and other governments about revitalizing international cooperation, the broader Middle East will be the 800-pound gorilla in the room. From an instrumental perspective, the United States will want to know how rebuilding international order and strengthening international institutions will help to create stability in Iraq, deny Iran nuclear weapons, defeat the Taliban in Afghanistan, and support a credible and sustainable Afghan state.

For many major powers, helping to meet those goals will be a high bar to clear. They will have to help the United States extricate itself from a war that they opposed. Some states may have to put short-term economic and energy interests aside to unify against Iran's pursuit of uranium enrichment. And some may have to put soldiers on the front lines in Afghanistan and commit themselves to engaging in a civilian state-building effort there.

Why would they even try to jump? We treat that question at length in chapter 10, but in short, the broader Middle East will be an immediate testing ground of a new U.S. commitment to diplomacy, consultation, and international order and of the major and rising powers' willingness to reciprocate with engagement and commitments of their own—not only because it will help consolidate international cooperation but because a stable Middle East is in their vital interest.

CONCLUSION

The inauguration of President Obama in 2009 creates an opportunity to begin building an international order that can effectively respond to today's transnational threats. The prospect of a U.S. recommitment to an international order based on the rule of law is real. President Obama can sell an agenda of international cooperation to the American people. Americans want their country to be respected, they want to lead in the global community, and they want U.S. engagement in other parts of the world to allow them to feel more secure. Finally, they know that U.S. unilateralism has undermined all of these core interests.

More than 75 percent of Americans are concerned that the United States has lost respect among the other nations of the world. They consider that a problem, and they want to improve the image of the United States. Americans clearly reject going it alone, but they are open to doing their fair share and focusing on international cooperation. Voters still believe that the United States needs to function as a world leader, but they feel that it is time for the country, instead of being a "bully" or a "policeman," to serve as a role model for democracy. Issues such as U.S. dependence on foreign oil, U.S. relationships with other countries, and global warming are reemerging as key concerns to U.S. voters. Even though Americans' first priority is to keep "America strong and secure around the world," they also want the nation to strike a balance between toughness and diplomacy.[23]

We do not argue that President Obama should embrace existing international institutions, warts and all. It would stretch credibility to believe that when so many of those institutions need repair, the United States would be unconditionally committed to them. Moreover, we recognize that it is not only the United States that needs to recommit to international order and institutions. Many states, especially the major and rising powers, have too frequently neglected their commitments and undermined rather than strengthened the mechanisms of cooperation.

What President Obama could say is that the United States is prepared to work hard to develop an international order that effectively addresses the new threats to national and collective security and that affirms key values such as human dignity and responsible sovereignty. In addition, it is essential that the Obama administration commit to binding the United States to that order when it is established. President Obama should underscore that such an international order is in the self-interest of both the United States and other nations. As the United States becomes more confident that a new international order is taking hold, it will attach fewer and fewer conditions to its commitment to maintaining that order.

Skeptics will likely counter that, in this day and age, no U.S. government can bind itself when it comes to the protection of the American people. Even President Clinton, they will argue, insisted "multilateral when we can, unilateral when we must." We understand that all heads of state, no matter what country they represent, need freedom of action in crises and that there may be times when they believe that acting alone is their only means to protect their citizens' safety—a principle that is hard-wired into Article 51 of the UN Charter (the provision for member state self-defense). In the end, we believe that international leadership is about the United States making four fundamental commitments: to act in partnership with others; to invest resources to encourage others to join and participate in international institutions; to energetically seek diplomatic solutions to crises; and to create robust, effective institutions that minimize the number of times it has to act alone.

International skeptics will say that many states will no longer trust the United States or accept its leadership, regardless of a new president, new rhetoric, or even new policy. Instead, some will argue, states will seek to go it alone or develop new coalitions to balance U.S. power. And there is no doubt that some states will take such actions. But we believe that the evidence suggests that a majority of leaders, in a majority of states, still recognize the inherent value of U.S. leadership in the international system and still recognize that U.S. power is an irreplaceable source of international order. Further, those states are still willing to engage constructively in a U.S.-led (although not U.S.-dominated) international system.

A sea change in U.S. foreign policy is a real possibility, and other great and rising powers can exert a powerful pull on the tides of change. Their reaction to U.S. reengagement with international institutions will help determine its sustainability, in terms of yielding tangible results and in assuring Americans that their country's global engagement is appreciated. For that reason, as we argue in the next chapter, a first priority of the new administration should be to bring the rising powers into a new international architecture that accords them the voice, influence, and responsibility that are their due.

THREE

POWER AND INSTITUTIONS
AN EFFECTIVE INTERNATIONAL ARCHITECTURE
FOR RESPONSIBLE SOVEREIGNTY

AN INTERNATIONAL ORDER based on responsible sovereignty will require a new U.S. foreign policy that seeks cooperation to mitigate transnational threats, invests in and strengthens international institutions to sustain cooperation, and signals its support for the international rule of law as the best guarantor of U.S. security and prosperity. It will also require a new U.S. leadership style that is based on consultation, listening, and openness to expanded participation from parts of the globe long ignored by the United States.

This is only a start, however, for the United States is not powerful enough to refashion the international order on its own. A second requirement for international order is institutionalized cooperation among the United States, other major powers such as France, Germany, the United Kingdom, and Japan, and rising powers such as India, China, Brazil, and South Africa.

Why set a goal for institutionalized cooperation among these countries? Because institutions are more than just devices for collective action: they are the infrastructure of order. They are reflections of underlying policy, but they are also mechanisms for shaping policy. When effectively designed, they allow states to identify and act on common interests, and in doing so, to build patterns of cooperation. And in their most crucial role, they can prevent direct conflict between or among the powers.

U.S. allies and rising powers alike express intense frustration about their lack of inclusion in the negotiating and decisionmaking processes that affect their security and prosperity. Their agenda includes expanding the UN Security Council and the G-8 and reforming the architecture of international trade, finance, and development. Although these issues are fraught with conflict and potential pitfalls, the longer they go unresolved the greater the frustration at the growing chasm between the distribution of power among today's states and the distribution of power within today's institutions.

Right now, if the United States or other leading nations were to seek to develop new arrangements for security, they would find only unsatisfactory options. The UN Security Council is sometimes effective, but often hampered by a lack of unity among the permanent members. By the time crises come to its attention, it is often too late to create consensus among its members. Nor is there any guarantee that all major powers will be present at any time; Japan, Brazil, India, and South Africa are not permanent members. Indeed, the council's lack of representation has eroded its legitimacy. The UN General Assembly, on the other hand, has legitimacy, but its universal membership dilutes its effectiveness. The United States and other major powers could turn to informal mechanisms, but they lack the structure, predictability, and legitimacy of long-term solutions.

Ultimately, this will have to be resolved by expanding the UN Security Council, but as we argue later in this chapter, this is the wrong place to start. Reforming the Security Council is difficult under any circumstances, and wrangling over expansion would detract attention from forging solutions to pressing transnational issues. Moreover, without shared perceptions and understandings among new members about today's threats, expansion would just as likely paralyze the council as make it more effective.

A mechanism does exist, however, that could forge patterns of cooperation among the major powers, including helping them to identify shared interests and understandings and build trust. Dissolving the current G-8 and creating a new G-16 that would include Brazil, China, India, South Africa, and Mexico (called the "Outreach Five"), along with Indonesia, Turkey, and one other country from Africa (likely Egypt or Nigeria), would create a means for the major and rising powers to construct shared interests and solutions to transnational threats.

It is easy to be pessimistic about institutional innovation at a time when many recent reform attempts have fallen short or stalled. Widespread disappointment about the outcomes from UN reform efforts in 2004–2005 was followed by poor performance from the UN Human Rights Council and a slow start to the UN Peacebuilding Commission. International Monetary Fund (IMF) and World Bank reform has been halting. But a better understanding of the relationship between power and institutional effectiveness and a close study of lessons learned from the record of post–cold war institutional innovation suggest otherwise. The period since the end of the cold war has seen substantial though ad hoc institutional innovation, including in the area of security.[1] This innovation was crisis driven, however, and institutions with partial capabilities and major coordination challenges proliferated.[2]

NINE LESSONS OF INSTITUTIONAL INNOVATION

During the remarkable period of institutional innovation and creation immediately after the Second World War, two great American statesmen issued cautionary pleas to their fellow policymakers about the future efficacy of international institutions. Dean Acheson warned of the folly of placing great responsibility on international organizations in the absence of governments infusing those organizations with power. Such, according to Acheson, was a recipe for disorder. And George Kennan foretold a challenge that reverberates to today:

> International political life is something organic, not something mechanical. Its essence is change, and the only systems for the regulation of international life which can be effective over long periods of time are ones sufficiently pliable, to adjust themselves to constant change in the interests and power of the various countries involved.[3]

Their prophetic advice rings even truer in a time of diffuse power and the need for international institutions to undergird cooperation against transnational threats.

Applying their insights to the record of post–cold war institutional innovation and reform, we derive nine lessons for designing effective institutional arrangements to meet current challenges:

1. U.S. consent is a necessary condition of success. Although the United States cannot dictate the course of institutional innovation or reform, it can block almost anything, and its position is pivotal. At times, others can lead, as Australia did in the creation of the Chemical Weapons Convention and the United Kingdom has in the area of humanitarian response. But the United States must at least support such initiatives, and in areas of core U.S. interests, the nation must show leadership, sometimes behind the scenes.

2. Rough alignment between the big players is a necessary condition for success. The biggest recent failure of institutional innovation was the creation of the UN Human Rights Council, which replaced the Human Rights Commission in 2006. Divergence among the United States, the European Union, Russia, and China about the composition and conduct of the proposed new council resulted in a compromise that satisfied no one and whose contribution to human rights is in doubt. The experience offers a sobering reminder to those who believe that new international institutions can be effective in the absence of major-power agreement about their purpose and operation.

The point is nuanced, however, by a subsidiary lesson, vital for future innovation. Not all the powers have to be on board all of the time for innovation to occur. As UN peacekeeping expanded in scale and scope, China was reluctant from the outset to support the deployment of peacekeepers in civil wars and mandates for "protection of civilians" or "responsibility to protect." Yet careful, patient, and sustained efforts have resulted in China acquiescing, supporting, and eventually even participating in UN peacekeeping operations with protection mandates.[4]

3. Big power agreement is necessary but not sufficient. Having the big players on board is not the same as achieving the broader support and legitimacy usually required to forge new cooperative arrangements. Achieving global results often requires an iterative process between smaller groupings that allow key states to forge rough agreement on the basic parameters of solutions, and more inclusive processes that forge wider agreement and the legitimacy this brings. Often these two types of negotiations will be coterminous, as when side negotiations between the United States and China enabled the World Health Assembly to adopt strong new International Health Regulations in 2005. Another recent example (which we discuss in chapter 4) is the tension between the

Major Economies Meeting (MEM) on climate change and the wider UN process, where the MEM's perceived competition with the UN process has undermined what might otherwise be a useful grouping of countries.

Inclusive multilateral bodies like the General Assembly can be helpful to the process, but a bad place to design new arrangements. Attempting to negotiate anything in a body of 192 states at best complicates the process and at worst produces lowest-common-denominator results. Such bodies are structurally biased toward inclusion over efficiency, which makes them better at negotiating new standards for state behavior than designing effective institutions. Consensus-based institutions can give even minor players an outsized influence on institutional design, for good or ill. But this point should not be overstated: well-managed negotiations in the General Assembly and similar, universal, or near-universal bodies can produce good outcomes, as the General Assembly did in 2005 with the Convention on Nuclear Terrorism. And if the big players broadly agree, they will usually be able to secure agreement from the wider membership of inclusive bodies.

4. Institutions or arrangements will need to be aligned to the shifting power balances among major powers, but in a way that can accommodate future changes to that balance and allow for action even when some of the major powers disagree. The failure to adapt decisionmaking processes to fit changing power relationships has begun to erode the vitality and legitimacy of current institutions. This has most obviously been true for the UN Security Council, the G-8, and the governing boards of the international financial institutions.

5. Institutions need flexibility to respond to changes in technology and society that render them less effective. Institutions must respond when new developments lead states and nonstate actors alike to discover new means for circumventing rules. As we describe in chapter 5, for example, advancements in technology have lowered the barriers to nuclear proliferation; nonstate actors have shared sensitive nuclear knowledge and devices; and terrorists, not just states, seek nuclear weapons. The continuing viability of the nonproliferation regime will depend on new rules, commitments, and capacities to address these challenges.

6. A more effective, better elaborated set of arrangements for interaction between regional and global bodies will be vital for building collective security. Regional arrangements have proved dynamic in some areas

where global arrangements are slow or even stuck. In some instances regional institutions have been able to mount responses when the United Nations cannot; a case in point is the African Union's ability to respond (partially) in Darfur when the United Nations was blocked by China's potential veto. Compared to global institutions, regional institutions in Latin America have responded more rapidly to coups and regional institutions in West Africa and Europe have a better track record on conflict prevention. Yet the ability to marshal resources, expertise, and political support from beyond any single region gives global institutions important comparative advantages as well.

7. The need for variable arrangements that engage the private and civic sectors continues to grow. Effective engagement with industry helped secure the Chemical Weapons Convention; neglect of it helped doom a verification protocol for the Biological Weapons Convention. Because of the enormous variation in the kinds of actors necessary for solutions, this is probably best managed at the issue-specific level. We need quite different arrangements, for example, to engage scientists, laboratories, and corporations in efforts to safely manage biotechnology (chapter 6) than we need to mobilize private-sector investment in clean energy technology (chapter 4). The common point, however, is to recognize that solutions to contemporary challenges will not be found by states alone—but that states create the incentives and means by which nonstate actors can engage and bring their assets to bear.

8. The need for cross-issue and cross-institution collaboration is growing as well. Peacebuilding efforts reflect this now: the United Nations Peacebuilding Commission has begun to forge links among financial, security, and political actors. It is equally true, however, of the intersections among climate change, nuclear energy, and nonproliferation, or of the interconnections among climate policy, energy security, and food security. Decisions in each have substantial impacts on the others—witness the tremendous negative effects on food prices, and on instability, of climate-driven policy to subsidize biofuels. International systems for monitoring the effects of policy decisions are currently sector specific, and no cross-cutting capacity exists through which to anticipate or monitor cross-sector effects of policy. Fluid mechanisms for bringing different institutions to bear on linked problems will be a central part of the challenge ahead.

9. Greater attention will need to be given to mechanisms that can better generate compliance—primarily through monitoring and accountability, but also through adjudication and the application of penalties, and in rare circumstances the use of force.

POWER AND RESPONSIBILITY: GREAT-POWER PRENEGOTIATION AT THE G-16

All this leads to the point that the single most important institutional innovation needed to undergird international order today is an institution to foster dynamic, cooperative interaction among the United States, other major powers, and the rising powers. The most achievable way to do this is to establish a G-16. We see this as the smallest grouping possible, drawn from the leading economies and the most populous states, regionally balanced. It replaces the G-8 (Canada, France, Germany, Italy, Japan, Russia, the United Kingdom, and the United States), and brings those countries together with China, Mexico, India, Brazil, South Africa, Indonesia, Turkey, and a second African nation, most likely Egypt or Nigeria.

The notion of expanding the G-8 or creating an additional, broader mechanism is now well established. The era in which the seven major industrial economies could meet with Russia and act collectively to solve global problems is over.

Former Canadian Prime Minister Paul Martin catalyzed the debate on expansion with his call for a Leaders 20 summit, and many have supported it. The G-8 partially recognized its own limitations and began to respond, inviting the Outreach Five (China, Mexico, India, Brazil, and South Africa) to meetings, but in a manner that actually aggravated these countries' feelings of exclusion. We need a fresh start.

Indeed, as this book was going to press in December 2008, an opportunity for a fresh start arose from the financial crisis. President Bush convened heads of state of the G-20 as equals because he recognized that the G-8 was insufficient to address the global financial crisis. The G-20 meeting does not close the debate on the precise composition of an expanded G-8—and below we explain why we arrived at sixteen members instead of twenty. (Oddly, the G-20 actually only has nineteen state members, with the European Central Bank making twenty. Four states that are not part of our discussion of a G-16 are members of the G-20: Australia, South Korea, Argentina, and Saudi Arabia; only one African state, South Africa, is part of the G-20.) However, what is more important is the conceptual breakthrough of institutionalized cooperation among major and rising powers, a central theme of this book.

If the basic logic is straightforward about creating something more than the G-8, proposals have been mired in endless debates: whether to create a new mechanism or simply transform the G-8; whether to have a fixed expansion or adopt a variable configuration; and whether to add a secretariat.[5] The resolution of those debates should derive from the new group's functions.

An expanded G-grouping should have three purposes:

1. It should be a prenegotiating forum, a place where the smallest possible grouping of necessary stakeholders can meet to forge agreements on the basic parameters of responses to major global challenges, and strategies for their implementation.

2. It should be a mechanism for building knowledge, trust, and patterns of cooperative behavior among the most powerful states.

3. It should be a device by which leading states encourage one another to take responsibility not only for the global impacts of their national actions but also for their global role in tackling common problems.

A G-16 could not make decisions for the rest of the world, but it could be a force for making the United Nations and other multilateral and regional bodies more effective. Policy discussions and institutional design efforts among 16 nations have much greater potential to be productive than a dialogue among 192 member states in the United Nations. Moreover, because these are the most powerful states in the international system, their ability to create shared threat perceptions could make the work of the UN Security Council more effective and render its expansion more likely and desirable.

A G-16 could work out trade-offs across nations that promote overall global security and prosperity. It could, depending on the issue, draw on the insights and energies of a far wider range of nations, large and small, in forging solutions. It could also tap the private and civic sectors for input; it would have the opportunity, if it chose, to be briefed by business community, consumer group, or labor representatives, and could use its cross-regional nature to promote corporate engagement on diffi-cult global issues, for example, on biosecurity. On most issues, we would not expect the G-16 to be an action body in itself—although on some issues, like carbon emissions and international finance, its collective con-tribution to the problems and the solutions would have global effects. Its convening power, the collective weight of its economies and diplomatic and military capacities, and its combined populations would create an unparalleled platform for catalyzing and mobilizing effective interna-tional action. In essence, a G-16 could be a steering mechanism with which to navigate the turbulence of diffuse power, transnational threats, and the changing distribution of power among key states.

The G-16 should have a fixed core to encourage predictability, accountability, and the development of networks and patterns of coop-eration. But it should also have flexible arrangements that allow it to bring a range of skills and perspectives to bear on complex problems, using "groups of responsibility" that are not limited to core G-16 mem-bers. For example, Australia, which is leading a multi-stakeholder process for revitalizing international arrangements on nonproliferation, could be invited to participate in discussions on that topic; or the group could invite Norway, which has advanced capacities for energy explo-ration, into discussions on energy security. The possibility of an invita-tion to the G-grouping would create incentives for smaller countries to contribute financial resources, issue expertise, and international legiti-macy to cooperative problem solving.

A secretariat should be avoided, lest the G-16 appear to be a rival to the United Nations; but the executive heads of the United Nations, the IMF, the World Bank, the IAEA, the World Trade Organization (WTO), and the World Health Organization should participate in relevant ses-sions and should be asked to help prepare inputs and agendas. Moreover, if the role is one of forging understanding, reviewing results, and guiding further action, de facto secretariats can be embedded elsewhere. For example, on climate change the de facto secretariat for monitoring the relationship between policy and technology and their impact on the envi-ronment should be the UN Framework Convention on Climate Change.[6] On nonproliferation and disarmament issues, the secretariat is at the IAEA, with the G-16 addressing the implications of IAEA findings for policy. Indeed, one of the advantages of the G-16 is that it could spur the kind of cross-institutional cooperation that many have called for but none has yet generated. Participating in the preparation for G-16 meetings would create major incentives for international secretariats to put forward their best analytical work and to develop informal networks across secretariat staffs to undertake the necessary cross-issue analysis.[7] Informal mechanisms like regular meetings of the chiefs of staff of those secretariats included in the G-16 would provide substantial benefits that would be hard to achieve through negotiated, formal relationships.

The G-16, in effect, becomes a mode of institutionalized dialogue that can improve policy. Its mandate is to find a path toward consensus and action.

The G-16 would schedule meetings flexibly: at leaders' level once a year, at foreign ministers' level more often; national security advisors might also meet informally. It would have the flexibility to invite other national leaders or leaders from foundations and the private sector; and it would have the ability to commission from the secretariats of the major international organizations inputs and agenda items that could help forge common solutions. It should also maintain a multiyear agenda, unlike the current G-8, to avoid the phenomenon of lurching from issue to issue without sustained attention.

The G-16 would not supplant existing, formal decisionmaking bodies. Were it to attempt to do so, it would run into a hard wall of perceived illegitimacy. If, however, outcomes from the G-16 were referred back to a formal mechanism—the General Assembly, the WTO, the IAEA Governing Board, and so on—the potential for a wider buy-in would be very high. If a rough agreement were forged on key issues in such a grouping, it would substantially increase the odds of reaching effective agreements in broader settings. The G-16 could also align its tactics for securing implementation of its proposals; a regular G-16 meeting of Ambassadors in New York, Vienna, or Geneva would help to this effect.[8]

Nor would the G-16 compete with the UN Security Council. In the entire history of the G-8, only once did it attempt to negotiate a crisis— over Kosovo. Given paralysis in the Security Council, the G-8's role in that instance was useful. But decisionmaking ultimately had to return to the Security Council to secure the result and authorize the necessary UN transitional administration. A G-16 will not have the day-in, day-out attention to crises that the Security Council has nor should it attempt to develop it.

The G-8+5 mechanism has basically established itself as the first wave of expansion. To consolidate this, and to give the body a heightened ability to carry its prenegotiations forward to implementation, three states should be added to the current thirteen to ensure adequate representation of large Muslim-majority states and of Africa. At this moment in history, any expansion of a grouping of this type that does not include the Muslim and Arab worlds would send a negative signal and contribute to further alienation and tensions. Expanding to sixteen would usefully bring in Turkey, Indonesia, and a second African state (Egypt or Nigeria).

This proposal will be resisted by many. And the details of membership and methodology will need to be negotiated. But the basic logic of an expanded and reconceptualized grouping has no credible alternatives. It brings together those with the power to solve global problems and creates the kind of ongoing relationships and networks that would allow them to find common ground and act upon it. Formal organizations will never have the kind of flexibility a G-16 could have; and larger, more inclusive institutions will never be nimble enough to deal with today's challenges. And as we address in greater depth in chapter 11, a Concert or League of Democracies may find it easier to agree on some solutions, but it will not have the power to implement them.

POWER AND LEGITIMACY: THE UN SECURITY COUNCIL

The G-16 would be a critical part of an international order based on responsible sovereignty. But it is not a substitute for the UN Security Council, which must remain at the core of international security. For the Security Council to live up to its purpose, however, requires giving a greater voice to the rising powers, eliciting greater contributions from them as well as from the five permanent members, and reforming procedures to help the council act even in the face of tensions between the major powers.

Among the earliest and thorniest issues that the next administration will be confronted with is expansion of the membership of the Security

Council. The case for U.S. leadership on this issue is strong. Bringing other responsible actors into the Security Council can increase both its legitimacy and its effectiveness—at only a small cost to its efficiency. Bringing Japan and India into the council would create leverage for dealing with Asian crises and security relations not available through regional forums. An expanded Security Council will include several of the world's other largest democracies.[9]

But the essential condition for effective expansion—a shared understanding of the nature of the collective security challenge that will confront the council—does not yet exist. Absent that shared understanding, an expansion of the Security Council will lead to more division, not less, and less action against threats, not more. Clearly that understanding must be built before expansion occurs. On the other hand, further delays will aggravate already inflamed sensitivities among U.S. allies and the emerging powers; forward movement on UN Security Council expansion would carry enormous symbolic value in signaling a decisive shift in the outlook of U.S. foreign policy. Reconciling these tensions, then, means first indicating a serious willingness to act on membership reform within a defined time period, then working within the G-16 and other informal mechanisms to build shared understandings of threats and appropriate responses, and in the meantime taking action on procedural and veto reform at the Security Council.

UN Security Council: Procedural and Veto Reform

Procedural reform of the Security Council sounds arcane, but its consequences are important. By extending its consultation with countries affected by particular decisions (troop contributors, financial contributors, and others with significant stakes in a given issue) the Security Council could substantially expand its legitimacy and support for its decisions. Few issues so irritate countries at the United Nations as being treated as second-class actors by the Permanent Five—especially when those countries' contributions are needed to implement proposed solutions. Greater and more predictable consultation is warranted.

In addition, we believe that the United States should lead on veto reform at the council. We do not advocate abolition of the veto. The veto offers an important reassurance to leading powers, including the United

States, making it more likely that they will actually bring issues to the council. It also prevents more frequent spurious use of the council to embarrass Permanent Five members by forcing them to make statements or adopt resolutions that have merely rhetorical value.

When it comes to the most serious aspect of the council's business, however, the authorization of the use of force, sanctions, or peacekeeping operations, it would substantially enhance the legitimacy of the Security Council were the Permanent Five to agree, informally, that they would not use the veto to block action unless at least two permanent members opposed that action.

For the United States, this would have two benefits. It would make it more difficult for another permanent member to block action against genocide or large-scale human rights violations; and it would avoid for the United States the diplomatic cost of being the sole actor on the stage blocking otherwise popular Security Council actions. Internationally, it would improve the legitimacy of council decisions. Of course, for this to be viable the United States would have to be willing occasionally to accept outcomes that are tangential to its interests. In most instances, however, the United States would be able to convince one other member of the Permanent Five to back its positions.

Most important, this reform would enable the Security Council to function even in times of tension between some of the major powers. (In extremis, of course, permanent members could have recourse to their veto rights enshrined in the charter.)

Voluntary reform of the veto power would have an additional benefit. It would ease the path to expanding the Security Council's membership without adding new vetoes, making the option of new seats without vetoes (the only feasible option) less discriminatory against incoming major powers.

Expansion of the UN Security Council

The United States and other leading powers should use informal mechanisms like the G-16 to build cooperative relationships around key security issues and to explore the effective basis for reform. When members share sufficient understanding of the role they expect the UN Security Council to play on issues like proliferation and terrorism, the United

States (after consultations with other members of the Permanent Five) should initiate membership reform of the council.

Seats in the Security Council should not simply be a reflection of power, but an inducement toward responsibility. Linking new seats to contributions to international peace and security would help ensure this. Expansion should also deal with concerns about a loss of the council's efficiency. The smallest possible expansion that can meet the goal of rebalancing and legitimating the Security Council should be pursued.

The experience of prenegotiating the council's expansion at the UN in 2005 proved one thing beyond doubt: no prospect exists, at this juncture, for adding new permanent seats, even without the veto. (The idea of new permanent seats with the veto is a nonstarter; most member states believe that the veto power should be curtailed, not expanded.) The coalition of those who would oppose new permanent seats is simply too broad, encompassing those who object in principle to expanding the permanent category, those who object specifically to a given proposed new permanent member (Italy objects to Germany, Pakistan to India, South Korea to Japan, and so on), and a broader set of actors who believe that their own influence would diminish with this kind of expansion.

A better option is creating renewable, long-term seats that would be open only to the leading contributors to the UN's budget, peacekeeping operations, and political functions within each region. Such a model has a serious chance of getting support from the General Assembly; indeed, in spring 2005 the "group of four" states pursuing a permanent seat—India, Germany, Japan, and Brazil—missed a window of opportunity to secure expansion on a similar model.

Of course, nonpermanent expansion does not fully meet the aspirations of the emerging powers or Japan. And in the case of India in particular, the scale and significance of the country make a nonpermanent expansion seem inappropriate. Marrying what is right with what is doable requires, then, a mechanism for long-term but nonpermanent expansion now, with a real option of creating new permanent seats within a defined time period. As one official from a government seeking reform told us, business-class seats are acceptable, so long as they come with the possibility of an eventual upgrade to first class.

The most effective approach would be to increase the total number of UN Security Council seats from fifteen to twenty-one, with no new permanent seats. The new seats should be long term (six to ten years); they should be renewable; and election to them should be limited to the top contributors to peace and security in each of the regional groupings. A date for review of these arrangements should be established, within fifteen years, and it should be made explicit that the review will consider the option of creating new permanent seats.

POWER AND EFFICIENCY: MANAGEMENT REFORM AT THE UNITED NATIONS

Throughout this book, we stress that the primary actors in tackling global threats are states; state power remains the principal driver of international order. But in many instances, states will choose to pool capabilities or coordinate their national resources through international organizations. Consider just one example: the UN Secretariat currently manages upward of 100,000 troops in twenty-one different operational theatres—more troops deployed around the world than any actor other than the U.S. government. Managing those organizations is thus an important part of how transnational threats will be mitigated.

For the threats discussed in this book, the relevant institutions are concentrated in the UN system, broadly conceived. Management reform is relevant to the international financial institutions as well, and certainly as the IMF and World Bank take on greater roles in climate change and postconflict reconstruction, their systems for recruiting, retaining, and rewarding personnel will have to be adapted to suit—but we leave a detailed examination of this issue to analysts with more direct experience of those institutions. Moreover, where the gap between expanding operational and political functions and stagnant management systems is greatest is at the United Nations. In addition to its dramatic expansion of peacekeeping, the United Nations has experienced an unprecedented demand to respond to global development and security challenges over the past decade. The growth of complex mandates, operations, and budgets has not been matched by commensurate improvements to its management system. As a result, the United Nations is falling short of its potential in dealing with collective security in the twenty-first century.

Like UN Security Council procedural reform, this issue appears technical and is often approached as a question of efficiency or effectiveness.

But the issue in fact is about power, both because it has become a consistent demand of the United Nations' most powerful member (the United States) and its second largest donor (Japan) and because management issues are the one place that smaller states exercise real influence in the UN system.

To non-American representatives at the United Nations, the U.S. preoccupation with management reform often seems specious. Most non-Americans viewed the vigorous campaign in 2005 by Republican members of the U.S. Congress against possible UN malfeasance during the "Oil-for-Food" program in Iraq as political retribution against statements then Secretary General Kofi Annan made during the U.S. election campaign that appeared to favor the Democratic candidate. Former U.S. Federal Reserve Chairman Paul Volcker's investigation of the scandal found scant evidence of corruption by secretariat officials but substantial evidence of malfeasance by UN Security Council members.

Volcker did find substantial evidence of mismanagement by the secretary general, especially on issues of personnel. In response, and under intense congressional and administration pressure, Annan proposed sweeping reforms that would link greater managerial authority for the secretary general with greater accountability and oversight. At the core of all of this was a series of proposals to shift management authority away from a budget committee comprising member states to the secretary general himself—to make him the chief operating officer of the institution as well as its chief diplomat.[10] It fell to U.S. Ambassador John Bolton to convince the rest of the UN membership that these proposed reforms were not simply designed to enhance U.S. power at the United Nations—without notable success. Bolton and his successor, Zalmay Khalilzad, have continued to push these reforms, but progress has been glacial. Some modest changes have occurred; more have been stymied.[11]

U.S. policy has repeatedly neglected that for most member states at the United Nations, management issues are not primarily about efficiency and effectiveness, but about power. The blunt reality is this: the only place where small states can exert power over the UN Secretariat is in the budget process. The UN Secretariat's budget process works by consensus, giving each of its members (the majority being small or developing world states) a veto. Ironically, it was the United States that insisted that it be so: the first Reagan administration introduced consensus-based budgeting to the UN Secretariat.[12] So for states that have no veto in the UN Security Council, no veto over the selection of the secretary general, no de facto veto (as the United States and the big powers have) over major political operations, the one place they can exercise power is in the budget committee. Unsurprisingly the United States has made little progress in convincing other member states to grant the secretary general greater control over the budgetary process.

If the United Nations is going to be asked to play important roles in managing transnational threats, it is fair and appropriate that it should be asked to play those roles effectively and efficiently. But here too a fresh start is needed. Recently Secretary General Ban Ki-moon introduced a new initiative that would stress accountability: in management terms within the secretariat, in oversight terms between the secretariat and the member states, and of the member states to their commitments to the organization itself. Although few details of this proposal have been elaborated, it does offer a feasible starting point: one that drives accountability across all power holders rather than attempting to shift power from one group to another without a compelling bargain. With respect to the budget, this approach envisages bringing the process into the sunlight, where the actions of individual countries in opposing or proposing expenditures can be scrutinized.

This initiative could usefully be expanded beyond the UN Secretariat, to encompass the UN operational agencies in security and development. This is where the United Nations most directly affects human lives, and it is also where the United Nations' money is spent. Although UN headquarters has substantial inefficiencies, its net budget of just over $4 billion is far less significant than the more than $25 billion spent in 2007 on peacekeeping operations and by UN development and humanitarian agencies. On these issues, the prospects for a winning coalition for reform are substantial. Some developing states that resist the secretary general's proposals for reforming headquarters are more amenable to reforms governing UN peacekeeping operations.[13] Other developing states have recently begun to agitate for greater transparency and accountability in UN agencies whose function is to help poorer states develop and build capacity. Western donors, even if less wedded to the United Nations' role in development, share an interest in accountability and transparency in how those agencies spend voluntary funds.

To achieve this reform coalition, the United States and Japan would have to build consensus among a core group of countries with the clout to turn this initiative from ideas to results, including but not limited to our proposed G-16. The members of the G-16, along with others,[14] could commit to support the secretary general's initiative and work to foster an extension of it to incorporate the rest of the ten largest UN spending activities, where those do not fall under the secretary general's direct management authority. (The secretary general's management powers over UN special agencies and programs are virtually nonexistent: each is managed by a separate system of member state boards, and the details of an accountability initiative would have to be negotiated separately in each of these.) The goals should be increased effectiveness, efficiency, and transparency in the United Nations' oversight and coordination of dozens of complex peacekeeping, humanitarian response, development, health, food security, and climate-related response efforts worldwide.[15]

POWER AND PROXIMITY: REGIONAL ARRANGEMENTS

Beyond the G-16 and the United Nations, regional organizations will play increasingly important roles in managing and implementing security arrangements, in many cases being the first responder. Just as in any neighborhood, the neighbors have a shared interest in secure surroundings. Of course, some regions, notably the Middle East, remain so riven by historical distrust that effective cooperation on security issues is absent. In these cases, the involvement of the United States as a global power and of global bodies like the UN Security Council is critical for articulating cooperative action.

Effective regional arrangements (formal or informal) are vital for ensuring state compliance. Whether on nonproliferation or conflict management, the mechanisms are similar. Global institutions are regulatory and normative devices, and sometimes the hub of operational response; but the diplomatic suasion and pressure often required to ensure state compliance, especially in managing escalating crises, reside equally if not more so at the regional level. Two basic reasons underlie this fact: by and large, states are more integrated economically at the regional than at the global level; and political elites have more extensive patterns of interaction, knowledge of one another's domestic realities, and thus more ability to use moral suasion than exists at the global level. The European Union's role in defusing the crisis in Ukraine and the Economic Community of West African States' role in heading off crisis in Guinea are two recent examples. The role of the Six-Party Talks on North Korea further makes the point.

Regional organizations also help provide regional public goods. This function is vital, for although many threats have global sources or causality, they are felt primarily in regional terms. This is especially so for developmental and environmental issues, as regional groupings of states are frequently bound together in common environmental or climate systems. But it is also true of security issues such as terrorism. For all of the transboundary nature of the modern terrorist threat, actual terrorists in actual organizations tend to have regional or subregional concentrations. Even global phenomena like pandemics have regional concentrations.

In some cases regional organizations provide mechanisms for rapid crisis response. Because the only global crisis management system, the United Nations, is comparatively new to the business and still underequipped and underresourced for rapid global crisis response, regional organizations can use their core comparative advantage—physical and political proximity—to rapidly respond to breaking crises. The progressive development of their capacities to do so will be a central part of any effective international system.

Finally, regional organizations have taken the lead in defining responsible sovereignty. Here, three mechanisms stand out. The African Union recognizes that each state within the region has responsibilities to its own citizens and to the other countries of the region; its charter allows for collective responses to internal crises. The European Union (EU), which has gone further than any other region in actually integrating national decisionmaking, supports common economic management and social programs—though not yet a foreign policy. The Organization of American States has been in the forefront on defining standards of democracy.

Some regional efforts need sustained support. In the African Union, we believe that a U.S. commitment to the emergence of a substantial African crisis management capacity is warranted. The United States and other major donors to the African Union should additionally take seriously their commitment, made in the 2005 World Summit at the United Nations, for a ten-year capacity-building program for the African Union. This will require not just business as usual, but multiyear legislative commitments of financial resources and sustained policy attention.

Asia has no magic formula for new regional security mechanisms. The current, fluid mix of regional and subregional mechanisms has its costs—forum shopping by the major players being the most obvious—but is responding to regional and subregional power dynamics. To a degree, the United States has neglected the evolution of regional arrangements in Asia, prompting some Asian states to align policy without U.S. participation, and in some cases specifically to frustrate U.S. action. Even so, U.S. policy remains pivotal in Northeast Asia and among the Asian powers. That policy must consider the need to involve Asian actors in managing global challenges; to avoid major-power confrontation; and to promote cooperative rather than conflictual relationships in this vital region. A U.S. strategy of multipronged engagement rather than an illusory search for the containment of China seems more likely to serve American interests and avoid regional or subregional conflict.

In the Middle East we believe the United States should and must play a more active and operational role in developing regional security mechanisms. As we argue in chapter 10, a U.S. initiative on Middle East regional security is urgently needed, and should be an early initiative of the incoming administration.

Europe and the Transatlantic Alliance

Europe's regional mechanisms are of a different nature than those of other continents; and in discussing Europe it is also important to highlight the global role of the transatlantic alliance and its institutional manifestation, NATO. The ever-tighter integration of Europe and the operation of the transatlantic alliance contributed to international order during the cold war and in the immediate post–cold war era, and still have vital roles to play in building an effective order to manage transnational threats.

Europe's institutions are different for two reasons: European states have more fully integrated their national decisionmaking; and by simple force of financial weight, the European Union has a global, not merely a regional role. The development of EU operational capacities for mediation (in the person of the High Representative for Foreign and Security Policy), civilian deployments, and the projection of force (in the form of EU battle groups) could constitute important contributions not just to European but also to global security. The United States for several years resisted the notion that the European Union should develop its own force structure, but more recently has come to recognize this as a positive step that need not undermine NATO.

NATO at the same time has been growing fitfully in members, functions, and geographical scope. In chapters on conflict management and terrorism we discuss elements of NATO's role in tackling transnational threats. Though no longer unified by a common territorial threat from the Soviet Union, NATO members are still unified by values. Their common understanding of the security challenges they confront, however, was sorely tested by the fusion of the "global war on terror" and Iraq. Key to NATO's future is whether its members can rediscover their common purpose and shared interest in success in Afghanistan.

We devote little attention to NATO in this book not out of a sense of its marginality but rather because it is the one international institution that no American administration has neglected. That NATO falls short of its new goals is evident in Afghanistan; but we believe that in an international order built on responsible sovereignty NATO will remain a central pillar of U.S. and European security. It will play that role, very likely, in an increasingly well-articulated relationship with the United Nations and the European Union.

POWER, COMPLIANCE, AND ENFORCEMENT

In the vision described in this book, states will redefine sovereignty to accept responsibilities—toward their own citizens, toward other states, and for the external consequences of their domestic actions. States will agree to take on these responsibilities, expecting others to reciprocate. International order will rest on predictable actions of states exercising their sovereignty responsibly. What we call "should act" norms in chapter 1 will become "do act" norms.

Throughout our consultations for this book we were frequently asked, "And what happens when a state is fundamentally irresponsible?" Our answer: whatever responsible sovereign states together decide. The order we describe is a self-enforcing one; that is, no leviathan or supra-national authority will magically police it. As with current international laws, treaties, and agreements, states must see it in their self-interest to comply, and when they do not comply, it is up to other states to enforce the rules.

The likelihood that states will comply with negotiated articulations of responsible sovereignty can be maximized in several ways. Institutions can be created through which states receive credible, unbiased information about their performance against agreed commitments. Mechanisms can be established to help resolve noncompliance. Major powers can create strategies to enforce compliance, including through the legitimate use of force.

In the order we describe, as is true today, the power to enforce compliance comes from powerful states. And, like today, enforcement depends on the ability of powerful states to reach common understandings about when the use or threat of force is justified, on their ability to wield force and diplomacy in unison to maximize compliance, and on the extent to which their use of force is legitimated by others. What is crucially different in a future international order built on responsible sovereignty is that institutional cooperation among the major and rising powers enhances enforcement.

TRUST BUT VERIFY, AND WHEN IN DOUBT ADJUDICATE

Because it cannot be stated too often, any proposed international order must promote the interests of those states capable of creating the order. If states believe that reciprocity and mutual compliance with rules are essential for long-term mutual gain, the prospect that cooperation could unravel is itself a force for compliance. The frontline defense of international order is the belief by states that if they do not comply, neither will other states, and all will lose. And of course states at any time can exercise their sovereignty to answer noncompliance with noncompliance.

When the risk and cost of institutional failure are high, states will generally choose to eschew the limited short-term gains of noncompliance. But states also want to be confident that others are complying, just as they are complying. In the contemporary international system, the capacity to solve collective problems is widely diffused across countries that do not have a shared history or established patterns of deep cooperation. In this context, President Reagan's injunction to "trust, but verify" is an essential basis for undergirding cooperation on critically sensitive security issues. Through monitoring and transparency, institutions can help assure states that their counterparts are living up to their commitments.

Some issue areas already have monitoring mechanisms to build on. In chapter 5 we discuss the important role of the IAEA in verifying state compliance with obligations under the nonproliferation treaty, and how the Additional Protocol and greater resources can strengthen the ability of the IAEA to do its job. The IMF needs to further expand its powers to monitor and report on national monetary policy. The WHO reports on state compliance with the International Health Regulations, a critical source of information in the battle for biosecurity.

More difficult is monitoring state compliance with actions mandated by the UN Security Council. These may be sanctions imposed by the council or more broad-based measures such as its requirements for counterterrorism and counterproliferation actions. Here, the council collects information that states must submit; the simple act of publishing these reports, and authorizing the Counterterrorism Executive Directorate to deepen its analytical and assessment capabilities, would go a substantial way toward creating the necessary pressure, national and international, to generate state compliance.

In a context of increasing civil-society activism and clearly articulated standards of responsible sovereignty, scrutiny, information, and market choices can help create substantial pressure for compliance. Groups in civil society have mechanisms for monitoring state action, and these have also started to show substantial promise. Notable examples include the work of Transparency International, which publishes highly credible information about corruption, and the Kimberly Process, which monitors state and extractive industry compliance to combat "blood" diamonds. In areas like climate change and human rights, such mechanisms are invaluable, and probably cannot be replicated through formal institutions. One could foresee in the order we propose a nongovernmental responsible sovereignty index that monitors the extent to which governments live up to their commitments across the range of transnational threats covered in this book.

An additional challenge facing international order is how to collect and publish information on nonstate actors, including civic and private ones. In chapter 4 we discuss one example where using an existing mechanism for private sector self-reporting (the International Standards Organization) could be a critical tool in the fight to reduce carbon emissions.

Even with credible information, occasions when states disagree about how to measure compliance are bound to occur, and dispute resolution methods will be required. In some issue areas, such as trade, states have created a formal mechanism to adjudicate questions of compliance. Such mechanisms succeed when the long-term gains of cooperation are high and the fear of costly institutional failure is palpable. For example, even though the WTO's Dispute Mechanism cannot compel state compliance with its outcomes, states accept its rulings because they see their interests served by participating in and preserving free trade. The WTO example makes the political point as well: nothing in the decision to join an international arbitration mechanism erodes sovereignty.

Inevitably, states must impose costs on those states that do not comply with their commitments. And like the content of responsible sovereignty, the question of costs and compliance mechanisms will have to be negotiated—by states, by issue area. The rules, costs, and procedures must be understood, transparent, and consistent. If states vest power in an adjudication body, they have to abide by its decisions to make it credible.

The Use of Force

Restoring a sense of predictability to the legitimate use of force is a critical part of an international order based on responsible sovereignty. Two controversial questions are crucial: who should authorize force and for what reason?

In the humanitarian field, the UN Security Council's decision to withdraw troops in the face of genocide in Rwanda, coupled with its inability to act in Kosovo, sparked discussions about creating alternative venues for authorizing humanitarian interventions, and the concept of the responsibility to protect. As we discuss in chapter 7, when states are incapable of or unwilling to protect their citizens from mass killing and atrocity, the responsibility to protect moves to the international community. This continues to mask important differences in interpretation, though. Everyone agrees the Security Council can authorize military force to protect victims in civil violence; many governments contend that regional organizations too can authorize such force.[16]

At a time when regions are differentially embracing the norm of responsible sovereignty, the principle of subsidiarity seems reasonable. Regions are taking the lead in defining what is expected of the states within them. New regional charters are being developed where states agree that how states treat their citizens is a key responsibility of their sovereignty. As these trends take hold, regional authorization of the use of force will grow in legitimacy. Several examples make the case: the European Union and NATO in Kosovo; the Organization of American States in Haiti; the Economic Community of West African States in Liberia and Sierra Leone; the European Union in Albania; and the Pacific Islands Forum in the Solomon Islands.

A second contentious debate centers on the preventive use of force in the face of a possible mass-casualty terrorist strike. Like others we distinguish between preventive use of force and preemptive use of force. And we agree with those who argue that the latter, the anticipatory use of self-defense in the face of an imminent threat, is covered by Article 51 of the UN Charter, which acknowledges the inherent right of nations to defend themselves.

The preventive use of force involves no imminent threat. The rationale for a preventive strike, and for the Bush administration's adoption of the doctrine of preventive force in its 2002 National Security Strategy, is that given the ability of a terrorist organization in possession of a nuclear or biological device to inflict major harm and the fact that such groups may well not be susceptible to deterrence, states may have cause to act before any such group poses an imminent threat of the kind that would fall under Article 51.

This problem motivated former Secretary General Annan to commission the High-Level Panel on Threats, Challenges, and Change. The panel charted a pragmatic course, rejecting the doctrine of preventive force but arguing in practical terms that "if there are good arguments for preventive military action, with good evidence to support them, they should be put to the UN Security Council, which can authorize such action if it chooses to. If it does not so choose, there will be, by definition, time to pursue other strategies, including persuasion, negotiation, deterrence and containment—and to visit again the military option."[17] The language implicitly recognized that there might be extreme circumstances where in the absence of Security Council authorization, a state, perceiving an overwhelming threat to its vital security interests, would act outside the Security Council framework—but that it was better to deal with such cases as they occur than to attempt to reformulate international law on the basis of such exceptions.

That position was reinforced by the conclusions of major studies by Brookings[18] and the Hoover Institution,[19] both involving substantial international consultations, which examined a range of circumstances under which preventive or preemptive force might conceivably be used. With respect to the threat of terrorist action, the Brookings study found that use of military force would be problematic in practical terms (see chapter 8). Meanwhile, the Hoover project , which focused explicitly on questions of preventive use of force, found grounds for real caution in adopting a preventive doctrine. The project concluded that the United States and other policymakers should exercise enormous rigor in assessing the pros and cons, with cons such as loss of allies, lack of legitimacy, and the erosion of international order potentially outweighing any national security benefit from using preventive force.

Legitimacy of force is one matter; its practical and effective use is another. At present, the humanitarian use of force is more legitimate than ever, but as we describe in chapter 7, international actors lack the capacity to shoulder the responsibility to protect. And as we see in chapter 5, with the hard cases of North Korea and Iran, it is extremely difficult to marry the UN Security Council's use of sticks to multilateral and bilateral strategies that can compel states to live up to key commitments in international security.

The examples of North Korea and Iran suggest, however, that the order we describe here will be an improvement on what we have now when it comes to enforcement. China, Russia, and India need to be on board for any strategy to work. Instead of the last seven years, imagine an institutionalized cooperation among the United States and the major and rising powers, and that this cooperation created ongoing policy relationships and networks and shared understandings of threats. Instead of American unilateralism, imagine creative American diplomacy that worked bilaterally and multilaterally to undergird international institutions. Imagine also a United States that others perceived to be committed to a rule-based international order. This is the order that we describe in this book, resting on the G-16 and a reformed UN Security Council, and it is much more likely to produce robust strategies that the major and rising powers can wield to maximize compliance with international commitments.

CONCLUSION

More than any innovation in the international architecture, the G-16 has the potential to be a game changer. It would recognize the larger transformation of global power and be a means to harness that power for greater global cooperation. It would create a venue for the United States, traditional powers, and rising powers to construct shared interests and common standards of responsible sovereignty across a host of difficult, complex issues.

From our discussion of power, we now turn to responsibility. The next chapters apply the principle of responsible sovereignty to today's most vexing threats, from global warming to poverty and economic instability, from nuclear weapons to deadly infectious disease, from civil war to terrorism. We suggest issue-specific institutions that can provide legitimacy, mobilize resources, and coordinate multiple actors toward common goals.

As we make clear in part II, solutions to these threats are not "one size fits all." Different combinations of actors, principles, and power are needed to address global warming than, say, nuclear nonproliferation or deadly infectious disease. But when one looks closely at each threat, it becomes clear that, though they may play different roles, the members of the G-16 keep showing up in the cast of characters needed to empower effective solutions.

PART **II**

RESPONSIBILITY

FOUR

ARRESTING CLIMATE CHANGE

CLIMATE CHANGE POSES an existential challenge: either all the world's major economies must join together to stop global warming or the world will risk a wave of catastrophe that will change life as we know it. A rise in global sea levels, changes in precipitation patterns, and an increase in extreme weather may be felt most severely by those living in developing countries, but the security and economic repercussions will reach into the industrialized world. Any solution will require radical changes in fossil fuel consumption and significant advances in technology. Yet few countries will sacrifice short-term economic growth to cut the greenhouse gas (GHG) emissions associated with energy use. Hence the dilemma before us—the need for an international agreement that protects all nations from global warming, yet also ensures economic growth and energy security.

Climate change will lead to severe flooding and droughts that will devastate food production in many countries, spread disease, and contribute to hundreds of thousands of deaths each year.[1] Across the developing world, global warming is predicted to push an additional 45 to 70 million people into poverty,[2] potentially negating the efforts of poverty-eradication campaigns of recent decades, driving migration, and exacerbating regional conflicts. Millions living in emerging economies such as China and India already face the impacts of climate change. In China a water crisis resulting from climate change is threatening the agricultural region that produces half the country's wheat.[3] In India leaders consider the impact of climate change on its deteriorating water situation to be the biggest risk facing the country.[4] Yet despite a growing awareness that irreparable damage to the environment could lead to economic and social disasters, these emerging powers cannot contemplate slowing their economic growth given the still high levels of poverty, rising populations, and soaring expectations.

Similarly, many American policymakers continue to operate under the illusion that the developed world will be insulated from the worst impacts of climate change. Hurricane Katrina was a glaring example of the dangers of this assumption, and Katrina's devastation may pale in comparison with future global warming scenarios.[5] If temperature increases remain on the current trajectory, parts of Florida and South Carolina could be under water within the next hundred years. Residents of the American Southwest already confront serious water shortages from changing rainfall patterns[6] and growing populations.[7]

Much like their American counterparts, Russian politicians have shrugged off the effects of warming. They might consider whether they would regret it if St. Petersburg were submerged under water, or whether they see a cautionary tale in the devastation of Canada's western forests.

The United States and Europe will face security threats brought on by climate change across the globe. Many countries and regions will face large-scale natural disasters and the potential for violent conflict because of competition for increasingly scarce resources. International stability and the global economy will be threatened if major energy consumers allow competition over diminishing supplies to escalate into war in regions crucial to energy security, particularly in the Middle East, Central Asia, and Africa. A robust international response would be needed to address these growing conflicts, compelling the international community to become more involved in conflict prevention, humanitarian intervention, and reconstruction.

Political leaders today do not imagine or articulate the scale of the devastation and economic burden that the international community will bear if global temperatures continue to rise at current rates. Even as scientists, environmental activists, and business leaders develop an increasingly nuanced understanding of climate change and its diverse impacts, public policies fail to match the seriousness of potential outcomes.

To create a more effective global framework to arrest climate change, policymakers must overcome two interrelated and equally significant challenges. First, they must use markets and prices to reduce global GHG emissions by creating better incentives for energy efficiency, alternative fuels, protection of forests, and innovation. Second, they must transfer technology, finance innovation, and support adaptation measures while bringing basic infrastructure to the world's poor—in effect, transforming our economies to halt global warming and redress its impacts. Both challenges are connected by policy choices to reflect the cost to our society of GHG emissions that cause global warming.

The United States must lead to break a global deadlock on these issues. Science tells us that decisions within the next decade will determine the depths of the crisis to come. We emphasize that the United States can benefit from measures to mitigate climate change if it accelerates commercialization of green technologies and the development of global markets in energy-efficient and clean-energy technologies. If it does, the scale and importance of the American market can be a driver for global change. If not, the United States will find that over time the opportunity for leadership will be replaced by crisis management of a scale well beyond the Katrina disaster.

INTERCONNECTED PROBLEMS: CLIMATE, SCARCITY, AND SECURITY

Climate change lies at the intersection of earth sciences, technology, economics, politics, and international security. It is central to the competition for energy, land, and water that increasingly threatens economic growth and national security around the world. Understanding the nature of this competition and how it relates to the science behind global warming is critical to arresting climate change.

As human and industrial processes release increasing amounts of carbon dioxide and other greenhouse gases, these gases remain in the atmosphere, trap the heat of the sun, and thus lead to rising global temperatures that alter the climate of the earth. The longer these gases are emitted, the more difficult it becomes to avoid the impacts on human life. The Intergovernmental Panel on Climate Change (IPCC) established that the maximum temperature increase that the world can sustain by 2050,

FIGURE 4-1. Global Temperature Change and Its Potential Impacts[a]

Global average annual temperature change relative to 1980–1999 (°C)

	0	1	2	3	4	5

WATER	Increased water availablity in moist tropics and high latitudes ··········► Decreasing water availability and increasing drought in mid-latitudes and semiarid low latitudes ········► Hundreds of millions of people exposed to increased water stress ···········►
ECOSYSTEMS	Up to 30% of species at increasing risk of extinction ———— Significant extinctions around the globe[b] ——► Increased coral bleaching ——Most corals bleached —— Widespread coral mortality ··········► Terrestrial biosphere tends toward a net carbon source as: ~15% ———— ~40% of ecosystems affected ——► Increasing species range shifts and wildfire risks Ecosystem changes caused by weakening of the meridional overturning circulation ··········►
FOOD	Complex, localized negative impacts on small-holders, subsistence farmers, and fishers ··········► Tendencies for cereal productivity to decrease in low latitudes ———— Productivity of all cereals decreases in low latitudes ········► Tendencies for some cereal productivity to increase in mid-to-high latitudes ——— Cereal productivity to decrease in some regions
COASTS	Increased damage from floods and storms ··········► About 30% of global coastal wetlands lost[c] ·········► Millions more people could experience coastal flooding each year ··········►
HEALTH	Increasing burden from malnutrition, diarrheal, cardiorespiratory, and infectious diseases ········► Increased morbidity and mortality from heat waves, floods, and droughts ·········► Changed distribution of some disease vectors ···········► Substantial burden on health services ········►

	0	1	2	3	4	5

Source: IPCC, *Climate Change 2007: Synthesis Report Summary for Policymakers* (November 2007), p. 10.

a. Impacts will vary by extent of adaptation, rate of temperature change, and socioeconomic pathway.

b. *Significant* is defined here as more than 40 percent.

c. Based on average rate of sea level rise of 4.2 mm/year from 2000 to 2080.

without causing irreparable damage, is roughly 2.5°C. Figure 4-1 illustrates that the higher the temperature change, the greater the devastation. Most experts accept the IPCC consensus that GHG emissions (carbon dioxide and equivalent gases, or CO_2e) must remain within 445–490 parts per million (ppm) to contain the earth's temperature within the 2.5°C mark.[8] Current global levels are estimated at between 420 and 445 ppm of CO_2e—in other words, we do not have much room for maneuver.[9]

Estimates of the level of reductions in global GHG emissions required to stabilize atmospheric concentrations between 445–490 ppm of CO_2e range between 50 and 85 percent (Table 4-1).[10] If we continue current trends, emissions will rise by 25 to 90 percent by 2030 and even more by 2050. The IPCC concludes that global CO_2e emissions must peak in 2015 to keep temperature increases under 2.5°C and avoid the worst changes in our environment. Assuming a two-term American presidency beginning in 2009, the policy choices of the next American president and his international counterparts will determine our environmental future.

The biggest driver of GHG emissions is the consumption of fossil fuels. The use of fossil fuels is central to economic growth, and rapid growth in developed and emerging economies is driving energy demand in ways that will continue to increase overall emissions unless radical changes are made in technology. The International Energy Agency (IEA) projects that by 2030 consumption of fossil fuels will increase by 53 percent to sustain global economic growth.[11] China and India account for close to 50 percent of that growth (see Figure 4-2).[12] The rate of China's rising energy demand is absolutely astounding. Since 2000 China's energy demand has doubled, and it has accounted for one-third of the increase in global oil demand during this period.[13] In 2005 and 2006 alone China's electricity generation increased by an amount equivalent to all the electricity required by the United Kingdom, and 85 percent of that electric power came from coal, the highest carbon-emitting fuel.[14] By 2030 China alone will add the equivalent of a European Union (EU) in electricity generation.[15] Unless economic growth is separated from fossil fuels and resulting emissions, particularly in emerging economies with the most growth in world energy demand, reducing global emissions will be close to impossible.

The competition for scarce energy has itself become a global security threat. For now huge fluctuations of fuel prices are the norm, the product of an oil market with little short-term flexibility on either the demand or supply side—at a time of insecurity in oil-producing regions and along transport routes. This includes conflict in the Middle East, the risk that the Iraq war will spill into the Persian Gulf, the risk of U.S. conflict with Iran, violence in the Niger Delta, populist governments in Iran and Venezuela, and the difficulty of securing major oil transport routes.[16] Add to this the power vested in energy-rich states—especially Russia, Iran, and

TABLE 4-1. Temperature and Stabilization Scenarios

Scenario	CO$_2$ concentration at stabilization (2005 = 379 ppm)	CO$_2$ equivalent atmospheric concentrations at stabilization, including GHGs and aerosols (2005 = 375 ppm)	Peaking year for CO$_2$ emissions	Percent change in global CO$_2$ emissions in 2050 (percent of 2000 emissions)	Global average temperature increase above pre-industrial at equilibrium, using "best estimate" climate sensitivity (°C)	Global average sea level rise in meters above pre-industrial at equilibrium from thermal expansion only	Number of assessed scenarios
I	350–440	445–490	2000–2015	−85 to −50	2.0–2.4	0.4–1.4	6
II	400–440	490–535	2000–2020	−60 to −30	2.4–2.8	0.5–1.7	18
III	440–485	535–590	2010–2030	−30 to +5	2.8–3.2	0.6–1.9	21
IV	485–570	590–710	2020–2060	+10 to +60	3.2–4.0	0.6–2.4	118
V	570–660	710–855	2050–2060	+25 to +85	4.0–4.9	0.8–2.9	9
VI	660–790	855–1130	2060–2090	+90 to +140	4.9–6.1	1.0–3.7	5

Source: IPCC, *Climate Change 2007: Synthesis Report Summary for Policymakers*, p. 20.

FIGURE 4-2. Increase in World Primary Energy Demand, Imports, and Energy-Related CO_2 Emissions in the Reference Scenario, 2000–06

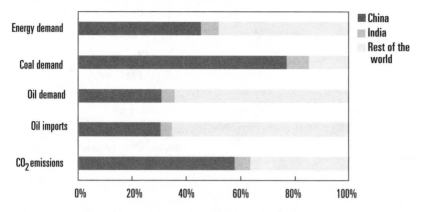

Source: International Energy Agency, *World Energy Outlook 2007.*

Venezuela—which have demonstrated that they are willing to use their energy market power to manipulate consumers and exert pressure on recipient states. In 2007 oil consumers paid $4 billion to $5 billion more for crude oil every day than they did five years before, transferring more than $2 trillion to oil companies and oil-producing nations.[17]

Moreover, the instability that has restricted access to energy supplies in some regions is driving a wedge between major powers and preventing them from cooperating on other threats. Tensions among the United States, Russia, and China regarding Iran's energy supplies are an obstacle in efforts to counter Iran's growing nuclear program. European dependency on Russian gas complicated a coherent response to Russia's incursion into Georgia in 2008. Major powers' oil interests in Sudan and West Africa have inhibited multilateral cooperation to stop the genocide in Sudan and address rising unrest in Nigeria. If climate change further disrupts access to energy supplies, the risk of clashes among consumers will become more acute.

Particularly in the United States, the tendency to view climate change through a lens of energy independence creates other vulnerabilities. The search for energy independence has led to investing in alternative energy sources without due regard for the consequences on other transnational threats. Nuclear power can help reduce fossil fuel consumption but, as we discuss in chapter 5, it creates its own risk of proliferation if not accompanied with controls over the fuel cycle and reprocessing. Similarly, more than $10 billion in annual subsidies for biofuels, especially in the United States and Europe, have had a series of adverse effects: land has been shifted out of food production, contributing 20–30 percent of increased food prices from 2006 to 2008,[18] while accelerating destruction of rain forests and scarcity of water—with little net savings on carbon emissions using current technology.[19] Deforestation now accounts for 20 percent of global GHG emissions and has put Brazil and India into the top five emitters of greenhouse gases.[20] By some estimates, the global community will have tapped all global fresh water supplies by 2050.[21]

Population growth will make all these problems worse. By 2050, the world's population is projected to grow from 6.7 billion today to 9 billion.[22] Already 1.6 billion people without electricity want it and should get it.[23] Add to that another 2.3 billion people on the planet in the next four decades, most of them in Asia and Africa.[24] Conservatively, this means that the world will need to accommodate 3.9 billion new electricity consumers by 2050. Building this capacity by replicating current patterns of energy use and economic growth will create a new form of mutually assured destruction. This underscores the urgency of action. A stable climate cannot sustain current rates of growth in energy use, GHG emissions, and use of limited resources while we wait for technological solutions. Instead, we must put all existing technologies to maximum use and create incentives to conserve in the present—and while we do all these things, enact policies to stimulate innovation that can transform our future.

RESPONSIBLE SOVEREIGNTY AND CLIMATE CHANGE

Climate change is a showcase for why responsible sovereignty must be an organizing principle for international engagement. First, because greenhouse gases contribute equally regardless of where they are emitted, all countries affect one another; the problem has no boundaries. Second, no country can isolate itself from climate change; each nation's welfare and security depend on and are interrelated with other countries' energy use and GHG emissions. Third, no country alone can succeed; restricting emissions in one country will have little net impact if investment and manufacturing grow in countries with "dirtier" technologies. Fourth, states must act now for the benefit of future generations—they must exercise responsibility across time and not just borders. Fifth, the issue is interrelated with other transnational challenges: climate change and misguided policies to address it will affect energy, water, land, and food scarcities, and all of these together will increase the risk of conflict.

This interdependence among nations and issues creates a common long-term incentive to solve climate change, but also complicates the short-term prospects to find workable solutions. The negotiator's nightmare is a harsh reality: any major emitter has a veto to a successful outcome. And this tension—between the need for responsible sovereignty on climate change and the capacity of any major power to undermine it—has characterized the nature of the current international framework. Although countries have recognized the need to restrict national emissions to halt global warming, the international regime remains weak because the major emitters have not been willing to participate.

At present, the rules and scientific foundations for responsible sovereignty on climate change center on the United Nations Framework Convention on Climate Change (UNFCCC) and the Kyoto Protocol, which set standards and goals for state actions, and the IPCC, which provides the scientific underpinning to those actions. Within this framework, a multiplicity of actors have operational roles, such as the UN Environmental Program (UNEP), the UN Development Program (UNDP), the World Bank, bilateral development agencies, and the European Union (EU). These operational agencies support investments ranging from energy efficiency to rain forest protection. The European Union runs the EU Emissions Trading Scheme (EU-ETS), which is a regional market for carbon. Coherence in the international framework is crucial to make the operational agencies effective.

Intergovernmental Panel on Climate Change

UNEP and the World Meteorological Organization (WMO) created the IPCC in 1988. Its membership includes the 190 members of the WMO, and a small secretariat within the WMO runs it. It convenes scientists, governments, and civil society to assess the process of climate change, options for its prevention, and how to adapt to its consequences.[25] The IPCC is perhaps the best example from any field of the valuable role the United Nations can play to achieve scientific consensus and serve as a watchdog on an issue of global concern. The 2007 Nobel Peace Prize to the IPCC demonstrates global recognition of its accomplishments.

Since its creation, the IPCC has fundamentally changed how the international community views and deals with global warming. Its first assessment report served as the basis for negotiating the UNFCCC, which has become the most important global forum on the issue. Subsequent IPCC reports presented decisive evidence of climate change and its devastating impacts and thus have made it a top priority worldwide. The IPCC's strength is that it collects scientific submissions from around the world and provides a forum to forge consensus on key findings. Its weakness is that it does not have the staff and resources to set and run its own analytic agenda. The IPCC can assess long-term trends in the relationships among GHG emissions, temperature, and the resulting impacts, but it cannot test and evaluate the effectiveness of specific policies within countries and regions or verify national emission levels.

United Nations Framework Convention on Climate Change

At the Rio Earth Summit in 1992 the United Nations created the UNFCCC as a forum of 192 countries to take actions to reduce the causes of global warming and to cope with its impacts.[26] The UNFCCC's notable endeavors include its ambitious goal of reducing industrial country greenhouse gas emissions by 25 to 40 percent below 1990 levels by 2020;[27] annual global summits among all parties to the convention to reflect on progress; and creation of the Kyoto Protocol to commit countries to reduce carbon emissions. The UNFCCC's greatest advantage has been its inclusive nature: countries around the world regard it as a legitimate, authoritative, and equitable forum. Its global membership is also its greatest disadvantage: it is an unwieldy and bureaucratic body, marred by politics and inefficiency because of the conflicting interests of its many members.

The UNFCCC process is based on the principle of "common but differentiated responsibilities and respective capabilities."[28] The principle recognizes that "the largest share of historical and current global emissions of greenhouse gases has originated in developed countries . . . and that the share of global emissions originating in developing countries will grow to meet their social and developmental needs."[29] In particular, it emphasizes that "responses to climate change should be coordinated with social and economic development . . . taking into full account the legitimate priority needs of developing countries for the achievement of sustained economic growth and the eradication of poverty."[30] The UNFCCC's members, including the United States, acknowledge that those who contributed most to the buildup of atmospheric carbon should do the most to cut their emissions, but also that all countries must take part in reducing global emissions. Success in the future depends on translating this principle into a legal framework that balances interests across countries in a way that they perceive as fair.

Kyoto Protocol

The Kyoto Protocol is an agreement by the parties to the UNFCCC that establishes binding commitments to reduce greenhouse gas emissions. It shares the objectives, principles, and institutions of the UNFCCC but significantly strengthens the convention by committing industrialized countries to individual, legally binding targets to limit or reduce their emissions. As delineated in Annex I of the protocol, 36 countries (all industrialized countries that signed the treaty) committed to reduce greenhouse gas emissions to levels specified for each of them.[31] These commitments add up to a total cut in GHG emissions of about 5 percent from 1990 levels in the commitment period from 2008 to 2012. Developing countries, defined by the protocol as Annex II countries, were not bound to emissions targets but rather committed to be more aware of their climate obligations.[32]

The Kyoto Protocol was an important step in international efforts to address climate change, but in recent years debates over its shortcomings have often overshadowed the more important issue of how to move forward at the end of its first commitment period in 2012. The point is not to declare a victor between Kyoto supporters and detractors, but to learn from the Kyoto experience to forge a more effective vehicle for future climate policy. Kyoto has been greatly constrained by two factors: the failure of some of the major emitters to ratify the treaty and tension between developed and developing country signatories. As a result, the Kyoto Protocol has not limited the emissions of four of the five biggest emitters of greenhouse gases. India and China do not have quantitative targets because they are considered "developing countries" under the protocol. Russia's targets exceed actual emissions because of the collapse of the Soviet industrial economy and therefore do not constrain its greenhouse gas emissions.[33] The United States, of course, never ratified the agreement. (Australia, the world's fifth largest contributor of emissions as of 2000,[34] ratified Kyoto under new Prime Minister Kevin Rudd only in December 2007.)[35] Absent support from the nations central to addressing the problem, the Kyoto Protocol could not mitigate the causes or address the catastrophic impacts of climate change.

The path toward achieving a new international framework on climate change has been complex. Officially, the UNFCCC orchestrates the process. A target has been set to agree on an international framework at the UNFCCC Conference of the Parties scheduled for Copenhagen in December 2009. Reaching an agreement, however, is complicated by substance—the wide divergence of the parties—and by process. In addition to the UNFCCC, negotiations have taken place among the G-8, the G-8 +5 (China, India, South Africa, Brazil, and Mexico), and the Major Economies Meeting (MEM) convened by the Bush administration. Although the MEM process was established on the reasonable presumption that the major producers of carbon must agree on a strategy to forge a global agreement, the juxtaposition of this meeting against other climate change forums has obfuscated leadership and the process to reaching consensus, causing the MEM process to be seen, especially among emerging and developing economies, as a rival to the UNFCCC rather than a means to help forge consensus.

LESSONS FROM MULTILATERAL EXPERIENCE

The foremost political challenge confronting a new climate regime is historical inequity. The industrialized world caused global warming and the concentration of greenhouse gases, yet the cooperation of emerging economies and developing countries is required to forge a solution. Developing countries justifiably argue that they should not bear the cost of a problem they did not create, but the crisis cannot be solved without them. Even if all high-income countries had zero carbon emissions as of tomorrow, the rising emissions of emerging and developing nations would still put them on a trajectory to climatic disaster and threaten the very economic growth and stability they desire.[36] If China and India alone continued on a trajectory of growth that brought them close to U.S. levels of per capita carbon emissions by 2050, their carbon emissions would be close to four times the "allowable" global concentrations.[37] Without the participation of emerging economies, an international response to avoid the worst impacts of climate change will not succeed.

The combination of inequities and interdependence has produced five blocs on climate change policy from which must emerge a new framework that embodies responsible sovereignty. The first is anchored by Europe and, with less fervor, Japan, and supports adopting an international treaty with common and binding global emissions targets. The second has been driven by the United States under the Bush administration and supports setting a long-term, internationally agreed goal on emissions levels and medium-term commitments that are binding only at the national level.

The third consists of emerging-market economies led by China and India, and has resisted any form of binding international targets. Emerging economies, stressing continued economic growth, have focused their demands on disseminating technology and financing clean technologies. The fourth group comprises developing countries, those that least contribute to greenhouse gas emissions but would bear the brunt of flooding, desertification, and other catastrophic effects. Unsurprisingly, they demand financing to adapt to the impacts of climate change. A subset of these emerging and developing economies includes those nations whose deforestation contributes 20 percent of global GHG emissions. International negotiations have yet to figure out how to create effective incentive structures so that governments of these countries, and their populations, have more to gain from protecting forests than destroying them.

An emerging fifth group is made up of energy suppliers who see the world shifting away from fossil fuels. Either they could emerge as facilitators of transition if they invest their wealth in technology dissemination and position themselves as winners in a greener international market, or they could be spoilers who drive up prices and profits to capture the greatest earnings during transition.

It is within this landscape of varied political interests and economic competition that a new international framework on climate change must navigate to stop global warming. Several critical lessons have emerged.

Support from the United States is essential, but the United States must first consolidate consensus on domestic policy before it can act credibly at an international level. The Clinton administration, sympathetic as it was to an international agreement to reduce emissions, was ultimately unable to build consensus on its urgency or forge a coalition to pass legislation. Despite Vice President Al Gore's best efforts to bring climate concerns to the top of the domestic agenda, the interests of labor unions and the politics of the North American trade treaty's ratification ultimately trumped the administration's environmental ambitions. President Clinton never submitted the Kyoto agreement to the Senate for ratification, knowing it had no chance of passing. President Bush failed for most of his administration to recognize climate change as a global problem. The Bush administration blocked domestic action and lost international credibility to lead on the issue. Without domestic support, the United States may be in a position to block international consensus, but it will not have the credibility to advance a positive agenda.

Developing countries, particularly China and India, must be part of a multilateral framework on global climate change. Their economic and population growth will increase global greenhouse gas emissions and energy demand, even as their governments strive to become as energy efficient as possible and still bring their populations out of poverty. The multilateral system must reconcile emerging economies' focus on growth with an awareness of their growing contribution to global warming. Over time a multilateral climate change framework must engage and assist developing countries to reduce their greenhouse gas emissions. Otherwise the potential exists for global CO_2 concentrations to balloon even as industrialized countries take drastic steps to change their behavior. A worst-case scenario is possible whereby investments flow to countries that are fast becoming the greatest emitters, causing a net increase in emissions.

Weak institutional capacities compromise the ability of the international community to combat global threats. The Kyoto Protocol has been plagued by well-intentioned but not well-structured internal mechanisms, with the Clean Development Mechanism (CDM) the most prominent example. CDM subsidizes companies to start green projects in developing countries, yet many of these projects might have happened anyway.[38] In addition, the proliferation of agencies and organizations within the United Nations and World Bank involved with fighting climate change has led to confusion and duplication. Too many UN organizational structures with too few resources address different facets of the problem, with little coordination and sharing among them.[39] A more efficient climate architecture must clarify and streamline the roles of various organizations, reform or do away with those that have proven ineffective, and expand financial support for others that show promise.

The private sector is a reservoir of capital and technology, and global and state institutions must leverage it. Many of the world's largest and most powerful multinational corporations support energy-efficient operations and reduced CO_2 emissions. Conoco recently publicly linked emissions from fossil fuels to global warning and lobbied for federal regulation of greenhouse gas emissions.[40] Six of the world's largest multinational companies announced a Supply Chain Leadership Coalition to require all their suppliers to release data about their carbon emission levels and strategies to mitigate climate change.[41] Companies as diverse as Wal-mart, GE, Shell, General Motors, and Sun Systems have all called for regulation to establish clear and common guidelines for all U.S. industries and stimulate conservation and technological innovation.[42] More than fifty major U.S. money managers, including Merrill Lynch and CalPERS (the country's largest public pension fund with $230 billion in assets), have also joined the chorus requesting U.S. domestic legislation to curb carbon emissions.[43] Companies across the world increasingly demand consistent regulation and carbon pricing because that will reduce risk and create a stable foundation for investment.

The nonprofit sector plays a crucial role in generating analysis, raising awareness, and calling attention to global warming. At every UNFCCC international meeting, nongovernmental organizations (NGOs) gather to scrutinize the proceedings and press states to act on issues ranging from cutting emissions to protecting rain forests to helping poor countries mitigate and adapt to the impacts of climate change. NGOs have pressed companies and countries to be more transparent in reporting their emissions. They are generally less well positioned to influence international legislation on binding commitments; advocacy efforts are often stymied by the vocal industry lobbies that stand to lose from such legislation. An improved multilateral framework on climate change could better channel diverse NGO voices, information sharing skills, and advocacy efforts into policymaking processes.

Perhaps the most important lesson that can be garnered from past and present efforts to address climate is that an extraordinary variety of actors must work together to make progress. It is one challenge to bring together governments to combat climate change, but quite a different one to mobilize companies, nonprofits, and individuals to work toward the same ends. The United States has a central role to play in linking these many players.

BUILDING A FOUNDATION FOR INTERNATIONAL AGREEMENT: U.S. ACTION

President Obama will be the most crucial actor in fundamentally changing U.S. and global climate policy. He will need to educate and motivate domestic constituents from many different industries and sectors and across the political spectrum. He will need to engage and build credibility with nations at varying levels of economic development, because each brings a distinct perspective of its own climate and energy dilemma. He will need to bring policy cohesion to an issue that fundamentally affects economic growth and national politics.

Pricing carbon must be the central tenet of U.S. policy to stimulate private investment, drive technological innovation, and encourage conservation. Three ways to price carbon are a tax on emissions, a cap-and-trade system, or fuel efficiency or renewable fuel standards that implicitly impose a cost. The three are not mutually exclusive. The last is politically easier because it hides the price, but it is less effective than transparent pricing. Europe began a cap-and-trade system in 2005, the EU-ETS. As the world's largest tradable permit system for carbon dioxide, it handles an estimated $30 billion market in emissions trading.[44] Australia is considering an innovative system based on long-term permits to emit carbon combined with annual sales of short-term permits, similar to how a central bank sells bonds and adjusts interest rates to manage monetary policy.[45]

Efforts to price carbon in the United States have stalled on two fronts. The first is political: pricing carbon will hurt fuel-intensive industries and labor groups in those industries. Because the Bush administration first denied the seriousness of climate change and then resisted legislation, the United States has still not debated the localized impacts and how to mitigate them. This will take time to negotiate. It will be harder in the midst of a financial crisis that creates fear about any actions that may hurt competitiveness and cut jobs. The second is a conundrum between science and technology. Given the political costs of pricing carbon, politicians have resisted emissions targets driven by science that current technology may not be able to achieve, yet delaying action will only exacerbate the problem.

The U.S. political environment is starting to facilitate progress. The Lieberman-Warner bill for an economywide cap-and-trade policy was favorably reported out of the U.S. Senate Environmental and Public Works Committee in December 2007. It did not pass because climate advocates realized that the Bush administration would have weakened the legislation and chose to wait for better prospects. Relative to 2005, the bill called for a 10 percent reduction in emissions by 2020, 20 percent by 2030, and 70 percent by 2050.[46] The Energy and Independence Act, passed in late 2007, included stronger implicit carbon pricing policies such as higher corporate average fuel economy (CAFE) standards, ambitious renewable fuel standards (RFS), and new energy efficiency requirements in lighting, buildings, and commercial equipment. [47]

In addition to movement in Washington, twenty-five states have enacted legislation to cut greenhouse gas emissions to levels far lower than proposed in pending federal legislation.[48] Despite an ongoing legal battle between the EPA and California on the latter's landmark climate change legislation,[49] state and regional efforts have generally enabled stronger federal action. States have already had to grapple with what kind of power plants to build and how to increase efficiency, cut emissions, and fuel their economies in environmentally sustainable ways.

President Obama should capitalize on this burgeoning interest and demonstrate leadership on state, federal, and international stages. To do so, he must move above politics and partisanship, which have too often misdirected America's domestic dialogue on climate change and thus clouded U.S. domestic policies.

First, President Obama will need to take on the role of educator-in-chief. He must explain why the United States must act, why Americans must take personal responsibility, and why we must absorb and mitigate the transitional costs that will come for specific industries and labor groups. Nationally, the United States must move away from framing energy and climate challenges under a single rubric of energy independence. Reliance on oil shale and corn-based ethanol may diversify America's energy sources, but will not help reduce its GHG emissions, and the latter will exacerbate international food shortages.[50] Energy security is central to national security, but so are the imperative and urgency to protect the planet. If global emissions do not peak by 2015, prospects to avoid catastrophic impacts seriously diminish.

Second, the administration should press for changes in national, state, and municipal regulation that will encourage the fastest possible spread of the available technological capacity of the private sector to create a more energy-efficient economy. In the southern United States, for example, the marginal cost of new solar power is already competitive with the marginal cost of new investments in gas and coal, but the current grid system precludes this head-to-head comparison. Innovative policies to distinguish new investments from municipal grids would immediately drive up the incentive for investments in solar power, and eventually larger economies of scale would make solar even more cost competitive. National building standards and investments in a smart grid are other examples of policies that could reduce emissions with existing technology and generate "green" jobs while reducing dependence on fossil fuels.

Third, President Obama will need to build consensus on a climate change policy that will unleash the technological innovation and investment needed to make the planet sustainable and prosperous in the long term. Failure to define a credible domestic policy has undermined U.S. influence on international policies that affect American economic, environmental, and security interests. The United States has relegated itself to being a "taker" of the impacts of climate change rather than a "driver" of policies to forge international consensus to forestall climate change and protect energy security. The United States must have a sound domestic foundation to drive consensus around goals articulated to and supported by the broader American public. It must create regulatory incentives to drive investment in available technologies to save and create renewable sources of energy. Pricing carbon is a necessary and fundamental tool to achieve these goals.

TOWARD A STRENGTHENED MULTILATERAL ARCHITECTURE

A new international framework on climate change must combine the inclusivity of the UN's negotiating forums with the powerful engagement of the world's major emitters. It must create incentives for the private sector to invest and innovate. It must institutionalize a role for NGOs to inject their insights, sustain scrutiny, and create pressures for compliance.

The principle of responsible sovereignty—the need for accountability for actions that reverberate across borders and time—combined with effective use of the UN and major-power negotiations, ideally through the G-16 we propose in chapter 3—together create the means to avert the looming climate crisis. The United States, because of the scale of its economy, level of emissions, and technical capacity, must be part of any solution. Europe, which has gone the furthest to create a regional climate regime, must continue to lead in setting goals that drive the international community to match its policies and actions with pressing scientific realities. Japan's technical prowess in energy efficiency can be a foundation for practical cooperation. Emerging economies must have confidence that an agreement will allow them to grow even within an international regime that curbs emissions. The process must engage the world's poorest countries on the impacts of climate change and the need to bring electricity to the 1.6 billion who lack it. In terms of substance and process, this is a tall order.

The goal must be a new, legally binding agreement to arrest global warming under the auspices of the UNFCCC. It should incorporate all the major economies and ideally include all the 192 signatories to the UNFCCC, and it should be built on the IPCC's scientific findings. Signatories to the agreement would commit that they will not allow the temperature of the planet to increase more than 2.5°C by 2050 relative to preindustrial levels, to reach a peak in global annual CO_2e emissions in 2015 and therefore to reduce CO_2e emissions by 50–85 percent by 2050.

To achieve these goals, the agreement must include two tracks that are separate but linked: (1) an "investment track" that gives nations the incentives and means to conserve energy, develop and commercialize technology, protect rain forests, and adapt to the effects of climate change; and (2) an "abatement track" that establishes the targets, timelines, policy framework, and accountability measures to control emissions. Because scientific understanding and technology continue to evolve, the agreement must be adaptable. It must include a formal annual review to tighten or loosen performance targets based on scientific evidence. It must explicitly call for NGOs to contribute to and monitor these reviews.

UN Secretary General Ban Ki-moon has called for completing a successor agreement to Kyoto at the Conference of the Parties to the UNFCCC scheduled for Copenhagen in December 2009. We endorse this target with caveats. The first commitment period of the Kyoto Protocol will end in 2012. An agreement in 2009 would give countries time to ratify it and come into effect when the Kyoto Protocol ends. Talks have been scheduled to negotiate a draft by the time of the Copenhagen conference. Yet it will be well into 2009 before a new U.S. administration and Congress could forge domestic consensus on a climate and energy strategy, solidify domestic constituencies, and ideally pass supporting legislation that would empower a U.S. negotiating position. China will not commit to an international strategy if the United States is silent. Even if the UNFCCC process can produce drafts for international reaction, these would be but opening positions until the United States and China align their strategies. Further, we described at least five major blocs of countries with widely varying agendas. The international financial crisis of 2008 will make it harder for every country to commit to policies that many perceive as constraining growth amidst a global recession.

Ideally both tracks of a new international agreement—on investment and abatement—would merge by the December 2009 conference. If they cannot, they should be separated and proceed in parallel, with the investment track closing in December 2009; an interim step on abatement could entail endorsing key principles that still must be translated into binding measures. An agreement on investment is within reach and will gain support from developed and developing countries alike that desire access to technology, resources, and other incentives to control emissions. Success on the abatement track will be far more difficult; key states remain far apart on politics and policy. If the tracks are phased, Copenhagen could endorse the principle of pricing carbon to promote conservation and innovation, plus reinforce a mandate for a G-16 Climate Group to formulate a proposal to restrict emissions and bring it to the

UNFCCC, with the aim of a binding agreement on emissions as soon as possible, with the end of 2010 as a target.

The phased introduction of a new agreement would reflect a meeting point between the realities of science and international politics. First is the imperative to agree to change investment patterns and peak emissions. Second, Copenhagen needs to sustain momentum among the parties and not explode a process that has no alternative to consensus. Better to have the parties emerge demonstrating unity and a sustained commitment for better results than leave a policy and procedural void, as occurred at the blowup of the Doha trade round in July 2008. Third, the parties should not simply settle on an ineffective substantive outcome for the sake of agreement. A bad outcome will not produce results, may not be ratified by parliaments, and could shatter prospects for compromise with little to show for it, rendering future negotiations harder. Better to create bargaining space for more effective policies when countries have more political will, and possibly more technological options.

Finally, to reach an agreement and set it on a constructive course, there must be clarity on the roles of two actors—the UNFCCC and the G-16.

The complex intersection of science, technology, economics, politics, international security, and bureaucratic politics demands one forum where all actors can voice demands and seek clarification. The UNFCCC must provide that forum and sustain a network among other key actors, particularly the IPCC, UNEP, the World Bank, and the Food and Agriculture Organization (FAO). For all its limitations in capacity, the UNFCCC has a mandate from 192 nations to act on their behalf to avert the catastrophic impacts of climate change. It has a forum and process for negotiations. Europe, China, Japan, and developing countries have engaged in that process, as has the United States, but with less commitment and usually with the intent to restrain rather than advance consensus.[51] The UNFCCC and the IPCC have already established a mechanism to incorporate scientific findings into the negotiating process, and that should be retained and not reinvented.

The second key body is a G-16 Climate Group (a "group of responsibility" that includes the G-16 plus other states central to the emissions debate). In chapter 3 we made the case for a G-16 to bring order to complicated negotiations with global significance and to bring its proposals to wider international bodies to seek legitimacy. This recognition of the value of a smaller forum has been a founding principle behind the MEM process put forth by the Bush administration in 2007. We agree with the principle behind the Major Economies initiative, but implementing it with no clear relationship to the G-8, the UN, or any other body has raised suspicions of its intent. The G-16 Climate Group should not be an alternative to the UN, but instead be established as a formal Subsidiary Body for Scientific and Technical Advice (SBSTA) within the UNFCCC, closing the gap between the MEM process and the UN process and, indeed, empowering the UN process. SBSTAs are already recognized as a forum to provide scientific advice to the Conference of the Parties of the broader UN climate change framework. Establishing a forum for negotiation among G-16 countries within an SBSTA would enable core countries to set objectives, rationalize priorities, create bargaining space, and set the foundation for actions within the larger UNFCCC process.

Recent international negotiations have seen debate over a possible new World Climate Organization (WCO).[52] Certainly, once negotiated, a new international agreement will need an effective coordinating mechanism, and a new agreement may well create demands for new capabilities and new mechanisms that could justify transforming the UNFCCC into a WCO. But negotiations over a WCO at this stage are putting the cart before the horse. Hence we call for keeping the UNFCCC as the central point for implementing any agreement until such time as new agreements require new mechanisms. Even then, a WCO should be conceived as a coordinating entity, mobilizing the many different capabilities that are likely to be needed to implement a robust international climate agreement. If a new agreement reaches consensus on carbon trading, appropriate mechanisms will be needed to set market rules and monitor performance. Multiple approaches will be needed to facilitate investment. Scientific capacities to stimulate innovation will rest in separate bodies. Even monitoring and verification of emissions will require different capacities for industry and agriculture. Attempts to fold all these capabilities into one organization would cause it to collapse under its own weight. Conversely, failure to define a central point of coordination within an orchestrated network would equally make an international agreement dysfunctional.

TRACK 1: INVESTMENT IN TECHNOLOGY INNOVATION AND DISSEMINATION

Success in addressing climate change requires technology and innovation. Most countries will not adopt binding restrictions on emissions that would keep them from providing jobs for their citizens. Investment in technology, both commercializing existing capacities and developing new ones, is essential to merge global interests in energy security and climate change. Japan and parts of Europe have demonstrated that through technology and innovation they can radically reduce energy consumption and still achieve rapid economic growth. Japan's current use of energy per unit of GDP is 43.75 percent less than China, 12.5 percent less than India, and 37.5 percent less than the United States.[53] The United States has already developed some new industries based on energy efficiency and clean growth. There is little doubt that we can discover new ways to achieve economic growth and still cut global greenhouse gas emissions. Yet the scale on which changes in efficiency and technology must be implemented has no precedent. That is the rationale for moving immediately with a technology track that has immediate impact and creates new possibilities.

The goals of Track 1 are to leverage resources, expand effective financing mechanisms, drive research, accelerate commercialization, and stimulate investment in energy and environmental technologies and infrastructure. Even more so in the wake of a global financial crisis and credit crunch, both policy and financial instruments are needed to reduce intertemporal risk and reduce disincentives to private investment with long payoffs. Track 1 on investment and Track 2 on abatement are related, most importantly through policies to price carbon. As argued earlier, prices will affect incentives to invest in technology and to curb emissions. We advocate separating the tracks only because an agreement to reduce emissions will take time, and many technologies are commercially feasible under current pricing scenarios.

The Track 1 agreement would give nations multiple investment channels to commit and disburse financing for technology: the GEF, World Bank, International Finance Corporation (IFC), UNFCCC's CDM, and regional development banks. Although nations will need to help finance public expenditures, especially for infrastructure in developing countries, public sector investment and finance will not be sufficient. The UN and partner multilateral organizations must unlock larger sources of private capital.

Track 1 will require flexibility and resources to address the distinct investment needs of countries at different levels of development around the globe: downstream investment in implementing and deploying existing energy-efficient technologies, and upstream investment in innovating technology and bringing new technologies to market.

For developed countries, private capital should finance most investments. Putting an implicit or explicit price on carbon is part of the answer, as growing technology markets in many European countries demonstrate. But better policies and risk mitigation mechanisms are still needed across high-income nations to create even stronger markets for already existing energy-efficient technologies. If industrial nations revamped their internal markets for clean technologies such as solar power, they could spur competitive investment in renewables and energy efficiency and reduce their GHG emissions.[54]

Emerging economies such as China and India have a different focus: attracting the fastest possible investments in technology that will increase efficiency, addressing both environmental and energy security concerns, yet still sustaining rapid growth. These nations can attract private capital for deploying clean technology, but have little incentive to shoulder the cost differential between business-as-usual technologies and energy-efficient technologies to solve a problem they did not create. New emissions from emerging economies now are the fastest drivers of climate change, but these governments rightly argue that their growth would not be an issue absent market failures in the industrialized world. For emerging economies, the two key issues are technology access and measures to share commercial risk globally and thus reduce the cost of capital. If Track 1 does not address these needs, emerging economies will not commit to an international agreement with binding emissions reduction targets.

Developing countries usually have limited access to private capital but require massive investments in energy infrastructure for economic growth. The IEA projects that even with $45 trillion in new global energy investments by 2050, an average investment of $185 billion each year, about 1.4 billion people will still remain without electricity.[55] If the poverty reduction objectives of the Millennium Development Goals are met, investing in energy infrastructure across the developing world will be even higher.[56] The developing world also has a related issue of how to finance investments in public goods such as creating or maintaining biological carbon sinks such as forests. Although poor countries have the least human capital, technology, resources, and resilience to cope with climate change, many will be struck first and hardest by droughts, floods, and reduced productivity. These countries will need public financing, particularly through the World Bank and regional development banks, to invest in infrastructure, rain forests, and adaptation to climate change.

A global climate change agreement cannot encompass every type of investment mechanism. Through the UNFCCC, however, it should provide a means for countries to pledge funds, designate vehicles to allocate funds, scrutinize national performance on commitments, consolidate reporting on the effectiveness of funding, and give nations and NGOs a transparent means to comment on funding priorities and vehicles. With that in mind, the following are illustrative funding mechanisms and priorities that should be strengthened under track 1.

Raising capital: The GEF should be recognized as the principal international mechanism to raise international donations for climate change and channel it to implementing UN agencies, the World Bank, regional development banks, national governments, and NGOs. Its role should be to assess needs, raise capital, set performance standards, set investment priorities, allocate funds, and report on performance. The GEF must put more emphasis on investing in abatement in the developing world and it should work more closely with the private sector—together with the IFC, regional development banks, and state-funded investment agencies—to leverage private investment in clean energy technologies or production.

Creating guarantee mechanisms: Mitigating risk can leverage private capital and reduce its cost, especially in emerging economies. One valuable model is the IFC's work with national banks to partially guarantee private bank loans to finance clean technology and renewable energy products. In China, demand for IFC assistance has outstripped available funding. The Multilateral Investment Guarantee Agency (MIGA), also part of the World Bank Group, should be tasked with working from the IFC model and establishing new products to address the intertemporal risk of investing in energy-efficient technologies. Both agencies should set standards for national risk-mitigation measures through investment insurance agencies such as Overseas Private Investment Corporation (OPIC).[57]

Sharing liability and insuring risk: Some technologies such as carbon capture and sequestration will require multiyear commercial testing before they can be used.[58] A global risk insurance mechanism, with waivers on national legal liabilities, should be created to foster international cooperation on challenging technological frontiers. Nations would need to agree on conditions in which they would approve such waivers. In addition, nations should implement domestic programs where they share liability with companies for demonstration of particularly risky and expensive products to bring to commercialization. France, for example, recently announced a carbon capture and storage (CCS) initiative in which it covers the liability costs for twelve CCS demonstration projects funded by private capital.[59]

Forming public-private investment partnerships: Currently, the CDM under the UNFCCC provides incentives for investments in developing countries to reduce greenhouse gas emissions. In doing so, CDM can support the growth of developing countries and steer capital to markets where investments will have the greatest environmental impact. Still, the CDM needs substantial overhaul so that it no longer pays industrial countries to carry out energy-efficient projects that might be financed anyway.

Leveraging development banks: The World Bank and regional development banks should continue to serve as the locus to finance energy infrastructure in developing countries and to support adaptation to climate change impacts. In 2008, the United Kingdom, United States, and Japan pledged $5 billion to $10 billion to support the World Bank Climate Investment Funds (CIF) to accelerate transformation to low carbon growth through innovation and deployment of clean technologies as well as to build climate resilience.[60] China has also demonstrated interest in funding green infrastructure in Africa that supports other Chinese investments. Energy and other commodity companies also share an interest in developing infrastructure in poor countries. The development banks should offer a mechanism to match private funding and set common standards. It would benefit developing countries to channel private and other aid through a common vehicle to ensure quality and to reduce the management burdens that multiple donors impose on developing country capacity, as we discuss in chapter 9.

Monitoring and protecting rain forests: UNEP, UNDP, and FAO launched in September 2008 the Reduced Emissions from Deforestation and Forest Degradation Program (UN-REDD) to assist nine developing countries (including Bolivia, Indonesia, and Zambia) in establishing systems to monitor, assess, and report forest cover. Norway donated $35 million to finance the initial phase. UN-REDD will be a critical field test of whether external financing can verifiably reduce the rates of deforestation.[61]

Developing innovative technologies: A renewable international fund of $10 billion should be created to fund competitive proposals for technical innovation. The IEA could run the fund, which would be open to public and private applicants. The focus would be on supporting technical innovation and establishing commercial viability. It would be oriented around reducing liability of investment in the riskiest of technologies and helping bridge the gap between the private sector and public research and development programs. A part of the fund could be reserved to support NGOs and programs that would build public-private partnerships for research and commercialization, such as the Civilian Research and Development Foundation, which has employed thousands of weapons scientists and institutes and linked them with commercial opportunities.

Creating networks of international research partners: A network would be created among national laboratories, research laboratories at universities, other centers of excellence, and private sector hubs of innovation and investment. The network would post developments in technical innovation and link scientists working in common areas. Those within the network could seek support from the technology fund and the broader venture capital community.

TRACK 2: EMISSIONS ABATEMENT

Climate change cannot be solved unless the major emitters buy into an international framework. The Kyoto Protocol will not significantly restrain emissions growth because the United States, China, and India have not participated. To date, the United States is responsible for having emitted the largest amount of energy-related CO_2 emissions into the atmosphere of any country (as of 2006, an estimated 320 billion tons of CO_2).[62] By 2030, energy-related CO_2 emissions from China are projected to account for 26 percent of the world total and 48 percent of the total coal-related emissions worldwide. If both China and India sustain their projected rates of economic and industrial growth over the next twenty-five years, they will together contribute about 60 percent of the global increase in carbon emissions.[63]

Track 2 on emissions abatement creates a process for the major emitters—a G-16 Climate Group—to shape a strategy to cut emissions and link their negotiations to a wider UNFCCC framework. As we indicated, a new international framework should limit global temperature increases and cut emissions, reflecting the IPCC's scientific conclusions. Track 2 should establish guidelines to achieve these targets based on the UNFCCC's core principle of "common but differentiated" responsibilities. Track 2 should be performance-based, emphasizing results rather than prescribing policies. As a core principle, it must recognize that GHG emissions must be priced to reflect the costs they impose through flooding, disease, scarcity, and conflict. Nations would choose how to do so: through some combination of a tax, a cap-and-trade system, or policies and measures for fuel efficiency and conservation.

Nations must have flexibility to adopt policies that reflect their political realities, yet the combined policy outcomes must be measured against science-driven targets. A carbon tax will be unpopular during a global recession. Cap-and-trade systems are difficult enough to establish nationally, much less globally or regionally. A global carbon market would have to manage key risks, such as a major player like the United States or China withdrawing from the market and causing its collapse. National cap-and-trade systems could be coordinated across countries, but comparable pricing mechanisms would need to be created. Regulatory targets on fuel efficiency and the use of renewables may create short-term momentum, but perhaps not the incentives needed to invest in new technology. These are just a handful of the complications that almost certainly preclude agreement at Copenhagen in December 2009.

Instead, Copenhagen could produce an interim framework that sustains progress toward a comprehensive package in 2010. The framework could:

Endorse IPCC goals: The temperature of the planet should not increase more than 2.5° C by 2050 relative to preindustrial levels.

Annual CO_2e emissions must peak in 2015 and be reduced 50–85 percent by 2050.

Commit nations to pursue national legislation to cap annual emissions in 2015: Even if not internationally binding, such a commitment would signal markets to change investment patterns and potentially encourage a shift to energy-efficient technologies.

Establish "best practices" for pricing carbon to be adopted in a comprehensive agreement: A comprehensive agreement on best practices would accomplish a number of objectives. Stability in long-term prices, not just short-term price spikes, would create investor confidence to change technologies and consumption patterns. Any pricing scheme would require a short-term safety valve or cost-containment mechanism to compensate for extreme economic contraction, comparable to the need for flexibility to adjust short-term interest rates. Incentives should drive investments where they have the greatest impact. For example, because Europe and Japan have already invested seriously in efficiency, incremental investments will have less impact in these economies than in China or India. "Common but differentiated" responsibilities could be met through time differentials as when emission targets constrain growth, thus preserving a common global policy framework but allowing flexibility on the timing to adhere to it.

Although the emissions abatement track should feed into one comprehensive treaty, we also urge flexibility on the final outcome, if needed, to allow nations to reach an informal arrangement. Given the domestic ratification procedures for treaties in the United States—a two-thirds majority in the Senate—and in other countries, a treaty might have to be so watered down to meet this political test that it could lose the core of its purpose. An arrangement among nations would not require ratification,[64] but would still create a legally binding relationship among countries. Experience with the Financial Action Task Force and the General Agreement on Tariffs and Trade (GATT) after the Second World War suggests the value of alternative models of international frameworks.[65] Nations would agree on common goals and implement nationally binding legislation to achieve these goals. In the United States, such an approach would require only a simple majority in both houses rather than the two-thirds majority in the Senate.

VERIFICATION AND ENFORCEMENT

Virtually every legislature will ask: How do we penalize countries that do not adopt comparable climate policies so that we do not reduce national competitiveness and export jobs to others? The premise is that tougher environmental standards elsewhere will decrease competitiveness and drive companies to relocate to China and India, resulting in a "leakage" of carbon to less environmentally responsible states. Concerns over lost competitiveness and leakage have led to proposals for a cross-border tax imposed on the carbon content of imported products from countries that do not have comparable policies. In the United States the intended target is China. In France such proposed measures originally targeted the United States. They are misguided and should be avoided.

Most U.S. emissions occur in transportation and housing, sectors that cannot be traded.[66] Energy generally constitutes a small percentage of total input costs in most manufacturing, making a higher price on carbon a small factor in total production costs.[67] For products such as steel, aluminum, cement, paper, and chemicals, which have a high energy and carbon content, less than 3 percent of U.S. imports come from China.[68] For all these reasons, less than 10 percent of the reduction in U.S. emissions from pricing carbon would be replaced by an increase in foreign emissions, and even then most modeling suggests that a border tax would reduce that 10 percent by half a percentage point.[69] Besides being ineffective, a border tax could prove noncompliant with WTO. India and China would argue that the United States is a greater culprit of climate change because of its contribution to aggregated emissions. Signatories to the Kyoto protocol could seek to apply such measures against the United States, which did not ratify it.

What should be the answer? As we suggested in chapter 3, compliance measures will need to be negotiated. To the extent that any individual state applies penalties unilaterally, it will create retaliatory risks that could undermine an entire regulatory regime. States need to understand the range of potential penalties and how they will be applied. They need to decide whether they will accept the scrutiny needed for external adjudication.

Just as important will be the pressures for compliance that can be created from the bottom up, forcing companies to reduce their emissions to compete in the marketplace and benefit from government contracts. To regulate carbon pricing, reporting standards are vital to account for emissions and enable emission trading schemes. Clear standards on acceptable emissions levels will compel states and businesses to be more transparent, empower investors to compare companies' carbon emissions, and thus increase market incentives for becoming energy efficient.

The International Organization for Standardization (ISO) has made considerable progress in setting standards to account for emissions and to verify them. In 2006, the ISO published its 14064 series standards as the first internationally accepted set of tools for measuring GHG emissions. A consensus for these standards has been growing.[70] They have been supported by the UNFCCC and IPCC, widely adopted by companies, governments, and regional institutions around the globe; further, companies and countries have greatly increased disclosing carbon emissions.[71]

The private and public sectors, including the UN, could continue to capitalize and expand on these ISO standards. Businesses would have incentives to integrate these practices into their commercial strategies to outdo competitors in efficiency rankings and publicize their achievements. Businesses could agree to establish partnerships and give preference to other firms that abided by the ISO 14064 series. Individual nations could adopt the ISO 14064 series as a regulatory standard for business, establishing comparable practice and reporting across firms. To compete for defense contracts, multilateral development bank contracts, and other state-funded procurements, firms would have to comply with ISO 14064.

The UNFCCC could provide further independent scrutiny by institutionalizing in its annual conferences a review of which members employ ISO standards effectively. The UNFCCC could use these occasions to highlight the best and worst firms within states. Organizations such as development banks and the United Nations could write these practices into their procurement regulations, requiring companies to be ISO certified before receiving funding. More powerfully, in the next round of trade talks ISO climate compliance standards could be negotiated into WTO rules on government procurement.

CONCLUSION

There is no harder issue than the climate crisis because it involves science, technology, economics, politics, and international relations. And the stakes could not be higher. The solutions, inevitably, will also be complex, involving many institutions and policies, with the expectations that both must change over time as good policy will accelerate technology and open up new possibilities. Logic tells us that this must be so— that in a complex world solutions to complex problems must evolve.

A successful framework on climate change must meet certain tests. The first is to set in motion the policies that will drive innovation and investment. The second is to bring together major and rising powers— which together will produce close to 90 percent of all carbon emissions by 2030.[72] That will require giving emerging economies time before pricing policies on carbon constrain their economic growth. In our judgment, better to get the G-16 moving toward these common goals now rather than pushing for targets that China and India will reject. The final test is to tap private capital, technology, and analytic capacity. In comparison to 1945 when most actors in the international system were states, we now have an array of national, regional, for-profit, and non-profit actors. Most resources and capabilities are outside of government, and those in the private sector must sustain pressure on government to improve policy.

In the next chapter we focus on nuclear security—an issue where policies on climate change and energy use are already driving many countries to develop civilian nuclear programs. Unless climate policy is coordinated with nuclear security, the gains in one area can create new risks of proliferation. The G-16 will again play a key role, both to reach consensus on nuclear security policies and to ensure that a common set of actors addresses the linkages across issues that must be considered together, not in isolation.

On climate change and nuclear security, U.S. policy is pivotal. For nations to engage collectively, they must share a mutual conviction that each will be better off. To set this tone, the United States must lead in action and not just rhetoric. If President Obama can see beyond short-term uncertainties to act responsibly for future generations, he will find that an aggressive climate policy can help restore America's international image as well as advance its energy security.

FIVE

THE SECOND NUCLEAR AGE

WE HAVE ENTERED a second nuclear age.[1] At the dawn of the first, the framers of the Nuclear Non-Proliferation Treaty (NPT) believed that they could create a firewall between nuclear technology for peaceful uses and nuclear technology for weapons. But in the 1980s, that assumption was proven wrong by Iraq and more recently, by North Korea and Iran. In the first nuclear age, proliferation was a problem only for states. No one assumed forty years ago that terrorists might seek a nuclear bomb, or that the sale of nuclear weapons materials and know-how would become a business opportunity for nonstate actors.

In the first nuclear age, nuclear power seemed to hold great promise, but it never became a leading energy source because of safety and environmental concerns. In the second nuclear age, concerns about global warming and the volatility of international oil and gas markets have revived the demand for nuclear power. Nearly thirty governments have announced a new intent to pursue peaceful nuclear programs.[2]

In the first nuclear age, the bomb was a weapon to deter others who had it; in the second, military planners in the nuclear weapons states now contemplate (apparently without irony) doctrines that make the weapons "usable" in the war against terror.[3] In the first nuclear age, the cold war rivalry between the United States and the Soviet Union served to limit the demand for the bomb; in the second, regional and global insecurities are generating new interest in the bomb, and some believe we now face a potential cascade of proliferation centered in the Middle East. In the first nuclear age, experts tacitly assumed that if the United States and Soviet Union disarmed, others would follow. Now it is not so clear. Nuclear states such as India, Pakistan, and Israel exist in their own regional insecurity complexes. If they were to give up their weapons, what international mechanisms would guarantee their security?[4]

No test of responsible sovereignty is more important than the effort to prevent the spread of nuclear weapons. The NPT, signed more than forty years ago, articulated key standards for responsible state action in dealing with nuclear technology. The consensus that animates those standards has eroded. The future health of the nonproliferation regime depends first on rebuilding that consensus. But that is not sufficient. New standards of responsibility are needed to adapt the regime to the twenty-first century.

The NPT's effectiveness rests on three agreements. First, the nuclear weapons states collectively agreed not to proliferate weapons to other states but instead to provide security guarantees. Second, the states that choose not to seek nuclear weapons and that comply with NPT obligations are entitled to nuclear technology for peaceful uses. And finally, those states that possessed nuclear weapons at the time of the signing of the treaty agreed to make good faith efforts to pursue disarmament.

During its first thirty years, the nonproliferation regime was an effective instrument in reducing state demand for nuclear weapons as well as limiting the supply of materials necessary to make such a weapon. This has been more tenuous since the end of the cold war, and the regime has proved much less effective in moving the nuclear weapons states toward disarmament. In the 1990s non-nuclear states grew frustrated about the inequity of the original deal and angry because the nuclear states were slow in meeting their commitments. That anger and frustration have festered, weakening the underlying bargains and the international commitment to stop the spread of nuclear weapons. Yet just when the consensus has broken down on the original deal, member states need to do more, not less, to stop the proliferation of nuclear materials, technology, and weapons.

Although the United States has an enormous stake in an effective nuclear nonproliferation regime, U.S. policy over the last seven years has weakened the existing regime by undermining the global consensus against the proliferation of nuclear weapons. The Bush administration created new instruments against proliferation, such as its 2003 Proliferation Security Initiative (PSI), but it treated its disarmament commitments with disdain. Key decisions by the Bush administration, which have included repudiating the antiballistic missile treaty and earlier U.S. commitments to disarmament, exploring the option of building new tactical warheads, and embracing preventive war and forcible regime change as national strategy—all while brandishing the potential use of nuclear weapons—have eroded the taboo against those weapons and diminished the perceived leadership of the United States as a guarantor of international security. At the same time, a cooling of relations between the United States and Russia has left both Russian and U.S. commitments to bilateral arms reductions in doubt.

President Obama must decide how to rebuild the global nonproliferation consensus and strengthen the regime. The United States will need to reengage with Russia on arms control and enter into talks with China about avoiding a new nuclear arms and technology race. The Obama administration must work with others to offer incentives for states to forgo the enrichment of fissile materials. U.S. leaders must cooperate with others so that the nonproliferation regime can meet the challenges of the second nuclear age. All this will be viable only if the United States leads by example to restore the disarmament agenda and aggressively cuts its nuclear weapons arsenal.

ASSESSING THE THREAT

Governments and citizens around the world differ dramatically in their perceptions of the nuclear threat. The possibility that terrorists could acquire a nuclear weapon is one reason the U.S. government treats nuclear proliferation with great urgency. An improvised nuclear bomb could result in levels of destruction foreshadowed by Hiroshima and Nagasaki in World War II. Such an attack would kill hundreds of thousands, and have devastating effects on international trade and finance, global economic growth, and the environment.

In other parts of the world, however, nuclear terrorism is seen as science fiction. Although some in Africa or Latin America recognize the threat to the United States and Europe, they do not see it as a threat to their own homelands. Some foreign officials go so far as to contend that the United States has fabricated the threat of nuclear terrorism to justify its pursuit of global primacy.[5]

Nonetheless, most countries agree that the spread of nuclear weapons, technology, and materials poses a grave threat to international peace and security. And terrorism is only one nightmare—the more states that possess nuclear weapons, the greater the potential for strategic miscalculation and accidental or deliberate use. Countries that obtain nuclear weapons for the first time lack reliable command-and-control procedures, raising the propensity for use.[6] The acquisition of nuclear weapons by one country could upset a regional security balance and compel regional competitors to follow suit. Nowhere is this possibility more likely and dangerous than in the Middle East and the Persian Gulf, particularly if Iran develops a nuclear weapon.

Other governments see all nuclear weapons as an existential threat, and insist that the nuclear powers pursue disarmament vigorously. Yet some of these very countries also benefit from a so-called "nuclear umbrella" from the nuclear weapons states, suggesting that disarmament must be coordinated with more than thirty non-nuclear weapons states. These states may support a disarmament agenda, but the scale, nature, and pace of disarmament can affect their security assumptions and policies.[7] Japan, for example, relies on the U.S. nuclear umbrella. If the United States were to disarm without coordinating with Japan, Japanese leaders could decide to reassess their nuclear policies, especially if there is any ambiguity about dismantling North Korea's nuclear program and weapons.

A serious threat is posed by the ability and willingness of individuals, companies, or governments to sell nuclear materials or technologies to aspiring nuclear weapons states or nonstate actors.[8] The sheer volume of global trade, the fact that technologies and materials can have dual uses, the fallibility of export control regimes in many countries, the existence of trading hubs with lax regulations, and the creative use of front companies and false end-user certificates by proliferators all pose challenges for detecting covert activity. We have already seen how easily the chains of controls and international safeguards can be circumvented. The network connected to Pakistani engineer A. Q. Khan demonstrated how a determined proliferator with the right access and contacts, together with keen knowledge of the international system, can circumvent the authorities.[9] Although it would seem unlikely that another covert network of that scope could escape detection, partial trading networks might endure.

High fossil fuel prices, the risks associated with energy suppliers and transport routes, and even policies to combat climate change—for example, the pricing of carbon—could accelerate a drive for civil nuclear power that could increase the proliferation risk. For economic, environmental, and security reasons, we should expect more countries to incorporate nuclear plants into the mix of their power generation capabilities. Will this be done safely and securely? Some countries that develop civil nuclear programs might be tempted to master and control all aspects of the fuel cycle. And once that occurs, the step to weaponization is dangerously close.

An increasing number of states have the technical capability to produce fissile material suitable for a nuclear weapon. Although there is no evidence that countries with a latent nuclear capacity wish to pursue a weapons program, intentions are notoriously fluid. If a non-nuclear state such as Iran develops a weapons capability, a domino effect could be set in motion as other countries, such as Saudi Arabia, Jordan, and Egypt, reevaluate whether to seek nuclear weapons.

In 2008, nine countries have nuclear weapons. Of the sixty states with some form of nuclear capacity, only twelve countries can enrich and commercially produce uranium.[10] Imagine if the number of countries producing enriched uranium were to double or triple as developing nations seek energy self-reliance and adopt carbon-free nuclear technology to produce electricity. This possibility calls for an intensified effort now, before a crisis arrives, to strengthen the firewalls between civil nuclear power and weaponization programs.

RESPONSIBLE SOVEREIGNTY AND THE INSTRUMENTS OF NONPROLIFERATION

People around the world might not agree about the threat posed by nuclear weapons, but agreement about what constitutes responsible behavior in the nuclear arena is remarkable. The NPT is nearly a universal treaty—188 of 192 UN member states belong. India, Israel, and

BOX 5-1. SOME KEY RESPONSIBILITIES OF STATES UNDER THE NPT

Article I

Each nuclear weapon State Party to the Treaty undertakes not to transfer to any recipient whatsoever nuclear weapons or other nuclear explosive devices or control over such weapons or explosive devices directly, or indirectly; and not in any way to assist, encourage, or induce any non-nuclear weapon State to manufacture or otherwise acquire nuclear weapons or other nuclear explosive devices, or control over such weapons or explosive devices.

Article II

Each non-nuclear weapon State Party to the Treaty undertakes not to receive the transfer from any transferor whatsoever of nuclear weapons or other nuclear explosive devices or of control over such weapons or explosive devices directly, or indirectly; not to manufacture or otherwise acquire nuclear weapons or other nuclear explosive devices; and not to seek or receive any assistance in the manufacture of nuclear weapons or other nuclear explosive devices.

Article III

1. Each non-nuclear weapon State Party to the Treaty undertakes to accept safeguards, as set forth in an agreement to be negotiated and concluded with the International Atomic Energy Agency in accordance with the Statute of the International Atomic Energy Agency and the Agency's safeguards system, for the exclusive purpose of verification of the fulfillment of its obligations assumed under this Treaty with a view to preventing diversion of nuclear energy from peaceful uses to nuclear weapons or other nuclear explosive devices.

2. Each State Party to the Treaty undertakes not to provide: (a) source or special fissionable material, or (b) equipment or material

especially designed or prepared for the processing, use or production of special fissionable material, to any non-nuclear weapon State for peaceful purposes, unless the source or special fissionable material shall be subject to the safeguards required by this Article.

Article IV

1. Nothing in this Treaty shall be interpreted as affecting the inalienable right of all the Parties to the Treaty to develop research, production, and use of nuclear energy for peaceful purposes without discrimination *and in conformity with Articles I and II of this Treaty* [emphasis added].

2. All the Parties to the Treaty undertake to facilitate, and have the right to participate in, the fullest possible exchange of equipment, materials, and scientific and technological information for the peaceful uses of nuclear energy. Parties to the Treaty in a position to do so shall also cooperate in contributing alone or together with other States or international organizations to the further development of the applications of nuclear energy for peaceful purposes, especially in the territories of non-nuclear weapon States Party to the Treaty, with due consideration for the needs of the developing areas of the world.

Article VI

Each of the Parties to the Treaty undertakes to pursue negotiations in good faith on effective measures relating to cessation of the nuclear arms race at an early date and to nuclear disarmament, and on a treaty on general and complete disarmament under strict and effective international control.

Pakistan—all nuclear weapons states—never joined; North Korea withdrew when it was found to be in violation. Box 5-1 shows key obligations of states under the treaty.

Through a process of "collective reassurance," the NPT seeks to counter both the demand for nuclear weapons and the supply of materials necessary to build them. The regime works first and foremost when states meet their nonproliferation and disarmament obligations. If all parties are convinced that cheaters will be discovered and handled appropriately, the system will function more effectively. In addition, if demonstrable progress on disarmament is achieved as pledged, non-nuclear states have added incentive and justification for not pursuing nuclear weapons.

Collective reassurance requires robust verification measures. Because verification relies on a state's willingness to comply, cheating is possible. The system is compromised when states believe it is failing and that certain states cannot be trusted. This perception encourages states to consider alternative options and runs the risk of unraveling the regime as confidence in the system diminishes.

The key verification arm of the nonproliferation regime, the International Atomic Energy Agency (IAEA),[11] operates by special agreement as an independent organization connected to the UN system. The IAEA promotes the peaceful exploitation of nuclear energy while preventing its use in weapons. Its primary means of enforcement is a system of monitoring and observing civil nuclear materials through "safeguards agreements," which are formally negotiated between the state and the agency. Under the NPT the countries designated as non-nuclear weapon states were required to reach a safeguards agreement with the IAEA within 180 days of signing the treaty. (The nuclear weapons states had a different arrangement, in which voluntary measures could be implemented on civil parts of their programs.)

Evolving Standards of Responsibility

Since the signing of the NPT in 1970, standards of responsible state action in the nuclear field have continued to develop. In the 1990s the IAEA came under considerable criticism for failing to identify the extensive clandestine nuclear program Iraq pursued in the 1980s. Despite IAEA monitoring, Iraq was able to operate an undetected weapons program at facilities it had not declared to the IAEA. After the 1991 Gulf War, inspection teams found evidence that Iraq was close to building a nuclear weapon.

This episode led to efforts to strengthen the safeguards regime. In 1992, the IAEA's Board of Governors—the agency's policymaking group—reaffirmed the objective of the safeguards agreements: to detect and deter the diversion of nuclear material from "peaceful nuclear activities to the manufacture of nuclear weapons or of other nuclear explosive devices or for purposes unknown." The board emphasized that the agreements apply not only "to nuclear material declared by a state," but also to "any nuclear material (and activity) subject to safeguards that should have been declared." In 1997, the board approved a model Additional Protocol to safeguards agreements that would give the IAEA greater investigative ability. Eighty-five states have signed and ratified the protocol and thirty-one have signed but not ratified it. This policy shift, however, was not matched with a corresponding increase in resources— not until 2003 did the IAEA receive more funds for verification, and then only about a 10 percent increase.[12]

Beyond the purview of the IAEA, other groups have taken steps to prevent cross-border transfers of nuclear technology. These efforts date back to 1971, when states that supply nuclear technology formed the Zangger Committee, with a mission to assist NPT parties in identifying equipment and materials subject to export controls. The committee established the "Trigger List"—items that required safeguards as a condition of supply.

In response to India's nuclear test in 1974, the suppliers sought to widen the cooperation to include states such as France that were not members of the NPT at the time. In 1975, the Nuclear Suppliers Group (NSG) was formed to establish guidelines on materials, equipment, and technologies that are subject to export controls. These guidelines were intended for implementation through national legislation by each member country. The group added technologies for control to the Zangger Committee's Trigger List. In addition, it expanded export controls to cover dual-use items that could have nuclear applications. Finally, NSG members agreed to apply their trade restrictions to all recipient states, not just those that were not party to the NPT. NSG membership now comprises forty-five states that supply nuclear materials.

Even though they are only voluntary groupings of states, the Zangger Committee and the NSG are important parts of the nonproliferation regime. In addition, their self-imposed restraints foreshadow the kinds of responsibilities that a broader grouping of states will have to adopt to handle the second nuclear age.

The Conference on Disarmament

One body intended to generate new norms and treaties for managing nuclear weapons responsibly is the Conference on Disarmament. Its sixty-six members include all the nuclear weapons states. Established by the UN General Assembly in 1979 as a single venue for discussing disarmament issues, the conference served as the forum where formal negotiations on a Comprehensive Test Ban Treaty (CTBT) began in 1994. At the 1995 NPT Review Conference, non-nuclear weapons states accepted a U.S. commitment to ratify the CTBT as a basis for indefinitely extending the nonproliferation treaty. In effect, this struck a deal in which the non-nuclear weapons states made a permanent commitment to forgo nuclear weapons.

But even though the United States signed the CTBT in 1996, the U.S. Senate voted against ratification in 1999, citing concerns about verification and the impact it would have on maintaining the U.S. nuclear weapons inventory. Even though a U.S. moratorium on nuclear testing has been in place since 1992 (initiated by the administration of President George H. W. Bush), this is not the same level of commitment as treaty ratification. The treaty will come into force after the forty-four "nuclear capable" states have ratified it. Thus far, only thirty-one have done so; among the holdouts, in addition to the United States, are China and Israel.

Following the acrimony surrounding the CTBT, the Conference on Disarmament deadlocked, unable to agree even on a work program. For more than eight years the conference has been unable to draft a single document on strategic disarmament, bringing the forum's utility into question. Part of the problem is the scope of the issues under discussion and how they intersect. In 2000, the NPT Review Conference proposed that along with general disarmament, the conference should discuss two specific issues: a Fissile Material Cutoff Treaty (FMCT) and negative security assurances (guarantees by the five NPT nuclear weapon states not to use or threaten to use nuclear weapons against states that have formally renounced them). After the United States withdrew from the Anti-Ballistic Missile Treaty in 2001, many members of the Conference on Disarmament, including Russia and China, felt that preventing an arms race in outer space should be a key consideration. The United States, however, views that issue as a potential hindrance to its ballistic missile defense aspirations and places a higher priority on controlling fissile materials. Other non-nuclear weapon states view progress on disarmament and negative security assurances as the most important issues.

The Specter of Terrorism after 9/11

After 9/11 the issues of terrorism and weapons of mass destruction (WMD) rose to the top of the global agenda. At the 2002 G-8 Summit, world leaders announced their commitment of $20 billion to a Global Partnership against the Spread of Weapons and Materials of Mass Destruction. Focused primarily on Russia, the Global Partnership covered the full range of measures designed to safeguard against WMD, including secure storage, nonproliferation, and counterterrorism.[13] This ambitious agenda has yielded some significant outcomes along with various funding and implementation problems.

Other international actions followed the formation of the G-8 Global Partnership. As part of the PSI created and led by the Bush administration, countries share information about shipments of concern—those that might contain components of WMD—with a goal of preventing them from reaching their destination. Although interdictions on the high seas are the headline-grabbing aspect of this initiative, its primary function is to help countries enforce their own export control legislation.

Another measure, Security Council Resolution 1540, requires member states to enact regulations that prevent illicit transfers of WMD materials and technologies. The most ambitious aspect of 1540, which was adopted in 2004, attempts to close some of the gaps in the export control regimes by widening their scope beyond the members of existing voluntary groupings such as the NSG and the PSI. To measure adherence to the resolution, a new UN committee was formed to receive states' declarations on compliance. A UN Convention on Nuclear Terrorism was also adopted by the General Assembly in 2005, giving a broader political base to efforts to combat that threat. As discussed in our chapter on terrorism, however, guaranteed resources for weak states that are willing to adopt regulations but have neither the experience nor capacity to do so, along with a mechanism to orchestrate collective inducement for states to comply, are needed.

EVALUATING THE NONPROLIFERATION REGIME

Debates among policymakers in the United States about the effectiveness of the nonproliferation regime tend to be overly swayed by the headline-grabbing cases. Some U.S. policymakers believe that the treaty is unable to distinguish between countries that are cheating and those that are not. Or they think that the treaty itself has failed because there are instances of failure (North Korea and Iran). Or they believe that it has failed because some countries that adhere to the treaty's responsibilities have not joined it (India).

Such superficial evaluations border on the reckless, for the value of the regime should first be measured against this question: Would the world be worse off or better off in its absence? Second, can the regime be improved? To build a better regime, we should then look at the causes of failures and what elements of the regime are at fault.

Taking into account its entire life span, the treaty has been remarkably successful. Its most important success has been to reduce the demand for nuclear weapons; since the NPT came into force, fewer countries have espoused and pursued nuclear ambitions. Almost forty years after its inception, around sixty states operate nuclear power or research reactors and at least thirty possess the industrial and scientific base to instigate a nuclear weapons program. Yet the number of countries that have actually become nuclear weapons states is relatively small (nine). Four countries inherited or acquired nuclear weapons but gave them up (Belarus, Kazakhstan, South Africa, and Ukraine). Others, like Brazil, started but discontinued nuclear programs.

Another indicator of success has been the ability of the nonproliferation regime to adapt over time. Many countries that were not original signatories to the treaty joined decades later. It is easy to forget that key states such as France, China, and Brazil joined the treaty only in the early 1990s.

TABLE 5-1. Nuclear Weapons Inventories, 1986 and 2006

P5 member country[a]	Nuclear weapons inventories of the P5 in 1986	Nuclear weapons inventories of the P5 in 2006
France	355	350
United Kingdom	300	200
Soviet Union/Russia	45,000	16,000
United States	24,400	10,000
China	425	100–400
Total	70,000+ (cold war high)	26,650–26,950

a. The P5 abbreviation refers to the five permanent members of the UN Security Council.

Analysts have consistently predicted the demise of the NPT, most recently after revelations about the Iraqi, Iranian, and North Korean programs. In part, the strength of the regime must be judged by whether it can adapt to new challenges. And it has, in part. For example, when it was revealed during the first Gulf War that Iraq had been able to build a clandestine nuclear program and was alarmingly close to building a bomb, the NPT developed the Additional Protocol to give the IAEA the ability to investigate more intrusively.

Even in terms of disarmament, which has stalled in the last ten years, there has been progress in reducing the number of nuclear warheads. Table 5-1 shows that, since the late 1980s, the number has decreased from a cold war high of more than 70,000 weapons to less than 30,000 today. Although this number is still way too high, and enough nuclear weapons are left to destroy the earth several times over, the task is to reinvigorate disarmament, not to start anew.

Progress on disarmament by the nuclear weapons states has relied heavily on bilateral talks between the United States and the former Soviet Union (now called Russia). Beginning in the 1970s, these countries took several steps to regulate and reduce their nuclear weapons holdings and strategic delivery systems. Of those still in force, the Strategic Arms Reduction Treaty (START I), which requires intrusive verification, expires in December 2009. Currently there are no plans to extend START I in its present configuration. Although the Moscow Treaty was signed in May 2002 and came into force in June 2003, it does not require the destruction of delivery systems, nor does it have any verification or inspection provisions.

Critics of the NPT claim that the 1990s proved that the underlying bargain of disarmament for nonproliferation does not exist. They argue that the decade showed the greatest reduction of nuclear weapons by the United States and Russia, but also the greatest amount of proliferation, with India and Pakistan developing and testing weapons and North Korea seeking to create its own bomb.

This is misleading, revisionist history. It is true that new nuclear weapons states emerged in the 1990s, but overall, the number of nuclear weapons states declined as South Africa and then the newly independent states of Ukraine, Belarus, and Kazakhstan gave up their weapons. Moreover, the 1990s achieved the indefinite extension of the NPT and an almost universal recommitment to nonproliferation. Nearly 130 states agreed voluntarily to place themselves under stronger inspections of the IAEA through the Additional Protocol. During the same period, states agreed on a treaty to ban testing of nuclear weapons.

Beyond cherry-picking the evidence that bolsters the case against the NPT, the critical view suffers from three additional problems. First, the critics focus narrowly on the proliferators by asking, "Is it really a lack of disarmament that drives North Korea and Iran to seek nuclear weapons?" Phrased this way, the answer is obviously no. A more relevant issue, however, is the lack of disarmament and its effects on the 183 non-nuclear weapons states that can help pressure the noncompliant. Clearly, some of these states have dragged their feet in condemning and opposing Iranian violations of the NPT because of what they perceive as a spirit of noncompliance by the nuclear weapons states for not fulfilling their disarmament obligations.

Second, the critics assume that states are either genetically programmed to seek or not seek nuclear weapons; in other words, those that do not seek nuclear weapons under the NPT would not seek them anyway. Those that do seek them are clearly undeterred by the NPT—therefore the treaty does not work. This ignores the host of reasons driving countries to seek weapons. Many non-nuclear states reject the weapons because the non-proliferation regime gives them assurance that they need not seek them as long as others do not. Perceptions of security are paramount. Perturbations in regional and global security, the rise of new threats, and failures of cooperation can drive states to seek self-help solutions. But the bottom line is that the treaty is important precisely *because* states are not predetermined seekers or avoiders of nuclear weapons.

And even as a lack of disarmament might not be a cause of Iranian and North Korean proliferation, actions of the United States—reneging on commitments to provide security guarantees, carrying out a policy of regime change, and brandishing nuclear bombs as usable weapons—all may have contributed to those countries' search for nuclear weapons.

What would the world look like without the nonproliferation regime? Without multilateral incentives, rules, and norms, a far greater emphasis might be placed on bilateral or alliance security guarantees. Questions about the strength of such guarantees would be warranted. Without the collective reassurance provided by the multilateral system, there would likely be a greater emphasis on unilateral strategies, including preventive war, to prevent proliferation. This in turn could encourage proliferation by reinforcing a belief that only possession of nuclear weapons could guarantee a state's security. And without any regulation on supply, it would be easier for states to obtain the necessary technology.

Dealing with the Hard Cases

Some would go so far as to say that the litmus test for the survival of the nonproliferation regime is how it tackles the hard cases of treaty violators like North Korea and Iran. Each of these cases has idiosyncrasies, but each also offers lessons that could be useful in strengthening the regime in the future. Both can be viewed as a failure of the nonproliferation regime, but they can more accurately be described as a failure of the Bush administration's nonproliferation policy. Both North Korea and Iran illustrate our central argument—that U.S. policy, and to an extent also that of major regional powers—are the pivots on which effective international regimes turn.

North Korea joined the NPT in 1985, but did not conclude a safeguards agreement with the IAEA until 1992. The IAEA uncovered a number of inconsistencies in North Korea's declaration, obtaining most of the evidence through the agency's own sampling and analysis and via satellite imagery supplied by the U.S. intelligence community. The evidence indicated that the country had separated more plutonium than it had declared, perhaps enough for one or two nuclear weapons. In response, North Korea gave notice of its intention to withdraw from the NPT in 1993, but diplomacy led it to suspend its withdrawal the day before it was to take effect.

Intensive bilateral negotiations between the United States and North Korea produced the 1994 Agreed Framework, in which North Korea committed to put all its nuclear facilities under IAEA monitoring and to work toward the denuclearization of the Korean peninsula. The key breakthrough came about when the United States realized that viewing the agreement solely as a nonproliferation treaty would be insufficient.[14] Led by a totalitarian, paranoid government, long out of touch with global changes, North Korea sought a framework that would address its broad security issues, including the promise of normalized relations with the United States. The Agreed Framework called on both sides "to move toward full normalization of political and economic relations," and included measures to increase diplomatic ties, trade, and investment between the United States and North Korea. As part of the agreement, a consortium of Japan, South Korea, and the European Union (EU) pledged to furnish a light-water reactor with which North Korea could meet its energy needs.

Beginning in 1993, when negotiations between the United States and North Korea started, and ending in 2000, the two countries engaged in more than twenty-two negotiations concerning a wide array of issues, including terrorism, missiles, food, and expanded nuclear inspections. Sixteen different agreements were produced. In the last days of the William J. Clinton administration in 2000, during Secretary of State Madeleine Albright's visit to Pyongyang, North Korea committed to negotiate an end to missile testing as part of the normalization of relations between the United States and North Korea.

Both countries implemented these agreements, including the Agreed Framework, sporadically and haphazardly. In the United States, the follow-through was bedeviled by domestic politics and the insistence that any concessions to North Korea were tantamount to appeasement. As long as the Clinton administration engaged at top levels, however, the North Korean proliferation issue was kept in check.

Negotiations between the United States and North Korea collapsed under the Bush administration in 2002. In 2001, a U.S. interagency team was authorized to travel to Pyongyang and offer a "grand bargain" that linked final denuclearization to diplomatic normalization. The trip was put on hold when intelligence suggested that North Korea was conducting a uranium-enrichment program outside the Agreed Framework. A U.S. team did eventually travel to Pyongyang in 2002, but this time the team's mandate was to confront North Korea with intelligence on its highly enriched uranium (HEU) program.[15] By this point, 9/11 had occurred, President Bush had named North Korea as part of the "axis of evil," and new administration appointees had taken up key roles in the U.S. State Department. When Pyongyang did not deny the HEU program, the U.S. team returned immediately to Washington. The Agreed Framework was terminated and a new policy of pressure and isolation was put in place.

This change in U.S. policy must rate among the most significant misjudgments of the Bush administration because it allowed North Korea to develop and test a nuclear weapon. In December 2002, North Korea expelled IAEA inspectors and disabled IAEA equipment at its Yongbyon reactor. The IAEA concluded that these actions constituted further noncompliance and reported the matter to the UN Security Council. North Korea subsequently left the NPT. Freed from IAEA inspections, North Korea assembled a nuclear weapon from reprocessed plutonium from Yongbyon, where IAEA inspectors had been present, and tested it in October 2006. Ironically, no nuclear material has been produced from the alleged HEU program that caused the United States to suspend the Agreed Framework and led North Korea to kick out IAEA inspectors. If the Agreed Framework had not been ruptured, and if the IAEA had been able to sustain its presence, we could plausibly argue that North Korea could not have obtained the fissile material to produce its nuclear weapon.

It then took five years of bilateral and multilateral diplomacy for the Bush administration to rediscover the wisdom of the Agreed Framework and the need to see North Korea as more than a proliferation problem. Key to this effort was intensive diplomatic attention and energy from China, which suggested that the governments most relevant to resolving the crisis (China, Japan, North and South Korea, Russia, and the United States) meet in what became known as the Six-Party Talks. China applied significant pressure to North Korea after the 2006 nuclear weapon test and helped create consensus within the Security Council to threaten sanctions. Combined with the Bush administration's renewed willingness to meet directly with North Korea and address its broader security, economic, and energy issues, this led to a new agreement in February 2007. But by then, of course, North Korea had joined the nuclear weapons club.

The challenge now is to denuclearize North Korea, which all analysts agree is a much more difficult problem than preventing North Korea from developing the weapon in the first place. Critics from both the left and right have argued that the February 2007 agreement is too lenient, and within the Bush administration there have been pressures to again suspend this agreement. Yet in mid-2008, this much is clear: the Yongbyon facility—the one confirmed source of nuclear material production in North Korea—is closed; it is being dismantled; and it will eventually take between eighteen and twenty-four months for North Korea to reassemble a similar capacity. The combination of pressure from the UN Security Council and China and engagement through the Six-Party Talks and bilaterally by the United States has produced more effective results than five years of suspending the Agreed Framework from 2002 to 2007.

Iran represents another hard case. The Bush administration's dismissal of disarmament as an essential component of the NPT cast a long shadow over Iran.[16] The country's clandestine nuclear activity was made public in August 2002 when an Iranian dissident group, the National Council of Resistance of Iran, identified an undeclared facility at Natanz that subsequently turned out to be a centrifuge enrichment facility. Ensuing investigations by the IAEA indicated that Iran had been hiding its nuclear activities for nineteen years.

In June 2003 the IAEA found Iran in breach of its safeguards agreement. In October 2003 after the United States threatened to bring Iran's breach to the Security Council, Iran agreed to give the IAEA "a full picture of its nuclear activities, with a view of removing any ambiguities and doubts about the exclusively peaceful character of these activities."[17] In seeking to keep this agreement, Iran signed the Additional Protocol (but never proceeded with ratification) and agreed to stop enrichment activity. The deal was brokered with the EU working through the IAEA. (Iran was explicit in stating that it would deal only with the IAEA.)

All of this took place in the context of the U.S. invasion of Iraq and fitful quasi-negotiations between Iran and the United States over cooperation in Afghanistan and Iraq. The war in Iraq, a common interest in a stable Afghanistan, and the fact that Iran's leadership was the most moderate since its revolution in 1979, created the possibility for a U.S.-Iran diplomatic opening. In May of 2003 Iran sent a long cable to the Secretary of State at the time, Colin Powell, suggesting the possibility of normalizing relations and expressing Iranian willingness to embrace full transparency for its nuclear program.[18] Sometime in the fall of 2003, again in response to possible referral to the UN Security Council, Iran disbanded its nuclear weaponization program.[19] The United States gave no substantive response to Iran's overture. In May 2008, Secretary of Defense Robert Gates alluded to this period when he bemoaned a lost opportunity to engage with Iran on a host of issues of mutual concern.[20]

Instead, the question of Iranian nuclear ambitions became stuck in a five-year morass of endless mediation, inspections, and recriminations. In November 2003, the IAEA found that although Iran had breached its safeguards agreement by its undisclosed enrichment facilities, there was no evidence that it had diverted declared material to a military program. The IAEA has repeated this finding in regular reports. At the same time worries about undeclared material and doubts about the exclusively peaceful character of Iran's nuclear program put Iran's continuing cooperation with the IAEA at center stage, and this cooperation faltered when Iran resumed uranium-enrichment activities in 2004. Although EU mediators demanded and achieved a halt to such activities that year, they found that their package of incentives to engage Iran lacked the biggest carrot of all—diplomatic talks with the United States on broad security and economic issues.

By late 2005 Iran had gone from intransigence to defiance. The election of Mahmoud Ahmadinejad ended Iran's moderate political turn. Rising oil prices and the U.S. debacle in Iraq led to immense confidence among Iran's leaders. The United States looked like a paper tiger, at the same time that energy demand was driving key rising powers like India and China to turn to Iran to meet their growth needs. IAEA reports chronicled a growing lack of cooperation from its Iranian interlocutors.

In January 2006, Iran reneged on its October 2003 commitments, and stopped cooperating with the IAEA's investigation. In February, the IAEA found Iran to be in noncompliance with its NPT obligations, and the

IAEA Governing Board voted overwhelmingly to report Iran to the Security Council. Hoping to move quickly to tough, hard-hitting sanctions against the Iranian regime, the United States, France, and the United Kingdom instead encountered foot-dragging from Russia and China, with both states generally opposing sanctions. In April 2006 Iran declared that it had enriched uranium.

In late 2006 and early 2007, the P5 plus Germany (P5+1), together with the EU's High Representative for Common Foreign and Security Policy, Javier Solana, pursued various avenues and options for negotiations, including direct conditional negotiations with the United States. This did not come to fruition, in part because by this juncture moderates within the Iranian regime had diminished influence with the leadership. Pressure on Iran was also weak because Russia and China feared that the United States would use Security Council resolutions as a pathway to war, and would agree only to weak sanctions. Moreover, key developing countries like South Africa and Indonesia were largely silent in the face of Iranian noncompliance with the IAEA.

After five years of investigations, the IAEA is still unable to deliver "credible assurances" that there are no undeclared nuclear materials and activities in Iran. In May 2008, the IAEA reported renewed concerns about Iran's nuclear weapons program. Moreover, it is extremely difficult to see how the IAEA can bring the case to closure because it has been drawn into the issue of *why* Iran breached its safeguards agreement. Seeking to uncover a weapons program is a different and far more subjective issue than proving noncompliance with a safeguards agreement.

In short, as in North Korea, U.S. underinvestment in diplomacy from 2002 to 2006, combined with a more general lack of trust between the United States and other major powers—especially Russia and China—have been critical variables leading to this poor outcome with Iran. This has enabled Iran to move further down the path of enrichment, and Ahmadinejad has used his resistance to more recent diplomatic overtures to burnish his political image as David standing up to Goliath. More and more countries in the broader Middle East—for example, the United Arab Emirates (UAE), Saudi Arabia, Egypt, Turkey, Bahrain, Yemen, Jordan, and Kuwait—have begun looking to obtain nuclear technology and know-how as a hedge against Iran attaining a nuclear weapon.[21]

Lessons from the Hard Cases

Can the nonproliferation regime handle the hard cases? The answer depends on two factors—the effectiveness of the organizations that monitor compliance, and the willingness of powerful states to create robust coalitions committed to bringing the hard cases into compliance. Key lessons learned in North Korea and Iran follow:

—From the perspective of noncompliant states, their proliferation activities reflect underlying security dilemmas and domestic political factors. Walking proliferators back into compliance requires addressing their behavior from a broad security and political perspective, not just a limited proliferation perspective. This took place in North Korea in 1994 and 2007, but it has never been done with Iran, although Iran's resistance to negotiations offered since 2006 certainly accounts for a major part of the problem.

—Violators in North Korea and Iran have sought relationships with the United States as a means for addressing their security dilemmas. This puts bilateral U.S. actions and strategies at center stage in crafting effective regional and global strategies. Multiparty negotiations increase leverage and influence, but do not eliminate the need for intensive bilateral diplomacy on the part of the United States.

—U.S. policies of regime change are at odds with its nonproliferation goals. The threat of regime change, combined with the IAEA's referral and the EU's diplomatic engagement, may have helped induce Iran to moderate its stance in 2003. But from 2002 to 2006, when wielded as a stick with no carrots and absent a formal framework, the main effect of regime change policy was to create incentives for North Korea and Iran to accelerate their search for nuclear capacity.

—Addressing noncompliance is easier when strong multilateral processes are coordinated with U.S. bilateral and Security Council actions. Dealing with North Korea was easier because the Six-Party Talks brought every major regional power together in a common effort. All those with leverage on North Korea spoke with a common voice, but it took North Korea testing a nuclear weapon to get there. The P5+1 initiative on Iran has not had comparable consensus on exerting pressure, especially because China, India, and Japan have continued to invest in Iran and purchase Iranian oil. Progress resulted when key powers temporarily sided with western efforts—for example, when India voted with the West in the IAEA on Iran's referral to the Security Council, and when China and Russia have supported Security Council sanctions.

—Security Council action should be a complement to, not a substitute for, a robust strategy. The Security Council is hampered because thus far it is solely a punitive body. It has few tools to offer positive incentives for compliance, so its utility is limited and can only be an adjunct to a larger strategy. Again, this reinforces our central argument that multilateral institutions can be effective only when the major powers take responsibility for overall strategy.

—It is difficult to breathe life into the nonproliferation regime during crises when the oxygen has been sucked out of it in between crises. The lack of alacrity with which many non-nuclear weapons states of the NPT have approached Iran is not surprising given their frustration and anger at the lack of interest of the nuclear weapons states in taking their disarmament obligations seriously. General disillusionment with U.S. foreign policy also diminished the ability of the United States to lead efforts to mobilize broader international pressure behind nonproliferation efforts.

In summary, the nonproliferation regime has been a valuable asset to U.S. and international security and has helped to contain proliferation. It can deal with the toughest cases, however, only when animated by broader strategies, which are usually enabled and enacted by the United States and other major powers. The policies of those powers, then, are central to the future evolution of the regime, and U.S. policy on nuclear weapons is particularly critical.

THE UNITED STATES, NUCLEAR WEAPONS, AND RESPONSIBLE SOVEREIGNTY

Tension between nuclear deterrence and the commitment to disarmament embedded in the NPT has existed since the treaty's inception. During the cold war, deterrence outweighed disarmament, fueling an arms race that defied logic because both sides more than exceeded a capacity for mutual destruction. Since the end of the cold war, neither the United States nor Russia has developed a convincing rationale for maintaining nuclear weapons. Significant disarmament is unlikely to undermine deterrence, yet without a clear vision of what role nuclear weapons should play in international security, action toward disarmament has languished.

The Clinton administration attacked this issue vigorously, but incrementally. Clinton and his advisers understood that the end of the cold war was a watershed, and that vast nuclear arsenals were no longer needed in the United States or Russia. They were quick to grasp the implications of loosely controlled nuclear weapons, fissile material, technology, and know-how in the former Soviet Union, and worked with then-Senator Sam Nunn (D-Ga.) and Senator Richard Lugar (R-Ind.) to sustain a strong bipartisan basis to address the problem. The administration worked hard to convince the new states of Ukraine, Belarus, and Kazakhstan to give up nuclear weapons that were on their territory when the Soviet Union dissolved. Administration officials engaged in serious negotiations to extend the NPT when it was scheduled to end in 1995. Clinton signed a CTBT, but could not convince Congress to ratify the agreement. The administration was willing to engage in negotiations for an FMCT.

Still, the Clinton administration never satisfactorily explained the role of nuclear weapons after the cold war. Were they still a deterrent, and if so, whom did they deter? Were they a usable weapon? How did they relate to the new threat of catastrophic terrorism? These were difficult questions, and it was not only the Clinton administration that was slow to answer them. Key American allies in Europe and Asia continue to this day to seek their security under U.S. nuclear weapons, yet there is no consensus on what they are protected from and whether nuclear weapons are still an appropriate tool in the absence of the Soviet threat. In this sense key governments around the world have been complicit in the failure of the United States to take more decisive steps toward disarmament.

Under the Bush administration, U.S. doctrine embraced nuclear weapons as a tool in the global war on terror, creating even wider divergence from NPT commitments to disarmament. The Bush administration understood that nuclear weapons made little sense as deterrents in an era when Russia was no longer an implacable foe. Bush and his advisers quickly jumped to the conclusion that terrorists or the states that might abet them could not be deterred, an important rationale for developing a policy of preventive war and regime change.

The Bush administration did identify the prospect of nuclear weapons in the hands of rogue states as a threat. The resulting policy had two facets: missile defense and the threat of preventive war, with an implied threat of using nuclear weapons as part of that strategy. Missile defense became a major feature of U.S.-Russia relations, with substantial costs in terms of negotiations with Russia on other issues, including Iran. And the threat of preventive war for regime change, as we have seen, created incentives for states potentially threatened by the United States to seek new anti-U.S. alliances, as well as their own nuclear deterrent.

The costs of this policy and its implications have been extremely high. Eroding the taboo against nuclear weapons erodes the international consensus against proliferation and weakens the nonproliferation regime. Notwithstanding the critics, that regime has paid important dividends to U.S. and global security and will be sorely needed in the years to come, particularly in the hard cases. Gaining the benefits of that regime will require a fundamental recalibration of U.S. nuclear weapons policy that acknowledges that reality and adapts it to a post–cold war world through the lens of responsible sovereignty.

STRENGTHENING THE RESPONSE

What needs to be done to ensure that the international architecture is more effective in this area? What would a policy based on the principle of responsible sovereignty look like?

Two key steps are necessary. First, the consensus underlying the nonproliferation treaty must be revitalized. States must live up to their existing commitments to standards of nuclear responsibility, and the nuclear weapons states, especially the United States, must lead. Second, as the nonproliferation consensus is rebuilt and trust is reestablished between nuclear and non-nuclear states, new standards of responsible sovereignty will need to be negotiated to adapt the nonproliferation regime to current challenges.

Revitalizing the Consensus

The 2007 initiative undertaken by former Secretaries of State Henry Kissinger and George Shultz, former Secretary of Defense William Perry, and former Senator Nunn opens a door for the Obama administration to reestablish U.S. bona fides in disarmament.[22] Renewing previous calls for the elimination of nuclear weapons, these dignitaries argue that leaders should acknowledge that the world has changed dramatically since the cold war, in ways that diminish the utility of nuclear weapons in securing international stability. In today's world, they insist, nuclear weapons actually generate instability, accentuating vulnerabilities, encouraging proliferation, and increasing the likelihood of use. Kissinger, Shultz, Perry, and Nunn support extensive cuts in U.S. and Russian arsenals, but maintain that the only way to truly diminish the prestige value of nuclear weapons is to eliminate them.

No one yet knows what a world free of nuclear weapons would look like. Most calls for nuclear disarmament assume that only nuclear weapons states would have obligations. But this is patently false. Because of the risk of nuclear breakout by any single country, the new non-nuclear world would see far greater international intrusion, surveillance, and inspection than today's world. All states would be subject to such highly intrusive surveillance, not just the former nuclear weapons states.

The tens of thousands of nuclear weapons that exist today are dangerous and expensive to maintain, and we most certainly can have a stable world with dramatically fewer of them. But before getting to zero, every nation would want to feel confident that this truly makes us all safer. Several considerations are paramount. First, the risks, temptations, and insecurities posed by low numbers of weapons or no weapons are unknown. Although research was conducted on this question during the cold war, it was based on assumptions of a bipolar world, where stability was assumed to be a function of mutual deterrence between the United States and the Soviet Union. What is stability in a world of low numbers with eight or nine nuclear weapons states, and tens of others with the latent capacity to build a weapon?[23]

Second, in creating a nuclear-free world, we do not want a return to the first half of the twentieth century, where wars between states were frequent and devastating in their consequences. At some point questions of nuclear disarmament must meet questions of conventional disarmament. New systems and policies must ensure that a nuclear-free world does not make it safer for countries to wage conventional war.

Finally, and related to the last point, questions of nuclear disarmament must eventually meet questions of collective security. What will guarantee the security of those countries that exist in insecure neighborhoods, such as Israel, or that live under the nuclear umbrella of an existing nuclear weapons state, such as Japan? What collective mechanism will bestow sufficient confidence on countries that possess the nuclear deterrent or live under extended deterrence?

We raise these questions not because we are skeptical of the initiative by Kissinger and others, but to outline an agenda that should be pursued now. Instead of focusing on the last missiles to go, we should concentrate on the first missiles to go. The United States must focus on five steps, enumerated in the list that follows.

1. *Unilaterally reducing arms while reenergizing bilateral arms reduction with Russia.* The United States and Russia possess by far the greatest share of the world's nuclear weapons. Both countries have acknowledged that their nuclear arsenals make little sense now that the cold war is over. Unilateral reduction of arms by the United States, followed by bilateral reductions by these two states, could dramatically reduce the nuclear peril overnight and reenergize the nonproliferation regime.

The one existing arms control agreement between the United States and Russia, START I, comes to an end in December 2009. In 2002, the Bush administration signed the Moscow Treaty with Russia, which commits each side to reduce its operational strategic warheads to a maximum of 1,700 to 2,200 by 2012. But there is no compulsion to destroy the warheads removed from service, nor is there a restriction on the number of nondeployed or reserve warheads. As a result, approximately 4,000 warheads will be retained on the U.S. side but not counted under the treaty; Russia is likely to retain a similar number. And the treaty has no provisions for verification.

An agreement without verification makes sense only in a strong relationship of trust and confidence. If START I is simply left to expire in 2009, there will no longer be any means for verifying and inspecting American and Russian nuclear arsenals at a time when tensions are resurfacing, especially in light of U.S. plans to deploy a missile defense system in the Czech Republic and Poland. The United States argues that this is a defensive system against rogue threats from Iran; Russia counters that the interceptors can be used preemptively against Russia. This combination of the collapse of a serious arms inspection regime and a growing distrust between the United States and Russia is not only dangerous, but it is destabilizing for the entire international community. One easy early win would be an agreement on both sides to take their nuclear forces off alert.

2. *Ratifying the CTBT.* U.S. ratification of the CTBT is a critical step toward restoring the credibility and vitality of the nonproliferation treaty. The United States committed itself to the CTBT in 1995 in exchange for non-nuclear weapons states' acceptance of the indefinite extension of the NPT. Moreover, the ban on testing is central in the geopolitics of nuclear power. A comprehensive test ban makes it harder for nuclear states to develop new weapons, which is sometimes called "horizontal proliferation." And the CTBT isolates those who seek to advance their quest for nuclear weapons. A comprehensive test ban would have the greatest impact on states that want to use civil programs as a platform for developing nuclear weapons. If any entity were to test a nuclear weapon, the test should be immediately detectable, and it should trigger sharp multilateral pressure to abandon the program.

3. *Starting a new diplomatic initiative to achieve an FMCT.* The purpose of such a treaty is to ban the production of fissile material for nuclear weapons and other nuclear explosive devices. The treaty would allow HEU and plutonium to be produced for nonexplosive purposes. The ban on producing fissile material together with a ban on testing would seriously complicate the manufacture of new nuclear weapons, in effect helping to put a cap on the world's nuclear arsenals. In particular, it could restrain the weapons buildup in Asia and the pressure to obtain nuclear weapons in the Middle East. The treaty could also bring other possessors of nuclear weapons—India, Pakistan, Israel, and North Korea—into the regime.

President Clinton first proposed the idea of an FMCT at the UN General Assembly in 1993. The concept has wide acceptance. Later in 1993 the General Assembly passed a resolution calling for a "nondiscriminatory, multilateral and internationally and effectively verifiable treaty banning the production of fissile material for nuclear weapons or other nuclear explosive devices."[24] In March 1995 the Geneva Conference on Disarmament mandated a committee to begin negotiations on a treaty. An extensive existing record of negotiations and materials should, with political determination from the major powers, make the FMCT within reach.

Except for China, all the nuclear weapons states have voluntarily suspended production of fissile material usable in weapons, and China is believed to have done so without a public declaration. China's participation in such a treaty would be extremely important to any progress. India has stated that it supports a treaty but is unlikely to participate without China. In addition, Pakistan has expressed support but will not be party unless India is involved. India, Pakistan, and Israel are believed to be producing fissile materials for their weapons programs.

The U.S. position on the proposed treaty changed in 2004, when the Bush administration asserted that it favored a treaty but no longer supported verification measures. Administration officials argued that inspections would be expensive, could compromise core national security interests, and would not actually be effective in monitoring compliance. A new diplomatic impetus on negotiations, though, should make it possible to explore measures that could enable some form of verification of existing stockpiles and excess fissile material. At least entertaining the possibility of a verification package would help to build confidence that a treaty could meet its aims. In the interim, pushing for countries to agree to a moratorium on producing fissile material could create political space for negotiations on verification details. Such an initiative could be undertaken in a G-16 context and potentially cut through the deadlock.

4. Adopting a "no-first-use" policy and affirming negative security guarantees. Since the end of the cold war, the United States has sent out confusing messages about the right to use nuclear weapons against non-nuclear states. Not only are such messages against the spirit of state responsibilities under the NPT, but they also exacerbate insecurities and encourage proliferation. U.S. signals might lead these states to conclude that the only way to reduce their vulnerability and deter attack is by developing or acquiring a nuclear capability. Adopting a no-first-use doctrine could help to diminish the significance of nuclear weapons and also strengthen U.S. counterterrorism strategy. Given that nuclear weapons produce indiscriminate terror, a no-first-use policy is consistent with delegitimizing terrorism.

5. Engaging both nuclear weapons states and non-nuclear weapons states to assess "getting to zero." To signal its willingness to explore complete nuclear disarmament, the United States should engage the other nuclear weapons states to analyze what would have to happen to achieve a world free of nuclear weapons; what would be necessary to achieve stability with few or no weapons; and what would be necessary to ensure a safer world. Similarly, it is crucial to engage the non-nuclear weapons states and assess their reactions. For example, how would Japan react to such a policy if it sees the nuclear umbrella eliminated? Work in this area has already begun in U.S. think tanks, and that work must be extended into official channels.

NEW STANDARDS OF RESPONSIBILITY
AND NEW TOOLS FOR NONPROLIFERATION

The future health of the nonproliferation regime depends on rebuilding the consensus that forms its foundation. But as we have seen, the existing regime is not sufficient. New standards of responsibility are needed to adapt the regime to the challenges of the twenty-first century, and new tools will be needed to bring those standards into effect.

Some non-nuclear states argue that Article IV of the NPT confers a "right" to develop all parts of the fuel cycle, including enrichment. With today's technology, however, the development of uranium enrichment and plutonium reprocessing capabilities brings states dangerously close to developing a nuclear weapon without actually violating the treaty.

Producing or acquiring the fissile material (HEU or plutonium) is the biggest obstacle to developing a nuclear weapon. The majority of uranium fuel used for power plants is enriched to about 4 percent. To achieve "weapons-grade" status, this uranium would need to be enriched further, increasing the proportion of the U-235 isotope to approximately 90 percent or greater. Reprocessing, or the process of separating plutonium from spent reactor fuel, is also used to produce fissile material.

Most states do not need either a full enrichment or a reprocessing capacity for modest commercial nuclear energy programs. Indeed, in most cases, enrichment or reprocessing is prohibitively expensive and makes little economic sense. Ten countries have an enrichment capacity, yet thirty-one countries operate commercial nuclear power plants, with most of those countries relying on enriched uranium supplied from abroad.

Given that in most cases acquiring an enrichment or reprocessing capability is economically irresponsible, and that in all cases it raises serious proliferation risks, a policy solution is needed to ensure that countries seeking civil nuclear power can forgo building an enrichment capacity and still be guaranteed a supply of nuclear fuel. At a minimum, incentives can be created to convince states to forgo enrichment or reprocessing. IAEA Director General Mohamed ElBaradei has proposed the creation of an international fuel bank under IAEA control.[25] As a supplier of fuel and a secure location for storage and reprocessing, Russia would need to be part of this agreement. As an added incentive, the agreement would generate massive commercial benefits for Russia.

Such a fuel bank would eliminate the need and cost for states to produce their own fissile materials, in addition to reducing the risk of access to such materials. An IAEA role is essential because its professionalism and impartiality lend important credibility to the guaranteed access to the fuel. All of this will discourage states from pursuing enrichment.

Over time, however, as the NPT consensus is rebuilt and states increase their willingness to meet existing commitments, all states should reconsider the interpretation of Article IV as conferring an inalienable right to the closed fuel cycle. To put it differently, in an international order defined by responsible sovereignty, inalienable rights come with inalienable responsibilities. In a world that moves toward small numbers of nuclear weapons, where nuclear fuel is cheap and supply is guaranteed by the IAEA, we can imagine governments negotiating a statement at a future NPT Review Conference that codifies a new interpretation of Article IV more appropriate for the perils of the second nuclear age. Similarly, NPT members should make the Additional Protocol mandatory.

For example, Iran's emphasis on its inalienable right under Article IV to full access to all nuclear technology as long as it is declared to the IAEA must be balanced against Iran's responsibilities. Civil nuclear projects should enjoy NPT protection only if the IAEA is able to draw up and implement its own criteria for what constitutes effective safeguards. In the case of Iran, the IAEA must be able to provide credible assurances that Iran's declarations are complete and correct and that the country has no undeclared nuclear materials and activities.

Standard inspections are insufficient to fulfill this mandate with any level of confidence. An important question arises from the scope of Iran's and North Korea's violations and their history of concealment: Would the IAEA ever be able to make such a determination? The IAEA is constantly constrained in its probing of Iran's past and present activities because Iran has little incentive for cooperating. Iran might fear that full disclosure of its pre-2003 activities would result in further punitive measures from the Security Council, possibly including forfeiting the country's right to enrichment technology. If the IAEA is unable to bring the case to closure, it should adhere to a strict interpretation of the NPT: Iran's right to nuclear technology under IAEA protection could legitimately be denied. The cost of noncompliance must be made greater than the cost of cooperation and compliance.

Finally, in a world of responsible sovereignty, no nation should be able to game the nuclear control system. States that have been found in breach of their safeguards agreements or noncompliant should be placed in a different category than states that have honored their agreements or are in compliance. The regime needs to be able to discriminate so that an offending state's right to nuclear technology is indefinitely premised on the IAEA's ability to verify that it is not cheating. In this way, a North Korea could not exercise its breakout option, whereby it acquired nuclear technology, developed a covert weapons program, was found to be noncompliant with its treaty obligations, and then exercised its right under Article X to leave the NPT but retain the technology it had acquired during its treaty membership. In a more just system, a country like North Korea could leave the NPT only if it first gave up, or disabled, the nuclear hardware.

Again, after the NPT consensus is rebuilt, it will have to be deepened. When future NPT review conferences are freed from the recriminations of the past, they can be the venue to bring understandings of the treaty in line with current and future challenges.

CONCLUSION

In 2009 President Obama has the opportunity to answer a key question: In a post–cold war world where nuclear weapons remain militarily unusable, what nuclear weapons policy should the United States adopt? The new administration's answer to that question will determine—in part—the likelihood of building an international order based on responsible sovereignty. If the administration affirms that the sole rationale for these weapons is to prevent others from using them, several actions can follow, all of them a boost for rebuilding the nonproliferation consensus. The United States can take unilateral steps to radically reduce its existing nuclear arsenal, it can revive bilateral processes for arms reductions with Russia, it can commit to seeking ratification of the CTBT, it can lead discussion about how to reduce the overall number of nuclear weapons while still maintaining international order, and it can ask serious questions about the possibility of attaining a nuclear-free world.

By revitalizing the nonproliferation consensus and building stronger norms of responsible sovereignty in the nuclear field, the Obama administration can reduce the danger from what has been an existential threat since the nuclear age began more than sixty years ago. Through cooperation, the United States can help build the standards and mechanisms for managing a second nuclear age, reaping critical benefits for U.S. and global security.

SIX

SECURITY IN THE BIOLOGICAL CENTURY

NEW KNOWLEDGE, TECHNOLOGY, and applications from biology promise to transform society, just as the industrial and information revolutions did in the nineteenth and twentieth centuries. Revolutionary discoveries in the life sciences have the potential to reshape the worlds of health, food production, energy, climate change, and economics, leading to fewer deadly diseases, new fuels, heartier food crops, longer life expectancy, and better quality of life.

The history of previous technological revolutions, however, provides a lesson that we ignore at our peril. As two of the world's foremost experts on biological weapons warn, "We know of no major technology with military utility that has not been vigorously exploited for hostile purposes."[1] A crucial test for responsible sovereignty will be to promote the benefits of the biotechnology revolution while ensuring that its potential harms—deliberate abuse by states, terrorists, or criminals or the accidental release of deadly pathogens—are prevented.

Biotechnology's benefits are needed to address myriad naturally occurring biological threats. Doctors, nurses, and public health officials do battle with bugs and germs that kill millions of people a year, most of them in the poorest regions of the world. Many of these frontline defenders of health fear that the bugs are winning. Mainline antibiotics have lost their potency, and new ones have been slow to take their place. New drug-resistant forms of tuberculosis and staph infections pose challenges in the developed and developing worlds. On average more than two new deadly infectious diseases emerge every year; in the last thirty years, they have included HIV-AIDS, SARS, Ebola, West Nile virus, and avian flu. One expert warns that it is 100 percent certain that in the next decades the world will face a new, deadly influenza pandemic, which could be as lethal as the 1919 pandemic of Spanish influenza, which killed 50 to 150 million.[2] In August 2008 the U.K. government published a report listing such an influenza as the most dangerous threat facing its people.[3]

International cooperation is essential to address this growing array of biological threats. The challenge is twofold. The first is to build a strong global public health regime that effectively responds to disease outbreaks and builds local capacity to sustain the health and well-being of citizens. Effective public health systems also are an important part of a multilayered response to potential bioterrorism. Given that developments in biotechnology will make the threat of bioterrorism as diffuse as that of cybercrime, prevention will be difficult; defenses—excellent global and local public health systems—therefore will need to be robust.

Beyond defending against disease and bioterrorism, there is a second challenge: to promote the bright side of advances in biotechnology while preventing their potentially dark side from appearing. The security opportunity of the biological century is to forge arrangements that produce beneficial results *for poor and developed countries alike*, with biotech applications that improve health, food production, and energy security for *everyone*. At present, however, our existing international arrangements are inadequate for promoting opportunities or combating abuses. Scientists, biotechnology companies, and universities must be centrally involved to create a regime that will work and the means to enforce it.

THE BIOLOGICAL CENTURY: TODAY AND TOMORROW

At the International Genetic Engineered Machines competition in October 2007, a team of high school students from San Francisco used gene-splicing techniques to create a synthesome, or artificial organelle. An organelle is to a cell what an organ, like a stomach or heart, is to an animal—a structure that performs a specific function. To prevent the synthesome from being eaten by a lysosome, an organelle responsible for disposing of unneeded molecules, the students had to create a DNA bar code that would fool the lysosome. Their creation has opened the door for possible future applications, such as programming yeast cells to make biofuels. Their accomplishment placed them in a group of six finalists, including students from the University of California at Berkeley who created "bacto-blood," or *E. coli* bacteria engineered to produce hemoglobin and a chemical that enables cells to survive freeze-drying. Another finalist was a group of undergraduates from Slovenia, who doctored the DNA of mammalian cells to create a virus trap, which could prove beneficial in the fight against HIV-AIDS. The winners of the contest were students from Beijing University who created tiny assembly lines out of bacteria.[4]

The contest brings students from around the world to engineer biological devices. It is sponsored by the BioBricks Foundation, created by professors at MIT who have compiled a library of several thousand standardized DNA sequences (BioBricks), which can be used to design and create new genetic machines. According to the foundation's website, scientists using BioBricks can "program living organisms in the same way a computer scientist can program a computer."[5]

Several aspects of the competition are noteworthy. The participants are young, ages seventeen to twenty-two. They are doing cutting-edge manipulations that just several years ago would have been deemed impossible. They are working without large capital outlays, public or private. Finally, they come from all parts of the world. The biotech revolution is global.

The breakthroughs engineered by these young scientists are among the many reasons that the twenty-first century will be known as the biological century. In the last thirty years, scientists have cloned pigs, sheep, and human embryos; genetically engineered human insulin and vaccines; discovered specific genes that cause cancer; carried out trans-species organ transplants; and genetically modified foods to make them more nutritious and plants to make them more resistant to insects. To imagine biotechnology's potential, one scientist predicts that within twenty to fifty years "genetically engineered carbon-eating trees" could reduce the amount of carbon dioxide in the environment by half.[6] In 2008 anyone who so desired could buy his or her complete genetic blueprint for

$350,000.[7] The goal of several biotech companies is to provide that service for $1,000, ushering in a world of medicine and disease prevention strategies designed for the individual. It also will bring us closer to what one scientist calls the domestication of biotechnology, whereby families will be as familiar with biological manipulation as they are today with personal computers.[8]

Before one shrugs this off as science fiction, consider that since the mid-1990s biotechnology has advanced faster than computer technology, which doubles in computational power every eighteen months.[9] Christopher Chyba, an astrobiologist at Princeton, observes that the speed of DNA synthesis has increased more than 500 times in fifteen years: "The synthesis of the polio virus, completed in 2002, took the [State University of New York] team three years of work. A year later, a research group at the Institute for Biological Energy Alternatives in Maryland manufactured a virus of comparable genomic length in just two weeks."[10]

A National Academy of Sciences committee tasked with reporting on globalization, biosecurity, and the future of the life sciences noted that several techniques, such as RNA interference and synthetic biology, came to fruition during the committee's mandate. The committee's report makes for sober reading:

> Neither of these developments could have been foretold even a few years back, pointing to the futility of trying to predict with accuracy what will come in the next few years. This leads to the second conclusion, that our task, the task of surveying current technology trends in order to anticipate what new threats may face us down the road, will be never ending. Our report, published in early 2006, will in some respects be out of date by 2007.[11]

Biotechnology's discoveries also have a dark side—they have the potential to cause immense harm through accidental or intentional release of a manufactured pathogen or through what the National Academy of Sciences terms "enabling technologies," such as acquisition of novel diversity, directed design, manipulation of biological systems, and enhanced packaging of biological materials, that can be used for weapons purposes.[12] The list of alarming scientific achievements includes

—synthetic re-creation of the virus that caused the 1919 Spanish influenza pandemic

—synthetic manufacture of the polio virus

—synthetic manipulation of the mousepox virus, making it much more lethal.

The work on the mousepox virus demands special reflection. The manipulated virus was fatal to rats that had been immunized against mousepox, raising the specter of what might be done with smallpox and humans. And it was an accidental discovery by researchers who were looking for ways to render rats sterile as a means of extermination.[13] Imagine new findings in biotechnology being used to attack the fertility of ethnic or national groups—or the entire human species.

The dark side could be pursued by an individual scientist with a grudge, a terrorist group intent on mass death and disruption, or states that covet novel offensive biological weapons. It also could be reached inadvertently through shoddy safety systems and careless contamination.

THE NATURE OF BIOLOGICAL THREATS

Governments perceive biological threats to security differently, just as they do many of the issues covered in this book. In the Global South, the most salient biological threat is an onslaught of deadly infectious diseases, the biggest cause of death in poor countries. For the developed world there are the threats of the *potential* outbreak of deadly infectious diseases (for example, a recurrence of a deadly influenza pandemic or the spread of a newly emerging infectious disease such as SARS); the *potential* use of harmful biological agents by other states; and the *potential* for biological terrorism, especially tied to the dramatic discoveries in the life sciences described above.

Any arrangement to promote biological security should start by acknowledging that examples of bioterrorism have been few and their effects small.[14] And while the potential harm of a pandemic of a deadly infectious disease in the developed world is hypothetical, the ravages of disease in the developing world are real and take their toll daily. Five people died in the 2001 anthrax attacks in the United States; five people die worldwide from infectious diseases every second.

We say that not to dismiss either the potential threat of pandemics to the developed world or the threat of bioterrorism, especially when tied to advances in biotechnology. Rather it is to underscore that if we need global cooperation to tackle biological threats to security effectively, then international approaches must also equitably tackle the primary threats to developing nations, whose priority is the ravages of disease.[15]

Deadly Infectious Diseases

Every year 15 million people die from infectious diseases such as HIV/AIDS, malaria, tuberculosis (TB), and cholera.[16] Such diseases are both cause and consequence of poverty. Up to 1.7 million of the deaths are due to illnesses caused by contaminated water and poor sanitation.[17] As one doctor insists, the greatest ethical problem facing the life sciences today is that life expectancy in the developed world is around eighty years, while in some poor countries it has fallen to about thirty years.[18]

The natural world of disease is not a static one. Between 1940 and 2004, 335 emerging infectious diseases, or diseases not previously recognized in humans, were reported.[19] The peak emergence of those diseases was in the 1980s, but they have continued to develop at alarming numbers since. The majority come from non-human animal sources; they are abetted by high population density, antibiotic use, and a host of ecological and environmental conditions that promote the transfer of pathogens from wildlife to humans.[20] HIV/AIDS alone has infected more than 70 million people worldwide and killed more than 30 million.

Infectious diseases are related to a host of other threats that we examine in this book. Food insecurity and malnutrition make populations more susceptible to disease; disease and poor health, in turn, weaken agricultural productivity. HIV/AIDS, malaria, and TB have been shown to reduce economic growth in countries hard hit by these diseases. The International Labor Organization estimates that between 2006 and 2020, should HIV/AIDS remain at its already high levels in Africa, the disease will cost more than $144 billion in economic growth.[21] Other research has shown similar effects of malaria, which reduces Africa's GDP by 1.3 percent each year, on average.[22] Poverty in turn contributes to the spread of infectious diseases because of poor public health and sanitation. As discussed later, poverty itself is a cause of civil war, and civil war facilitates the spread of disease by destroying health systems, forcing populations to move, and overwhelming the carrying capacity of local communities.[23] In addition, the failure of governments to provide for the health of their populations contributes to their lack of legitimacy, which in turn makes them vulnerable to rebels and insurgents.

The extent of global travel means that the United States along with every other country is at risk from emerging infectious diseases and a global influenza pandemic. (In 2007 there were more than 830 million international air passengers and another 1.2 billion domestic air passengers. In 2006 the United States alone welcomed 52 million foreign visitors, while Americans took 60 million trips abroad that year.)[24] Although the public health systems in developed countries may be better equipped to respond to any potential outbreak than are those in less developed countries, there is no national defense against this transnational issue. Biological security anywhere, including in the United States, is only as good as global biological security.

Despite the need for international cooperation in fighting infectious diseases, issues of equity have created real barriers to joint action. The developing world resents that only 10 percent of the $30 billion spent globally on health research and development is spent on the diseases of the developing world.[25] In 2007, the government of Indonesia refused to share strains of avian flu with the World Health Organization, charging that any vaccine that might be developed from the strains would be unlikely to reach Indonesia.[26] And the measure required to stanch avian flu—the indiscriminate elimination of poultry flocks—has disproportionately hurt the poorest farmers in Asia.[27]

Bioterrorism

Given the wide diffusion of biological technologies and materials, the likelihood is greater that terrorist groups would be able to obtain the means to manufacture bioweapons than nuclear or chemical weapons. Moreover, there is evidence of intent: documents found in al Qaeda training camps in Afghanistan revealed rudimentary experiments with bioweapons.[28] Nonetheless, terrorist attacks using biological weapons have been few. Turning bioagents into weapons is difficult, and an attack of real magnitude remains a challenge. The lack of bioterrorism has led some to conclude that the threat has been exaggerated.[29] As one analyst points out, an American is 235 times more likely to be hit by lightning than to die of anthrax poisoning.[30]

But, as in the world of investing, past performance is no guarantee of future results, and it is precisely because of the revolutionary transformation of the life sciences that we should be concerned. The key is to create policies and institutions that help safeguard that transformation while building strong global public health defenses against natural and intentional disease outbreaks wherever and however they might occur.

Cultivation of Pathogens for State Programs

In the 1990s it was revealed that several states—the Soviet Union, Iraq, and South Africa—had created large-scale offensive biological programs.[31] In the Soviet Union, scientific experiments led to large-scale production of weaponized anthrax; an accidental release of a plume of anthrax killed at least sixty-four people in the town of Sverdlovsk in 1979.[32] Soviet scientists also experimented with the transfer and modification of genes in order to destroy the human immune system as well as with genetically engineered pathogens that could induce autoimmunity, which when tested on animals proved nearly 100 percent lethal.[33] In July 1995, the government of Saddam Hussein admitted to UN weapons inspectors that it had an extensive offensive biological weapons program; the inspectors in turn dismantled and destroyed Iraq's declared facilities and others that the regime had not declared.[34] In the 1980s, the South African apartheid regime attempted but failed to develop a vaccine that would render black women infertile.[35] To the question of whether advances in biotechnology could be used for the dark side, the answer is that they already have been.

States have a legal right under the Biological Weapons Convention to invest in biodefense, which by implication involves the development of agents that could have an offensive purpose. However, the criteria for defining offensive and defensive are not objective, and definitions depend largely on assessment of intent. The expansion of biodefense programs in response to the increasing threat from bioterrorism and the diffusion of biotechnology are arguably increasing the potential threat of diversion of both knowledge and materials. By the nature of their access and research, scientists inside state programs pose a considerable potential threat because they could circumvent controls on access to pathogens and technology under the cover of national security. That seems to have been the case with the American scientist accused of carrying out the 2001 anthrax attacks, Bruce Ivins.

A critical question is whether we are likely to see in state biological weapons programs what happened with nuclear weapons in the 1990s, with rogue state weapons scientists using their knowledge and technology to create proliferation networks. In the 1990s the United States and United Kingdom feared that a leading scientist in South Africa's bioweapons program was selling his secrets to Libya. There are now more than 400 U.S. institutions with access to live bioweapons agents and 14,000 individuals approved to handle them. Will one of them or some other scientist elsewhere in the world turn out to be the A. Q. Khan of bioweapons?

Biotechnology

Global growth in this industry now generates annual revenues of more than $60 billion. In thousands of laboratories around the world, scientists are using cutting-edge technologies to understand the causes of diseases in order to prevent and treat them. Similar activity is occurring in the areas of farming, plant and animal biology, and energy. Other scientific disciplines (nanotechnology, information technology, materials science) not normally associated with biotechnology are becoming integrated in ways that are generating new technological applications in the life sciences.

Advances in biotechnology greatly expand the reservoir of potentially lethal agents. The growing understanding of the mechanisms of both infectious diseases and the immune system creates the potential for genetically tailoring agents. The possibility increases of developing "stealth" viruses, which could be introduced secretly into the genomes of a given population and then triggered later by a signal and "designer" disease pathogens, which could be used to attack the genome of a given population on command.[36] As Claire Fraser and Malcolm Dando observe, such possibilities represent "an order-of-magnitude change in potential offensive capabilities."[37] Ever-expanding microbial genome databases now provide a parts list of dangerous genes from which to pick and choose the most lethal combinations. There is danger in the misuse of large-scale databases containing information on the genetics of specific populations, just as there are potential risks in openly publishing complete sequences of dangerous pathogens.

The pace of change within biotechnology poses an almost unprecedented security threat, demanding a high level of responsiveness from international institutions. Today's capabilities in the life sciences and related technologies have already changed the nature of what is possible. The accelerating pace of discovery has fundamentally altered the threat spectrum. It may be futile to predict with any accuracy what will come over the next few years.

A considerable burden of responsibility falls on companies and individual scientists to ensure that they understand the harm that could be caused by the abuse of biotechnology in biowarfare and by terrorists. Irresponsible and careless behavior within the industry could have significant implications. Yet most scientists who are concerned about the potential dangers of biotechnology admit that there is no scientific consensus about the dark side, and there is plenty of opposition to any hint that regulation may be needed to address misuse of the science or its application.

At one remove that is understandable: for those who face the ravages of disease every day, the promise of biotechnology cannot be realized too soon, and it may seem misguided to express caution about potential scientific discoveries that could address those ravages. On the other hand, scientists often display a knee-jerk reaction against challenges to scientific inquiry and openness. In this case, however, they do so at great peril.

The likelihood of realizing biotechnology's promise will depend on popular confidence and trust in the technology. We start with an already immense amount of popular skepticism and doubt about where the life sciences are headed. Worldwide opinion surveys show much distrust in the safety of genetically modified food and seeds, and such distrust would be exacerbated by a devastating incident, either accidental or intentional, involving biotechnology.

RESPONSIBLE SOVEREIGNTY AND BIOLOGICAL THREATS

As with the other issues addressed in this book, possible solutions to the biological threats to security rest on a near-universal commitment of states to standards of responsible sovereignty, which provide a useful foundation for building an effective regime. Here we focus on three important agreements: the Biological Weapons Convention, the International Health Regulations, and UN General Assembly Resolution 60/1. Together, these agreements define the current state of responsibility in the biological field. Responsible sovereignty includes rejecting the development of offensive biological weapons, preventing groups or individuals within state borders from accessing dangerous biological weapons, cooperating in the event of deadly disease outbreaks, building local and public health capacity throughout the world, and working to reduce disease and its effects in poor countries.

The Biological Weapons Convention

Evidence of repulsion against the use of biological weapons dates back thousands of years and across civilizations. In the twentieth century, in reaction to the horrors of the use of chemical and biological agents in World War I, states signed the 1925 Geneva Protocol, which prohibited the use of such agents on the battlefield. In 1975 states brought into force the Biological and Toxic Weapons Convention, which has been signed by 162 countries and ratified by 149. The convention puts forward several state obligations:

—to prohibit the development of biological agents for military offensive purposes

—to prohibit the transfer of such agents between states

—to prohibit any persons within the jurisdiction of the state from developing bioweapons

—to facilitate the transfer of knowledge, equipment, and materials for peaceful purposes.

Although the convention did not foresee a revolution in the life sciences or the fact that future weapons may be based on different scientific discoveries, its language implies that the convention applies to new developments and their application to bioweapons. Moreover, the convention does suggest that since governments have responsibility for prohibiting anyone in their jurisdictions from developing bioweapons, they must take responsibility for ensuring the security and safety of biotechnology.

Such an obligation can also be inferred from the International Convention on the Suppression of Terrorist Bombings (1998), which requires states "to make the creation, detonation, dissemination, and discharge of biological agents or weaponry criminal offences under their domestic criminal codes."

The International Health Regulations 2005

The principle of sovereignty as responsibility is well-established in the field of international health. Long before what we now call globalization, governments understood that outbreaks of devastating infectious diseases were a problem of international consequence, no matter where they occurred. In 1951 the member states of the World Health Organization adopted the International Sanitary Regulations, which focused on border controls to prevent the spread of five diseases: cholera, plague, smallpox, typhoid fever, and yellow fever. In 1969, the first International Health Regulations were adopted, creating a legal framework for reporting and responding to those diseases.

By the 1990s public health experts understood that the 1969 regulations were inadequate to ensure global health security. First, there was the challenge of emerging infectious diseases that were not covered by the regulations. Second, because border control was found to be an ineffective response to disease outbreaks, it would have to give way to thorough disease surveillance and response, with an emphasis on rapid expert intervention to diagnose and stanch outbreaks at their source. Third, changes in information technology meant that the World Health Organization should no longer rely simply on governments to report outbreaks; Internet networks could provide earlier indications of worrying symptoms than many ministries of health could.

In 2005 the International Health Regulations were thoroughly revised. The 2005 regulations require that states work to prevent and control outbreaks of infectious disease, protect their citizens against such outbreaks, and cooperate with the World Health Organization and other states against events (naturally occurring or caused by humans, accidentally or intentionally) that pose international public health risks.

The 2005 regulations are a universal agreement among states. States must report evidence of international public health threats to the World Health Organization, including laboratory results, the source and type of risk, number of cases and deaths, conditions affecting the spread of disease, and health measures employed. States also must develop a national response plan and coordinate their actions with hospitals, health personnel and organizations, and government health agencies at domestic points of entry (airports, water ports, and land crossings) in the event of an infectious breakout or instance of contamination.

States are expected to collaborate with each other in detecting and responding to health risks. That includes providing technical cooperation and logistical support in developing public health capacities as well as mobilizing financial resources to implement an adequate response to health hazards. States must aid each other in formulating domestic laws to ensure effective implementation of health regulations.

To understand how far and how fast responsible sovereignty has come in the world of public health, consider that when the World Health Organization began the quest to renegotiate the 1969 International Health Regulations in 1996, one legal expert questioned that strategy, arguing that "what is scientifically and medically necessary to combat emerging diseases may not be what states are willing to agree to undertake."[38] The same expert rightly observed later that the subsequent 2005 regulations constitute "a major development in the use of international law for public health" that "imposes serious responsibilities that significantly affect sovereignty."[39]

UN General Assembly Resolution 60/1

The 2005 World Summit, a high-level plenary meeting of the UN General Assembly, reached decisions on development, security, human rights, and institutional reform of the United Nations. It also evaluated the progress made toward achieving the Millennium Development Goals, a set of targets for the year 2015 that states adopted in 2000, which include reducing child mortality by two-thirds, reducing the maternal mortality rate by three-fourths, achieving universal access to reproductive health care, and a host of measures to combat HIV/AIDS, malaria, and TB.

One outcome of the summit was General Assembly Resolution 60/1, which emphasizes the need for an international response to build the capacity of developing nations to help realize health-related millennium goals. All states are responsible for increasing investment and improving the infrastructure of health care systems in developing nations, including by ensuring that they have sufficient health care workers, management systems, and supplies to reach the Millennium Development Goals by

2015. States also must work toward improving investment strategies that promote the capacity of healthcare systems in developing nations. States are expected to contribute funding for academic and industrial research and for the development of vaccines, microbicides, diagnostic kits, and drug treatments to address major pandemics, tropical diseases, and other infectious health risks, such as avian flu and SARS. Finally, General Assembly Resolution 60/1 reinforces the 2005 International Health Regulations and calls on states to continue to ensure the implementation of obligations set forth in the regulations.

EVALUATING THE INTERNATIONAL ARCHITECTURE

Governments face a challenge that is both a multifaceted threat and a significant opportunity. In response, they have built important assets to help promote biological security, among them the World Health Organization, a competent first responder to disease outbreaks and strong coordinator of global and national health responses to pandemics; the International Health Regulations (2005), a universal agreement that places clear obligations on states to cooperate in responding to infectious disease outbreaks and to build strong global public health systems; and the Biological Weapons Convention, an agreement based on a long-standing repulsion against the use of diseases and pathogens as weapons of war. Nonetheless, the present international architecture is insufficient in scope and responsiveness and inadequate to tap the capacity of the private sector and individual scientists to address the dynamic nature of this challenge.

WHO

From 1990 to 2008, the World Health Organization transformed itself from an institution in crisis, foundering in its search for a role in meeting the health challenges of globalization, to an institution that has regained global respect and that is a key player in the fight for global public health. Its performance during that time shows that dynamic leadership is needed to anticipate challenges and aggressively position international institutions to perform in crisis.

WHO began as a technical agency with a narrow focus on disease control, and in the 1960s it achieved a major success in eradicating smallpox.[40] Less remarked upon, however, is that during that time WHO also attempted to rid the world of malaria, a campaign that failed after showing positive results early on. In the 1970s, the organization rightly drew the conclusion that different diseases require different strategies and that achievements in medicine and immunization were not enough in the face of crumbling public health infrastructure. Toward the end of that decade, WHO and its director general, Halfdan Mahler, made primary health services—especially building public health infrastructure and delivering services to poor countries—central to WHO's mandate. Two WHO-led initiatives—an international code on baby formula and regulation of essential drugs—led to a clash with key wealthy member states, including the United States. In retrospect, however, it is clear that WHO was out in front on issues that were harbingers of global health challenges in the post–cold war era.

Poised to be a leader in global health at the end of the cold war, WHO instead retreated to issues of narrow medical competence. That sharp downward trajectory coincided with the disastrous choice of a new director general, Hiroshi Nakajima, in 1988. Nakajima led WHO into an era of intense bureaucratic politicking, low morale, and constant allegations of corruption and incompetence.

WHO's freefall could not have come at a worse time. In 1988, there were about 7 million cases of HIV/AIDS. The director of WHO's AIDS program, Dr. Jonathan Mann, resigned in 1990, citing undue infringement on his work by Nakajima and a lack of strategy and leadership in addressing what would turn out to be the worst global pandemic since the plague. [41] When the United Nations created the Global Program on AIDS in 1993, it wrested control from WHO and made it a bit player in a larger multiagency program.[42] By the 1990s the World Bank was arguably a greater player in global health than WHO.

AIDS was not the only emerging infectious disease challenge that WHO botched. In 1994 there was a reemergence of plague in India. Nakajima's handling of the outbreak was so obviously incompetent that it brought respect for WHO to an all-time low and threatened to discredit its work in infectious diseases, long a strength.[43] In 1998, the member states of WHO chose a dynamic new director general, Gro Harlem Brundtland, a three-time prime minister of Norway and a medical doctor by training.

Brundtland initiated important changes at WHO, but we want to focus on one issue in particular: her repositioning of WHO as the global leader and coordinator on issues involving deadly infectious diseases. First, under Brundtland, WHO advocated a change from international health to global health—health issues that transcend borders. WHO made revision of the International Health Regulations a priority and worked to fill the gaps between the old health regulations and the imperatives of public health in a globalized world. Under Brundtland, WHO created the Global Outbreak Alert and Response Network (GOARN) to coordinate the response to outbreaks of deadly diseases. Finally, WHO returned to its advocacy role, emphasizing primary public health and the need to strengthen local, national, and global capacity.

HARD CASE: SARS. Inept in confronting an outbreak of plague in 1994, WHO proved invaluable in stopping severe acute respiratory syndrome (SARS) in its tracks nine years later. SARS emerged somewhere in the southern Chinese province of Guangdong in late 2002, with outbreaks in several cities. On January 31 one victim caught a hyperinfective case of the disease and while being treated by three different hospitals infected an estimated 200 persons, most of them hospital workers. News of the outbreak reached WHO through electronic reporting systems, prompting GOARN to ask the Chinese government about the epidemic. China confirmed an outbreak of an infectious disease, which by that time had infected 300 persons and killed five in Guangdong. But Chinese authorities misattributed the outbreak to a commonly known bacterial agent, thereby unduly reducing alarm.

The disease spread outside of China on February 21, 2003, when a Chinese physician infected twelve people who were staying at the same hotel in Hong Kong. Within twenty-four hours, those twelve people traveled by air to Singapore, Vietnam, Canada, Ireland, and the United States, generating most of the 8,000 cases of the disease worldwide.

Global response was prompted by a February 28 report from Dr. Carlo Urbani, a WHO physician in Hanoi, identifying a patient with a high fever and atypical pneumonia. That triggered GOARN to send investigative and containment teams to Hanoi and Hong Kong, where reports of a mysterious, deadly infectious disease continued to find their way to the Internet. Dr. Urbani himself died of the disease.

According to a National Academy of Sciences evaluation of the response, WHO issued a global alert on March 12, "describing outbreaks of the yet-unnamed respiratory disease in Hong Kong and Vietnam, and instituted worldwide surveillance. A second alert on March 15 named the condition, listed its symptoms, and advised travelers to have a high level of suspicion of SARS and report to a health worker if they had SARS symptoms and had visited an area where SARS was known to be occurring. Two further alerts provided recommendations for airports to screen passengers and for travelers to avoid areas where SARS had been detected."[44] The warnings to avoid travel to infected areas were "the most restrictive in the history of the organization."[45]

In March GOARN, using secure communications, created a virtual network among eleven laboratories in nine countries to hasten identification of the cause of the disease. The disease was identified a month later.

GOARN also succeeded in the difficult task of pressing China's health authorities to cooperate with its efforts to stanch the pandemic. Key to its success was a warning that "if SARS was not brought under control in China, there would be no chance of controlling the global threat of SARS."[46] Within days of GOARN's first intercession, China agreed to cooperate. GOARN specialists, however, grew frustrated over China's continued slow response to treating the disease. On April 16 WHO publicly criticized the Chinese authorities for "inadequate reporting" of cases. The Chinese reaction was swift. On April 20 a "nationwide war" on SARS was declared and several officials, including the minister of health, were fired for their inadequate response to the disease. For the next two months, Chinese health officials worked intensively to halt the spread of the disease, which they accomplished in late June.

On July 5, 2003, a little more than four months after GOARN responded to Dr. Urbani's report from Vietnam, WHO declared that SARS had been broken. It had spread to thirty countries on six continents, infected more than 8,000 people and killed nearly 800 of its known victims. The epidemic's toll on the economies of the hardest-hit countries was estimated to be $40 billion.

The Institute of Medicine of the National Academies of Science in the United States deemed the international response to SARS a great success: "the quality, speed, and effectiveness of the public health response to

SARS brilliantly outshone past responses to international outbreaks of infectious disease, validating a decade's worth of progress in global public health networking."[47]

A key part of this story was that Director General Brundtland pushed for WHO to exert autonomy and influence way beyond its authority and mandate. SARS was not covered under the existing International Health Regulations, but WHO demanded cooperation and openness nonetheless. Brundtland issued travel warnings and advisories without the legal authorization to do so and amidst some criticism from member states.

WHO's activism was tolerated, then championed, and ultimately enshrined in the new International Health Regulations negotiated in 2005, because governments all around the world came face to face with the health implications of a globalized, interconnected world. China's role in this story is crucial; when it realized that China's economic stake in an open international system was at risk and that its failures of response were bringing it unwanted global attention, it decided that its security and prosperity demanded a cooperative response.

SARS also showed the wisdom of creating the Global Outbreak Alert and Response Network. GOARN is a consortium of 140 technical partners in sixty countries, coordinated at WHO in Geneva, where it runs a situation room twenty-four hours a day, seven days a week, to monitor deadly infectious disease outbreaks around the world. With its network approach and reliance on fast communication, GOARN spotted SARS before any report from the Chinese government appeared; within twenty-four hours it had put together an international team under WHO auspices to investigate. While SARS was GOARN's most public work, it responded to seventy outbreaks of deadly infectious diseases between 2000 and 2005.

Nonetheless, the National Academy of Sciences study cautions that the success in addressing SARS also contains several warnings. National capacities were overstretched: in Toronto, for example, where two different outbreaks of SARS swamped public health officials, authorities asked for help from the United States. In the United States, the Centers for Disease Control was at the forefront of the response but quickly found itself overextended, with too few experts and scientists.

Moreover, as deadly as SARS was, it is not in the same league as an influenza pandemic. The transmission rate for SARS was slower than that for influenza. An official from GOARN admits that SARS put it under maximum stress and that it does not have the capacity to address a large-scale influenza pandemic. In response to concerns about such a pandemic, WHO took the global lead in coordinating efforts to prepare for it by creating a special coordinator with a dedicated staff devoted solely to surveillance and response to avian flu.

The Biological Weapons Convention

The Biological Weapons Convention (BWC) has a limited mandate: to cover state-run biological weapons programs. Unlike nuclear and chemical conventions, the BWC lacks a verification mechanism to prove states' compliance; that means that it has no effective capacity to deter cheating by raising the possibility of discovery. In that regard the inability of the regime to prevent the Soviet Union and Iraq from developing sophisticated bioweapons capabilities over a sustained period is a significant failure.

Yet even if a verification mechanism existed, it is not clear how effective it would be in detecting noncompliance. The inherent difficulty of distinguishing illegitimate offensive bioweapons programs from legitimate defensive research adds to the dilemma, as does the practical problem of conducting inspections that actually yield substantive evidence. Even with such a process in place, parties to the treaty would still have little faith that verification could actually catch the cheaters. To reiterate a key theme of this chapter, the ability to detect offensive bioweapons programs will only get more difficult as experimentation in biotechnology becomes more widespread—down to the level of individual businesses and scientists and eventually households. Moreover, in a world of business competition over cutting-edge applications in the life sciences, neither states nor industry will have an interest in compromising confidential and proprietary business information.

Efforts to strengthen the BWC have for the most part failed. A 2001 draft protocol was rejected by the United States, which claimed that the verification procedures proposed would be ineffectual. Major opposition from industry led the United States to argue that confidential business information could be compromised; the United States also contended that potential proliferators could use the protocol to undermine international export control regimes such as the Australia Group, a group of

41 governments that has created stringent rules restricting the export and shipment of potential bioweapons agents and technology. Iran, for one, argued that as a party to the BWC, it should be allowed free trade in all biological materials.

While some of the proposed monitoring techniques might be useful, many experts agreed with the U.S. government that there were significant deficiencies in the verification regime. The inspectors would be too few in number, they would lack essential skills, and they would not be deployed to sites long enough to generate reliable findings.

The United States emphasized instead that BWC members should take measures to strengthen their own domestic legislation and develop codes of conduct for enhancing biosecurity. However, one problem with this individualistic approach was that there was no articulation of an acceptable international standard for biosecurity. In the absence of agreement on a standard, national legislation could be weak and inadequate. While national legislation could be the first step, without a high standard and extensive global participation in creating domestic biosecurity legislation, the likely outcome would be a patchwork of rules and regulations with clear and significant gaps that determined proliferators or terrorists could seek to exploit.

Gaps in the Architecture

The safety and security of biotechnology is an area in which a traditional type of arms control agreement has only limited utility; it can be but one thin layer in a multilayered solution to the challenge. Several problems remain: lack of universal biosafety and biosecurity standards, data deficits, the role of nonstate actors, and the question of who should attend to the fast pace of technological advances and their corresponding threats.

BIOSAFETY (WORKING WITH PATHOGENS). The World Health Organization defines biosafety as practices implemented to prevent unintentional exposure to pathogens or their accidental release. In many cases facilities and research centers are aware of the need for such measures but they are not necessarily obligated to abide by regulations. For example, government-funded organizations in the United States must follow the biosafety guidelines of the Centers for Disease Control and the National Institutes of Health, but adherence is optional for other institutions. National biosafety regulations could be effective, but allowing governments to set their own standards in this area would not necessarily lead to an overall strengthening of the regime.

BIOSECURITY (PRECLUDING UNAUTHORIZED ACCESS TO AGENTS, TECHNOLOGY, AND KNOWLEDGE). While signatories to the BWC are prohibited from making biological weapons, individuals generally are not restricted from possessing biothreat agents. Not all countries have enacted legislation criminalizing the development, production, and use of biological weapons by individuals. The 1996 BWC Review Conference "strongly urged" states to pass criminal legislation barring offensive biological weapons research. Yet, as of 2001, only twenty-seven of forty-five states that provided any information to the United Nations said that they had done anything in that regard, while ninety-eight states failed to submit any data whatsoever. Again, if left to individual countries, the outcome may not be acceptable.

At the industry and university level, laboratories may be familiar with biosafety issues, but they are generally unaccustomed to the concept of biosecurity—for example, the need for enhanced on-site security measures, access and transfer regulations for pathogens, or even monitoring of the stocks of pathogens or toxins that they possess. Often such measures are perceived by scientists to be ineffective, intrusive, or too costly or as an obstruction to research, resulting in skepticism of their value. Self-regulation of biosecurity by facilities, including R&D facilities, is therefore unlikely to be adequate. Formal government oversight arrangements, including legislation, probably are necessary, yet such regulations must be developed in consultation with the scientists who are expected to implement them if they are to have any chance of being adopted and followed.

Only a small number of countries have enacted legislation that specifically addresses biosecurity, and again, as with biosafety, it is not clear that leaving it to individual countries to set their own standards is appropriate. In the absence of agreed-on universal standards, they could merely enact weak legislation. Although self-regulation by individual states may further biosecurity in some countries, it does not by itself provide a disincentive for states that are noncompliant.

DATA DEFICIT. Large numbers of laboratories around the world possess dangerous pathogens or toxins or conduct work on them, but there are no data on exactly how many such laboratories exist. Moreover, no comprehensive records exist on bioscience experts who have worked with lethal pathogens, nor is any sophisticated global structure in place to track and identify dangerous germs or critical equipment; consequently, there is no information on the scale and quantity of global transfers.

Voluntary measures have been proposed through the Biological Weapons Convention to close some of the data deficits, but they have proved singularly ineffective. At the 1986 BWC Review Conference, member states agreed to provide annual data on issues relating to biological research, high biosecurity laboratories, and suspicious disease outbreaks. In 1991, BWC members further agreed to provide more detailed data to the UN to promote transparency about their compliance with the BWC. During the first ten years when such data exchanges were to occur, not once did a majority of BWC member states participate—not even to check the "nothing to declare" box on the reporting form.[48]

NONSTATE ACTORS. Traditional arms-control measures such as the BWC have concentrated almost exclusively on state programs. While state programs remain important, the activities of nonstate actors demand further attention. Today, a strategy is needed that focuses on denying knowledge and material to terrorists as well as interdicting their networks before they attack. Clearly not enough is being done to track potentially dangerous bioscience programs within the private sector. The system for detecting wrongful conduct and investigating suspicious activity at a national and international level is woefully inadequate.

KEEPING TABS ON THE EVOLUTION OF THE THREAT. As biotechnology advances, so do its possible applications to offensive bioweapons. Today it might be possible to, among other things, enhance the antibiotic resistance of biological agents, modify their antigenic properties, or transfer pathogenic properties between them. That could make them harder to detect, diagnose, and treat, increasing their military utility and thus increasing the temptation to pursue offensive programs. Should development of a new generation of offensive biological weapons programs occur, what might happen in a decade or two as the genomics revolution consolidates and spreads around the world?

An international regime must be supple enough to evolve with developments in technology. Given the widespread development and use of technology, the regime will require the active engagement of scientists, universities, and businesses to have any chance of detecting and acting on violations, yet to rely on voluntary participation alone, as argued above, would be folly. Hence, a biotechnology security regime requires clarity and strength from the top down and bottom up in order to create the breadth and strength of response needed to succeed.

STRENGTHENING THE INTERNATIONAL RESPONSE TO BIOLOGICAL THREATS

The biological threats to security are diverse. They include old and new infectious diseases, potential outbreaks of new disease, use of diseases as weapons by states or terrorists, and the intentional or accidental release of new pathogens or agents produced by revolutionary developments in the life sciences. Despite the diversity of threats, efforts to defend against any or all of them must have several common features: strong global, national, and local public health systems; willingness of states to cooperate with other states and international organizations in the face of public health emergencies of international concern; and a strong World Health Organization to promote cooperation.

As with the other threats that we examine in this book, prevention is a primary goal. In the case of naturally occurring disease, WHO has shown that it is possible to take actions and put in place strategies that can help minimize the deadliness of the next influenza pandemic. But what of the threat from bioterrorism? It may be that the biotech revolution will render complete prevention impossible. What *can* be done, however, is to make it more difficult for groups or individuals to use the life sciences for nefarious purposes. And the universal adoption of strong safety procedures and the creation of a culture of safety can minimize the risk of accidental release of a devastating pathogen.

Two challenges are clear. The first—the need for a strong defense based on global public health systems and strong international cooperation—is not controversial. The dogged work of WHO in forging the 2005 International Health Regulations, its role in addressing avian flu, and the performance of the Global Outbreak Alert and Response Network against SARS have led to remarkable agreement on how to build public health security. What is needed now is the full implementation of the 2005 regulations and the creation of the necessary capacity to ensure that they succeed.

The second challenge—the creation of a new international regime to promote the safety and security of the life sciences and biotechnology—is contentious. As mentioned, the biotech industry is global, diverse, decentralized, competitive, and growing. Scientists and industry bridle at restraints—the former for fear of losing freedom of scientific inquiry and the latter for fear of being put at a market disadvantage. At the same time, the general public itself distrusts some of the key products of the biotech revolution. And many governments have not modified their assessment of the threat of bioweapons to meet the exponential pace of technological change.

A new regime for biotechnology safety and security will need to look and to be different from any existing international regime. Effective regulation, not heavy regulation, is required. The regime must engage industry, scientists, and the public. It is possible to sketch some of its features: universal standards for biosafety and biosecurity; national legislation to regulate domestic industry, universally applied; codes of conduct for scientists and industry; collection of information about what kinds of research are being done, by whom; awareness of scientific advancements and the dangers that they might produce; and a focal point for sharing information.

The first step toward building this regime is to create the scientific consensus, international trust, and knowledge necessary to forge a common perception of the problem and spur the collective action necessary to deal with it.

Capacity Building for Full Implementation of the International Health Regulations 2005

What the WHO calls public health security depends on a robust defense against disease that rests on strong surveillance, international and local preparedness, and international and local response. As WHO insists, such a defense must include "governments, industry, public and private financiers, academia, international organizations, and civil society."[49] The International Health Regulations 2005 lay out in detail the key responsibilities of states:

—strengthen national disease surveillance, prevention, control, and response systems

—strengthen public health security in travel and transport
—strengthen WHO global alert and response systems
—strengthen the management of specific disease risks.[50]

Implementation of the regulations requires developed countries to assist poorer countries in building national health systems; that in turn imposes the obligation on governments to cooperate globally with other states and with WHO in addressing public health emergencies of international concern.

The vital missing link is local capacity in much of the developing world. There is a widespread desire among governments, international organizations, and nongovernmental organizations to fight disease in the developing world and an unprecedented amount of private resources, such as funds from the Bill and Melinda Gates Foundation, to realize that goal. But as Laurie Garrett points out, the key issues for many of the disparate health projects of the last several years are scalability and sustainability—and the key to both are local talent in the form of trained health care professionals, facilities that the poor can access, and dependable flows of resources to sustain programs.[51] What remains unknown is whether basic public health in the developing world can be strengthened through a sectoral approach that just targets health care or whether it requires broad systemic reform of governance, a topic examined in chapter 9.

In 2008 WHO called for governments and nongovernmental organizations to shift their emphasis to primary health care and to governance reforms to bolster national public health systems.[52] As a first step in that direction, WHO should use implementation of the International Health Regulations to provide a strategic framework for donors to integrate infectious disease programs into general public health systems and to help developing countries adopt best practices from other nations to build effective and sustainable capacity.

Steps toward Implementation of a Universal Regime

The U.S. position on bioweapons control since the 2001 rejection of the BWC Protocol has been to move away from legally binding multilateral measures toward voluntary national actions. However, for a number of other countries the ultimate goal remains to develop a multilaterally negotiated, legally binding verification regime.

Members of the European Union, along with Latin American and Caribbean leaders, issued a political declaration in May 2002 in which they underlined their "conviction [that] the latter Convention [BWC] is best enhanced by the adoption of a legally binding instrument to oversee the prohibition of the development, production and stockpiling of Biological and Toxic Weapons and their destruction."[53] In the lead-up to the 2006 BWC Review Conference, however, many states had started to look beyond the protocol, recognizing that there was more to an effective BWC than the open-ended and divisive debate over whether and how verification should be pursued.

The United States needs to reengage and reassert its leadership role in this area to promote a range of multilateral actions on biosecurity that need not undermine the BWC and that could even strengthen the prospects for establishment of a multilateral, legally binding verification regime in the long term, which is the ultimate goal of many states.

Several incremental steps can be taken to increase the costs for terrorists who try to obtain the capability to make a bioweapon and the probability that illicit activity will be detected. If fully implemented, such steps could form the basis for a global regime.

First, the United States could begin a dialogue with the G-16 and other countries of responsibility in the field of biotechnology to negotiate standards and facilitate uniform national action to improve biosecurity and biosafety. As a first step, lists need to be compiled that categorize pathogens, toxins, and new technologies that could be used for bioweapons and rank them by urgency. Such lists would change over time, and there would need to be a mechanism to ensure regular reassessment not just of pathogens but also of the trajectory of future research on "next-generation agents" and to identify techniques and technologies that might apply directly to biowarfare. Second, common models could be developed for access, transfer, and chain-of-custody regulations for select pathogens and toxins. The proposed dialogue would have to enlist scientists and the biotech industry as partners in formulating both standards and practices.

On the basis of the negotiated standards, the G-16 could work toward mandatory implementation of standards through national legislation and regulation. The only way to ensure that the agreed-on standards are being applied is for countries to establish a national regulatory mechanism to provide oversight of facilities working with dangerous pathogens and engaged in research involving genetically modified organisms. Again, the participation of scientists and the biotech industry is crucial, and it would play a role in detecting and interdicting illicit conduct. While regulatory oversight is necessary, it needs to be complemented by measures, such as codes of conduct, best practice protocols, and dedicated training, to improve self-regulation within the life sciences and the biotech industry.

The goal of regulation is to protect legitimate scientific and business inquiry, research, and operations and to make it easier for authorities to detect illicit activity. That would require government registration of legitimate facilities, as well as audit declarations of activities from academic, research, industry, and government organizations. Again, the purpose of such reporting is not to restrict legitimate activity but to close some data gaps so that governments can better target illegitimate activities.

In the longer term, agreement among the G-16 and countries of responsibility, bolstered by national legislation and regulation, could be a step toward implementation of a universal international regime. The G-16 would need to work toward encouraging wider adoption by other states. Some countries have not even enacted legislation criminalizing the development, production, and use of biological weapons by individuals. The final step to ensure implementation would be to create an international body to coordinate and promote national legislation and its implementation, update standards, and provide a formal mechanism for sharing information on suspicious activity.

This approach is not a complete answer, but its emphasis on registering legitimate activity and detecting illicit activity makes it more difficult for groups or individuals to use advances in biotechnology for nefarious purposes. Global adoption of mandatory practices would help close some of the gaps that bioterrorists may try to exploit and increase the costs of achieving an offensive capability.

An "Intergovernmental Panel on Safety of Biotechnology"

Cooperation does not happen without trust and knowledge, and two initial steps can be taken to promote both. The first is to take a page from the battle against global warming and create an "Intergovernmental Panel on Safety of Biotechnology," an independent scientific group, akin to the Intergovernmental Panel on Climate Change (IPCC), to analyze objectively and assess the risks inherent in biotechnology's discoveries in health, food, agriculture, energy, and security. The IPCC, winner of the 2007 Nobel Peace Prize, was founded for two reasons: to bring the best scientific judgment about climate change to a debate that was otherwise highly politicized and to involve scientists from around the world, especially from developing countries, in a global scientific process of assessment and evaluation. Scientists from all over the world have the opportunity to submit peer-reviewed research to the IPCC for consideration, thus establishing a forum for systematic debate and the formulation of scientific consensus. The resulting assessments of the IPCC have been instrumental in creating trust among scientists from different parts of the globe and in creating knowledge about climate change that people and governments can trust.

Disagreements about the safety of biotechnology and appropriate measures to address its risks resemble the debates on climate change twenty years ago. In the past year, for example, the Prince of Wales dismissed all genetically manipulated food as an unmitigated environmental disaster, while the chief scientist of Great Britain declared such food to be a key tool for addressing world hunger. In Africa in the past several years, cultural suspicions about biotechnology have led a head of state to refuse donations of genetically modified food even as his country teetered on the brink of famine and a regional governor to refuse to carry out polio vaccinations, leading to a global outbreak of the disease.

In the field of bioterrorism, similar differences exist. A National Academy of Sciences panel could agree on key risks of biotechnology, especially various experiments of concern, yet its findings and judgment have not entered into the mainstream scientific debate.

The IPCC has created policy networks among scientists who work on climate research and among scientists, government officials, and advocates from nongovernmental organizations. To replicate its success, a similar institution on biotechnology would need to emulate the IPCC's scientific openness and dialogue and, more important, its essential commitment to scientific rigor, peer review, and objectivity.

"DNA for Peace" Program

While the creation of an Intergovernmental Panel on Safety of Biotechnology can go a long way toward producing the trust and knowledge to support international cooperation in making biotechnology safe and secure, a second initiative could also work toward that goal: creation of a "DNA for Peace" program to help developing countries build their own expertise and capacity in biotechnology in exchange for implementing high standards of safety and security in their new life sciences industry.

It is all too easy to dismiss the potential contribution of the biotech revolution in improving the lives of the world's poor. Some seek to trivialize the potential impact of the billions of dollars spent on new research by pointing out that much of what contributes to the health woes of the poor can be addressed by simple technologies, applied with sustained commitment.

But it is wrong to claim that a choice has to be made between spending resources on high-tech solutions and spending them on sustained application of simple technologies. We have advocated a strong international commitment to building local and national public health systems and surveillance and treatment of infectious diseases, all of which can improve the health of billions of people. And advances in biotechnology can play a role there too. The Gates Foundation commissioned a panel of top doctors and scientists from around the world to imagine a dream list of products that could have a huge impact on the health of the world's poor.[54] These are just a few of the products that they listed:

—vaccines that do not require refrigeration

—needle-free delivery systems for vaccines

—creation of new vaccines

—a genetic strategy to deplete or incapacitate disease-transmitting insect populations

—creation of a full range of optimal bioavailable nutrients in a single staple plant species

—new drugs and delivery systems that minimize the likelihood of development of drug-resistant microorganisms.[55]

The "DNA for Peace" initiative is the brainchild of the Canadian McLaughlin-Rotman Centre for Global Health, which has warned that global efforts to combat bioterrorism are on a collision course with legitimate biotechnology pursuits.[56] They argue that what is needed is a network of scientists who will promote biotechnology research to fight disease, hunger, and poverty in the developing world and to keep vigil against the misuse of biotechnology. They contend that the key is to develop the capacity of poorer countries to participate in the biotech revolution and bolster their ability to use its remarkable advances to address the health problems that are most relevant to them. Investing in and fostering biotech development around the world will create a better environment in which to fight bioterrorism by building the network of experts needed to spot attempts to misuse the science.

CONCLUSION

Like nuclear energy in the twentieth century, the development of biotechnology in the twenty-first brings with it the potential for existential danger to the human species. Like computer technology in the twentieth century, biotechnology and its applications will be diffuse and domesticated. There will be broad potential for both benefits and harm. Promoting the former while preventing the latter will pose unprecedented challenges for development, security, and responsible sovereignty. Neither heavy government regulation nor self-regulation by industry and science alone will do. A new international regime will have to seek the active participation of science and industry to develop national legislation and regulations and appropriate international standards. Science and industry will need to help enforce compliance in order to sharpen the line between bright side and dark side activities. International cooperation for information sharing, monitoring of compliance, and updating threat assessments will be required.

A first step must be to create a common foundation for progress. As in the case of climate change twenty years ago, there is insufficient global and scientific consensus to move forward. That then is the urgent task, and it should be pursued immediately. The threat of biotechnology's dark side is only growing greater; should it be realized before that consensus is reached, the policy reaction will likely stifle the technology's positive potential.

In the meantime, there is the challenge of defense—against the ravages of disease and against the potential harm of bioterrorism. Both require a robust global health system, with strong disease surveillance and response. Both require national health systems that provide citizens in countries around the globe with adequate health care. A global initiative to build such systems would provide a win-win result for development and security.

In large parts of the world, however, such an initiative can succeed only in conjunction with concerted efforts to end ongoing civil wars and rebuild failed states, both of which devastate public health and local health capacities. We turn to that challenge in the next chapter.

SEVEN

MANAGING CIVIL VIOLENCE AND REGIONAL CONFLICT

FAILED STATES ARE BOTH cause and manifestation of a breakdown in international order. States that cannot maintain the rule of law or provide for the well-being of their citizens are closely associated with civil violence and amplify the risk of transnational threats such as terrorism and deadly infectious disease. Civil violence often crosses borders and draws regional and international actors into its vortex. Today's cases—Afghanistan, Congo, Iraq, Kosovo, Lebanon, and Sudan—demonstrate the consequences: lives lost, futures diminished, regional rivalries inflamed, and the credibility of international institutions cast into doubt.

A sea change has taken place in international views and policies toward civil wars and fragile states. When violence erupts, international mediators are expected to produce peace agreements. When peace agreements are signed, peacekeepers are expected to implement them. This expansion in mediation and peacekeeping has achieved important successes in countries around the world, such as El Salvador, Guatemala, Mozambique, Liberia, Sierra Leone, Côte d'Ivoire, and East Timor.

The current demand for peacekeepers has reached an all-time high—an estimated 180,000 individuals are currently serving in more than 20 conflicts.[1] The growth of peacekeeping during the last decade, however, has stretched its capacity to the breaking point. In addition, this growth has not been accompanied by effective peacebuilding, creating the risk of squandering this investment.

At the same time, popular expectations about what international actors should do to stop civil violence have increased. This is directly related to demands that states exercise their sovereignty responsibly and live up to their own stated commitments to protect victims caught in the maelstrom of mass atrocity.

It could be argued that peacekeeping has reached high tide and will now recede. Today's level of United Nations (UN) deployments is higher than the organization's previous record, but that record came during the war in Bosnia, when the United Nations was discredited and its deployments plummeted. Serious failures in Lebanon or Darfur—or other major centers of UN forces in Africa—could result in a similar loss of credibility and an associated retreat. Likewise, the pressures on the North Atlantic Treaty Organization (NATO) in Afghanistan might cause alliance leaders to conclude that they should not venture beyond Europe. The African Union's (AU) Sudanese and Somali trials might erode its appetite for future missions. The scale of today's peacekeeping operations does not guarantee that they will survive, and they could be reversed rapidly.

The consequences would be extremely damaging to international security and U.S. interests. A severe reduction of peacekeeping in Africa would permit recently concluded and semidormant wars to restart, guaranteeing humanitarian disasters. It would also undermine the gradual but unsteady progress toward building lasting security institutions in Africa to address future conflicts. Retreat from Lebanon could destabilize moderate governments in the Middle East, and open new havens for terrorist groups. A major setback in Afghanistan would signal that even if they work together, the United Nations and NATO cannot sustain a major operation in support of a fragile state.

In this chapter, we assess the threat and evaluate current international performance. The UN Security Council and its operational organizations loom large in this analysis. Not only have the past several years highlighted the importance of the legitimacy Security Council action provides, facts on the ground show that the United Nations is ever more critical to an effective response. We then focus on four issues: improving the capacity of international actors to prevent civil violence and better mediate conflicts; solidifying and enhancing peacekeeping capabilities; substantially enhancing the ability of the international system to help weak states build the capacity to govern, especially in the area of the rule of law (both to prevent conflict, and to recover from it); and improving the response to large-scale atrocities. Implementation of these proposals would not only enhance international conflict management, but would also help to achieve counterterrorism and counterproliferation objectives.

THREAT ASSESSMENT

Civil wars have declined dramatically since the end of the cold war. From a 1993 peak, by 2005 there were roughly 40 percent fewer civil wars.[2] By the best measures of intensity and by measures of consequences (number of refugees, number of internally displaced persons, and other factors) the scale of wars declined along with their absolute number.

This broad trend, however, hides important regional variations. For much of the 1990s, Africa was the sole continent exempt from this otherwise positive pattern, experiencing ongoing internal wars and huge spikes in deaths in places such as Rwanda. At the turn of the twenty-first century, more people were being killed in wars in Africa than in the rest of the world combined.[3]

More recently, some mixed patterns have emerged. In a positive trend, beginning in the late 1990s, wars in Africa began to show the same pattern of decline as the rest of the world.[4] Still, the number of conflicts in the Middle East increased slightly, and a similar increase was seen in the number of interstate wars, after a long period in which there were few. These negative trends are connected, and related to U.S. military posture and policy shifts in the Middle East since 9/11.

Indicators about what is ahead are worrisome. First, a number of large, relatively populous countries face risks of serious political instability (Pakistan)[5] or institutional collapse (Nigeria),[6] with enormous economic, humanitarian, and security implications spreading beyond their own borders. The international system lacks effective mechanisms for promptly addressing the underlying sources of such instability or for identifying and proactively responding to potential triggers of conflict. Second, several zones of conflict in the Middle East are increasingly linked to one another—sectarian and terrorist violence in Iraq, Iran's perceived rise in the region, the Israeli-Palestinian conflict, the internal Palestinian conflict, and Lebanon's struggle against Syrian influence.[7] (So grave are the consequences of conflict in that region that we single it out for specific treatment in chapter 9.) In other parts of the world—such as the Horn of Africa—similar subregional conflicts pose new challenges to regional and international security.

Connection to Other Threats and Implications for U.S. and International Security

Internal wars can spill across borders, destabilize neighbors, and create refugee flows. Even when seemingly resolved, war heightens the risk of further war—the greatest single predictor of a new war in a country is a war that was fought within the past five years. Roughly one-third of countries recovering from civil war face the risk of renewed conflict within the first five years of reaching a peace agreement.[8]

Humanitarian and moral issues are also at stake. When conflict management fails, the risk of widespread suffering is high, as is the potential for large-scale human rights abuses or even mass killings. The international system's ability to halt such atrocities is weak—as we have been witnessing in Darfur.

There are also links to other security threats. In the Middle East and Central Asia, internal conflict and weak or fragile states produce a major risk of transnational terrorism, including the specter of terrorist access to nuclear materials (also an issue in South Asia). In the same regions, interstate tension and conflict threaten to encourage nuclear proliferation. In Africa, small wars may not carry significant international security risks. But internal wars and state collapses generate humanitarian crises and provide fertile ground for international criminal networks and drug trafficking. African states weakened by conflict also can become important way stations for transnational terrorists and arms proliferators.

Afghanistan is a compelling case in point. Neglect of Afghanistan after the withdrawal of the Soviet army in 1989 compounded the collapse of state institutions and led to the takeover by the Taliban movement, which in turn afforded safe haven to al Qaeda's Osama bin Laden after his ouster from Sudan. After the U.S. invasion and defeat of the Taliban regime in 2001, inadequate conflict management and reconstruction efforts have had serious consequences. Afghanistan has emerged as the world's leading supplier of opium. The Taliban is resurgent, and the threats to central order and the government remain virulent. The tribal area on the Pakistan border has emerged as a new safe haven for the Taliban and for al Qaeda, which has used this base to regain much of its former strength. Turmoil in the tribal areas is threatening the stability of Pakistan—a populous and arguably now very fragile state armed with nuclear weapons. The collapse of Pakistan would have nightmarish consequences for the region and for U.S. and international security.

After 9/11, the Bush administration elevated the threat of state failure to a top national security concern: "America is now threatened less by conquering states than we are by failing ones."[9] A long-term view suggests a strongly shared U.S. and international interest in effective systems for preventing conflict, mediating and managing conflicts once they have begun, supporting stabilization and reconstruction efforts in their aftermath, and strengthening state capacities for the rule of law and public order—both before and after conflict.

CIVIL VIOLENCE AND RESPONSIBLE SOVEREIGNTY

The rules relating to conflict between sovereign states are well developed. The responsibility to avoid interstate war is embedded in the UN Charter itself, which calls on states to use peaceful means, including adjudication, to resolve disputes, and to avoid using force except in self-defense. These provisions apply to wars between states, and help explain why the number of wars between states has remained extremely low despite the quadrupling of the number of states (from 51 to 192) since the United Nations was founded in 1945. When it comes to the issue of internal war, the normative question becomes more complex, as does the relationship between national and international responsibility. Traditionally, internal violence was the preserve of domestic sovereignty. Norms have been evolving, however, as encapsulated in the United Nations' *2005 World Summit Outcome,* in which member states acknowledge that "Each individual State has the responsibility to protect its populations from genocide, war crimes, ethnic cleansing and crimes against humanity. This responsibility entails the prevention of such crimes, including their incitement, through appropriate and necessary means. We accept that responsibility and will act in accordance with it."[10]

But if responsible sovereignty is built on the precept that sovereign nations must take responsibility for actions that spill across borders and threaten global security, internal conflict poses a special challenge precisely because the state itself will be under attack or involved in perpetuating a war. Consequently, in defining the "responsibility to protect," the *2005 Outcome* also underscores that external actors must bear specific responsibilities: to help states to exercise their responsibilities; build state capacity; and undertake diplomatic, humanitarian, and other peaceful efforts to protect populations from genocide, war crimes, ethnic cleansing, and crimes against humanity. Most notably, the UN General Assembly affirmed that when national authorities "manifestly fail to protect" their populations from such crimes, "We are prepared to take collective action, in a timely and decisive manner, through the Security Council, in accordance with the Charter, including Chapter VII."[11] This is UN language for using force where necessary to step in when a state has failed in its own responsibility to protect.

This, however, is a paradigmatic example of what we refer to as the adoption of "how it should be," not "how it will be" norms. Although adopting the responsibility to protect represented a significant step forward in conceptual terms, it has not yet been matched by action in cases like Darfur or by efforts to ensure that the United Nations or other organizations have a "capacity to protect." Nor have developed states yet shown credible commitment to their "responsibility to build."

THE INTERNATIONAL RESPONSE

During the cold war, superpower rivalry constrained international efforts to resolve civil wars. In Africa and Asia the United States, the Soviet Union, and China backed different factions in the attempt to prevent their clients from losing. The result was protracted wars, some lasting decades. In the Middle East, the UN Security Council sought to freeze conflicts to prevent escalation and direct confrontation between the United States and the Soviet Union. Since the end of the cold war, international institutions—primarily the United Nations and NATO, but also increasingly the European and African unions—have been far more active in managing conflicts.

Prevention: Internal and Interstate War and State Collapse

At the United Nations, secretary generals Boutros-Ghali and Annan used the more open political atmosphere of the 1990s to create an array of diplomatic tools to address potential and active conflicts. They also instituted policies on prevention and management, including the establishment of early warning mechanisms. The secretary general's office deployed dozens of special envoys and special representatives to help to mediate an end to ongoing conflicts or to oversee the implementation of peace agreements. The UN Security Council increasingly applied sanctions and other policy tools to advance a range of conflict prevention and management goals. The Security Council and regional organizations also undertook fact-finding missions and mandated preventive deployment.[12]

In the same period, other actors became progressively engaged in preventing and managing conflict. Regional organizations and states adopted some of the same practices as the United Nations, including the deployment of representatives or presidential envoys.[13] Nongovernmental organizations (NGOs) also became involved in a range of activities, often focusing on a specific sector or topic. Although many of the mediation efforts by these actors in the 1990s were episodic, poorly structured, and inexperienced, more recent successes by governments such as Norway and Switzerland, and by NGOs such as the Center for Humanitarian Dialogue (the HD Center, based in Geneva), signal a new level of maturity in the field. Successful efforts by the European Union (EU) high representative have been particularly instrumental in shaping thinking about non-UN options for responding to crises.

Given the costs of violent conflict and long-term reconstruction, the case for building international capabilities to anticipate and effectively respond to potential conflicts and regional instabilities is compelling. The alternative is to watch conflict and tension develop into full-blown violent crises in multiple theaters. Yet implementing a policy of prevention is not easy. Intrinsic difficulties are found in correctly understanding and anticipating the actions and strategies of political actors in any situation, and the international mechanisms designed to do just this—discussed in the sections that follow—are deficient in many respects.

LONG-TERM OR "STRUCTURAL" PREVENTION. The thorniest challenge in conflict management is preventing state failure. Ironically, once war has started, international actors have political openings to wield such tools as mediation, the threat of sanctions, and peacekeeping to help bring conflict to an end—sometimes after wars have endured to a point of exhaustion, but sometimes much more rapidly. Before war starts, however, the shield of sovereignty is hard to pierce. Governments typically resist outside engagement on domestic political and economic issues even when internal tensions are rising.

Africa has learned this lesson the hard way. In negotiations at the United Nations in 2005 about establishing the Peacebuilding Commission (PBC), African negotiators gave voice to the lesson, arguing for the PBC to have a preventive as well as a postconflict role. In the words of one African ambassador: "Why do we have to wait until war breaks out before we can turn to the international community for help to reform our judicial sector or build our police?" In recent years, a few Latin American and Caribbean countries have also quietly reached out to the United Nations for help in building up their domestic capacity or constitutional mechanisms to prevent civil violence.

The African ambassador's focus on assistance to build the rule of law was apt. Although conflict is closely correlated with poverty—statistically, low-income states have a 14 percent chance of internal conflict within any five-year period—the causal relationship between poverty and war is complex.[14] Some of the world's poorest states (Malawi and Tanzania) have avoided internal conflict. Between poverty and war are several intervening factors: economic inequality;[15] the degree of economic dependence of the state on exploitable natural resources;[16] and the nature of social and ethnic relations within the country. But over time, the closest predictor of conflict within poor states is the nature of the regime and the process of political transition.[17] In short, governance is pivotal.

This does not remove poverty reduction from the menu of long-term prevention. Below a certain level of resources, even the best-intentioned state will not have the capacity to govern effectively or responsibly. In chapter 9 we examine the elements of a holistic strategy for reducing poverty and building state capacity.

That, however, is a project for a generation. In the interim many states will still be at risk of conflict and state collapse. They will warrant close attention to reforming government and the security sector, investing in rule-of-law capacity, and putting in place similar processes that can reduce the risk of conflict.

Of course, governance reform is often part and parcel of a process of political transition and regime transformation. The challenge here is that such transitions are fraught with risk. Proponents of democratization as a pathway for reform have been sobered by consistent findings that the process of transition from authoritarian to democratic regimes actually *increases* the risk of conflict in the short term.[18] There are, however, pathways for reform that reduce that risk.

International actors seeking to support or urge governance reform or regime transition without inducing conflict face two quite different obstacles—weak tools with which to support domestic demand for reform and limited influence over governments that resist such processes.

The past eight years have highlighted the folly of believing that democracy can be imposed from the outside. Although this point should be obvious, given the recent conflation of democracy promotion with military intervention, it needs restating. There are exceptions at the extreme—in the aftermath of surrender, for example, Japan's democracy was imposed by U.S. postwar occupation authorities. But absent such conditions, democracy can arise only from within.

There are other lessons from this period, as well as from ongoing efforts through the United Nations and other multilateral mechanisms to promote or support democratization. The hard-learned lesson is that democratization is a long-term process that involves many dimensions of social and political practice—including the development of civil society and the transformation of political culture. Democracy is not to be conflated merely with elections. A further lesson is that although U.S. support for democratization has been vital in several important cases, including Ukraine, Serbia, and South Africa, regional mechanisms (where they are developed) can achieve both a degree of penetration of the political culture and a legitimacy that bilateral efforts can rarely garner. International mechanisms can play important roles as well. One of the most neglected facts about the United Nations is that its development arm (the UN Development Program [UNDP]) and its electoral arm (the Electoral Affairs Division) have supported democratic transitions in the majority of the more than ninety countries that have emerged as democracies since the 1970s. Peacekeeping has played a similar role since the end of the cold war, as has the European Union's ascension mechanism. The establishment of the UN Democracy Fund and the UNDP/Organization for Economic Cooperation and Development (OECD) Partnership for Democratic Governance shows the potential for deepening such work, and we see further promise in the fact that UNDP's governing board has adopted the promotion of democratic governance as a core function for that agency.

The role of regions and regional powers is particularly salient in the toughest cases, those where the state has the diplomatic capacity to resist pressure from the United Nations or the West and where the economy depends less on external aid than on domestic production and regional trade. Examples include Zimbabwe and Myanmar. For good or ill, neighbors and regional powers will be heavily influential in such cases, and U.S. or Western efforts to induce regime transition are unlikely to succeed without support from regional powers.

At first view, this argues for working within the G-16 where major regional actors will be present alongside the major Western powers—to forge shared strategies and approaches to the prevention of state failure. In practice, though, there will be limits to this. At least in the near term, the Western powers and the rising powers will have different views about the role of democracy as a tool for conflict prevention. We can see potential, however, in Indonesia's vocal arguments within the Association of Southeast Asian Nations (ASEAN) for that body to take a more assertive stance on democracy. Nevertheless, support for democratic transformation in the short to medium term is likely to remain largely the preserve of bilateral action by Western donors and regional/multilateral bodies. Joint analysis and joint initiatives by those donors would increase their potency.

There is, however, a shared interest among potential G-16 members in stabilizing states and avoiding their collapse. For all of South Africa's reluctance to pressure Zimbabwe's Robert Mugabe to bow to internal pressure for democratic change, it is hard to see how South Africa would profit from Zimbabwe's collapse into internal war. Similarities can be drawn with China and Myanmar, as evidenced by China's pressure on Myanmar, which ultimately led the regime to accept the appointment of UN Special Envoy Ibrahim Gambari after its crackdown on Buddhist demonstrations. Brazil's leadership of the UN military mission in Haiti since 2004 shows a similar interest in investing in processes to avoid state failure or contain their effects. A shared interest in stabilization is an important starting point for building a broader consensus on the importance of investing in governance reform, strengthening the rule of law, and establishing accountability mechanisms—both in terms of broad policy, but perhaps also in specific cases. Still, the difficulties of forging agreement on these issues within the G-16, or of getting effective results without the regional powers, should not be underestimated.

Building bilateral and multilateral capacity to support governance reform and political transition should anticipate the needs and demands of domestic actors. Much of this is already occurring. Consider, for example, the expanding role of the European Union in civilian spheres, new activism by UNDP in responding to national requests for support on governance and constitutional reform, the recent establishment of a standing police unit and a rule-of-law and security institutions pillar at the UN Department of Peacekeeping Operations (DPKO), and the increasing investment of bilateral actors in necessary civilian capacities to engage in rule-of-law and governance reform programs.

Here, the obstacles are largely found in bureaucratic impediments to effectiveness. For example, OECD rules stipulate that money spent on critical elements of the rule of law—most importantly, on security sector reform—cannot be counted toward a country's 0.7 percent target of spending for overseas development assistance. This creates important political and bureaucratic pressures against targeting spending on these vital issues. With greater political awareness of the costs and security risks associated with state collapse, however, there is new political interest in overcoming these obstacles.

Reform of bilateral development agencies will be more difficult. The governance efforts of these agencies are still characterized, perhaps even more in this area than in traditional development activities, by an extreme degree of incoherence, competitive bilateral "branding," and out-of-date business practices. Again, though, growing political understanding of the consequences of these characteristics is starting to open new space in which to tackle the bureaucratic and technical obstacles to reform. Lessons learned in Afghanistan have been influential in highlighting the costs of ineffective development agencies. This is perhaps reflected in the fact that former U.S. Ambassador to Afghanistan Zalmay Khalilzad and former Afghan Finance Minister Ashraf Ghani have been two of the more eloquent critics of U.S. and other bilateral and multilateral action in the realm of building state capacity. Indeed, Ghani has articulated a compelling case for root-and-branch reform and set forth a road map for achieving such reform.[19]

SHORT-TERM OR "OPERATIONAL" PREVENTION. Even if a long-term approach to prevention were to succeed, it would be at least a generation before the full effects of this approach were realized. Meanwhile, both current and incipient conflicts will need to be confronted.

When it comes to short-term conflict prevention, usually associated with the deployment of special envoys and the like, the focus of analysis tends to turn back to the United Nations. Here, however, assessments suggest a need for skepticism, or at least for improvement.

Even though the United Nations plays a lead role in peacekeeping and in ending civil wars, the organization has important disadvantages when it comes to preventing internal war. Indeed, a 2003–04 study for the UN Department of Political Affairs found no evidence of UN effectiveness in preventing internal conflicts.[20] The United Nations faces several barriers in attempting to mediate internal conflicts, including the UN Charter's silence on such issues as democratic governance and minority rights, a lack of established norms and regulations on how to interact with non-state actors, and resistance from governments.

That this is so should not be surprising. Stopping governments and potential rebels from starting a war is difficult at the best of times, even for peacemakers more powerful than the United Nations. Yet this is one area where regional organizations appear to have a better track record. Consider several examples: the Organization for Security and Cooperation in Europe (OSCE), the European Union, and NATO together helped to prevent an outbreak of conflict between Serb and Albanian groups in Macedonia; the European Union helped prevent a conflict in Ukraine; the Commonwealth helped cool off all sides after two coups in Fiji; the Organization of American States (OAS) helped reverse coups in Latin America and avert conflict between Colombia and its neighbors; and the Economic Community of West African States (ECOWAS) had a role in reversing coups and preventing conflicts in Guinea and Togo. The United Nations has a better track record in preventing interstate war—for example, between Iran and Afghanistan in the late 1990s, and between Nigeria and Cameroon in the early part of this decade.

Diplomacy aimed at preventing incipient conflict is often kept quiet for tactical reasons. As a consequence, the effectiveness of specific efforts or institutional mechanisms can be difficult to measure. Evaluations indicate, however, that efforts offering a variety of carrots and sticks are more effective at preventing deadly conflict than other strategies. The challenge then becomes coordinating such efforts among international institutions and neighboring countries.

Mediation

The United Nations has been more successful in mediating civil wars. Important examples include El Salvador, Mozambique, Guatemala, and Nepal. It is now commonplace for governments, regional organizations, international organizations, and NGOs to rush to resolve a conflict once violence has erupted. As a result, more civil wars have ended through negotiated settlements since the end of the cold war than in the previous 200 years. A major compilation of data on such efforts, the *Human Security Brief 2006*,[21] points to increased international peacekeeping and diplomacy as a reason violent conflicts are on the decline, especially in sub-Saharan Africa. Recognizing the modest investment in mediation elevates the significance of this achievement.

Two very different approaches have worked. First, comprehensive peace agreements have been negotiated—usually through the good offices of the secretary general or another third-party diplomatic actor—to end internal wars. Second, cease-fire or cessation-of-hostilities arrangements have been imposed—usually by the Security Council—to halt wars between states.

The United Nations has several advantages in negotiating peace agreements to resolve ongoing internal conflicts. The organization is perceived as legitimate and impartial, and it has the capacity to convene parties and set standards of practice (for example, rules that preclude UN mediators from accepting blanket amnesties for human-rights abuses.) It also has accumulated experience in many countries through its development and humanitarian programs. Nonetheless, it does suffer from important weaknesses. In recent cases the United Nations has not been capable of confidentiality (to the detriment of its diplomacy). Representatives have had difficulty initiating discussions with nonstate actors, including groups designated as terrorists. The emergence of a growing number of well-organized, well-financed unofficial mediation groups is testimony to the limitations of the role of the United Nations.[22]

When it comes to imposing a cessation of hostilities in interstate wars, the United Nations has both advantages and disadvantages, depending on context. Where such wars directly engage one of the permanent five members of the Security Council (China, France, the Russian Federation, the United Kingdom, and the United States), of course, that member can block any UN action. On the other hand, because states tend to seek the legitimacy that only the Security Council can bestow, the council potentially wields significant leverage.

More challenging is a war between a state and a nonstate entity, such as the fight between Israel and Hezbollah in the summer of 2006. In the end, the Security Council resolution to end hostilities (after active U.S. and UN joint diplomacy)[23] relied on the Lebanese state to assert its authority over Hezbollah (in word, if not yet in deed), because the council had no ability to make demands of, or even reference, a nonstate actor such as Hezbollah. In certain cases, the secretary general might be able to step into the vacuum and mediate with nonstate actors as well as governments, but in this case the secretary general was politically constrained from meeting with, let alone negotiating with, Hezbollah. (Before deploying their forces, however, the French—who led the UN's troop deployment—engaged in quiet negotiations with Hezbollah.)

Experience indicates the potential benefits of strengthening cross-institutional capacities. In the Balkans and Libya, withholding economic aid has proven effective in getting actors back to the negotiating table when used in conjunction with diplomatic pressure or threat of force. The United States and Australia stopped the massacres in East Timor in 1999 by coordinating the insertion of troops with the threat of cutting off economic support to Indonesia from the IMF. Effective peacemaking requires strategic planning and adaptability, along with a nuanced understanding of the characteristics of the conflict, the actors involved, and the legitimacy and efficacy of external leverage.[24]

The United Nations has always been under-resourced to perform its peacemaking function. To illustrate, at the 2005 World Summit 192 member states agreed on the importance of enhancing the secretary general's capacity to engage in mediation. That led to the creation of a "mediation support unit"—with a grand total of two staff members and six consultants. As a point of comparison, there were more than 200 U.S. staff members engaged in the Dayton process for Bosnia alone.[25]

Postconflict Peacekeeping

When conflict management succeeds, it is often followed by the deployment of peacekeepers to help implement agreements and contain the risk of relapse. But peacekeeping is not merely a military tool; it is a continuation of conflict management and prevention by other means. It is the essential platform for broader postconflict reconstruction and stabilization, or peacebuilding, which has at its core the extension of state authority within an agreed-on legal framework.

Peacekeeping operations have become an increasingly important tool in the last decade. In the mid-1990s, failures in Bosnia, Rwanda, and Somalia appeared to have discredited peacekeeping. But subsequent efforts to broker or enforce peace in a number of volatile regions (including the Western Balkans, West Africa, the Great Lakes region of central Africa, and the broader Middle East) resulted in a new generation of peace operations. From January 2000 to January 2007, the number of UN military and police personnel deployed around the world jumped from 18,600 to 82,000, and is on pace to rise to more than 100,000 in 2008. Deployments by regional organizations including NATO, the European Union and the African Union are on an upward trend after a period of gradual decline. In 2006 alone, the number of troops deployed by these organizations leapt from 53,000 to more than 70,000. By early 2008, the global number of troops in the field exceeded 160,000.

The figures are still short of the military forces that the United States can bring to bear globally. But United Nations and non–United Nations peace operations can play a significant role in bringing about short-term stability and in providing a framework for longer-term peacebuilding and reconstruction in areas torn by conflict. These include areas—such as Darfur—where an obvious moral imperative for international action exists. But they also include places that can act as havens for terrorists (such as Afghanistan and Somalia); serve as bases or conduits for international criminal activity (such as Haiti); or are located at the hub of regional conflicts central to U.S. regional policies (such as southern Lebanon).

Although cases such as these are of direct concern to U.S. policy, experience has shown that they can often be addressed through multilateral cooperation. In Haiti, the subject of repeated U.S. interventions in the past, a coalition of Latin American states led by Brazil is now sustaining a robust peace operation under the UN banner. In Afghanistan (as of mid-2008), Canadians and Europeans are supplying—through NATO— about 28,000 of 62,000 international troops.[26] In southern Lebanon, the 2006 crisis prompted rapid pledges of peacekeepers not only by European states, but also by regional actors including Turkey and Qatar. They were joined by other countries aiming to show their commitment to international peace and security, including China and Indonesia. And after much diplomatic friction, the African Union, the European Union, and China have now committed themselves to an AU–UN force in Darfur, an initiative that Washington has persistently promoted in the face of Sudanese opposition.

In such cases, peacekeeping operations can make a double contribution to international security. In operational terms, they bring direct security to troubled territories. In political terms, they build frameworks for international cooperation in conflict management—whether through military alliances such as NATO or ad hoc coalitions. The United States thus has dual incentives to build confidence in and through peacekeeping operations, as well as to fulfill the responsibility to protect populations facing genocide or mass slaughter by ensuring a capacity to protect.

This plays out primarily in Africa, the core of the United Nations' operations, where it deploys upward of 75 percent of its Blue Helmets, and in the greater Middle East, where the United Nations and NATO combined have deployed more than 70,000 peacekeepers. In both contexts, the international community has increasingly turned to "hybrid" peace operations, which involve the simultaneous or sequential deployment of missions by two or more international or multinational actors. This process is rarely easy. The institutions involved typically aim to keep their chains of command distinct, although organizations have accepted integrated command structures in some cases, such as the cooperation between the United Nations, the European Union, and the OSCE in Kosovo since 1999. Forming these hybrid missions, however, has given the international community an added degree of flexibility in responding to crises. This flexibility has been strengthened by the emergence of a number of "regional peacekeeping formations," in which missions have been deployed in neighboring countries to handle conflicts spreading across borders. These include clusters of UN missions on the West African littoral, the Great Lakes region of central Africa, and Sudan and the Horn.

Peacekeeping has begun to succeed more frequently. A RAND study of eight current UN-led peace operations found that seven of these countries are still at peace.[27] In second chances in both Haiti and East Timor, UN missions have made progress despite massive underfunding and huge political complications, although Congo could yet again unravel. But a number of problems—including locating suitable troop contingents and mobilizing early funding for recovery—have recurred, especially in hard cases. To maintain the current level of UN military personnel in the field requires the rotation of approximately 130,000 to 140,000 troops per year. Even though the United Nations has been able to find sufficient numbers of infantry for its current operations, it usually has great difficulty acquiring more specialized assets, such as helicopters and light armor, necessary to mount credible operations in hostile environments such as the Democratic Republic of the Congo and Sudan/Darfur. Additionally, there is a shortage of long-range airlift available to rapidly deploy new missions.

Such problems are not confined to the United Nations. Through 2006 and 2007, NATO commanders publicly complained about their lack of access to specialized resources, especially helicopters. The AU mission in Sudan has suffered particularly grim challenges. Its troops have only light weapons in a region where many militias are far more heavily armed, and in 2007 it had fewer than thirty helicopters for a force of 7,000. In addition, personnel shortages have prevented units from being rotated on schedule. In 2008, some AU troops had gone unpaid for months, indicating another major challenge—locating and facilitating the financial resources necessary to sustain long-term missions.

The United Nations has a special problem. Because the bulk of troops that it uses are not predesignated for UN operations, as troops are for NATO, there is little or no pretraining of forces. As a remedy for this shortcoming, the possibility of developing standby forces has long been discussed in the United Nations. Some limited progress has been made;

in particular, the European Union has established standby battle groups for deployment to UN mandates. Major troop contributors such as India have also indicated a readiness to predesignate and train standby battalions for UN operations, but financial donors (including principally the United States) have not yet agreed on funding mechanisms for such reserves. The growth of peace operations is also placing a major strain on the staff at headquarters of the responsible international organization, especially the United Nations and the African Union. As of September 2007, the UN's DPKO had just 555 civilian staff members to oversee its operations—although these were supplemented by managerial staff in other departments—giving it an overall ratio of headquarters staff to field staff of 1:149. Figures for the African Union vary, but it is estimated that in 2007 no more than 10 to 20 staff members were fully focused on peacekeeping. NATO is somewhat better off with a 1:4 ratio of headquarters to field staffers. In short, the organizations with the fewest resources (the United Nations and African Union) are the most likely to see rising numbers of operations.[28]

Finally, the United Nations is constrained in carrying out its multidimensional mandates. Where peacekeepers are deployed to implement agreements after civil wars or in response to state collapses, they do not undertake only political and military tasks; instead, roughly since the late 1990s, they have frequently been mandated (especially by the Security Council) to take on important governance, capacity-building, rule-of-law, judicial, policing, and economic functions. As they operate under these multidimensional missions, then, the peacekeepers contribute not just to military stabilization, but—in theory—to the broader stabilization and reconstruction effort as well. UN operations face substantial problems in implementing these mandates. And indeed, the broader set of international mechanisms for peacebuilding is far weaker than current mechanisms for peacekeeping in the narrow sense.

Peacebuilding, or Restoring State Capacity

Peacebuilding operations seek to build a peace that is self-sustaining long after the peacekeepers leave. Peacebuilders seek to foster effective public institutions that establish a consensual framework for governing within the rule of law. The imprecise science of peacebuilding goes beyond military peacekeeping, inevitably crossing into a spectrum that includes development and institution-building activities. Yet we have learned enough about the process to understand what we can do to increase the chances for sustainable peace.

First we have to understand in broad terms how peacebuilding can fail. From a security perspective, it can fail to constrain spoilers who want to disrupt the process. From a political perspective, it can fail to resolve issues not settled in the peace agreement. And it can fail at state building, which encompasses putting in place necessary and effective local capacity and achieving the legitimacy required to sustain peace.

More positively, the international community has learned important lessons from recurrent experience. As a starting point, peacebuilding is a process that demands time. To understand its nature, the types of international skills required, and the local capabilities that must be developed, consider the five elements of peacebuilding in the list that follows. All five can work concurrently, but progress in one can coincide with reversal in another. For peace to become sustainable, some degree of progress is needed at every level, although the relative importance of each varies from conflict to conflict.

1. Stabilizing the situation. This is the first priority after any conflict. It is incumbent on peacekeepers to guarantee peace and impose law and order in the absence of a widely accepted rule of law. In addition to providing basic security through peacekeeping, there is a "window of necessity" for meeting humanitarian needs and giving people confidence in the future. Key goals are to restart basic social services and stimulate jobs that create economic alternatives to taking up arms. The process must start to disarm, demobilize, and reintegrate warring opponents. Some form of political activity must begin, often locally, that will lead to credible governance. Elections are often viewed as necessary, although they can be detrimental when conducted too soon. Badly timed elections can invite competition among previously warring factions before wounds have healed and also have the potential to entrench criminals or warlords in political office.

2. Building the infrastructure, laws, and institutions of democratic governance and a market economy. The process of helping countries build the foundations of their societies is generally the most time-consuming and complicated stage of transition. Laws and regulations must be written and adopted, people trained in new forms of governance, investments made in appropriate infrastructure, and governance theory and training turned into practice. The challenges extend from building economic capacity (markets, banking and tax systems, and fiscal viability) and political institutions (parties, functioning parliaments, and accountable executives), through administering the rule of law (via constitutions, legislation, judges, lawyers, and penitentiary systems), to transferring control of security structures (police, military, and new defense and interior ministries) to civilians. After a conflict, a society seeks to transform from relying on imposed order to establishing order based on freedom, openness, and competition. Such transitions require time and local ownership.

3. Nurturing civil society. Outsiders cannot build civil society, but they can offer training to media representatives, civic organizations, business groups, environmental activists, and others who can advance community interests and guard against abuses of power. In some contexts, the role of women is especially important because they often take a practical stance on issues such as health care, education, and water and land use, a stance that can contribute to an environment of trust.

4. Unraveling the past. Eventually, societies recovering from violence must address the factors that drove them to conflict in the first place. If this does not take place, these issues can resurface and contribute to the cycle of war that plagues almost half of all postconflict states. Root issues might include exclusion from politics, persecution of ethnic or religious groups, lack of trust in formal systems of justice, massive poverty, corruption, failing state enterprises, land and water disputes, and income inequality. Addressing these drivers of conflict, though, can in itself be destabilizing. Privatizing state industry, for example, can lead to more unemployment and political unrest. Going after corruption can lead to former elites using money and influence to sabotage the political transition. Part of the challenge is to judge when and how to tackle these issues when stabilization is also an imperative.

5. Restoring state capacity. By definition, internal war constitutes an important challenge to state authority. In long wars, especially those that play out in poor states, countries can emerge from conflict with minimal capacity to enact the rule of law, supply and manage public goods, impose basic regulation of the economy, or manage basic social services and welfare. The restoration of state authority is a critical function of stabilization and recovery, and that requires investment from the first moments after a cease-fire. Efforts to improve rule-of-law capacity building within the United Nations, the European Union, and elsewhere have so far been partial and incomplete. A survey of UN peacebuilding strengths and weaknesses by the secretary general's office found that reforming public administration was one of the United Nations' weakest capabilities.

Across these stages of transition, certain practices can increase the chances for success. All things being equal, peace agreements should be written and clear about expectations, with achievable mandates for the international community.[29] Physical security is a prerequisite for economic and political progress.[30] Adequate forces are needed to enforce the peace, but the use of force without a peace agreement is not sustainable.

Resource-rich countries have a greater chance of falling back into conflict because they can divert funds to finance war. Accountability for wealth must be sought from the outset, and peacebuilding missions must have a plan for dealing with resource-management issues.[31]

Peacebuilding entails the redefinition of the state's social contract with its citizenry. If citizens do not believe in the new state, it cannot succeed. Hence, international institutions must involve and seek to empower locals from the outset. Building local capacity takes time, often more time than the international community is willing to give to sustain financing and troops. If the evolution from stabilization to other stages of transition is to proceed more quickly, locals must play a greater role in the process.[32]

Assessing Performance: General Trends

UN and broader international peacebuilding operations have recorded some significant successes. But far more frequently they have underperformed. There are policy reasons for this, but more important are the diffuse and ill-coordinated structures, often redundant, used to implement such operations.

Until the Peacebuilding Commission was formally created in 2005, there was no UN body formally tasked with coordinating peacebuilding activities across the UN secretariat, agencies, and departments. The UN Security Council is responsible for the use of force and for peacekeeping, but maintains no oversight of the agencies central to building a sustainable peace.

Despite the promise of its name, the PBC has at best a soft mandate and limited capacity for its purported function. As of mid-2008, it had engaged in four pilot countries (Guinea Bissau, Burundi, Sierra Leone, and Central African Republic). Also, as of mid-2008, the Peacebuilding Support Office (PBSO), which staffs the PBC, was authorized at about 20 positions, or 2 percent of the personnel dedicated to peacekeeping.[33] Even if it operated as a coordinating staff office that drew on capabilities across the UN system, the PBSO would be overwhelmed if tasked to manage strategy for multiple concurrent operations.

Because of this legacy of limited coordinating capacity, each UN-related entity operating in peacebuilding has tended to function independently. DPKO has the largest staff and in many cases, such as in Haiti in 2005, has run peacebuilding operations effectively in the field. In other cases the UN Development Program (UNDP), the UN Office for the Coordination of Humanitarian Affairs (OCHA), the UN High Commissioner for Refugees (UNHCR), and the World Bank have played concurrent roles through separate field operations. The United Nations has made considerable headway in integrating its actors in the field using the "integrated mission" model, in which its development and humanitarian coordinator serves as deputy to the mission head, providing a tool to link political/security and development/humanitarian action. The model, though, has its limits, notably that several of the crucial peacebuilding actors—major bilateral donors, regional organizations, and most critically, the international financial institutions—do not have a place in the integrated mission structure. The goal should be to create a coordinated and effective delivery capacity on the ground.

In large missions, the United Nations' overall capacity to deliver is often strained, particularly in the ability to provide civilian personnel to assist in state building. Of 4,967 civilian personnel deployed in peacekeeping operations around the globe in 2007, only a small fraction (fewer than 100) were employed in governance functions.[34] Of these, just a small fraction were recruited explicitly for these skills (although in cases such as Kosovo, the United Nations also had personnel seconded from other organizations such as the European Union and the OSCE engaged in the mission). This slightly overstates the situation, because relevant staffers from the UNDP's Bureau for Conflict Prevention and

Recovery (BCPR), the UN Office of the High Commissioner for Human Rights (OHCHR), and similar outfits should be added to this complement. But even these numbers are in double digits globally. The absence of a core capacity to provide rule-of-law and state-building support to countries emerging from conflict is a critical weakness of the overall conflict management system.

On the positive side, peacekeeping has been responsible for helping to usher in democratic transitions in several postconflict states since the early 1990s, by providing election monitors, support to national election processes, support to national constitutional processes, and the like. A weakness in this effort has been in building the civil society mechanisms that can provide the deeper substance of democratization.

Dealing with the Hard Cases

International capabilities are especially weak for what we call the "hard cases." The scale and strategic significance of these cases require a great volume of resources and a high number of significant actors. Even in Iraq, where U.S. appropriations and Iraqi oil funds provided billions in resources alongside 130,000–160,000 U.S. and other coalition troops, the challenge of mobilizing, deploying, and coordinating such resources and personnel in an effective strategy is daunting. The job of managing the hard cases presents extra challenges across the spectrum of prevention, mediation, peacekeeping, and peacebuilding.

The challenge of preventing or managing conflict is most complex in countries that have significant economic, military, and diplomatic capacity, along with strategic significance. In crises involving large states, major powers must consider broader priorities such as counterterrorism, energy, trade, and regional stability. They will also always be responding to public pressure. These considerations can diminish or overshadow the immediate goals of preventing or managing conflict. And the competing interests of major powers can stymie efforts to formulate policy through international institutions or mechanisms.

But these are challenges that must be grappled with, because the major conflicts ahead require cooperation on a global scale. Currently, there is an urgent need to invest simultaneously in stabilizing fragile improvements in Iraq while moving toward resolution on the Israel-Palestine and Israel-Lebanon fronts. There is no military solution to the broad, multidimensional crises in the Middle East, although specific aspects of that crisis may ultimately require the use of force. Neither the United States alone nor existing UN regional mechanisms can manage the many dimensions of this perennial crisis—but it cannot go unattended.

Iraq and Afghanistan represent exceptionally hard cases in which the United States has taken the lead and the United Nations has played a secondary role. Iraq is especially difficult because it has endured both a civil war and a state failure, and because the U.S. presence there is so widely contested. To build peace in the context of a civil war, experience has shown that peace agreements are an essential first step, although alone not necessarily sufficient to guarantee peace.[35] Because Iraq has been a failed state in the midst of war, the parties themselves cannot be expected to reach a political settlement without an outside broker. Even then, external forces are needed to create an environment of stability that allows local entities to make progress toward building peace.

An even greater challenge is posed when internal conflict or state failure or both are accompanied by mass atrocities. In the last few years, the United Nations has tried to mobilize against such outrages. Recall that the General Assembly adopted the concept of the responsibility to protect in 2005, and the Security Council approved a somewhat more cautious version in 2006.

Even in the absence of such a doctrine, though, NATO acted to halt atrocities in Kosovo after the Security Council was stymied by a threatened Russian veto. That case, however, had the distinction of taking place in Europe, and most of the continent—and many countries beyond—backed what was regarded as a necessary action. In the years since, several African countries—notably Rwanda—have joined a smattering of Latin American and smaller Asian countries in accepting the basic principle that sovereignty must be seen in light of responsibilities. The major non-Western powers still exhibit a great deal of nervousness about this concept, however.

The doctrine of the responsibility to protect was first tested in the Sudan/Darfur context. That episode revealed some of the difficulties of acting on the basis of a noble principle. In early August 2007 after much negotiation, the Security Council authorized 27,000 peacekeepers to deploy to Darfur to halt the ongoing atrocities. Although this is a significant response, it had initially been called for at least two years earlier.

And during 2007 and 2008, those troops were deploying at a snail's pace. Deployments are not always so slow—the United Nations sent a robust force of 12,000 to southern Lebanon in less than two weeks. But in Darfur the United Nations was thwarted by a lack of logistics capacity; by strained supply lines (Darfur is 1,500 miles from the nearest port and roads into the area are abysmal); by Western governments' unwillingness to contribute high-end military units and equipment such as attack helicopters; and most of all by the Sudanese government's intransigence, which ranged from insisting on an all-African force to blocking the deployment of equipment crucial to ground-force mobility.

A failure? In many respects, yes. But we must also assess the realism of authorizing a force in early 2005 when the Sudanese government would not have accepted it, and evaluate the chances that an international peacekeeping force could fight its way across Sudan over the opposition of the Sudanese army. What humanitarian consequences, how many lives saved or lost, in this instance? Short of a full-scale intervention led by the United States, no protection force will be able to deploy, much less sustain, a ground presence in the absence of the consent of the government in question. The acid test of the commitment of Western governments to the concept of the responsibility to protect is their willingness to provide troops to a robust multi-national force for Sudan.

Nevertheless, for circumstances short of the very toughest cases, if the United Nations is to be given the *responsibility* to protect, it should surely be given the *capacity* to protect. Of late, peacekeepers have grown increasingly robust in the use of force. UN mandates now contain references to the protection of civilians almost as a matter of course. For example, UN forces acted assertively against armed groups in both Haiti and the eastern Democratic Republic of the Congo with significant successes. Difficulties arise where peacekeepers are required to act against opponents with a greater potential to fight back. Faced with operating in proximity to Hezbollah, UN member states negotiated intensively in the Security Council on their precise rules of engagement before agreeing to deploy. The NATO operation in Afghanistan and the EU force sent to reinforce the United Nations in the Democratic Republic of the Congo were both hampered by caveats on the use of force and by fear of casualties.

Qualms about the use of force will continue to influence governments contributing troops to peacekeeping missions. The United Nations and NATO routinely incorporate into regular operations the use of force against opposing combatants and for civilian protection. But many nations (several European countries and Japan, among others) place sharp restrictions on their troops' availability for the hard edge of combat. In Afghanistan, for example, of the thirty-seven countries participating in the International Security Assistance Force, only four—the United States, the United Kingdom, Canada, and the Netherlands—have deployed on the front lines of Helmand province, where the toughest fighting has occurred. Those four countries have taken the lion's share of casualties to date, and if they continue to suffer disproportionate losses, protests about the sacrifice will increase back home.

Contemporary peacekeeping operations that take on the hard cases, then, have substantial weaknesses. Even if Iraq and Afghanistan are not typical challenges, they have sorely tested the limits of the United States and—in Afghanistan—UN and NATO capabilities as well. From these shortcomings, we should take lessons for building a more effective multilateral peacekeeping capacity.

This leaves the international community with one real alternative. Before its institutions are faced with the collapse of a large, populous state, international leaders must build up the world's peacekeeping and humanitarian capabilities. First, such a buildup would allow current missions to be handled more successfully. A surge capacity buildup (preferably with resources on standby) would follow, preparing the international community to respond to at least one large-scale catastrophe.

LESSONS AND CHANGES

As we argue throughout this book, solving today's transnational threats takes more than the willingness of governments to cooperate. States must develop a sense of responsibility, not only for the well-being of their citizens, but for the effects of their policies and the well-being of people far beyond their borders. Sustained attention and investment in policy tools are necessary for reforming the international system's capacity to avoid conflict, to prevent spillover into neighboring countries, and—in extremis—to respond to mass atrocities.

Adequate security forces are needed to uphold the peace and enforce law and order immediately after a conflict. In Bosnia and Kosovo the troop-to-population ratios were 19:1,000 and 20:1,000, respectively. In Iraq and Afghanistan the ratios were 7.5:1,000 and 1.5:1,000, respectively.[36] The subsequent insurgencies in Iraq and Afghanistan should not be a surprise. Once a mission loses control over the use of force and criminal activity, it creates the space for insurgency.

Indigenous security forces must assume responsibility for law and order, but building their capacity takes time. In Afghanistan new defense and interior ministries had to be created, and the initial failure to address such restructuring, especially of the police, delayed the establishment of effective local capabilities by three or more years. Still, the only viable strategy for sustained peace is building effective state institutions within a framework of the rule of law—precisely the function for which international response mechanisms are least well suited.

At some point, peacebuilders must turn over responsibilities to local actors, giving them a stake in the system. But precipitous elections when the legal foundation is weak and few governmental checks and balances are in place can create rather than solve problems. A process run badly can favor majority groups and become its own driving force for insurgency by bringing warlords and criminals to power or producing flawed legislation such as the Iraqi constitution.

Creating jobs and building infrastructure are essential to establishing a tangible sense of progress. But these require enough security to permit large numbers of civilians to move and act freely. Without that underlying sense of peace and stability, progress in these areas is unrealistic. Yet failure to mobilize civilians to help rebuild their country will also undermine security. So goes the catch-22 of today's overstretched peacebuilding system.

The growing scale and complexity of peace operations underscores the need for multilateral engagement to sustain an international role for years. Yet to be effective, that role cannot be ad hoc. The United States and other international actors face a strategic choice. They can stretch the current operational system past the point of viability by placing new demands on the United Nations, NATO, and other organizations without increasing their resources, or they can seize the moment of opportunity to achieve greater operational coherence and cooperation.

Across the spectrum of action, we believe that the UN Security Council and the United Nations' operational arms have a central role to play. The bulk of resources, whether they are troops, funds, or diplomatic heavyweights, will always reside with member states. But the UN Security Council is a vital legitimating mechanism, and the UN Secretariat can play a catalytic role—as it did, for example, in Lebanon—in forging effective joint action by member states. In the following sections, we consider how the United Nations might serve as a catalyst for crisis response; how NATO might be strengthened in its peacekeeping functions; how the major donors can act more purposefully to help prevent state failure and galvanize recovery; and what standby capacities will be necessary if there is to be a capacity to protect. We offer recommendations in the areas of prevention and mediation, peacekeeping, and peacebuilding.

Prevention and Mediation

In chapter 9 we address some of the actions necessary to tackle state capacity building, effective governance, and poverty eradication. But investment in short-term prevention is warranted as well.

Coordinate among international institutions. Links between the political mechanisms of the United Nations and major financial actors—particularly the World Bank, the IMF, and bilateral donors—could help develop strategies that marry sophistication with actual leverage to prevent state collapse. The UN Security Council, as well as the secretary general, would manage these approaches. Facing conflict or widespread violence somewhere in the world, the secretary general could exert diplomatic pressure with a number of tools at hand, integrating positive incentives for compliance into sanctions regimes.

Form a joint scenario-planning team. The United States, the United Kingdom, and other major donors analyze early warnings and scenarios for likely future conflicts. These separate efforts tend to feed into separate strategies, and the resulting early warnings often go unheeded. Forming a joint scenario-planning team would help to develop shared strategy, bring greater attention to early warnings, and foster coordinated action to prevent impending crises.

Build UN capacity for mediation and political analysis. The UN Department of Political Affairs (DPA) should be realigned and where necessary, restaffed. [37] It should have the capacity to lead UN mediation efforts or support UN-sanctioned mediations. Where the secretary general is involved in preventive efforts, DPA should contribute the political analysis for crisis prevention strategies. Before and during peacebuilding operations, DPA should lead in developing political strategy for peacebuilding efforts, including strategies for political transition and building local capacity. The PBSO should have the overall lead for peacebuilding strategies, of which the political tactics would be one element.

Cultivate "anticipatory" relationships. The personal factor is always significant in conflict management, and there is no policy or institutional substitute for relationships among leaders. Where there are potential flash points, however, the U.S. president, the UN secretary general, the EU high representative, and the heads of relevant regional organizations (especially the African Union, the OAS, and ASEAN) can engage in deliberate efforts to build relationships with other leaders, who in turn may be in a position to contribute to conflict management in emerging crises.

Support informal diplomatic capacities. Kofi Annan's mediation in early 2008 to forestall further escalation of the violence that followed contested elections in Kenya highlights the important role that unofficial diplomats can play. In this case, a key to Annan's success was that UN Secretary General Ban Ki-moon, U.S. Secretary of State Condoleezza Rice, and the African Union all backed Annan, signaling to the parties that they were behind any solution he could broker. Thus faced with a unified international front, the Kenyan president and the head of the opposition struck a deal. In a precedent-setting example of integrating resources behind a single mediation lead, Annan was also backstopped by an integrated office comprising senior staff from the Center for Humanitarian Dialogue, the UN DPA, and the UN country team.

Peacekeeping

The surest way to avoid a new generation of wars is to invest adequately in securing and stabilizing the peace in conflicts that have ended by building up effective peacekeeping and peacebuilding capacities.

Mitigate the shortage of specialized peacekeeping assets. Using military and diplomatic incentives, the United States and its donor partners should cooperate militarily and diplomatically to build up specialized capabilities for peace operations in other countries. This might include creating incentives for militaries to focus on peacekeeping training and acquire more specialized assets (such as transport helicopters). These could be funded through military aid agreements, but with the condition that they become part of a roster of forces on standby for UN and other peace operations. This would reflect existing European arrangements for UN support and ongoing efforts to develop an African standby force, while shifting emphasis to high-quality and predictably available specialized assets.

Address the lack of strategic airlifts for peace operations. The United States and its partners can reduce logistical problems for peace operations by developing a system of voluntarily funded (or partly subsidized) lift support. This would build on the current NATO and EU support to the African Union in Darfur and on comparable U.S. and European initiatives elsewhere. This system would be based on a coordinated process of assessing needs and identifying capacity by planners from missions and potential lift providers.

Improve NATO's ability to mount multidimensional operations. NATO suffers from the absence of a civilian or political component of its operations. Initial efforts to develop a comprehensive approach have been halting and warrant acceleration. Much of this could be achieved by overcoming the dysfunctional relationship between NATO and EU planning mechanisms, allowing NATO operations to draw more heavily on the EU civilian capacities that are being built up to a substantial level.

Develop an interinstitutional framework for strategic projections and joint planning for peace operations. To develop overall guidance for the assets resulting from these initiatives, the United States and its partners should emphasize a three-tier approach to strategic planning for peace operations: (1) increase international funding for planning capacities at the United Nations and the African Union; (2) establish a formal or semi-formal process for interinstitutional and intergovernmental conferences focused on strategic projections for peace operations; and (3) develop a standing operational framework for headquarters-to-headquarters communications during hybrid operations, possibly overseen by a standing "coordination cell." These capacities should be tested through regular exercises, for which there is precedent.

Create a more structured funding pool for AU and other African missions. Specific priority should be given to creating a new standing fund for African operations and capacity building. The fund should be based on current U.S., EU, and other donor initiatives, but funding release and reporting procedures must be clarified. Particular attention should be given to functions that are currently the least funded, such as mission planning and niche capacity building.

Promote an intermilitary, intergovernmental doctrine for peace operations. Building on recent experiences, the United States and its partners should facilitate an ongoing and open discussion of peacekeeping doctrine, with particular attention given to the issues surrounding responses to violent threats. The goal should be shared doctrine, at least among the four major global peacekeeping platforms: NATO, the United Nations, the African Union, and the European Union.

Broaden the system of standby reserve capacities for peacekeeping. This action is needed for the United Nations and for regional organizations. To have the capacity to respond effectively and with adequate speed in peacebuilding operations, the United Nations must have access to 50,000 peacekeepers, or five operational brigades, on standby. Several standby forces are planned in Africa for AU purposes. In addition, the European Union has developed a joint standby battalion for rapid deployment to UN missions, which was used for the first time in the Democratic Republic of the Congo in 2007. To deepen this capacity, individual countries or regional organizations would designate their contributions to a UN force and guarantee the availability of such forces. The United Nations would be responsible for designating performance standards and qualifying training programs that would be run at the national or regional level.

Establish a target for net global capacity of up to 300,000 peacekeepers. This would involve a net increase of 120,000 peacekeepers from the 180,000 already deployed—a realistic growth target. They could be mandated through existing programs such as the Global Peace Operations Initiative, through reorganization of armed services in NATO countries, and through increasing participation by new contributing countries such as China and Indonesia.

Peacebuilding

These investments in peacekeeping will be effective only if matched with investment in the tools for peacebuilding.

Create a UN strategic planning capacity supplemented by national and regional capabilities. The UN Peacebuilding Commission should be transformed into an entity that coordinates strategic plans for peacebuilding, incorporating the capabilities and contributions of diverse donors. This would require a team of at least 150 full-time staff members, which could be drawn from the Peacebuilding Support Office (PBSO), other parts of the UN Secretariat, relevant UN organizations, and the UNDP's Bureau for Conflict Prevention and Recovery. The goal would be to build the capacity to plan and coordinate five major concurrent missions. Each mission would require a core staff of 20 individuals, along with another 50 at headquarters to compile lessons, establish procedures, run training programs, and manage overall operations.

Once the PBSO has established core competencies, it should be designated the lead international entity for developing strategy and planning for multilateral peacebuilding missions (unless there is an obvious regional or national entity that can credibly assume such a role). The PBSO should base a planning framework and sectoral checklists on the best international experience to create a common foundation for planning across donors.[38]

National and regional entities need comparable capabilities to oversee coordinated contributions as part of—or in parallel with—UN missions.

Establish a response corps to run field missions. The United Nations must have access to a core group of at least 1,000 specialists available at any given time to staff coordinated field operations. Such specialists would range from senior representatives of the secretary general to staffers in core technical competencies. They would reside in UN departments and programs, national governments, NGOs, and other institutions, but be available on standby arrangements. In addition, the United Nations should have an in-house capacity to plan and establish mission structures. The goal would be to have the capacity to establish a coordinated field office within thirty days.

National and regional entities must build comparable response capabilities to give them an effective field capacity, which is usually the most critical level for coordination.

Build an expanded international network of skilled providers to implement programs. In addition to peacekeepers, the United Nations should maintain a pretrained network of 20,000 police officers, police trainers, and rule-of-law experts through an international reserve system arranged with national and regional entities. These law enforcers should be ready to deploy within sixty days. The United Nations should also refine and expand its database of contractors, NGOs, and other service providers in key peacebuilding areas, increasing its ability to draw on proven, and whenever possible, local expertise.

Regional and national entities should establish their own reserves and contractual networks that can be used in coordination with or as part of multilateral operations.

Ensure $2 billion in predictable funding for UN peacebuilding activities. Such funding is needed to allow peacebuilding operations to mobilize rapidly once authorized by the UN Security Council. By shaping dynamics early on, rapid deployments will shorten operations and save funds. Funds would finance rapid deployment of peacebuilding operations other than peacekeeping forces, which would still be financed through existing mechanisms. Funding should be adjusted to cover six months of unplanned peacebuilding operations based on annual surveys of actual costs. Contributions should be an assessed cost because all countries benefit from the effectiveness of a mechanism that can limit the spillover from conflict and state failure. Regional and national entities should establish comparable mechanisms to allow for rapid deployment of peacebuilding contributions.

CONCLUSION

None of this will be achieved without active U.S. engagement and substantial U.S. investments. Those investments alone, of course, will be far from enough. Many other states, including the rising powers, have vital contributions to make in strengthening international conflict management efforts. The European Union has also emerged as a significant political and financial actor on these issues. Of particular note is Prime Minister Gordon Brown's call for establishing a stabilization force and strengthened capacity for early recovery. Many of the recommendations outlined in this chapter could form part of such a capacity. The United Kingdom has an established track record of leading important reform in the United Nations, particularly in the field of humanitarian response. With support from the United States and others, the United Kingdom could lead on this set of reforms.

Finally, it is worth stressing that UN member states from all regions have continued to view prevention, mediation, peacekeeping, and peace-building as critical institutional functions. Consequently, reforms in this area should proceed in a way that preserves north-south mutual engagement and reinforces perceptions of shared interests in effective conflict management. Of the wide range of issues requiring attention from President Obama, this may rank among the easier opportunities for making headway. An early signal from the United States that it is willing to work with and invest in UN conflict management mechanisms—and that it is prepared to follow as well as lead reforms—would energize international cooperation.

EIGHT

COMBATING TRANSNATIONAL TERRORISM

TERRORISM WAS A CONSTANT COMPANION to war and ideological struggle in the twentieth century, and at the start of the twenty-first, al Qaeda represents the most virulent form of the phenomenon the world has yet faced. Although the threat posed by terrorism has often been exaggerated, the prospect that a network like al Qaeda could gain access to a nuclear or biological weapon represents a serious threat to U.S. and international security.

No state, however powerful, can defend itself unilaterally against transnational terrorism. Terrorist networks move operatives, money, and material across borders and through the crevices of the global economy. Only through extensive cooperation on financial flows, intelligence, and police action, and parallel action to reduce the social and political appeal of terrorism, can the risk be reduced. The most dangerous form of terrorism, involving nuclear and biological weapons, requires the most extensive cooperation.

The struggle against terrorism rests on four facets of responsible sovereignty. Effective strategies to combat terrorism require states to (1) fulfill universal responsibilities not to sponsor, aid, or abet transnational terrorism; (2) take responsibility for the external impacts of conditions within their borders; (3) take responsibility for the well-being of their citizens, thereby diminishing the risk of terrorism; and (4) build adequate capacity to implement their responsibilities. The capacity-building point underscores an important concept—that powerful states have an incentive based on self-interest, along with a positive responsibility, to assist weak states. If states want to create an international system that helps them protect the territory within their own borders, they need the cooperation of all states. That creates an imperative to build the capabilities of even the weakest links in the chain.

As the victim of the largest terrorist attack in history and with its global reach, the United States should be the leader in cooperative efforts to combat terrorism. In the immediate aftermath of 9/11, the United States enjoyed support for robust action against al Qaeda from a broad coalition that encompassed all the major powers and much of the Arab world. The months after 9/11 also saw new energy at the United Nations, and in regional organizations, aimed at filling gaps in the normative, legal, and institutional infrastructure of effective counterterrorism.

The war in Iraq, however, destroyed that unity of purpose. The rhetoric and tactics of the U.S. "global war on terror," along with the ill-founded justification of the war in Iraq as part of the fight against terror, have alienated the Arab and Muslim worlds and caused a loss of U.S. standing on the critical issues of human rights and democratization. The diminished standing of the United States has undermined counterterrorism efforts and the broader prospects for cooperative action against other shared threats.

The credibility and capacity of global counterterrorism efforts will flounder without a policy shift in the United States. Going forward, U.S. policy should encompass a dedicated operational and diplomatic focus on al Qaeda and its related groups; support national efforts against various terrorist organizations, which in turn should be based on a law-enforcement and rule-of-law strategy and grounded in human rights; contribute to efforts to reduce the social and political appeal of terrorism; and embed U.S. efforts within a robust framework for international cooperation against terrorism.

Current international mechanisms to promote state and collective action against terrorism are comprehensive but not authoritative. State responsibilities are increasingly well articulated, through the now 16 UN conventions and protocols, UN Security Council resolutions, the UN General Assembly's unanimously adopted counterterrorism strategy, and regional declarations and conventions. Of these, however, only the Security Council's elements are authoritative. Little has been done to develop effective mechanisms for building local capacity to combat terrorism or for supporting the development of national strategies. In addition, a proliferation of actors has led to a lack of coherence. There is no shared concept of enforcement.

In the midst of this rather muddling performance by formal bodies, the G-8 has been a useful venue for promoting cooperation on tactical counterterrorism, in law enforcement and financing, and for spawning new, informal tools for cooperation, such as the Proliferation and Container Security initiatives.[1] The work of the G-8 has been limited, though, by its lack of widespread legitimacy in the Global South (the nations of Africa, Central and Latin America, and most of Asia).

As a major threat to security and order in the twenty-first century, terrorism demands a more deliberate and effective response. We support the creation of a new instrument that could help to expand the scale and improve the quality of national counterterrorism strategies. Such an organization, grounded in existing treaties and established international frameworks, could also set standards for state action and, ideally, monitor state performance. To be efficient, it should build on existing capacities such as the UN Office on Drugs and Crime (UNODC). And it should operate in a manner that reinforces the central role of the UN Security Council in addressing threats to international peace and security. Although such an organization could take many forms, effectiveness and legitimacy would best be combined by creating a High Commissioner for Counterterrorism Capacity Building, modeled on the UN High Commissioner for Refugees (UNHCR).

Creating a more effective response to the changing threat of terrorism will not be easy. But with new U.S. policy and a concerted effort to build consensus—first within a new G-16,[2] then within the broader UN membership—this goal can be achieved, and the effort can help to heal broader divisions that have undermined U.S. and international security.[3]

ASSESSING THE THREAT

Data about terrorism are notoriously weak, and analysis of its causes controversial.[4] Part of the challenge is the international community's persistent effort to find a single explanation for this widely diverse phenomenon. Terrorism ranges from, for example, the radical Salafist Wahhabi (an archconservative brand of Islam) extremism al Qaeda practices on a global scale to the targeted Maoist terrorism the Naxalites carry out locally in India's northern provinces. Just as war takes myriad forms with diverse causes (such as great-power, interstate, internal, irredentist, and separatist), terrorism takes many forms for which there is no a priori reason to assume the same cause.

Moreover, efforts to explain terrorism must account for the attitudes and actions of distinct sets of actors: the senior leadership of a terrorist organization; its henchmen, especially those who engage in operations; and its supporters within a population; or state sponsors. The motivations of these groups can differ within a given terrorist campaign. Iran's motives in supporting Hamas operations in Gaza, for example, are evidently grounded in efforts to combat U.S. influence in the region. The leadership of Hamas itself, however, has been primarily motivated by the desire to be seen as leading the Palestinian national struggle in a fight against Israel. Meanwhile, operatives join for a combination of reasons, including feelings of humiliation and rage about the occupation, lack of future prospects, and incentives created in the form of substantial monetary payments to families of "martyrs." Popular support for Hamas has numerous sources, but seems particularly influenced by disaffection with the corruption and ineffectiveness of the Palestinian Authority. Various causes or factors influence these actors to differing extents.

Does poverty cause terrorism? If it did, terrorism would be prevalent in the third world and rare in the rich world. In reality, though, every single Organization for Economic Cooperation and Development (OECD) country has experienced terrorism, both homegrown and imported, while only a fraction of less-developed countries have been victimized. In the contemporary period, terrorism is closely associated with middle-income countries.[5] Moreover, repeated studies have shown that terrorist leaders and even terrorist operatives tend to be better educated and have higher incomes than average.[6] Nevertheless, in some cases (Nepal, for example), poverty and inequality—and marginalization from a political process—appear to contribute to popular support for terrorist organizations.[7]

Does religion drive terrorism? Survey data covering 90 percent of the world's Muslim population indicate that it does not. Politics, not religion, seems to be the driver of terrorist action, even among Salafist communities.[8] Religion does not explain who is a radical or who is a moderate. Those who condoned the 9/11 attacks did so on the basis of politics. Many of those who condemned the attacks did so on religious grounds. At least some of the al Qaeda leadership does appear to be genuinely motivated by religious beliefs. There is, however, a need for a great deal of caution on this point. To describe Salafist Wahhabism (which is dominant in Saudi Arabia and among the al Qaeda leadership) as a cause of terrorism is to profoundly overstate the point and to neglect the tens of millions of Wahhabis, including Salafists, who are not involved with terrorism in any way. Similarly, the Palestinian population's support for Hamas increased between 2005 and 2006, not because Palestinians became more religious or more extreme in their religious views, but because Hamas appeared less corrupt and more credible than the Palestinian Authority, which had lost the popular confidence that it could either govern or negotiate with Israel effectively. Iraqis in Anbar province initially supported al Qaeda as a counter to the U.S. occupation, and then withdrew their support when confronted with the realities of al Qaeda's brutality; neither support nor loss of support pivoted on religious issues.

Does the denial of human rights contribute to terrorism? Perhaps in part. Recent evidence suggests that in the current wave of terrorism, a high percentage of terrorist leaders and activists come from countries with limited political freedoms. In this regard, the fact that much contemporary terrorism emanates from the Middle East, the region with the lowest scores on civil rights, is salient, including in terms of recruitment for al Qaeda, the Muslim Brotherhood, and other regional networks.[9] But how do human rights issues explain the participation of second-generation Muslims in terrorist attacks in London or Madrid? Or participation in the Baader-Meinhof Gang, which terrorized Germany from roughly 1968 to 1977?

Does military occupation cause terrorism? There is strong support for this argument. A very high correlation is seen between large-scale suicide terrorist campaigns and foreign occupation of territory—in, for example, the Palestinian territories, Iraq, and Sri Lanka—irrespective of the religion of the group involved.[10] On the other hand, Colombian groups waged terrorist campaigns for decades with no reference to any question of occupation. Nor can questions of occupation explain attacks linked to al Qaeda in Jordan or Turkey.[11]

Given these variations in causes or factors, counterterrorism strategies must be tailored to the specific realities of distinct terrorist networks or campaigns. There is no one terrorism threat; there are several, and they are different. Terrorism in East Asia, for example, is primarily linked to ethnonationalist struggles and religious minorities (as in Thailand and the Philippines).[12] Along India's northern border, terrorist activities are tied to leftist ideologies, underdevelopment, and exclusion (as in Nepal, Assam, and Bangladesh).

Complicating this divergence is evidence of sporadic tactical cooperation between a subset of these diverse groups and al Qaeda. In some instances, such as the Bali bombing by Jemaah Islamiyah, evidence points to direct tactical cooperation between the two outfits. On the other hand, no evidence of such cooperation was found between al Qaeda and local groups involved in the Madrid train bombings. In that case, al Qaeda appears to have provided inspiration instead of operational support.

Al Qaeda and Its Offshoots

Because al Qaeda stands out as a unique phenomenon, it poses a special threat to U.S. and international security. Unlike most terrorist organizations whose efforts are linked to a specific territorial or ideological struggle, al Qaeda has defined its relationship to terrorism quite differently. Terrorism is not merely a tactic of al Qaeda, it is essential to the organization's identity, purpose, and strategy. Moreover, al Qaeda's targets—the United States, U.S. interests, U.S. allies, the United Nations, and the basic structures of global order—are strategic, not limited (although al Qaeda has an additional, more focused objective of overthrowing secular Arab governments, especially those backed by the United States, including Saudi Arabia, Egypt, and Pakistan).

The Bush administration has argued that al Qaeda's power has been substantially diminished by the war in Iraq, contending that "we are fighting them there so that we don't have to fight them here." Putting aside for a moment the colossal insensitivity of that argument for public diplomacy, there did appear to be some truth to the administration's case for a period after the fall of Saddam Hussein's regime. Al Qaeda's public statements and captured correspondence revealed that after the defeat of its Afghan partners, the Taliban, the organization was concentrating its efforts on battling U.S. forces in Iraq.[13]

By July 2007, however, the U.S. National Intelligence Council's (NIC) national intelligence estimate (NIE) on al Qaeda made clear that the U.S. occupation had, among other effects, led to the creation of a major offshoot, al Qaeda in Iraq.[14] The NIE estimates that al Qaeda in Iraq is the strongest of al Qaeda's affiliates and is capable of directly attacking the United States. By mid-2008, the "Sunni Awakening" movement backed by the U.S. military surge had made inroads in combating al Qaeda in Iraq; how durably remains to be seen. According to the NIE, the invasion of Iraq had also created a training ground for a new generation of sophisticated jihadists inspired by al Qaeda. Finally, the NIE points out that the invasion distracted the United States from the key battle against al Qaeda and the Taliban in Afghanistan and on the Afghanistan–Pakistan border.

This last effect is the most dangerous. The Taliban and al Qaeda central are now resurgent inside a safe haven and newly capable of posing an ongoing threat to the United States. They have mounted an increasing challenge to Pakistan, a populous Muslim state with a critical role in the stability of West Asia and nuclear weapons.[15] In a paper for the MGI project, Bruce Riedel described Pakistan (even before the tumultuous political and economic events of 2008) as "the most dangerous country in the world."[16]

Al Qaeda has transformed into three entities or phenomena: (1) the remaining core, still led by Osama bin Laden's inner circle, based in and around Waziristan; (2) linked affiliates, which range from those with close operational connections—such as al Qaeda in Iraq—to those with looser financial or logistical ties; and (3) an organizing principle or a rallying point, not just for several other groups that fly under the al Qaeda flag, but for a spreading movement of political and cultural anti-Americanism. That movement is attracting ever more recruits, not to a central organization, not even to Salafist jihad, but to the cause of standing up for Islam against the United States as both symbol and driving force of modernity and globalization. On the other hand, a 2007 Human

Security Report brief showed a substantial decline in the number of terrorist attacks worldwide, outside of Iraq.[17]

Connection to Other Threats

Terrorism in general and al Qaeda in particular are connected to other threats. Nuclear proliferation by states increases the availability of material and technology necessary for a terrorist to acquire a nuclear weapon. Internal and interstate conflict, including occupation, foments grievances nurtured by terrorist organizations to aid in recruiting and mobilization. The erosion of state capacity also helps the terrorist cause. The ability of nonstate actors to traffic in nuclear matériel and technology is aided by ineffective state control of borders and the relative ease of transit through weak states. Weak states are often unable to provide for basic social services such as universal primary education, allowing this vacuum to be filled by social organizations linked to groups with extremist ideologies. In addition, weak states often lack the capacity to exercise territorial control, leaving a power and security vacuum that terrorist organizations have exploited to maintain safe havens, training facilities, and bases for launching terrorist operations.

Response Strategy

Given the diversity of terrorist organizations, specific local strategies must be a major part of counterterrorism. Lessons from Afghanistan, Iraq, and previous counterterrorism efforts suggest that those strategies should incorporate a multidimensional approach (as recently recognized, though arguably not implemented, by the Bush administration).[18] In addition to the necessity to capture and kill proven terrorists, the core elements of those strategies must include the following:

—Eroding the support for terrorist organizations using political, human rights, community development, and other strategies specific to the context

—Isolating and creating costs for state supporters of terrorist organizations using regional and international legal and political mechanisms to isolate, penalize, and ultimately sanction state supporters of terrorism

—Denying safe havens, in part by using peacekeeping and peacebuilding capacities to restore government control over territory where it has eroded

—Using advanced law-enforcement, not military, methods to prevent, deter, and capture terrorist leaders; gain intelligence; and freeze terrorist finances

—Persuading communities to withhold local support using local leaders, education systems, and other means to reduce the extent to which the social context animates support for terrorists

—Defending human rights.

Any counterterrorism strategy will inevitably be confronted with dilemmas. In some cases, countering terrorism cannot escape working with national authorities that sponsor, support, or at least give succor to terrorist groups. Most difficult of all will be instances when the national authority ostensibly supports counterterrorism, but tepidly so, while retaining an authoritarian grip over political life and oppressing human rights. In many such cases, regional or subregional actors may have relationships, access, cultural ties, and other assets that are not likely to exist in the United States or at the international level. Regional law-enforcement and counterterrorism capacities could be developed to aid in this effort.

The Case for a U.S. Policy Shift

In 2008, the approach of a U.S. presidential election occasioned a debate about whether the global war on terror has been actual strategy or mere rhetoric. In our view it has been both, equally counterproductive. As a rhetorical device, the global war on terror is diplomatically counterproductive. As a strategy, it allowed broad, global concerns to trump local, specific strategy; it put undue emphasis on the military dimensions of what should be a multidimensional response; it facilitated the worst aspects of a state-of-war mentality without generating domestic or international mobilization in support; and it allowed a loss of focus on al Qaeda and its direct supporters. At best, the term "global war on terror" has been a useful political device for some U.S. politicians, but it has proved dysfunctional and damaging beyond U.S. borders.

U.S. policy has been weakest of all in trying to root out terrorists from failed and weak states. These include Afghanistan, where the United States underinvested in both military capacity and state building, and where corruption, an inadequate international response, and poor relations with Pakistan have weakened central state authority. In Iraq, a failure to establish law and order after the U.S. invasion, together with neglect of state building and reconstruction planning, created conditions that favored the insurgency and terrorist organizations, including al Qaeda in Iraq. And in Pakistan, an excessive emphasis on military approaches to the terrorist problem and neglect of the democratic process eroded political support for the regime of Pakistan President Pervez Musharraf, who resigned under pressure in August 2008, creating a political and institutional crisis that now fosters further opportunities for terrorist destabilization. Somalia is another example of failed strategy.

U.S. counterterrorism and Middle Eastern strategies have driven a deep wedge between the United States and other major and emerging powers. The poorly conceived rhetoric of the global war on terrorism and the association with Iraq have eroded unity of purpose where counterterrorism once united the United States, the major powers, the western world, and the status quo states of the Middle East and Asia, it is now an issue that divides the United States from its traditional allies, from the rising powers, and indeed from the majority of other states. It has fueled anti-American sentiment worldwide, diminishing the prospects for U.S. leadership.[19] Perhaps most worrisome, the unpopularity of U.S. policies on terrorism, Iraq, and the Middle East has created a sense of unjust U.S. policy toward Islam itself, and this appears to be generating a shift in loyalties among Muslim minorities—especially in the western world—away from their adopted nations and toward Islam as the *ummah* (the "global nation" of Islam). In some countries, notably the United Kingdom, France, and Spain, this has led to a rise in Muslim minorities' support for "radical" Islam, which is seen as the only potential bulwark against the perceived injustices of U.S. policy.[20]

This trend is particularly problematic given the nature of al Qaeda, which has immediate political goals that require local support. Al Qaeda and its affiliates must be able to hide and operate in local communities. Strategies to break al Qaeda or even contain it are unlikely to succeed without the help of these communities, including those in the Arab world, as evidenced in Anbar province in 2007–08, when local groups sided with the U.S. military against al Qaeda in Iraq after successive al Qaeda in Iraq brutalities. Right now, however, the unpopularity of U.S. policy in the Middle East is such that it alienates these communities, even from their own governments when those governments are allied with the U.S. war on terror.

U.S. human rights behavior since 9/11—consider Guantánamo, Abu Ghraib, and the administration's "extraordinary rendition" policy—has also undercut U.S. leadership. This is particularly unfortunate because more and more evidence suggests that it is the denial of civil rights, not poverty or other causes, that is most closely correlated with al Qaeda recruitment and the rise of its necessary support from domestic populations.

Loss of credibility on these issues damages core U.S. security interests, with the most salient recent experience coming from Pakistan. Five years ago, U.S. support for Musharraf was a critical asset to his government; by 2008, it had become a fatal embrace. U.S. backing weakened Musharraf and damaged support for his counterterrorism efforts. It has also contributed to a sharp decline in the ability of the United States to influence policy, let alone foster democratic change.[21] In short, despite seven years of intensive U.S. policy focus on counterterrorism, international terrorism is not only undiminished, but mounting in terms of the magnitude of the threat it poses to U.S. and international security.

The United States is the only actor whose policy has global implications, and effective U.S. policy is certainly a necessary, if not sufficient, condition for response. U.S. policy will be an important factor in enabling or constraining counterterrorism action in directly affected countries. The United States can make a positive impact by supplying money, police assistance, intelligence, and tactical cooperation in support of local strategies. On the other hand, U.S. policy can diminish the legitimacy of national actions, especially among local community leaders who face revolt if they are seen as too closely tied to Washington. Yet it is precisely those local leaders whose backing is most crucial to eliminating support for terrorism.

A new U.S. policy should have four core elements:

1. Shift strategy and rhetoric away from a general war against terror and toward a specific war against al Qaeda and its affiliates. This will involve continuing offensive operations against al Qaeda in Afghanistan, including devoting the necessary resources and attention to that operation, as well as sanctioning individuals and states that support or facilitate al Qaeda operations.

2. Support local strategies, where that support is requested, against local or subregional terrorist groups or networks. After al Qaeda, four

clusters demand attention, roughly in order of importance—the Levant, South and Southeast Asia, the Horn of Africa, and in the Tri-border (where Paraguay, Brazil, and Argentina meet) and Andean regions of Latin America.

3. Continue to improve U.S. tactical cooperation against terrorism—involving law-enforcement personnel, intelligence-gathering operatives, and financing investigators—at the bilateral level. Building multilateral capabilities to support this cooperation is another part of this core element. In the near term, this capacity building could take place through the existing G-8, and over the longer term, through a G-16 that we advocate creating in this book.

4. Engage in a broad diplomatic effort to bring peace and stability to the Middle East. This will help to improve the political context for both U.S. and international counterterrorism efforts and will be beneficial for other reasons as well (see chapter 10 for a more detailed discussion of this element).

In addition to changing its counterterrorism policy, the United States will have to work to resuscitate the nuclear nonproliferation regime (chapter 5) and lead international efforts to promote biosecurity and biosafety, in part to reduce the risks associated with terrorist use of biological weapons (chapter 6). Bolstering conflict management mechanisms (chapter 7) will have adjacent benefits for counterterrorism efforts.

COUNTERTERRORISM AND RESPONSIBLE SOVEREIGNTY

Substantial progress has been made, especially since 9/11, on articulating the responsibilities of states in dealing with terrorism at the regional level. Groups such as the Organization of American States (OAS), the Organization for Security and Cooperation in Europe (OSCE), and the Asia Pacific Economic Cooperation (APEC) forum have adopted summit declarations, joint statements, or similar commitments to tackle terrorism.

This has also occurred at the global level. Two weeks after 9/11, the UN Security Council adopted Resolution 1373,[22] which obliges member states to enhance legislation, strengthen border controls, coordinate executive machinery, and increase cooperation in combating terrorism. By imposing general counterterrorism obligations on all UN member states, the resolution went beyond existing conventions and protocols, which bind only those that have become parties to the existing agreements. Resolution 1373 took provisions from a variety of treaties that did not have universal support, in particular the UN Terrorism Financing Convention, and incorporated them into a resolution that is binding on all states.

Similarly in 2004, the Security Council adopted Resolution 1540,[23] which mandates that all states (1) refrain from providing any form of support to nonstate actors that attempt to develop, acquire, manufacture, possess, transport, transfer, or use nuclear, chemical, or biological weapons and their means of delivery; (2) adopt and enforce appropriate effective laws to that effect; and (3) establish domestic controls to prevent the proliferation of nuclear, chemical, or biological weapons and their means of delivery. The resolution also established a committee of the Security Council to report on implementation of these provisions, and called on states with the capacity to do so to assist states needing help to develop the legal and regulatory infrastructure for fulfilling the requirements of the resolution. In a related decision, the UN General Assembly adopted the International Convention for the Suppression of Acts of Nuclear Terrorism in 2005.[24]

The advantage of the Security Council's resolutions is that they require all states to act. But the process of having the council "legislate" such actions has generated substantial objections—not just to these specific resolutions but to the role of the council itself. Many states with crucial roles in counterterrorism resist the council mandating action in their domestic affairs without serious consultation. Indeed, this legislative action has become a touchstone in calls for procedural and membership reform of the Security Council.

In 2006, at the urging of then-UN Secretary General Kofi Annan, the UN General Assembly adopted the "General Assembly Counterterrorism Strategy." Based on the secretary general's report,[25] the strategy sets out broad responsibilities. The first set of responsibilities compels states (and international organizations) to address the conditions that foment the spread of terrorism, such as prolonged unresolved conflicts; the absence of the rule of law; human rights violations; ethnic, national, and religious discrimination; socioeconomic marginalization; and the absence of good governance. These measures pay particular attention to meeting the UN Millennium Development Goals as a means of eradicating poverty and ameliorating the conditions that can facilitate the recruitment of terrorists or create sympathy for harboring terrorists.

The second set of measures addresses state obligations to prevent and combat terrorism by refraining from facilitating, financing, encouraging, or tolerating terrorist activities and by denying terrorist groups safe haven. States are also expected to cooperate in extraditing and prosecuting any person who supports, facilitates, or participates in the planning, preparation, financing, or perpetration of terrorist acts.

The third set of responsibilities requires states to aid in building each other's capacity to prevent and combat terrorism, in part by sharing technical information and best practices. A final set of measures requires states to ensure that any person who participates in the financing, planning, preparation, or perpetration of terrorist acts is prosecuted under domestic criminal law or extradited to another country for prosecution. Criminal prosecution must take into account the severity of the crime, while still respecting international human rights standards. Taken together, these regional and global declarations and agreed strategies constitute a partial framework of sovereign responsibilities for counterterrorism.

In addition, an emerging norm is embedded in the UN General Assembly's strategy document and is common to virtually all regional declarations. It requires nations to work to resolve conflicts (including military occupation), fight extremism, combat poverty, and in other ways address issues that generate popular support for terrorism. That norm does not yet include, however, a commitment to expand political participation, which is necessary because excluding people from a role in their society is an important driver of political support for terrorism.

International standards of responsibility are least developed on the issue of what penalties should be levied against those who do not comply with international conventions or even binding Security Council resolutions. Guiding principles for when the use of force might be appropriate to deal with potential or actual terrorist actions are also lacking.

INTERNATIONAL COUNTERTERRORISM ARCHITECTURE

An effective response against the al Qaeda threat and terrorist activities in general will require extensive international cooperation and infrastructure. Stronger capabilities are needed to authorize and support offensive efforts against al Qaeda; to build national capacity and support local strategies against terrorism; to implement a robust legal and normative framework; to further articulate state responsibilities; and to support tactical cooperation on intelligence and financing.

Supporting an Offensive Strategy against al Qaeda

The UN Security Council adopted targeted financial sanctions against al Qaeda and the Taliban in 1999. This measure came against the backdrop of previous resolutions that condemned al Qaeda's role in the Tanzania and Kenya bombings in 1998 and demanded that the Taliban regime hand over Osama bin Laden. In its 1999 resolution, the UN Security Council called the Taliban's refusal to surrender bin Laden and cease support for terrorist training and other activities a "grave threat to international peace and security"—language that invokes the possibility of coercive measures. Those measures were initially limited to aviation and financial sanctions against the Taliban, and then extended to include an arms embargo. After 9/11, sanctions were expanded to require countries to freeze the assets of any entity on the list maintained by the al Qaeda and Taliban Sanctions Committee, a subsidiary body of the Security Council.

Although the travel ban and arms embargo associated with the al Qaeda sanctions produced few tangible results, the financial sanctions led to the freezing of some $100 million, most of it in the months after 9/11.[26] Of course, the broad objective of compelling the Taliban to hand over bin Laden was not met—setting the stage for the dramatic aftermath of 9/11.

On September 12, 2001, the Security Council not only condemned global terrorism and the 9/11 attacks, but asserted the right of the United States to act in self-defense under the UN charter, which established an important precedent.[27] During the U.S. invasion of Afghanistan, the UN Secretary General led efforts through a special envoy, Lakhdar Brahimi, to negotiate the Bonn Accords, an arrangement for an interim government in post-Taliban Afghanistan. To help implement the Bonn Accords, the United Nations established the Assistance Mission in Afghanistan, which played a critical role in building key national institutions. Finally, in December 2001, the Security Council authorized the International Security Assistance Force for Afghanistan, creating a multilateral framework through which North Atlantic Treaty Organization (NATO) members and forty other countries could contribute forces to the ongoing effort to contain and defeat the Taliban.

Since 2002, NATO has been at the heart of the international response in Afghanistan. NATO members have deployed more than 50,000 troops to carry out counterinsurgency and stabilization functions. NATO provides direct security to the Afghan president and senior officials, security in and around Kabul, and—to lesser or greater extents—security in each of the Afghan provinces. Three constraints have hampered its work: the lack of capacity to ensure that coordinated (or "comprehensive," to use NATO terminology) development assistance is rendered through civilian entities when an area is secured; poor coordination between the U.S.-led coalition and the UN political presence; and extensive national caveats on how forces can be used within Afghanistan, which has proved most troubling. Several NATO members set detailed limits on where their forces can be sent and what kind of fighting they can do, forcing NATO to rely on a handful of troop contributors in the toughest provinces.

We can see, then, that even though the United Nations and NATO operations have made critical contributions to stabilizing Afghanistan, they have suffered from all the frailties normally associated with peacekeeping and peacebuilding operations deployed to hard cases. Continuing corruption within the Afghan government, especially within police institutions, has eroded the legitimacy and authority of national institutions. Resultant reversals, combined with the ungoverned space in western Pakistan where the Taliban finds sanctuary, have led to a resurgence of the Taliban, especially along the Afghanistan–Pakistan border. This development has also contributed to further instability in Pakistan.

The case of Pakistan reveals the hard limits of multilateral instruments. In Pakistan to date, there has been neither significant multilateral engagement in counterterrorism efforts nor any significant multilateral effort to assist in internal stabilization.[28] Should the situation in Pakistan destabilize further, perhaps through well-organized and well-aimed al Qaeda attacks, demand for international action would mount. But this would only reveal the limitations of international security mechanisms in two key areas—counterterrorism support to local authorities and prevention of state failure. Neither the United Nations nor most regional bodies have the right tools to support domestic actors in counterterrorist operations. In addition, international mechanisms for the prevention of state failure are rudimentary. Furthermore, the United Nations in particular has historically encountered significant difficulties in involving itself in large or diplomatically influential member states, and Pakistan, for all of its frailties, certainly qualifies as such a state. All of this may appear to be an indictment of multilateral institutions, but we should recall that the United States too, even when President Bush was directly engaged, has not had a coherent, effective policy toward either Afghanistan or Pakistan.[29]

Taking Action against the General Threat of Terrorism

A number of strategies, discussed in the sections that follow, are necessary to effectively combat terrorism.

BUILDING NATIONAL CAPACITY. Because counterterrorism is a critically sensitive internal issue that is likely to generate intense resistance to any intervention by international bodies, supporting local capacity and local strategies must be central to any effective effort. The international capacities to support local counterterrorism, however, remain underdeveloped, despite the fact that strengthening the counterterrorism capabilities of all states has been near the top of the international agenda.

Strengthening capabilities is one of the few counterterrorism issues at the United Nations that has not been affected by the divisions over the Middle East. The Security Council's Counterterrorism Committee (CTC, established in 2001 by Resolution 1373) was intended to assume a leading role in identifying capacity needs of all member states, first by helping them to prioritize needs, then by reaching out to donor states and organizations to garner the necessary assistance. Nearly six years since it was established, though, the committee has yet to adequately fulfill its mandate, lacking resources, expertise, and broad political support from donor and recipient states. The UNODC has played a small but important role—largely based on voluntary funding—in helping states to develop effective counterterrorism legislation and training. The International Atomic Energy Agency has helped a small number of states, especially in the former Soviet Union, develop effective border monitoring against the smuggling of radiological or nuclear material.

In 2003, dissatisfied with the lack of concrete results from the CTC, the United States pushed the G-8 to create the Counterterrorism Action

Group (CTAG), which was intended to coordinate the delivery of assistance from the major donors. The group, however, like the G-8 itself, is an ad hoc political mechanism with no permanent secretariat or capacity. CTAG also lacks the necessary legitimacy in the Global South to assume a role in coordinating global, multilateral, and nonmilitary counterterrorism efforts. It has yet to deliver significant results.

Financing counterterrorism efforts is another challenge. Most donor states have budgets for overseas development assistance, but spending through such budgets is restricted to programs that the OECD considers "developmental." Spending through larger military budgets tends to skew programs toward military aspects. Spending for international cooperative efforts in nonmilitary security areas is not yet a normal part of the budget structure of most governments. Proposals have been made for establishing and tracking a new category of budget spending at the OECD, which would be allocated to international cooperation on common global threats—including terrorism—but little progress has been made.[30] Strengthening civilian police forces would seem to be a logical way to combat terrorism. But even in postconflict contexts, where funding has historically been more flexible than in regular development settings, there is significant underspending on police institutions.

SUPPORTING LOCAL ACTION. Building counterterrorism capacity is one thing; developing an effective local strategy to fight terrorism is another. States requiring support to implement strategy can expect little of it from regional or international organizations. The international system has no standing or effective mechanisms to support police work in this area (or any other), or to support rule-of-law institutions in counterterrorism investigations. Nor does the international system have any mechanism that can serve as a repository of best practices and lessons learned, or of training in counterterrorism strategy and tactics. States can seek bilateral assistance—for example, the U.S. Federal Bureau of Investigation and the United Kingdom's Scotland Yard have occasionally loaned capacities to states to assist in specific investigations—but this can have costly political ramifications. There are two exceptions—but both within significant limits, as discussed previously—UNODC's work in helping states draft counterterrorism legislation, and the work of the Counterterrorism Executive Directorate of the Security Council in disseminating best practices on issues related to UN Security Resolution 1373.

CONSTRUCTING LEGAL AND REGULATORY FRAMEWORKS. In an attempt to dissuade actors from resorting to terrorism, the international community has, over the past four decades, promoted and adopted numerous legal instruments. Given the continuing lack of agreement on a comprehensive definition of terrorism, the approach has been to outlaw specific acts. The UN General Assembly and UN special agencies have adopted 16 international conventions, most of which criminalize specific acts of terrorism such as actions against certain means of transport or facilities, acts against specific categories of persons, hostage taking, use of certain substances or devices for terrorist purposes, financing of terrorist activities, and bombings, among others.[31] These conventions, supplemented by seven regional conventions, have laid an important foundation for setting global norms against international terrorism.

These measures are complemented by legal instruments that provide comprehensive measures against organized crime, in particular drug trafficking and money laundering, activities that are often connected with international terrorism. These conventions allow for international cooperation through, for example, extradition of drug traffickers and criminals and transfer of proceedings.

What has not occurred, however, is universal adherence by states to these treaties. Although accessions and ratifications to multilateral conventions have dramatically increased since 9/11, this is less a function of the U.S. global war on terrorism than of the fact that 9/11 put the threat squarely on the international agenda. Nevertheless, as of June 2004, approximately one-third of UN member states still had not ratified the two conventions (terrorist financing and terrorist bombings) that are key to international counterterrorism activities.[32] Moreover, little monitoring of state compliance with various treaty obligations takes place—a point to which we will return.

SUPPORTING TACTICAL COOPERATION—FINANCING AND LAW ENFORCEMENT. Since 9/11 perhaps the best organized, albeit informal, global cooperation has been in the area of financing and law enforcement. Interpol, for example, has undergone important changes to enhance its capacity to support police cooperation on counterterrorism. It now can issue notices to arrest suspected terrorists.[33] It has created a global database of suspected terrorists and developed a state-of-the-art global communications system. But many states lack the capacity to participate in this system, and others, concerned about leaks, are still reluctant to share sensitive information with Interpol and prefer bilateral cooperation.[34]

The G-8's Lyon-Roma Anticrime and Terrorism Group (Lyon-Roma), a group of experts established before 9/11 to link justice and interior ministry officials of the G-8, has emerged as a central actor, especially in fostering guidelines for security in travel and border controls. Working through this group, G-8 states have developed counterterrorism standards on a wide variety of law-enforcement and border-security issues, some of which were later adopted by UN bodies such as the International Civil Aviation Organization (ICAO). Rosand notes that Lyon-Roma has been successful in breaking down barriers to cooperation, including within governments.[35] This has become possible because the involvement of top national executives in the G-8 process creates incentives and mechanisms for collaborations within, among, and across governments.

Because participation in the G-8 and its subgroups is informal and flexible enough to allow a wide assortment of experts to participate, the G-8 has been able to produce concrete results more quickly than formal multilateral bodies. Its rotating presidency and lack of a secretariat, however, often impede the necessary follow-up to make such initiatives sustainable. And the G-8 also lacks broad legitimacy in the Global South.

The new sense of global cooperation against terrorism extends to the battle to prevent terrorist financing. Under pressure from the United States, the international financial institutions adopted antiterrorist standards and established a task force to promulgate them. Organized under the auspices of the OECD, the Financial Action Task Force (FATF) has developed a series of recommendations on terrorist financing and money laundering, and has pursued their adoption with substantial success. Even though FATF is housed at the OECD, it held far wider influence because it reviewed the financial vulnerabilities of all states and offered recommendations to improve weaknesses. The task force also made clear that it would publicize the weaknesses of the banking systems in those states that did not comply. Fearing that their banks might be blacklisted in international financial transactions, nations have moved to comply with FATF's recommendations. National regimes have improved radically, in turn creating a more effective international system to prevent the use of banking systems for terrorist financing. The most recent innovation is the Egmont Group, which is composed of national financial intelligence units. The group's objective is to increase the sharing of terrorist financing information and promote financial transparency.[36]

Broadly speaking, the impact of the FATF speaks to the effect that a few of the largest economies can have through the power of markets. Although the large economies have no formal authority to stipulate policy at a global level, their common actions can create an enormous incentive for compliance simply because the world needs access to their markets.

LINKING HUMAN RIGHTS AND COUNTERTERRORISM. Given a relationship between the denial of human rights and the support for and recruitment to terrorist organizations, the promotion of human rights and counterterrorism actions should be mutually reinforcing. But this is not always the case, because counterterrorism strategies can themselves negate human rights concerns. In addition, the weakness of the human rights regime itself can prevent symbiosis in this area.

The bulk of counterterrorism capacity training is undertaken bilaterally. Even when democracies supply such assistance, their counterterrorism support does not automatically emphasize human rights. Strategic issues frequently interfere. Several recipients of large increases in U.S. foreign assistance and counterterrorism support since 2001 have had very poor human rights records. As an example, U.S. assistance to Uzbekistan increased sharply after 2001, then decreased after the Andijan massacre in May 2005, when human rights abuses in Uzbekistan captured international attention.[37] Even more grounds for concern about human rights are rooted in the decision of the Shanghai Cooperation Organization (whose members are China, Russia, Kazakhstan, Kyrgyzstan, Tajikistan, and Uzbekistan—none exactly a bastion of human rights) to begin counterterrorism activities that include cooperation with Iran.

U.S. neglect of human rights considerations in its counterterrorism relationships with authoritarian regimes has seriously dented the nation's standing on human rights and democratization issues generally. But that is not to suggest that cooperating with authoritarian regimes on global counterterrorism is easy. One must often cooperate with regimes with poor human rights records, but the mere fact of doing so can reinforce perceptions that human rights and democratic standards are readily sacrificed on the altar of security. Both the United States and the international community must find a formula that allows them to sustain what seem to be contradictory policies—support for human rights and indigenous democratic movements and engagement with national authorities (sometimes authoritarian) against terrorism. The only way to manage such a dilemma is to be open about the contradictions and clear about the purposes, while recognizing that democracy must be internally driven and cannot be imposed.

This issue cannot be addressed abstractly but must be tackled in its most difficult context, the Middle East. Take Egypt—a leading Arab and Middle East state, a necessary partner in the pursuit of Middle East peace, and a forceful actor in many international forums including the United Nations, the African Union (AU), and the Nuclear Non-Proliferation Treaty—so much so that many of our international interlocutors believe that a G-16 will not have the desired impact on global issues unless Egypt is incorporated. Yet it is also a country where a lack of democratic freedoms has fueled support for the Muslim Brotherhood, a powerful network that crosses the Arab world and supports terrorist organizations both financially and politically. Efforts to push democratic reform from the outside, including the Bush administration's Greater Middle East Partnership Initiative, have had little impact on human rights or democratic reform within Egypt and have generated a backlash in Cairo against U.S. policy on counterterrorism and nonproliferation. The lesson? The only available strategy is a long-term approach that acknowledges the short-term tensions between stability and counterterrorism objectives and the long-term coincidence of those objectives with the principles of democratic reform and human rights. This strategy informs our proposals in chapter 10 for a regional stability mechanism in the broader Middle East that would marry stabilization objectives with economic and political reforms over the medium term.

Managing this dilemma would be easier if mechanisms and institutions to advance human rights and to counter terrorism were linked and reinforcing and if the entire regime that promotes human rights were strong. This is problematic not only from a human rights perspective but from a counterterrorism standpoint as well.

ENSURING COMPLIANCE. The Financial Action Task Force works because publicity about noncompliance can have huge financial costs that most governments and their private sectors are unwilling to bear. Few countries can afford for other financial institutions to shun their banking systems. Mechanisms to ensure compliance with other international standards on counterterrorism, however, are much more limited.

Also important is the UN Security Council's Counterterrorism Committee (CTC). States are required to report to the CTC on their compliance with its provisions. At its inception, the committee was hampered in carrying out its broad mandate, and had no ability to check on the quality or accuracy of these reports. After months of contentious negotiations among Security Council members and between the council and the UN Secretariat, however, the council established a more substantial body, the Counterterrorism Executive Directorate (CTED). The CTED is now staffed and authorized to conduct field visits to monitor member state compliance with Resolution 1373. This, of course, has a limited scope—the CTC can determine only that states have established the relevant legislation and mechanisms—not that they have fully implemented those measures.

A far more limited exception is a mandated two-year review of progress on the General Assembly counterterrorism strategy. In principle such a review could shine a spotlight on noncompliant states, but in practice the UN Secretary General has no resources and no powers for conducting the necessary investigations. It could be possible to examine progress at the level of international institutions, not at the state level, where the core responsibilities lie.

ENFORCEMENT. Even more problematic is the question of enforcement: If the Security Council were properly informed about state violation of agreed international standards, how should it enforce compliance?

In Libya, Sudan, and Afghanistan, the Security Council imposed sanctions in response to evidence of state support for terrorist organizations or direct involvement in terrorism action; in Libya and Sudan the sanctions were effective in helping to shift policy. Below this high threshold, however, the international system has no tools to encourage compliance, identify and name noncompliant states, or create even limited sanctions against states in sustained noncompliance. And this pertains only to the limited resolutions of the UN Security Council. The more comprehensive General Assembly strategy does not even refer to enforcement.

In theory, the CTC could publish the results of its reviews of state compliance, creating "name and shame" mechanisms. In practice, however, the CTC, working as it does on the basis of consensus, is unlikely to agree to such a step. A major gap exists, then, in the vital process of monitoring—a task for the new organization we propose later in this chapter.

THE USE OF FORCE. And what about the use of force as a counterterrorism tool? UN Security Council Resolution 1368 strongly condemned the 9/11 attacks and expressed the United Nations' solidarity with the United States, but it also specifically referred to Article 51, the UN Charter's provision for member state self-defense. In effect, the Security Council signaled that if the United States took military action in response to those attacks, the action would be justified by self-defense provisions and would have Security Council support. That might sound self-evident, but the combination of the UN resolution and the organization's engagement in helping to restore the Afghan government after the overthrow of the Taliban mean that, in effect, the United Nations established a precedent that affirms the legality and legitimacy of military response to a state that had harbored a terrorist group responsible for an attack.

Preempting a terrorist strike is a more complicated issue. Although Article 51 is silent on preemption, a widespread interpretation based on customary law argues that it gives states the right to act in self-defense to preempt an imminent attack. Especially because of the precedent set in Afghanistan, it would be reasonable to infer that using force against a state hosting a terrorist movement to preempt an imminent terrorist attack would be legal under the charter. The challenge comes in establishing a solid case for imminence, given the difficulties inherent in gathering and sharing intelligence and assessing terrorist organizations.

Far more divisive is the issue of preventive force, in which military means are used to disable a terrorist group's capacity to strike before the attack is imminent. The logic for such a strike, and for the Bush administration's adoption of the doctrine of preventive force in its 2002 national security strategy,[38] is rooted in two factors: (1) a terrorist organization that possesses a nuclear or biological device has the ability to inflict major harm, and (2) such groups may well not be susceptible to deterrence through the threat of a response. In light of these considerations, states may have real cause to act before the group is able to pose the imminent threat.

As we discussed in chapter 3, this is more problematic and difficult than it first appears. Rare are the circumstances when a military strike can be pinpointed against a specific individual or group. Rare also are those circumstances when such strikes are sufficient to claim a "victory" over terrorism. As we have seen in Iraq and Afghanistan, the fight against terrorist groups can draw outside actors into a sustained battle, and those struggles are usually far more complicated than simply a battle against terrorism. In Afghanistan the fight against the Taliban is entangled with narcotics, corruption, and poverty. In Iraq, the struggle against al Qaeda is secondary to an internal civil war. Even when force is relevant, it must be accompanied with support for building indigenous policing and counterterrorism capacity, and usually for building governance capacity as well. Success in such circumstances requires an international and local partnership, where there is internal political will to make the changes in governance needed to administer the rule of law and win the support of a nation's citizens.

In other words, force alone is not an effective means for combating terrorism. Surgical strikes against specific targets are rarely feasible and even more rarely definitive. When force is needed, it is usually not enough to make a difference in combating terrorism in the absence of a local capacity to enforce the rule of law.

FILLING GAPS: A NEW COUNTERTERRORISM BODY

The existing architecture, then, has some key gaps: inadequate mechanisms to assist states in building their capacity to meet counterterrorism objectives and requirements; few tools to support states in establishing and implementing local or subregional counterterrorism strategies; insufficient monitoring of and reporting on state compliance with treaty responsibilities; and no shared approach to penalizing states that do not comply with UNSC resolutions. These gaps in coverage, together with the rapid increase in counterterrorism efforts since 9/11, have led to growing calls for greater cooperation and enhanced synergies of effort.

Specifically, reformers are calling for the establishment of a more effective, more coherent counterterrorism organization.

In examining the weakness in counterterrorist structures and the coordination challenge, Sebastian Einsiedel and Eric Rosand note

> Despite the global threat that terrorism continues to pose and the increase in counterterrorist activity worldwide, this issue remains one of the few global, let alone security, issues that does not have a dedicated international body. The need to fill this lacuna has become more apparent with the continuation of terrorist attacks around the globe; the proliferation of counterterrorism programs and initiatives at the global, regional, and subregional levels and in different substantive areas since 9/11; and the UN's uneven performance in this field.[39]

Functions of a New Counterterrorism Organization

This idea takes more and less ambitious forms. At the less ambitious end, a new body could provide a forum for leading international players to collaborate on a range of counterterrorism issues, including efforts to reverse the growing radicalization and extremism that fuels Islamist terrorism, an issue for which no broad-based and effective forum exists. A new body could also serve as the focal point for coordinating counterterrorism technical assistance, a role that would help the international community make better use of the limited funds and expertise available. A new organization could improve coordination, cooperation, and information sharing among states and the different multilateral bodies engaged in counterterrorism. Finally, a new entity could set global counterterrorism standards in areas where none currently exist and identify and help correct vulnerabilities in countries at risk of becoming terrorist safe havens.[40]

At a more ambitious level, a new body could also oversee the implementation of the entire UN global counterterrorism framework and monitor state compliance with treaty commitments; identify noncompliers and—in extreme cases—propose action or sanctions; publish reports on persistent noncompliance, and/or refer noncompliant countries to the Security Council for appropriate action.[41] Such an entity would engage proactively with nongovernmental organizations (NGOs), give those

NGOs a mechanism through which to raise concerns and recommendations, take advantage of the decentralized networks of NGOs and their capacity to collect data, and ensure that human rights issues are made central to the counterterrorism agenda.

This more ambitious set of tasks would require adoption of a comprehensive counterterrorism convention, a document that has been stuck in UN legal debate for years—though one that could move forward if progress were made on the Israeli-Palestinian issue. In the short term, the prospects for a treaty as a basis for a new organization are dim, and efforts to strengthen capacity building and support for national efforts should not wait.

Such a body could be established inside or outside the United Nations. Creating a new body outside the United Nations might be easier if the intention is to have limited membership, but the costs would be substantial. For example, the new organization would be unlikely to have the legitimacy that the United Nations could confer or the ability to promote inclusive strategies among states that may not be willing to join a new body but have important roles to play in countering terrorism. A new body would also undermine the responsibility (and accountability) of the Security Council for dealing with threats to international peace and security.[42]

After weighing the pros and cons of different models, we conclude that the best prospect for effective change would be to move toward establishing a UN High Commissioner for Counterterrorism Capacity Building, modeled on the UNHCR. The G-16 could prenegotiate the major elements of such a body, and then bring the issue to the General Assembly for further negotiation and decision.

A high commission, functioning as a sort of halfway house between a UN Secretariat department and a stand-alone agency, would have several advantages. First, the commission's board would be available to all member states that demonstrate full compliance with all existing counterterrorism conventions and treaties and show evidence of their commitment to combating terrorism. This would create a self-selecting group of states committed to tackling terrorism, but the group would be based on standards, not ad hoc political criteria. As new conventions and treaties are passed, they could be added to the required elements for election to the high commission's governing board. Given the likelihood that this group would be politically, regionally, and religiously diverse, as well as a treaty-based UN body, its policies and capacities could command substantial legitimacy, especially within states uncomfortable with U.S.-backed counterterrorism strategy. And such an organization would be well placed to foster compliance with the General Assembly's strategy—and, more broadly—to encourage adoption of and compliance with UN counterterrorism conventions and treaties.

High commissions form part of the UN's regular budget, but they are governed by more efficient rules and systems than the secretariat per se. They also typically manage operational resources and programs more effectively. In short, they can (if well led) combine the best of predictable funding with efficient and flexible management.

And because high commissioners are senior UN appointees (at the undersecretary general level), identified by the secretary seneral but endorsed by the Governing Board, a UN high commissioner for counterterrorism capacity building would have the political weight within the UN system to coordinate efforts to build capacity, improve training, and coordinate with other UN and international bodies that are central to the counterterrorism agenda. The commissioner would also have the political standing to engage with the NGO community and would be able to assess NGO reports and findings, follow up on their recommendations, and translate them into effective programs.

The establishment of such an entity would mark a significant evolution in the traditionally ad hoc and largely improvisational response of multilateral bodies to global terrorism, particularly within the United Nations. It would signal an end to at least some of the institutional rivalries and divisions that have characterized much of the UN's program. It would also finally give the United Nations an institutional framework with the necessary political legitimacy and technical capacity to launch and implement a wide range of counterterrorism initiatives.

In addition, it would help to improve coordination and cooperation among the seventy or so different formal and informal bodies that now pursue counterterrorism.[43] The new entity could incorporate and rationalize some existing capacities. It would depoliticize and enhance the technical capacity-building focus of the current effort and, in doing so, give priority attention to those regions that lack the necessary institutional capacities to address the complex and evolving threat effectively. Finally, it would develop a more holistic approach to countering the threat—an approach that includes strategies for addressing terrorism's underlying conditions.

A CATALYTIC ROLE FOR A NEW G-16. If the United States took a lead role in reshaping the institutional counterterrorism architecture, it would go a long way toward reassuring other countries that its commitment to rebuilding international order is real. Supporting a new global counterterrorism body within the United Nations would clearly show such resolve, in addition to making the United States and others safer from terrorism.

Movement on this, however, cannot be delivered by the United States alone. Here, we see a catalytic role for the new G-16 that we proposed in chapter 3. As we see it, the G-16 would serve in part as a confidence-building forum, strengthened by its regionally balanced membership. It would build on the G-8's vitality in achieving tactical cooperation against terrorists, and it would address the political limitations on that cooperation. We propose that the G-16 establish "groups of responsibility" on specific issues to allow it to work with a broader set of engaged states. Terrorism is an issue that could well lend itself to such a forum.

Prenegotiations among the G-16 members on the parameters of a new high commission could establish a solid basis on which to enter General Assembly negotiations required for its creation. Broad agreement within the G-16 would help ensure that those negotiations would be fruitful, building support and legitimacy but not veering away from core requirements of effectiveness and efficiency.

CONCLUSION

G-16 initiatives can build on and extend both the reach and legitimacy of prior G-8 actions on counterterrorism. An international architecture that is both strengthened and streamlined can help to promote standards of responsibility in counterterrorism and to build national capacity and support local strategies.

The impact of these approaches, though, will depend in substantial part on the broader questions of promoting development and effective state capacity, as well as on the spread of human rights and democracy. We turn to these issues next: first examining the challenge of fostering the economic underpinnings of peace and security, and then by considering the issue of democracy promotion. In the last section of the book, we apply this examination to the broader Middle East, where the struggles among al Qaeda, more general forms of terrorism, and political reform have emerged as a central challenge for security in the United States and abroad.

NINE

STRENGTHENING THE PILLARS OF ECONOMIC SECURITY

IN THE AFTERMATH of the global depression of the 1930s and World War II, forty-four nations agreed to create the Bretton Woods institutions and the General Agreement on Tariffs and Trade (GATT) to promote economic stability and peace. As the principal architect of the Bretton Woods system, Harry Dexter White, put it, "The absence of a high degree of economic collaboration among the leading nations will . . . inevitably result in economic warfare that will be but the prelude and instigator of military warfare on an even vaster scale."[1]

More than sixty years later, the nature of international security threats may have changed, but White's premise still holds. Countering twenty-first-century security threats and promoting prosperity in the coming decades will require international cooperation and global institutions designed to sustain open yet stable systems of trade and finance, build resiliency to economic shocks, tackle the poverty that still traps billions of people, and ensure that the benefits of globalization are shared more equally.

Global institutions and the international cooperation they foster, though, must be geared to a new economic landscape. The rise of new economic powers—China, India, the Gulf States, Brazil, Mexico, and many countries across East Asia—has shifted patterns of capital concentration and natural resource consumption. With globalization and greater integration, volatility in the international financial and trade system is increasingly shared. As exemplified by the 2008 mortgage and financial crisis in the United States, economic calamity in a single sector or country can reverberate throughout the world, underscoring the need for effective oversight and regulation—not just at the national but also at the global level.

Countries that have taken advantage of the international trade and financial system have reaped vast benefits. Yet fear of instability and the impact of globalization on the competitiveness of domestic products and labor are giving rise to a tide of protectionism that threatens to block further progress on liberalizing trade. This is happening precisely when further gains in the international trading system would begin to make the benefits of globalization more accessible to the poor. Despite the booming global economy of the last decade, much of sub-Saharan Africa and substantial populations in the Middle East and West Asia have been left behind.[2] At the beginning of the twenty-first century, many countries are worse off—in absolute terms—than they were in the 1960s. Poverty in these countries remains a direct threat to their populations. Globally, 30,000 people die as a result of poverty *every day*.[3]

Moreover, the cyclical effects of poverty pose a direct and immediate challenge to global stability. Extreme poverty has been both cause and consequence of state weakness, undermining the basic unit of the international system.[4] Poverty can erode a state's ability to exercise good governance, undercut human capital, ignite grievances about inequalities, and challenge individual freedom and dignity. Poor and poorly governed states are the least able to safeguard the well-being of their own citizens and to fit cooperatively into a community of nations. Put another way, they are the least able to uphold the demands of responsible sovereignty.

Combating poverty and promoting well-governed states tied to a stable and prosperous global economy promises to become even more complex as resource scarcity, population growth, and climate change become more acute. The United Nations projects that the world's population will reach 10 billion by mid-century. Limited supplies of oil, food, water, land, energy, and "atmospheric space" to absorb carbon emissions mean that the world is poised for severe economic and social adjustment problems.[5] Already, food shortages caused unrest across dozens of countries in 2007 and 2008. Issues of scarcity and strategies for building resilience to those issues are likely to emerge as increasingly central to sustainable development.

Promoting and sustaining economic security will depend on four interconnected pillars: (1) a stable financial system; (2) an open and resilient trading system that benefits the poor; (3) more robust and effective delivery of international assistance; and (4) improved governance and democratic institutions.

These four pillars rely on one another for success. Globalization has resulted in record levels of wealth, but the international system needs mechanisms to ensure that the world's poor can take advantage of these possibilities. The international system must also be resilient to shocks and contagion that can undermine the progress of all. International aid is crucial to help countries build human capacity and infrastructure to tap into international markets. Aid will be wasted, though, unless recipients govern effectively, combat inequality, and become accountable to their citizens. The risks, opportunities, and accompanying responsibilities will need to be shared—among the public and private sectors, the major and rising powers, and the developing world.

RESPONSIBLE SOVEREIGNTY AND ECONOMIC SECURITY

The collapse of the Doha Development Round (the Doha Round, or Doha) of the World Trade Organization (WTO) in July 2008—the first failure of a major international trade negotiation since the 1930s—underscored the complexity of sustaining an international economic system where power is more diffuse, interests are more diverse, and the ties across economies are manifold and not always complementary. Similarly, the financial crisis of fall 2008 highlighted the interdependence of global credit markets and the risks of weak oversight. States need to move urgently to fill a void before ad hoc improvisation and protectionism make it more difficult to achieve global solutions that benefit both rich and poor nations. As indicated by the concept of responsible sovereignty, if economic instability is to be avoided and prosperity effectively promoted, states will need to take responsibility for the external effects of their domestic economic actions. Building on existing commitments within the International Monetary Fund (IMF) and the WTO, world leaders will need to articulate a new understanding of what it means to exercise economic sovereignty responsibly: new agreements will be needed to strengthen financial management at home, to build an open and inclusive international system of trade and finance that maximizes economic opportunity, and to boost the capacity of weak states to join in these arrangements. The United States will find itself in a new role— not just as a leader, but also as a participant, inviting scrutiny by other members.

Responsibility Begins at Home

The 2007–08 mortgage and financial crisis in the United States was a wake-up call that highlighted weaknesses in the U.S. domestic regulatory environment and underscored both the positive and negative side of a new global economy.[6] Some economists argued that the market boom in Asia and in other emerging countries built enough momentum that these economies can stave off the impacts of the U.S. crisis.[7] During our 2008 consultations in China, however, policymakers were increasingly concerned that China would be unable to insulate itself from the U.S. shock or find alternative markets if U.S. demand continued to diminish. In India in February 2008, local high-tech firms told us that slowdowns in the U.S. economy had shaken investor confidence in firms dependent on U.S. outsourcing. The financial crisis of September–October 2008 quickly and inevitably went global as banks failed across Europe, markets plunged in Asia, and Russia lost two-thirds of the value of its stock market. Around the world, major and rising powers have begun calling for an overhaul of the Bretton Woods institutions to create new mechanisms for oversight and accountability.

Add to the economic crisis deep structural weaknesses in our international economic system. Today's current account imbalances and those projected into the future may drive economic volatility on a scale not seen for decades.[8] Between 2000 and 2005, U.S. debt grew from 14 to 25 percent of gross domestic product (GDP), creating huge current account surpluses in Japan, China, and other Asian and European economies as well as in energy-exporting countries.[9] If the United States wants to reduce its dependence on and vulnerability to its creditors, it must take responsibility for national deficits and consumer spending. Holders of U.S. debt also carry a responsibility because deliberate undermining of the U.S. economy would undercut the largest single market for their products.

An evolving regime of responsible economic sovereignty will also require correcting well-intentioned mistakes, such as ethanol subsidies that contributed to the 2008 food crisis. Prices for staple foods like rice, corn, and wheat skyrocketed by more than 180 percent from 2005 to 2008.[10] Part of the problem was a drought that affected key producers such as Australia and Ukraine. Exacerbating the impacts were combined financial and social pressures—the global population burgeoned; climate change continued to shrink available agricultural land; meat consumption increased (also increasing feed-grain consumption) as income levels rose in emerging economies; protective tariffs diminished trade in food supplies; and energy prices soared, further increasing prices of food produced using mechanized agriculture. Although disputes continue about precise impacts, there is no doubt that U.S. subsidies for biofuels took land out of food production and worsened the global crisis. The poor—who spend a disproportionately large share of their income on food and water—felt the most profound impact.

The lesson for most of the world is not surprising. What happens in the U.S. economy matters. If the United States succeeds, the rest of the world is better off, yet other nations have few levers to influence U.S. policy. The global interest in effective U.S. oversight and regulation is evident. But it would be short-sighted to believe that the United States will be the sole source of globally significant crises. With new capital concentrations come new potential sources of vulnerability. The regulatory environment in emerging economies will soon become every bit as important as that in the United States. Stabilizing policies depends on national action, yet in most emerging economies the instruments to execute fiscal and monetary interventions are untested. Already, three of the largest six banks in the world are Chinese.[11] Japan is the only Asian state, however, that claims comparable monetary policy capacity to the United States. For the United States, then, effective global oversight of the international economic and financial system has a clear, long-term protective function.

One source of potential oversight is the IMF. The IMF has a broad surveillance role over stability of the international financial system, but its leverage to enforce its recommendations extends principally to borrowing states—and IMF lending was only $600 million globally for 2007, with loans extended primarily to poor countries.[12] Even in poor and transitioning states, the post-Soviet experience from the 1990s demonstrated that conditional loans cannot substitute for national consensus on sound economic policy. The global financial architecture, then, faces several challenges. There is a growing need for global pressure, scrutiny, and dialogue involving the major economies. Best practices that allow states to implement sound economic policies with a stabilizing impact globally must be shared. And at the same time, the sovereign rights of nation-states to develop and implement such policies must be respected.

Responsibility for International Order

The post–World War II economic system began with the GATT, grew into the WTO, and has been supported by monitoring and investments by the World Bank and the IMF. The Monterrey Consensus of 2002, discussed later in this chapter, established basic standards of state responsibility for combating poverty by setting out a bargain between developed and developing nations that matched policy reform with access to global markets for goods, technology, capital, and services. Specialized mechanisms like the Financial Action Task Force (FATF) have created guidelines to establish open and safe international banking systems. All of these mechanisms require that states commit to national legislation that abides by international rules to promote stability and predictability.

The consistent pattern of refining the rules for international trade and finance came to a halt with the crash of the Doha Round in mid-2008, raising the question of whether the international community has the political capacity to manage domestic transitions in economic competitiveness while sustaining global markets critical to economic prosperity. The fact that the Doha Round settled eighteen of the twenty topics on its agenda reflected the stakes.[13] Doha collapsed because of Indian and Chinese demands for agricultural safeguards, affirming that the international trade environment has fundamentally changed and the West can no longer single-handedly set the terms. As emerging countries acquire greater economic power and the capacity to block action, they must simultaneously take on greater responsibility, recognizing that a prosperous international economy serves their interests and may require compromise.

But the dominant lesson from the Doha experience is that if nations use trade policy to compensate for domestic structural weaknesses, such as inadequate education and poor safety nets, they will make decisions that hurt them domestically and internationally. First and foremost, national governments have a responsibility to their own citizens, but such responsibility requires that they understand the dynamics between national policy and global trends.

The challenge to our international trade architecture—despite Doha and perhaps especially after Doha—is how to forge rules and promote responsible behavior by all states that will keep the international system of economic governance open, dynamic, and resilient to short-term shocks.

The Responsibility to Build

Responsible sovereignty includes a "responsibility to build," which means encouraging the development of stable and well-governed states that can lift their populations out of poverty and serve as responsible stakeholders in the international system. An index of state weakness published in 2008 established that a substantial majority of the world's failed and critically weak states are the world's poorest.[14] Poverty undermines a state's ability to protect against environmental degradation, including deforestation—for example, burning firewood now accounts for 24 percent of global carbon dioxide emissions.[15] Poverty also contributes to the spread of diseases. According to the World Health Organization, low- and middle-income countries (LICs and MICs) suffer 90 percent of the world's disease burden, yet account for only 11 percent of health-care spending. Poor, weak, and lawless states—or underdeveloped and under-governed parts of middle-income states—become easy training grounds for terrorist groups and provide an environment ripe for the transnational crime that can finance terrorism.[16] Although there is as yet no such formally articulated responsibility, the developed world certainly has a long-term interest in building effective state capacity in the less developed world. Adopting a specific responsibility to this end could be warranted both in terms of that interest and as part of the bargaining about state responsibilities across issues that will be a necessary part of managing global threats.

The ability of countries to link to global trade and finance networks is vital for spurring development and combating poverty. In 1981, 64 percent of China's population lived on an income below a dollar a day; by 2001, that statistic was reduced to 17 percent—largely due to China's ties to the global economy. But rising inequality, the persistence of poverty, and a market that has left entire regions behind demonstrate that these systems alone are inadequate for achieving prosperity. To combat poverty, poor states need to adopt effective policies. Wealthy states need to help poor countries build better-functioning governments that allow them to participate effectively in global markets.

The international response to global poverty has reflected this dual responsibility. At the Millennium Assembly of the United Nations, held in New York in September 2000, delegates adopted eight Millennium Development Goals (MDGs). These goals committed the world to a series of targets including sharp cuts in poverty, disease, child mortality, and environmental degradation, along with improved maternal health care, education, and gender equity. The eighth goal represents a compact between rich and poor to achieve the first seven, calling for increased development assistance, debt relief, and trade liberalization.[17] Then in March 2002, world leaders met at the International Conference on Financing for Development in Monterrey, Mexico, and signed the Monterrey Consensus. Developed countries accepted responsibility for their side of the equation, committing to encourage private foreign direct investment and restating a long-standing UN target of 0.7 percent gross national product (GNP) for official development assistance (ODA).[18] Developing countries acknowledged their own responsibilities, and committed to improving performance on governance, human rights, corruption, and research and technology acquisition.

In recent years, the debate about antipoverty policies has often devolved into a false argument between disciples of the MDGs and followers of the Monterrey Consensus. Those focused on achieving the MDGs have been characterized as fixating on increased assistance flows as the silver bullet for poverty alleviation, and emphasizing the failure of the developed world to deliver aid. Their opponents have cited the Monterrey Consensus, often arguing that assistance will have little impact unless accompanied by policy reform in recipient countries. Trends of growth and inequality, however, suggest a more complex picture than just aid versus trade. The world economy and developing countries in particular have rarely grown faster than over the past two decades. The number of extremely poor (living on less than $1.25 a day) is 1.4 billion (one in four) in 2008 compared to 1.9 billion (one in two) in 1981. These data, though, show marked regional differences. Poverty in East Asia has fallen nearly 80 percent since 1981 but the poverty rate in sub-Saharan Africa remains unchanged at 50 percent.[19]

The need to use all tools strategically to combat poverty is clear. These tools include our four pillars: access to international capital through a stable financial system, access to an open and resilient trading system, effective and targeted ODA, and strong policies and governance in poor countries. Indeed, this assessment of economic security suggests that we need these pillars not just to fight poverty, but also to sustain a stable and prosperous world economy.

LESSONS FROM NATIONAL AND GLOBAL MARKETS

Establishing economic security in a transnational environment involves a continuous dynamic between national and global markets and the ways in which we govern both. Market access to global capital, technology, and labor (for producing goods) and to international markets (for selling those goods) has driven the success of wealthy nation-states (for example, the United States, the European Union, Japan); emerging economies (for example, China, India, Brazil); and energy-rich states (for example, the Persian Gulf, Russia). But these global markets also drive competition and potential disruptions that spark calls for protectionism and isolationism. Worse yet, the dynamic of growth sweeps by those who cannot access these markets and widens the gap between rich and poor. In this section, we assess the lessons from this dynamic between national policy and global markets to identify the areas where the international system can be stronger. This, in turn, reveals where we should target our efforts.

Financial Scrutiny and Targeted Investment

Even though the last two decades have been characterized by rapid and accelerating global growth, the world has also seen three crises driven by financial difficulties of a global nature—the fall 2008 global financial crisis; the Asian financial crisis of 1997, which spread to Russia and Latin America; and the 2001 burst of the dot-com bubble. Deregulation in the market has led to booming prosperity, but also to the spread of risk to corners of the market that were previously protected.

Many economists link future systemic crises to the unwinding of global economic imbalances—notably the U.S. current-account deficit—and the potentially devastating repercussions for the United States and the global economy. Those most concerned about global imbalances worry that the U.S. deficit will lead to a "sudden stop" of capital flows to the United States, in turn causing a significant sell-off of the dollar and a "hard landing" for the United States and the global economy.[20]

The international institutions charged with economic governance have not kept pace with today's volatile and integrated economy. Many of today's institutions must be reshaped to anticipate and address systemic financial risk and to encourage states to take responsibility for economic actions that reverberate throughout the global economic system. A system is required that combines regulation and early warning with incentives for dynamism and innovation. For the poorest countries, net financial flows from international institutions are declining, which means that the poor have less aid to help them access global capital markets.

Representation in international financial institutions also does not reflect the rise of new players in the global economy. By 2050, experts anticipate that global prosperity will be generated in large measure by industrializing countries, including India and China. By that time, the world's financial center may shift to Asia.[21] Economies in all stages of development will share a common interest in transparent and sound regulation. That includes the emerging economies, which must accept the intrusion of regulatory scrutiny to sustain their own economic growth. In turn, these emerging powers must be given a greater voice in economic governance—both in terms of "board" powers at the international financial institutions and in the selection of the leaders of those institutions.

UN Development Program (UNDP) Administrator Kemal Dervis has voiced this concern: "It does not seem right that Brazil and India have less of a vote in the boards of the IMF and the World Bank than very small European countries. . . . It does not seem right that the 'emerging South' still is allowed only a minor role in the big decisions on the top management positions in the international system."[22]

Ideally, IMF and World Bank member states will build on initial reform measures passed in April 2008 to give emerging and developing economies a greater voice and thus build confidence in greater scrutiny for the common good. If not, we can expect either emerging countries or regional blocs to create their own ad hoc governance mechanisms that exclude the current major powers. Without governance reform, the international financial institutions threaten to atrophy, with their relevance and influence undermined at the expense of all.

Global Trade and National Competitiveness

In the last two decades, global trade has emerged as a key engine of growth. For example, in fast-growing East Asia and the Pacific region, trade increased from 47 percent of GDP in 1990 to 87 percent in 2006.[23] Those who favor free trade view it as the key engine of world growth that spreads ideas, improves productivity, exploits economies of scale, and reduces poverty. But building an open and resilient trading system inevitably intersects with national politics on issues such as protection of subsidized sectors, job competition, and equity in labor and environmental regulations. Trade negotiations are inherently political, and development issues often take a back seat.

Globalization of labor markets has made the issues more complex; for example, a company's profitability does not necessarily secure employment within a country if that company can source labor offshore.[24] That has made protectionism increasingly tempting for leaders in the United States and Europe, responding to even a temporary loss of jobs among important domestic constituencies. In a volatile global economy, there is also a risk that countries will "race to the bottom" on tax rates and regulations to attract investment, creating the impression of unfair trade.[25] Conversely, rich countries place their highest tariffs on imports vital to developing countries, such as garments and agricultural products.

What is without dispute is that countries that have embraced aggressive export-led strategies have progressed. Globalization has given these countries unprecedented access to capital, technology, and markets. Exports of goods and services accounted for 38 percent of China's GDP in 2006, double the share of a decade earlier.[26] For India, once largely closed to the global economy, trade in goods and services as a proportion of the GDP has risen from 16 percent in 1990 and 1991 to 49 percent in 2006 and 2007.[27] In contrast, in oil-importing low-income African countries, exports of good and services in 2006 accounted for only 25 percent of GDP.[28]

The challenge for long-term economic security is to achieve a global trading system that includes the poor. But that is much easier said than done. The Doha Round, launched in November 2001, put developing countries' priorities at the center of the agenda for the first time in WTO negotiations. The fact that the Doha Round collapsed because India and China sought stronger protection for their farmers from import surges— surges most likely to come from Brazil or other emerging economies— underscores the risk of new protectionist coalitions even among those who have benefited most from an open global trade regime.[29]

Global markets mean global competition. That creates two types of tensions. The first is the immediate dislocation of national products and labor, whether textiles in the United States, or agricultural products in India, or assembly plants in China or Taiwan. The second is the pressure to continue to seek higher value added jobs to compensate for dislocation. That means not just shifting workers across sectors, but training them in new skills, which takes time and often requires geographic relocations. Stopping this process of transition would stymie innovation and growth. But ignoring the short-term costs will exacerbate gaps between rich and poor within countries and would be suicidal for politicians. In the future, if Doha succeeds or if there is a successor agreement, the tensions that caused this round to collapse will become only more acute as poor countries enter into competitive niches now dominated by China, India, and other emerging economies.

World Bank President Robert Zoellick has warned that if economic isolationism is not halted, we "will reap the losses, not the gains, of globalization."[30] If battling isolation turns into a proliferation of bilateral and regional deals with different terms across the globe, the race to the bottom we cautioned against earlier becomes even more likely. For international leaders, the inescapable ties between national and global markets and competitiveness will make trade the issue they most want to avoid, and for the viability of their economies, the one they can least afford to ignore.

Improving the Quality and Quantity of Aid

Combating global poverty cannot ignore the central importance of linking to global markets. Yet it will also require nuanced approaches that reflect the diverse realities facing the poor. Seventy percent of the world's poor (living on $2 a day or less) still reside in middle-income economies.[31]

Their plight reflects the unkind face of market-based growth—rising income inequality within states. Improved policies and responsive governance will be needed to narrow the gap between rich and poor.[32]

In both the quantity and quality of aid, the international community is not keeping pace with its commitments. Much larger and sustained increases in aid will be needed to reach the target of a $50 billion increase in real terms by 2010 that was set at the 2005 G-8 summit in Gleneagles, United Kingdom, to meet the MDGs. Total net ODA from Development Assistance Committee (DAC) donors was $103.7 billion in 2007, $15 billion higher than its 2004 (pre-Gleneagles) level, but total net ODA must reach $130 billion in 2010 to match the Gleneagles commitment.[33] Under the Monterrey Consensus, sixteen of twenty-two OECD donor nations have achieved or are on track with their commitments to 0.7 percent of GNP for development aid; six countries are not (Australia, Canada, Japan, New Zealand, Switzerland, and the United States).[34]

Many point to the United States as the largest missing element in financing the MDGs, almost half of the foreign assistance shortfall. If the United States spent just one-tenth of its defense budget on foreign aid, it would double its funding to fight poverty. The share of U.S. gross national product (GNP) devoted to helping the poor has declined for decades and is only a fraction of what the country has repeatedly promised.[35]

In addition, most ODA does not translate into funds available for projects and development programs. Aid flows are often used for special purposes such as debt relief, humanitarian and emergency spending, technical assistance costs (such as salaries for western workers in developing countries), administrative costs, and food aid. Net aid available for direct assistance to the poor (known as country programmable aid, or CPA) was $38 billion in 2005.[36] In these "real" terms, official aid dropped by 5.1 percent in 2005, the first decline since 1997. If CPA to Iraq and Afghanistan is excluded, net CPA was lower in 2005 than in 1985 in absolute terms. Sub-Saharan Africa is hardest hit by the gap between ODA and CPA. It received $12.1 billion in CPA in 2005—representing almost no increase over the preceding decades.[37]

Aid coordination mechanisms should be broadened to include emerging economy donors and to reflect private capital flows. The international aid system must also take better advantage of private capital flows and nontraditional players in poverty alleviation. Bilateral development assistance from countries such as China, India, Thailand, Turkey, and Brazil is growing and promises to change the international aid landscape. Private flows, from corporate partnerships to philanthropic activities, now amount to more than twice the level of global ODA. Warren Buffett's $37-billion donation in 2006 to the Bill and Melinda Gates Foundation enabled Gates to disburse more in grants than the U.S. Millennium Challenge Corporation (MCC) disbursed in the same year.[38]

Finally, there is the challenge of donor governance. With a proliferation of new public and private development actors, there has also been a growing fragmentation of aid. The amount of aid passing through new bilateral donors, NGOs, and new corporate philanthropists now is higher than through traditional official channels.[39] Multilateral aid agencies (around 230) now outnumber donors and recipients combined.[40] Each of these aid providers pursues its own focus areas, goals, and constituencies, resulting in an enormous coordination burden on recipient countries. On the ground, development agencies often hire away the best local personnel with the offer of high salaries, and valuable government time and limited capacity is wasted coordinating multiple donor requirements. The Paris Declaration on Aid Effectiveness by the Organization for Economic Cooperation and Development (OECD) in 2005 sought to improve the harmonization of aid, but gains have been muted by an increasingly complex and crowded development landscape.

Governance, Politics, and Cycles of Poverty

The Commission for Africa, comprising African and international experts convened by Tony Blair, emphasized in a 2005 report to the G-8 that the way states function is increasingly seen as one of the most important factors affecting development in the poorest countries. Paul Collier cites poor governance as the greatest challenge that must be overcome to pull the bottom billion out of poverty.[41] Achieving the MDGs will require governments that can deliver services to their citizens, protect human rights, and spur economic development. Good governance is essential for creating the policies that address inequality and stabilize fragile and failed states. Sound governance is also necessary for managing shocks and external pressures, such as climate change and scarcity issues, that can interrupt economic growth and threaten stability.

During the cold war, the United States spent huge sums wooing partners such as Sudan, Zaire, Somalia, the Philippines, and Egypt with little sustainable development impact. In 2008, the Democratic Republic of the Congo (formerly Zaire), Sudan, and Somalia may represent the most acute sources of instability in Africa. The lesson is clear: resources spent in bad policy environments are wasted, and may further entrench elites, corrupt practices, and languishing performances. As Larry Diamond stresses, it is the natural tendency of elites everywhere to monopolize power rather than restrain it.[42] Once they consolidate power, uncontested elites limit economic competition to benefit themselves instead of society at large.[43] Pledging resources to these states often only reinforces bad behavior.

Nearly 30 percent of all people in extreme poverty live in fragile states.[44] By 2015, extreme poverty in these countries is projected to increase by more than 50 percent (from the 1990 percentage).[45] Fragile states with weak governance, sometimes plagued by conflict, present perhaps the biggest conundrum in development. By definition, these states do not have the governance capacity necessary to meet the needs of their people, attract private investment, and tap into global markets. Aid supplied in this context can be wasted. Yet withholding assistance from poor states until they govern effectively is a recipe for continued poverty. These states need help to change their performance. To sustain progress, that support must build local capability.

Studies of the impact of governance on development conclude that countries can derive a very large "development dividend" from better governance.[46] A country that improves its governance from a relatively low to an average level could almost triple per capita income in the long term and similarly reduce infant mortality and illiteracy.[47] Sub-Saharan Africa, after averaging no annual per capita growth between 1970 and 2000, has begun to grow at about 5 percent annually, driven by countries that have embraced good governance, instilled stronger macroeconomic management, and in turn received significant debt relief.

The relationship between democracy and development is also strong, in part because democracies encourage accountability and good governance. Although some have questioned whether authoritarian states such as China, Singapore, and now Vietnam offer an alternative political path for developing countries, democracies generally perform better than autocracies.[48] Better governance helps in the fight against poverty and improves living standards. Research by the World Bank Group's Worldwide Governance Indicators Project over the past decade demonstrates that improved governance encourages development, not the other way around. When governance is improved by one standard deviation, infant mortality declines by two-thirds and incomes rise threefold. Good governance has also been found to enhance the overall effectiveness of development assistance.[49]

From a different perspective, autocracies that govern well—in particular those that uphold the rule of law, enforce contracts, and allow markets to drive their economies—can sustain economic growth, but they are the exception rather than the rule. Based on the Weak States Index, 60 percent of critically weak states in the world are ranked by Freedom House as "not free." As states move up the ladder toward greater state stability, more countries are democratic—80 percent of developing and emerging economies in the top quintile of state stability are ranked as "free" and just 3 percent as "not free."[50] For authoritarian regimes, the attraction of the so-called "China model" is the desire to maintain political control. To follow the China model, however, most authoritarian regimes would need to liberalize their economies, increase competition, enforce the rule of law, and prosecute corruption. As China and Singapore have begun to experience, over time there are real tensions between liberal markets and restricted politics.

As understanding has grown about the links among economic performance, good governance, and democracy, both official and nongovernmental donors have integrated support for good governance with development assistance. Traditional aid donors such as the United States Agency for International Development (USAID), European agencies such as the UK Department for International Development (DFID) and the UNDP provide more than $1 billion per year for good governance assistance.[51] Hundreds of international NGOs, foundations, and private companies have entered the democracy promotion business.

Many regional and international organizations also make democracy assistance a core component of their work. Through UNDP and the UN Electoral Affairs division, the United Nations has supported democratic transitions in the majority of the more than ninety countries that have emerged as democracies since 1974. The Community of Democracies

(CD), an intergovernmental organization comprising more than 100 democracies and democratizing countries, affirmed in its 2007 *Bamako Ministerial Consensus on Democracy, Development and Poverty Reduction* the importance of strengthening democratic governance "as an essential means to reduce poverty and support equitable and sustainable development."[52] In July 2005, then-Secretary General Kofi Annan announced the establishment of a UN Democracy Fund, an idea first articulated by President George W. Bush in 2004 and now embraced by 141 nations. The Partnership for Democratic Governance (PDG), a new project housed at OECD, with support from UNDP, the OAS, and OECD's thirty members, helps democratizing countries find certified assistance providers that employ international best practices.

Still, developing countries and donors are learning how to incorporate democracy and governance assistance into effective development strategies, as illustrated by both the success and the limitations of the MCC. The MCC invests in "compacts" with developing countries that achieve performance targets across independent and transparent policy indicators related to governance such as ruling justly, investing in people, and encouraging economic freedom.[53] The prospect of major, multiyear funding commitments is intended to increase the incentive for countries to improve performance. The MCC's limitation is that it excludes developing countries with weak governance that cannot meet the eligibility criteria.

A related issue is the challenge of promoting governance reform in conflict-affected states, particularly in postconflict states that require investments in building indigenous security structures. As we noted in chapter 7, the international development system is poorly organized, and in some cases has little capacity to support the development of effective police forces, the rule of law, and democratic oversight of security systems. Without basic security and prospects for political stability, investment and economic development lag. Among the challenges is that the international guidelines for development spending, developed by the OECD, limit counting security sector reform as part of a government's 0.7 percent commitment to ODA. In addition, many donor countries, such as the United States, have legal limitations on using development aid to reform civilian security systems even if they are fundamental to the rule of law.

Even more complex is the political climate to support democracy. Democracy promotion has become mired in political division. U.S. rhetoric and action in Iraq, more than any other single factor, has led to a conflation of democracy promotion with violent and unilateral regime change. Many countries believe that international interventions to assist democracy are a breach of national sovereignty. Others point to U.S. violations of the Convention against Torture and Other Cruel, Inhuman or Degrading Treatment or Punishment (at Guantánamo Bay and Abu Ghraib), or to selective U.S. support for election results (rejecting Hamas in the Palestinian territories), or even to mixed signals on support for democratic movements (in Egypt). These critics deduce that for the United States, global efforts to combat international terrorism take precedence over democracy and human rights. In this climate, many Europeans and other donors often avoid programs to support democracy. If they undertake such programs, they prefer relatively technical and "safe" interventions on governance, such as reforming public services and helping to draw up budgets.

The roles of good governance and democracy in eradicating poverty and building international stability and prosperity will put responsible sovereignty to the test. Pursuing both serves nation-states well. Authoritarian leaders may desire neither. Regional and international actors are most secure when states are well governed and democratic. Yet without the cooperation of authoritarian and often poor leaders, assistance and progress may not be sustainable. Perhaps at one point leaving such states to fail might have seemed plausible. In an interconnected world, the consequences are too severe.

MOVING FORWARD TOWARD GLOBAL ECONOMIC SECURITY

Global economic security defies a simple grand solution. As we argue in this chapter, it depends on four pillars: a stable financial system; an open and resilient trading system that benefits the poor; more robust and effective delivery of international assistance; and improved governance and democratic institutions. If states commit to responsible sovereignty in order to strengthen these pillars, they will create the conditions for global economic growth and stability.

The G-16 can be an asset in this endeavor, even if it often operates in smaller "groups of responsibility." The G-16's engagement within international financial institutions, the UN, and the WTO can help create patterns of cooperation that build confidence. In many weak states or states at risk of failing where policy change is needed, many of the emerging economies among the G-16 often have stronger trade relationships than western donors through which influence can be wielded.

Leadership and Coherence

To enhance leadership and coherence among and within nations, we recommend creating a focal point for a sustained and coherent agenda on economic prosperity. No such focal point currently exists. Some of the tools to promote prosperity lie within the UN system, some outside. UN leadership on prosperity issues would logically fall to its Economic and Social Council (ECOSOC), just as the UN Security Council is the preeminent body on security issues. But when we consulted with representatives of advanced and developing economies alike, the mention of ECOSOC usually provoked disdain. We found no donor country that supported a strong ECOSOC role. In the developing world, views were similar, except that representatives from developing countries did not want to say so on the record. Although the logical step would be to advocate abolishing ECOSOC, doing so would immediately raise the diplomatic ire of developing countries who would argue that they have little voice in the international financial institutions (IFIs) and that they would lose the one body where they have a voice, however negligible its influence.

Complicating the picture are innumerable parallel bodies that have a stake in tracking and guiding international economic policy.[54] No one entity assesses the collective impact of policies and practices by institutions, donors, and emerging and developing economies on trade, finance, and development. The proliferation of functions across agencies has intensified without a strong magnet to bring the system together—a central body for consolidating the multiple efforts to reduce poverty.

To establish such a body, which we call a "Center of Excellence for Economic Prosperity," we recommend using the 2010 summit on the MDGs as a target for action. Well in advance of the summit, the UN secretary general and the president of the World Bank should propose and create the center, with members appointed by the heads of the World

Bank, IMF, UNDP, WTO, OECD, UNICEF, and DESA. Networks should be created with top research institutions around the globe to draw on their expertise. The UN secretary general and the president of the World Bank would appoint a prominent international figure to head the center, supported by a secretariat seconded from participating institutions. Although the center would *operate* independently, analogous to how a central bank develops and assesses monetary policy, it would not be able to *set policy* independently—a major and significant restraint.

The Center of Excellence would assess and consolidate recommendations on research and analysis conducted by the wide range of actors on finance, trade, and development. It would present points of consensus; identify causal trends in poverty eradication; assess interrelationships among trade, finance, and development measures in specific countries; investigate pressures and remedies for protectionism; call attention to vulnerable nations and economic trends; and consolidate indicators of both donor and recipient performance. The center would also consolidate the vast array of existing performance reports on MDGs and financing into a "poverty clock," a concept proposed by our Brookings colleague Homi Kharas to show how overall poverty rates change over time within individual countries and regions.[55] The clock could also track changes in inputs and policies—for example, changes in ODA flows, investment trends, new technologies, trade patterns, and governance practices—to develop data-driven recommendations on the tools needed in particular countries and regions for poverty alleviation.

The center's work would be debated at the annual meetings of the IMF and World Bank. This is the right forum, with all of the world's leaders on finance and development. A special session would be needed to include civic organizations. Findings would feed into the 2010 Millennium Summit, which would look ahead to the final five years in which the MDGs must be achieved.

There are certainly reasons for skepticism. For example, even though the Intergovernmental Panel on Climate Change (IPCC) helped forge consensus on global warming, consensus on problems and remedies becomes more difficult as we stray farther from hard science. But the current track of competing analyses with neither a forum nor mechanisms to forge consensus is destined to create further divides.

In the sections that follow, we give our recommendations for strengthening each of the four pillars of economic security.

Pillar One: A Stable Financial System

The goal of the international financial system should be to promote stability and provide predictability, transparency, and skilled management when crises emerge. In the 1990s, emerging markets were the major cause of shocks, but in 2008 they were an important source of capital and stability. For the future, risks are greatest in countries and regions that have large capital concentrations, limited oversight, and limited capacity or experience in managing financial crises, such as parts of Asia and the Middle East. To get greater international oversight and scrutiny in vulnerable areas, countries will seek a reciprocal voice in governing international economic institutions. For poor nations, the challenge is one of access and capacity. In the following recommendations, we see the G-16 or relevant subsets coordinating strategies and tactics within the IMF and the World Bank, producing proposals that can be brought to the executive directors of these institutions for consensus.

REFOCUS THE IMF. The IMF must be retooled to provide surveillance, early warning, and crisis management and to build the capacity to work with rich and poor governments on financial sector reform. Greater IMF scrutiny must include transparent and independent surveillance over the policies of emerging economies with limited experience in managing financial crises and regulation, as well as the United States, Europe, Japan, and other systemically significant countries. The IMF would be the repository for global best practices on financial management, setting standards and reporting on how countries regulate and manage financial institutions and markets.

When global financial crises loom, the IMF should ideally play a preventive role, alerting the international community to the weaknesses in the system before a full-blown crisis unfolds. By sparking dialogue, conducting in-depth analyses, and carrying out independent assessments, the IMF can serve as an "honest broker" among countries facing a crisis and issue recommendations based on best practice. In addition, the IMF should continue its work to lead regional and international negotiations on ensuring that global imbalances even out while sustaining global stability and growth.

TARGET WORLD BANK INVESTMENTS. Mandated to assist poor countries left behind by the global economy, the World Bank's traditional leadership role in global development has eroded. The World Bank could improve its operational effectiveness by building relationships with other donors, including emerging donors like China and private donors. The Bank should also refocus on its relative advantage: promoting inclusive and sustainable globalization, particularly by helping developing countries link to the global economy. In addition, the Bank should help emerging economies bridge the divide between rich and poor within their own borders. On climate change, its role will be critical—sharing the cost differential for clean technologies with emerging economies, investing in energy infrastructure in poor countries, and helping countries invest in adaptation strategies.

The Bank has also taken on an important role in helping countries recover from conflict. World Bank President Robert Zoellick listed assisting conflict-affected countries as one of the Bank's six top priorities. The bank has developed effective relationships with the United Nations in conflict settings, particularly through its partnership with the UN Development Group (UNDG) and the World Bank/UNDG postconflict needs assessment process. In addition, the Bank has cooperated increasingly with the UN Peacebuilding Support Office and the UN Department of Peacekeeping Operations to link recovery and development strategies. The Bank should now take the next step to increase its effectiveness in conflict zones by rapidly deploying resident missions with conflict expertise that have the authority to oversee and act on trust funds and accelerate loan applications.

WIDEN REPRESENTATION IN ECONOMIC GOVERNANCE. The legitimacy and effectiveness of the IMF and the World Bank will depend on their ability to reflect the interests of emerging and developing economies as capital balances shift away from the United States and Europe.[56] This is also in the interest of traditional economic powers, which will benefit from stronger oversight that includes these new and influential economies.

In April 2008, the IMF adjusted the formula by which it allocates votes and financial contributions according to economic size, reserves, and other measures. The shares of votes from emerging economies, however, still do not match their economic and political weight and the old power pattern still dictates the top jobs—the World Bank is run by an American, and the IMF by a European. To incorporate future changes in relative economic power, the IMF needs a rebalancing formula, which must be viable for the long-term governance of the IMF.[57] Similarly, the World Bank's legitimacy has been undermined by an outdated distribution of shares, votes, and chairs. The Bank should give stronger voice and more votes to its key clients (developing countries) and new donor countries, while simultaneously maintaining a lead role for major donors.

One way forward, suggested by Brookings colleagues Colin Bradford and Johannes Linn, would be a "grand bargain." First, the United States would give up its veto right at the IMF and the World Bank in exchange for the Europeans giving up shares, votes, and chairs. The U.S. veto in both institutions has become anachronistic. If wielded, the veto would likely undermine rather than advance broader U.S. interests.[58] European shares would be reallocated to emerging and developing countries, particularly in Asia. Second, say Bradford and Linn, the United States and Europe should give up their lock on the leadership of the two institutions. The Europeans have signaled their willingness to relinquish the IMF's managing director position, but are loath to take the first step. To complete such a package, all shareholders would accept the kind of scrutiny proposed earlier in this section as part of the IMF's redefined role.

ENGINEER A FINANCIAL "SOFT BALANCING." The explosion in U.S. borrowing poses risks to competitiveness and economic security. The crisis scenario is a hard landing: investors dump dollar assets, the Federal Reserve is forced to raise interest rates, and global growth is curtailed. A policy of just "leaving it to the markets" is risky. We defer to scores of economists on how to reintroduce incentives for savings and fiscal responsibility to the U.S. economy. As a national security matter, though, President Obama should encourage markets and currencies toward a soft balancing to unravel the massive debt the United States has accumulated with its international creditors. Within the United States, this means curtailing demand. Internationally it must involve negotiations with China and its regional trading partners in East Asia on exchange rate policies. Simply revaluing the Chinese currency will shift deficits within Asia.[59] To manage the discussions, the parties need an honest broker; this should be the first test for the IMF's role as a sponsor of regional negotiations.

Pillar Two: An Open and Resilient Trading System

The 2008 collapse of the Doha Round underscored how national politics constrains international trade negotiations. Major progress on the international trade agenda is not likely before 2010, after elections in the United States (November 2008) and India (May 2009) and the appointment of a new European Commission (late 2009). Still, the world's trading powers need to start setting the tone now to sustain an impetus for a future global trade agreement. The fundamental goal—an open and inclusive trading system that benefits the poor—remains critical. To succeed, that system must help countries attend to painful internal transitions in competitiveness.

SUSTAIN THE COMMITMENT TO A GLOBAL TRADE AGREEMENT. The shock that emanated from Doha's collapse and the efforts made to avoid its failure reflect a latent understanding of the need to bring poor countries into the global trade regime. Some will argue that key players such as the United States and Brazil should refocus attention on regional and bilateral agreements. Although there is a compelling short-term logic for doing so, there is also a risk of diverting attention from a wider global agenda. The proliferation of bilateral deals has made trade agreements harder to negotiate and enforce. Moreover, the very transnational problems on agricultural subsidies and industrial protection that have thwarted a global agreement will continue to prevail bilaterally and regionally. To those contending that the Doha Round is permanently dead, the best counterpoint would be to demonstrate continued demand for a global agreement to address transnational issues that defy bilateral solutions.[60]

The progress made in the 2008 negotiations should not be lost. WTO Director General Pascal Lamy should publish the eighteen (of twenty) trade areas that were agreed on during the negotiations.[61] Even if they have no formal legal standing, these eighteen points should be the starting point for new negotiations to avoid retreading old ground. And even if some states then back away from the eighteen points, better to establish clarity going into the next round and to force states to explain any departures from agreed positions.

The principal trading partners—starting with a G-16 subgroup of trade ministers from the United States, the European Union, India, Brazil, and China—must make clear that they expect new trade negotiations by 2010. They must not leave room for speculation. Because these countries will shape the nature of the trading regime, they should create a process to commission research and policy options on the issues that have blocked consensus. They should look ahead to new areas and potential problems, not the least of which is climate change, where border adjustments for carbon content could unleash a new wave of protectionism.

President Obama should also seek ratification of pending bilateral trade deals with Colombia, Panama, and South Korea. That may seem contradictory with a focus on global agreements, but having gained commitments from others to open themselves to U.S. exports, the United States would be well served to pass these agreements. Korea has endured massive protests against U.S. beef. Colombia is gaining control over narcotics traffickers and guerrillas and needs markets for legitimate products. A Panama FTA would help to build on a long-standing strategic military and commercial relationship. U.S. credibility in leading future trade negotiations would be shattered if it will not stand by agreements negotiated to its benefit.

MAKE TRADE ADJUSTMENT ASSISTANCE A NATIONAL AND INTERNATIONAL PRIORITY. Recent studies have shown that trade is not always to blame for the loss of jobs: 90 percent of U.S. manufacturing job losses result from companies that shed workers as they become more technologically advanced.[62] But even if trade is wrongly blamed for displacement, transition is socially painful and politically lethal, affecting workers globally as countries move through niches of competitiveness. The major trading economies should put this issue squarely on the international agenda.

If it were already formed, this would be an ideal topic for the Center of Excellence for Economic Prosperity. Given time lags, the heads of the WTO, the World Bank, and the IMF should establish a special commission to examine the cyclical impacts of trade on displaced workers, extract lessons for effective trade adjustment assistance programs around the world, recommend best practices for national action, and propose potential international mechanisms to help countries manage such transitions. G-16 trade and finance ministers should strongly support this step and call for discussions at the IMF and World Bank annual meetings. The commission might assess, for example, whether the World Bank Group's Multilateral Investment Guarantee Agency (MIGA) could guarantee loan facilities for businesses absorbing displaced workers. If global trade negotiations reconvene formally in 2010 as we propose, trade adjustment measures should be part of the agenda.

Within the United States, the Obama administration must retool the Trade Adjustment Assistance (TAA) programs (administered by the U.S. Department of Labor's Employment and Training Administration), whose benefits do not adequately support either the transition to new jobs or the costs of those transitions.[63] For displaced workers, for example, income support at $260 per week is below the poverty line; out-of-pocket expenses for health care are, on average, double the benefit; and job search and relocation allowances cannot exceed $1,250.[64] In building a case for free trade, the president and Congress will also need to propose measures to expand education and training, increase income and health benefits during transitions, increase job search and relocation allowances, and compensate more significantly for permanent salary differentials.

OFFER TRADE FOR DEVELOPMENT. A comprehensive trade policy for development could include providing duty-free, quota-free market access for all the least developed countries and simplifying various regional programs by bringing them all under one umbrella. Such a program could build on the lessons of the African Growth and Opportunity Act (AGOA, first signed into law in 2000), but should avoid AGOA's greatest shortfall: because oil accounts for nearly 90 percent of all African exports to the United States, the program's benefits accrue to only a subset of African countries.[65] U.S. policymakers might be concerned about the impact of this type of initiative on U.S. producers. But if duty-free, quota-free access is extended to all the least developed countries, the impact on U.S. production of textiles, apparel, and sugar, for example, is likely to be a revenue reduction of less than 1 percent.[66] A trade-for-development program could also focus on promoting "aid for trade," which helps countries address "behind-the-border" constraints on their capacity to exploit trade opportunities. Aid for trade could be particularly helpful for the least developed countries, most of which are in Africa and face poor trade-related infrastructure and customs services.[67]

Pillar Three: Effective International Assistance to Alleviate Poverty

Having argued that international aid alone is insufficient to help countries emerge from poverty, we turn now to the challenge—how to structure international assistance so that flows are adequate and well targeted to contribute to effective results when countries govern competently. The focus of these recommendations is to sustain scrutiny and focus on both the quantity and quality of aid, ensuring that it will help nations build the capacity to link to international markets for trade and finance.

DEVISE NATIONAL DEVELOPMENT STRATEGIES. Documented poverty reduction strategies are central to effective development. These country-owned strategies, often written as position papers, organize donors around specific objectives and ensure that their assistance is tailored to a particular country's challenges. These national strategies are also essential for developing country-based plans to achieve the MDGs. In 2007, 13 percent of the least developed countries were deemed to have effective operational frameworks. Another 67 percent had taken significant action to create them.[68] Where a national strategy does not exist, national governments should co-chair a consultative process with the UN resident representative and the appropriate World Bank country director to form one.[69]

MEET FUNDING COMMITMENTS. As discussed previously, CPA has declined when Afghanistan and Iraq are excluded. This particularly hurts a region like sub-Saharan Africa, where international assistance accounts for about two-thirds of all capital inflows.

A Center of Excellence for Economic Prosperity should establish the definitive view of donor performance. As a first step, the center should focus on CPA, increasing the global total from $38 billion in 2005 to $60 billion by 2010. The amount of CPA going to sub-Saharan Africa should double from current levels, rising to $30 billion. The second step is to use the combined tools of a recipient peer review and the Center of Excellence to achieve—by 2015—the bargain struck under the Monterrey Consensus: transparent progress on policy reforms met with donor support at 0.7 percent of their GNP. Underpinning both these steps must be the IFI reforms that we discussed earlier in this chapter, particularly those recommended for the World Bank, as well as improved governance within poor countries to stimulate trade and investment. Progress must be assessed as a package—how aid, markets, and national policies work together.

DOUBLE U.S. FOREIGN AID AND IMPROVE ITS EFFECTIVENESS. The United States can help restore its international reputation by acting on long-held values—combating global poverty and inequality, assisting in establishing democracy, and protecting human rights and dignity. The Bush administration's fiscal year 2009 budget request included $38.3 billion to fund the civilian-side foreign affairs and foreign aid budget.[70] In comparison, the President asked for $515 billion for the Department of Defense's core budget, before factoring in the cost of waging war in Iraq and Afghanistan.[71] The United States is also tied for last out of the 22 donor nations of the Organization for Economic Cooperation and Development (OECD) in terms of international aid as a percentage of gross national product.[72]

By committing to double the U.S. civilian foreign affairs budget by the end of a first term in 2012, President Obama would demonstrate that civilian—not military—tools are the primary means with which to build a secure and prosperous international community. He could elevate the nation's "development arsenal" to the level of diplomacy and defense, promoting a more effective, efficient, and well-resourced USAID along with a better resourced and staffed Department of State.

A doubling of funding alone is necessary but not sufficient. Decades of development experience have illustrated that a diverse toolbox—which includes trade, aid, political incentives, and security—is necessary to alleviate poverty. The new administration must also better coordinate development efforts among U.S. agencies. The innovative MCC, which targets countries that demonstrate progress on objective indicators, holds promise to get greater resources to good performers. But that approach is irrelevant for fragile states. For those states, the priority is tackling critical obstacles to governance and the rule of law.

To build its own capacity, the United States must invest in a stronger on-the-ground presence in developing countries. Ambassadors must be held accountable for the coherence of development aid proposals coming from their posts. Country teams must integrate assistance, policy, and diplomacy to drive both growth and sustainability. In Washington, coherence must be restored among the twenty-two government agencies that furnish some form of foreign aid. In many cases, this may mean simply stopping some agencies from engaging in well-meaning but marginal programs. Most radically, President Obama should propose to Congress a partnership to rewrite the Foreign Assistance Act to restructure the accounts that fracture the allocation of assistance.

FOSTER DONOR COHERENCE. UNDP and the World Bank should deepen their work to produce self-regulatory guidelines to help all donors coordinate in the field, including to the nongovernmental community. Using the UNDP and the World Bank for this process makes sense because both organizations have country missions around the world and have worked together to create tools for jointly assessing country needs and strategic plans. The objectives should be to ensure that external assistance supports national development strategies, to reduce the drain on host governments pressured to work out strategies with tens (if not hundreds) of official and nongovernmental donors, and to stop the exodus of talented personnel from public and private jobs in developing countries to donor agencies.

A donor coherence process should give impetus from the top and build on experience from the ground. As with overall leadership on economic policy, ECOSOC would logically launch such a process, but it lacks international credibility. Instead, the UNDP and the World Bank would pick a cross-regional subset of fifteen countries and ask country missions to convene all official and nongovernmental donors, along with the host governments, to garner recommendations based on practical experience. The United Nations would contribute lessons from its initial experience to build a "one UN" process, but if it is to have an impact, the exercise must go beyond the United Nations. The goal would be to issue guidelines by 2010 that official and nongovernmental donors and aid recipients would commit to uphold.

Pillar Four: Strengthening Governance and Democratic Institutions

Supporting good governance and democracy presents an inherent tension between national commitment and international action. The issue is not with poor states committed to governing accountably. For them, mechanisms exist to invest in governance—through international institutions (UNDP, the World Bank, OECD); bilateral donors (USAID, MCC, and most European aid agencies); and scores of NGOs and semi-independent organizations. The challenge is with states that are poorly governed and have weak institutions, especially states facing internal conflict. Examples include Burma, Cambodia, Zimbabwe, Guinea, Sudan, Congo, Haiti, and Chad. Focusing on this group, our goals should be to change the incentives that drive those who wield power, whether in or out of government, to put national interest over personal gain; to build local capacity in key sectors, especially the rule of law and civilian security services that can leverage wider systemic change; and to change misperceptions of democracy as externally imposed.

STRENGTHEN MECHANISMS FOR REGIONAL ACCOUNTABILITY AND MEDIATION. Regional organizations are well placed to avoid debates about infringements on sovereignty and generally more familiar with regional security, economic, and political challenges. The African Union, the Organization of American States (OAS), the European Union, and the North Atlantic Treaty Organization (NATO) have adopted good governance and democratic norms in their membership criteria, establishing an indigenous base for accountability. Neighbors may try to avoid criticizing others that might return the scrutiny, which hampered the old Organization of African Unity. But change is possible. The African Union's proactive stance in Kenya after election fraud in 2008 may have averted a wider crisis. The AU split over Zimbabwe's stolen election and South Africa's weak stance were disappointing, but the African Union did not give up, seeking a renewed political process in Zimbabwe. In Burma, the relatively weak Association of Southeast Asian Nations (ASEAN) helped open doors so that the United Nations and NGOs could provide humanitarian relief. Regional organizations should recognize their critical roles and receive international support where necessary.

WIDEN REGIONAL AND INTERNATIONAL PEER REVIEWS. The European Union has a transparent and ongoing review process for current and new members. African countries moved in this direction when they created the New Partnership for Africa's Development (NEPAD) in 2001. The partnership's rationale was that African states had to create a foundation for good governance and a means to monitor and drive their commitments. The partnership launched the African Peer Review Mechanism (APRM), which initiates periodic reviews of participating governments in the areas of democracy and political governance, economic governance and management, corporate governance, and socioeconomic development. Fellow Africans conduct the review, which is overseen by a panel of eminent African leaders. The process is not ideal—sometimes too slow and not sufficiently incisive—but it is a start toward accountability.

The principle of "neighbor influence" should extend internationally. Africans have an opportunity to lead the process by setting an example of intensified scrutiny. NEPAD could join with the African Development Bank, the UNDP, and the World Bank to create an international cadre of peer reviewers, including representatives from academic and civic organizations. Other regional organizations, starting with the European Union and OAS, could be invited to join. A peer review process will give recalcitrant states less room to claim that they are being subjected to "external values."

CONSOLIDATE AND EXTEND EXPERTISE. There is no lack of international institutions that assess international performance on governance and democracy. The World Bank Institute and Transparency International, for example, set out well-respected ratings on corruption. And Freedom House and the Bertelsmann Foundation publish annual performance reports on governance and democracy for all countries.

But a consolidation of experience, lessons, and standards on governance and democratic practices is not so readily available. A base has been established at the PDG, whose association with the OECD, the UNDP, and several regional organizations provides a useful foundation for expansion. To build credibility, it is necessary to bring in the African Union and partners from developing countries. The International Institute for Democracy and Electoral Assistance (IDEA), an intergovernmental organization specializing in democratic institutions and processes, should also be drawn into the network. To help transfer expertise, the PDG should create a formal financial relationship with the UN Democracy Fund, thereby tapping into its capacity to reach a wide range of UN members. If the OECD, which houses the PDG, can sustain such a broad network, it can set a useful precedent for OECD outreach beyond its high-income membership.

STRENGTHEN SUPPORT FOR GOVERNANCE IN POSTCONFLICT STATES. As we argued in chapter 7, fragile and failed states require security assistance combined with support for the rule of law, governance, and political transition. The experience of UN peacekeeping and peacebuilding missions offers many lessons. The UNDP should lead in addressing governance in such transitional situations. It is uniquely placed to bridge in two directions—to the UN's Department of Peacekeeping Operations for peacekeeping and police functions, and to the World Bank and other development organizations to make the transition from stabilizing a country after an emergency to building indigenous institutions. Especially given the central role of police in creating the legal conditions for economic development, OECD guidelines should be changed to count support for indigenous police as ODA.

REFRAME THE DEMOCRACY AGENDA. The Universal Declaration of Human Rights, which is part of the founding documentation of the United Nations, remains the strongest international statement on democratic practice. It has been echoed in other declarations, conventions, and covenants produced by the United Nations. Rooting advocacy for democracy in the Universal Declaration of Human Rights will reaffirm to the world at large that these rights are not "imported concepts." And there are indeed receptive audiences. Despite the recent backlash against how the United States promotes democracy, most of the world still covets democratic government.[73] That gives the Obama administration an opportunity to reframe an agenda on democracy and good governance. First, though, the new administration must restore the reputation of the United States in the eyes of the world and commit to working through international institutions. This includes embracing the Geneva Conventions, rejecting the use of torture, and closing Guantánamo.

The biggest challenge to giving democracy a central place in foreign policy comes in the broader Middle East, a theme we address in more detail in chapter 10. It is a difficult and complicated agenda, and can be managed only if nations acknowledge that advocating democracy and dealing with authoritarian regimes must coexist. Democracy, by definition, cannot be imposed and must come from within a nation. For democratic forces to develop, they must have some political space in which to operate. At the same time, nations must engage these authoritarian regimes on issues where the state is critical: counterterrorism, peace in the Middle East, energy supplies, and regional security. Politically, the only way to cope with such an agenda is to drop pronouncements about good and evil, and acknowledge that we must work in a world of gray transitions.

Operationally, greater sophistication is needed to promote democracy. A starting point is to recognize that effective democracy depends on checks and balances among branches and levels of government, and between government and civil society. It requires a legal framework to guide the rule of law. The state must hold a monopoly on the use of force, which means that de facto militias should be banned from the political process. Participants in the political process must commit to succession through electoral means to avoid the phenomenon of "one person, one vote, one time." If all these pieces are not in place, elections may not deliver democratic results and should potentially be deferred while other aspects of the political process are built.

CONCLUSION

The past two decades have demonstrated both the potential and the risks of globalization. Its positive side is the innovation and prosperity made possible by global access to ideas, capital, labor, and technology. The negative side is that mistakes reverberate around the globe, potentially bringing down governments and causing extreme dislocation.

Leadership will be imperative to continue to build a more stable and prosperous global economy on a number of fronts—from the United States, given the scale of its economy and because it drives most global imbalances; from the G-16 leaders, because they must sustain an open and inclusive trading system; from emerging economies, because their willingness to open their markets to scrutiny will build confidence in areas of vulnerability; and from developing countries themselves because poverty cannot be eradicated for them. The Monterrey Consensus started with the premise of a governance partnership between developed and developing countries: "We commit ourselves to sound policies, good governance at all levels and the rule of law."[74] That sense of partnership, a key to the concept of responsible sovereignty, is fundamental to a shared commitment on mobilizing trade, financing, debt relief, assistance flows, and technical cooperation.

Now the stakes are higher than even in 2000, when the UN Millennium Declaration resolved that "The central challenge we face today is to ensure that globalization becomes a positive force for all the world's people."[75] The gap between those who tap into the positive forces of globalization and those who are left out promises to grow wider, forming two vectors moving at divergent angles and differing speeds. No formula for closing that gap will work unless the world's major powers take the initiative, form the partnerships, and build the systems necessary to bring prosperity to all.

The same combination of U.S. leadership and robust cooperation with the major and rising powers is foundational to the broader order we envision in this book. Financial crises will be a test of that order, perhaps providing an impetus for action. We turn in Part III to another immediate challenge that can either derail international security and prosperity or galvanize new action toward it—the interlocking crises in the broader Middle East. We conclude by highlighting the urgency of this vision.

PART **III**

ORDER

TEN

THE HARDEST CASE

THE BROADER MIDDLE EAST

THE THREATS DESCRIBED in earlier chapters are real and mounting, but nowhere are they more acute than in the broader Middle East.[1] From the Lebanese, Syrian, and Israeli-Palestinian crises to Iraq, Iran, Afghanistan, and Pakistan, security challenges in the region have systemic implications. The threats run the gamut from interstate and internal conflict to transnational terrorism and nuclear proliferation. Spillovers from the region's turmoil—and from the deep unpopularity of U.S. policy there—have destabilizing impacts across Asia, Europe, and the Horn of Africa as well as on the global economy. In short, the region is a case study of the mix of transnational threats that challenge the global security system. This chapter addresses how a new approach to regional security based on the concept of responsible sovereignty can advance peace and security in the Middle East.

The United States remains an indispensable player in any regional or international strategy to orchestrate a regionwide, cross-issue diplomatic offensive to underpin and sustain regional stability. Having tried unilateral approaches in Iraq and having neglected political mediation in the Israeli-Palestinian conflict for most of the George W. Bush administration, U.S. policy must now shift toward sustained and predictable international cooperation. Inasmuch as all countries in the neighborhood will find it in their interests to settle the region's conflicts, end terrorism, and create an environment for economic growth, all will need to make political compromises to achieve sustainable outcomes. To take that risk, they must believe that the United States will remain engaged. U.S. core interests in Israeli security and energy security will remain central to that engagement, but a wider framework and broader consultation in shaping U.S. policy and posture in the region will pay dividends in greater burden sharing and new diplomatic opportunities.

Other international actors—particularly the United Nations, the European powers, Russia, India, China, and key Muslim and Arab states—also are crucial. Their political leverage, resources, and security forces are vital to any effort to help stabilize Iraq and Afghanistan, find solutions in Iran, and make progress on the Israeli-Palestinian conflict. Although these states have divergent interests in the broader Middle East, they share a long-term interest in stabilization and in containing nuclear proliferation and terrorism. And even though none can compete for influence with the United States, each can help search for solutions— or, conversely, hinder their attainment. The United States must leverage these states' interest in stability.

Progress in the Middle East would reverberate throughout the world. During consultations with government leaders in India, China, Latin America, East Asia, and Europe, we were told repeatedly that the Middle East is central to tensions over international security. Many governments abhor Washington's Middle East policy. Concerns about unilateralism often reflect distress about the limited diplomacy and lack of consultation that have characterized U.S. policy in the Middle East. The flip side of a more consultative U.S. strategy is that neighbors and major powers will need to join forces with the United States in forging stable solutions, not simply take heart in watching the United States reap the consequences of its policy failures.

Iraq policy is one potential beneficiary of a more consultative U.S. strategy. The United States will need support within the region if it hopes to produce a reliably secure environment in Iraq. The substantial decline in violence during the winter of 2007–08 must now be perpetuated. Whatever credit for the lull is given to the U.S. military surge, consolidating the relative peace will require the "diplomatic surge" recommended by the Baker-Hamilton study of the war.[2] Absent that effort, Iraqi political institutions are unlikely to recover sufficiently to sustain peace. The surge must involve engagement with Iraq's neighbors, who have the ability to reinforce or undermine any political progress.

If a diplomatic surge in Iraq produces enhanced regional engagement, the United States could use the opportunity to lay the groundwork for a regional security arrangement in the broader Middle East that could begin to create mechanisms to reinforce stability and incentives for political reform within the region. Global institutions like the United Nations have proven better at responding to crises in the Middle East than at preventing their outbreak. Better ways must be found to promote peaceful change and prevent the region from becoming a flash point for conflict between major powers. That will require not just the crisis-management capabilities of the United Nations and other global bodies but also investment in a regional architecture capable of guaranteeing long-term stability.

In other words, the process of consolidating security can become something more: a start toward elaborating the kind of responsible sovereignty that can produce lasting stability and prosperity. Nowhere does the prospect of order based on a nation's responsibility toward its own people and its neighbors seem more distant, but nowhere is investment in a combination of regional institutions and security arrangements that can serve that goal more essential.

If Iraq needs a diplomatic surge, Afghanistan will require a coordinated political, developmental, and security-stabilizing surge if international policy there is to succeed. That will of necessity involve the North Atlantic Treaty Organization (NATO) and the United Nations. Afghanistan will likely be an early focus of the Obama administration, a proving ground for new relationships, and an important test of the emerging capacity of multilateral institutions to handle hard cases.

Across our consultations, we found that multilateral organizations are judged primarily by their performance on the hardest cases. From the standpoint of evaluation, such judgments are misleading, and from a normative standpoint, they are unfair. But from the political perspective, they are a fact of life. A strong UN peacekeeping performance in Burundi or Sierra Leone matters greatly in humanitarian terms and in terms of African security, but it does not affect political support in Washington or Brussels or Cairo. By contrast, the performance of the United Nations or NATO in a hard case like Lebanon or Afghanistan does affect political support. In the years ahead, proponents of a strong multilateral system will have to demonstrate that reforming and investing in multilateral institutions creates the capacity to deliver results on hard cases. Including ourselves in this admonition, we focus in this chapter on how the recommendations that we set out in this book can contribute to a more stable regional order in the broader Middle East

DIMENSIONS OF THE CONTEMPORARY CRISIS

In the immediate aftermath of 9/11, the United States enjoyed a moment of unrivaled, even unquestioned supremacy in the broader Middle East as well as broad international support for the war against al Qaeda. States like Syria cooperated with the United States in the counterintelligence effort against al Qaeda, and Iran cooperated in the effort to stabilize Afghanistan after the Bonn Accords. The rapid destruction of the Taliban put al Qaeda on the defensive and served as a compelling demonstration of U.S. power and resolve. The moment brought with it hope for resolution of the Israeli-Palestinian conflict, and it encouraged renewed diplomacy, notably in the form of a "vision statement" from President George W. Bush. That statement was later endorsed in the road map to peace agreed by the diplomatic Quartet (the United States, the UN Secretary General, the European Union, and Russia) and by two UN Security Council resolutions.[3]

That support was ruptured, however, by regional and international reaction to the war in Iraq and to the subsequent U.S. occupation. The fallout from Iraq, combined with cooler U.S. attitudes toward Egypt and Saudi Arabia after 9/11, created a tectonic shift in the Middle East—and not in the direction of the "new Middle East" imagined by the Bush administration in early 2004. Instead, by 2006 the entire region had become ensnared in a multifaceted crisis.

A Regional Conflict in the Making

At the core of the region's crisis is a struggle to survive or profit from the reordering of the regional balance of power that resulted from the U.S. overthrow of Saddam Hussein's regime. Iran and the United States are the two actors most able to gain in regional influence from that reordering, and the outcome has enormous implications for Saudi Arabia, Egypt, and others, to say nothing of Iraqi citizens. Much of the current dynamic of conflict in the region is linked to efforts by U.S.-allied or Iran-allied forces to gain the upper hand in political as well as military terms. Taken as a whole, the region's crises potentially pit the United States, Israel, and Sunni governments against Iran and its regional allies.

Although Iran began the post-9/11 period by cooperating with the United States in Afghanistan, it also continued a clandestine nuclear enrichment program, in violation of the Nuclear Non-Proliferation Treaty (NPT)—a move understood in the region as a step toward developing its capacity to produce nuclear weapons.[4] Iran's initial motives for continuing enrichment even when it had been brought to the attention of the International Atomic Energy Agency (IAEA) and the UN Security Council may have been defensive: President Bush had denounced Iran along with Iraq and North Korea as a member of the "axis of evil." In addition, the country then watched the United States overthrow the other non-nuclear member of that club and encamp on its own border. The election of President Mahmoud Ahmadinejad amplified tensions, especially with his threats of genocide toward Israel. As the United States became bogged down in Iraq, Iran's strategy evolved into a broader play to tie down the United States and challenge its regional power. That move was evident in Iraq, where Iran augmented its support to Shia insurgents, political parties, and government officials and in Afghanistan, where the Iranian Revolutionary Guard began supplying operational support to a resurgent Taliban. Iran also provided operational support to Hezbollah in the buildup that culminated in the Israel-Hezbollah war in 2006 and increased its support to Damascus-based factions of Palestinian Islamic Jihad and Palestinian Hamas.[5]

The connections between these groups and Iran have led analysts to describe the region in terms of a mounting Sunni/Shiite split or, as some have argued, a Shiite resurgence that seeks to transcend old Arab nationalist networks and has put the region's Sunni elites—including America's most important Arab allies—on the defensive.[6] There is much to that assessment, although the region also now hosts important alliances of convenience, notably an anti-American alliance that cuts through sectarian divides. Such an alliance is visible, for example, in Sunni al Qaeda's support for Shia Hezbollah's struggle for power against Western-backed political parties in Lebanon.

By 2006 Saudi Arabia and other Sunni governments were attempting to mount a cross-regional alliance against Iran and its substate allies, even to the point of tacit cooperation with Israel.[7] As they had done immediately after 9/11, the region's Sunni states, notably Saudi Arabia, raised the prospect of normalization with Israel after a fair settlement to the Israeli-Palestinian crisis. The most concrete of those indicators included Riyadh's restating its peace initiative and participating alongside Israel at a diplomatic conference in Annapolis, Maryland, in November 2007.

These protoalliances were complicated, however, by the fallout from Iraq. Saudi Arabia may have seen the geopolitical wisdom of shoring up its U.S. alliance to counter Iran, but it also had to contend with the domestic unpopularity of that position. The Saudis' decision to invite President Ahmadinejad to participate in the Hajj in Mecca in December 2007, a month after the Annapolis meeting, illustrated the complexity of their situation.

Turkey, too, found itself torn between its strategic relationship with the United States and concerns about instability emanating from Iraq. Popular support for the United States in Turkey eroded in the lead-up to the Iraq War, resulting in the decision to refuse the United States permission to use Turkish territory as a base for attacks on Iraq. Tensions heightened in July 2007, when Turkey stationed masses of troops along the Iraq border, and escalated five months later when Ankara staged a series of limited cross-border raids against members of the Kurdistan Workers Party (PKK) inside Iraq. Washington forestalled any further deterioration of its Turkish alliance and kept the fighting in check by backing the inviolability of Turkey's border with Iraq.

In Lebanon, Afghanistan, and—in a different sense—Pakistan, tactical alliances were forming to challenge U.S. forces and U.S.-backed governments. They took form in Iran's support for Hezbollah and the Taliban but had a broader, popular base.[8] In the fall of 2008 the most worrying aspect was the mounting political and security crisis in western Pakistan and its implications for Afghanistan. With the Taliban given a safe haven in the frontier areas of Pakistan, cross-border disruptions have continued unabated, not only calling into question Pakistan's own strategy for controlling terrorists but also eclipsing the capacity of both the United Nations and NATO to gain traction in their support for a viable Afghan government.

A Nuclear Proliferation Crisis

The regional crisis links to broader international security issues in several dimensions—beginning with the regional nuclear proliferation crisis. In March 2006, the IAEA reported Iran to the UN Security Council after concluding that Iran's enrichment program had violated the nonproliferation treaty. The November 2007 U.S. National Intelligence Estimate (NIE) concluded that Iran had suspended its nuclear weapons program, yet Iran continues to develop its capacity to enrich uranium. In 2006 Iran rejected a proposal from the P5+1 (China, France, Russia, the United States, and the United Kingdom, plus Germany) to provide Iran with guaranteed fuel supplies, calling into question why Iran seeks enrichment capacity.[9] Even though Iran began to make overtures toward diplomatic engagement in mid-2008, few in the region doubt that the country has nuclear weapons ambitions.

The widely perceived Iranian nuclear threat is driving the entire Middle East and North Africa toward a dangerous nuclear race.[10] Iran, Saudi Arabia, Bahrain, United Arab Emirates (UAE), Yemen, Syria, Jordan, Egypt, Tunisia, Libya, Algeria, Morocco, and Turkey already have some form of civilian nuclear program or have declared their intent to start one.[11] Should Iran acquire a nuclear weapon, there is little doubt that others will try to follow, creating a new form of regional competition among nuclear powers that will make the nuclear tensions between India and Pakistan pale in comparison.

A Terrorist Threat

Containing the terrorist threat from the region has been a driving force in U.S. policy since 9/11. Arguably, however, the singular focus on terrorism has been counterproductive. Although preventing the emergence of a more virulent terrorist threat has been a core goal of policy, in some cases the outcome has been the strengthening of terrorist organizations and their backers in the region.

Part of the problem with U.S. counterterrorism policy in the broader Middle East has been its failure to understand and act on the principal threats facing countries in the region. The United States underestimated the resiliency of the Taliban and al Qaeda in Afghanistan and diverted attention, troops, and resources from its attempt to stabilize the country when it began the war in Iraq. The United States ignored Turkey's concerns over the PKK almost until too late, coming to the brink of letting another front open in Kurdistan, the one part of Iraq that showed promise of stabilizing.[12] In Lebanon, the United States has not worked out a strategy to counter Hezbollah's dominance in the south and, increasingly, in national politics. In these cases, by ignoring the biggest threats to countries in the region, the United States inevitably lost support for its counterterrorism priorities.

Conversely, the fixation on terrorism in relations with Pakistan produced few sustainable results during Pervez Musharraf's presidency. The political rebuke to Musharraf's party in the February 2008 parliamentary elections demonstrated how deeply he had alienated Pakistan's moderates, and the resentment toward Musharraf carried through to the United States.[13] In turn, Pakistan's new government has distanced itself from Musharraf's counterterrorism strategy in the frontier areas with Afghanistan, facilitating the resurgence of the Taliban and al Qaeda in Afghanistan, along the Afghanistan–Pakistan border, and in Pakistan itself. Another collapse in Afghanistan would pose a serious threat, but nothing like the dangers of substantial destabilization in Pakistan, a nuclear-armed state that borders Afghanistan, India, China, and Iran.

In the West Bank and Gaza, Hamas has strengthened its operations through cooperation with Damascus-based groups backed by Iranians and its political position through the absence of a viable political process and the economic collapse that followed Israel's withdrawal from Gaza in the summer of 2005. In Lebanon, Hezbollah quickly recovered from its 2006 war with Israel. The terrorist presence in the Levant is of a different type, more deeply grounded in national politics, than the more explicitly international terrorist presence in the Gulf, although connections between the two are growing.

As elaborated in chapter 8, the crisis in Iraq has fueled a broad process of radicalization across the region, serving as a seedbed for terrorist organizations and as an incentive for disaffected Muslims around the world to join them. From a global perspective, Middle Eastern tensions and the U.S. role in fueling or not resolving those tensions—particularly as a result of the Iraq War and the Bush administration's refusal to engage in political negotiations on the Israeli-Palestinian conflict until 2007—have stalled efforts to develop a more robust counterterrorism architecture. The cooperation of Muslim-majority states is crucial to the effectiveness of any international initiative to combat terrorism, yet those who have cooperated with the United States have seen little gain. Conversely, closer ties with the United States in fighting terrorism have become associated with the worst of U.S. policy failures and lapses in the Muslim world, creating political liabilities for leaders seen as allied with the United States.

Economic Risk and Opportunity

Record-level global energy prices through September 2008, followed by massive price volatility, have the potential for seismic socioeconomic and political ramifications that have yet to play out. Unprecedented wealth combined with economic inequality within and between countries is already creating political expectations among winners and resentment on the part of those who see few changes in their lives.[14] Some parts of the Middle East have become hubs of vibrant economic activity as oil increased from $27.69 per barrel on average in 2003 to more than $140 per barrel in 2008, only to fall to about $60 per barrel when the global recession collapsed consumer demand. Saudi Arabia, for example, saw its gross domestic product (GDP) increase by well over $130 billion, and according to International Monetary Fund data, per capita GDP in Qatar surpassed $70,000, the third-highest amount in the world.[15] Energy-rich states now must face unaccustomed budget constraints.

Although economic, social, and political reform has often accompanied economic growth in other parts of the developing world, many Middle Eastern countries have seen few changes.[16] Income inequality remains severe in many Middle Eastern states. Policies to promote more inclusive and sustainable growth have been thwarted by the power of authoritarian rulers. Reform measures threaten business elites, who have ties to the politically powerful.[17] Oil income has historically reinforced authoritarianism, making it easier to buy off dissent and centralize authority.

The region is also on the precipice of a significant demographic shift. In 2008, 37.1 percent of the population of the Arab world was under fifteen years of age. As those youths enter the job market in the next two decades, they will demand 80 million new jobs.[18] That demand is set against the backdrop of currently increasing unemployment—in the Middle East, youth unemployment rates are nearly twice the world average.[19] Resources from diminished oil wealth could help manage the demographic boom, but centralized government power means that benefits go to only a few. Moreover, if the global recession becomes protracted, oil wealth may not be able to keep pace with the pressures a young population places on social services and labor markets. The combination of elite power, increasing inequality, and a burgeoning youth population is a recipe for volatility in a region central to the maintenance of global energy supplies and critical to the stability of the international financial system.

There is still a chance that stability will prevail. If the region is able to capitalize on its wealth, manage the accompanying financial risks, and put sound social policies in place, it could find itself in an era of opportunity. A positive outcome requires simultaneous political, social, and economic reform. That includes political change to nurture competition and accountability, check corruption, manage inequality, and promote political freedom. It includes economic reform to promote investment in stagnant economies and to diversify the economy in energy-dependent ones. The right development policies now could pave the way for prosperity and stability in the Middle East.[20]

A Diplomatic Crisis

The deepening crisis in the Middle East and the perceived ineptness of the United States in dealing with security in the region has eroded U.S. diplomatic standing in the region and around the world. Historically, the region's governments and people have had two attitudes about the United States—they have resented its dominance but relied on the umbrella of security that it provides. The U.S. misadventure in Iraq, Iran's ascendance in the aftermath, and U.S. neglect of the Palestinian issue all contribute to a rising sense that the United States is powerful but not politically competent and certainly not powerful enough to secure an unstable region. That worst-of-all-worlds perception leads the regions' governments to adopt a self-help posture (for example, the pursuit of nuclear programs) and to dabble in anti-U.S. rhetoric and dealmaking. At present, only the threat posed by Iran is keeping traditional U.S. alliances together and then only weakly. Beyond the region, the unpopularity of U.S. policy is complicating diplomatic support for U.S. policy goals across a range of issues.

A Conflict on Energy Politics in the Making

The Middle East is the focus of a growing contest among the United States, China, and India for energy resources and relationships with energy suppliers. The United States remains the region's dominant customer and hegemon. But increasing Chinese investment in Iran and Sudan and Indian efforts to gain access to Middle East oil and gas—the source of 75 percent of its energy imports—show the potential for tension among major powers about the politics of energy relationships.

Oil and natural gas in the Middle East are produced almost exclusively by state-owned companies. When China, India, and the United States invest in energy production in the region, it is as a partner with a local company. Those investments add to the global supply of oil and gas, although physical limitations restrict the number of markets that gas can reach (liquefied natural gas markets eventually will change that). In principle, all energy importers benefit from investments that increase global supply. It is a misperception that foreign investors "lock up" such supplies. Instead, seen from the U.S. perspective, the point of political tension lies in China's and India's relationships with energy suppliers such as Iran and Sudan; seen from the international perspective, it lies in U.S. relationships with Saudi Arabia and other Gulf states. These commercial interests have complicated attempts, for example, to forge a common international stance against Iran's nuclear weapons program or to deploy peacekeepers in Darfur.

The second issue is one of energy wealth and pure volatility. Until the recent collapse, astronomical oil prices accorded Iran and other countries throughout the Middle East a new degree of global influence in politics and economics. Such wealth allowed Iran to resist international calls for transparency in its nuclear program. It made Middle Eastern sovereign wealth funds into global financial players, affecting the viability even of venerable Wall Street financial institutions. Residual wealth could still give the energy-producing nations of the Gulf a unique role in climate change. If they use their wealth to invest in alternatives to fossil fuels, they can create the foundations to diversify their own economic growth. Conversely, if they oppose policies to price carbon as part of a global climate change strategy, they can complicate already difficult negotiations on a new international agreement.

THE CASE FOR U.S. ENGAGEMENT AND POLICY SHIFT

No U.S. president can avoid engagement in the Middle East. Presidents William J. Clinton and George W. Bush both ended their tenures by launching personal diplomatic initiatives on the Israeli-Palestinian track. Although the Clinton administration had been involved in the Middle East peace process from its earliest days, Clinton's personal initiative at Camp David was launched too late to bear fruit. Bush's 2007 Annapolis initiative will suffer the same fate. President Obama would do well not to wait. Not only has U.S. standing been damaged by the country's Middle East policy, but left unchecked the region's interlocking crises have the potential to undermine relations between the United States and other major powers with interests in the region—particularly Russia, India, and China—and to erode existing global security regimes, especially in the areas of nonproliferation and terrorism.

During consultations for this project, we often found that calls for a U.S. return to multilateralism reflected a desire to see the United States return to diplomacy in the Middle East—specifically, to engage in direct negotiations with Iran and commit to a serious Israeli-Palestinian peace process. The widespread support for the November 2007 Annapolis meeting illustrated the potential diplomatic gains from an active U.S. policy. Failure to change perceptions of U.S. neglect on issues critical to Muslims (the Palestinian question, local terrorist threats, and economic development) and of U.S. incompetence on others (Iraq and Afghanistan) would leave the United States handcuffed in a region where its interests are enormous. Popular distress has made it difficult or impossible for even democratic governments in the region to align themselves with U.S. policy, not just on crises like Iran but on the broader questions of terrorism and proliferation.[21]

Of course, the Middle East is a graveyard of well-meaning diplomatic initiatives. Fortunately, few if any leaders in the region or beyond view immediate progress as a condition for support. Instead they are looking for evidence of *sustained* commitment. The elements of that commitment are in place. As mentioned, the United States remains the pivotal actor in the region. It would gain important credibility and leverage if it could demonstrate bipartisan support for a long-term strategy. And although there have been important discontinuities between Democratic and

Republican policies in the region, we argue that there are also important continuities, especially on the Israeli-Palestinian track.

Like the Annapolis process, engagement on the Middle East peace process should be embedded in a regional strategy. The Israeli-Palestinian crisis is interconnected with many others, including instability in Lebanon. There can be no solution in Lebanon that leaves out Israel and Syria; no agreement with Syria that does not involve the regional management of Iraq; no regional management of Iraq without resolving the question of Iran's ambitions, and so forth. The development of a broad regional view and regional engagement on the interlocking crises in the Middle East will be critical to conflict resolution in any specific arena.

This strategy must be led by the United States, even as it encompasses and, of necessity, engages others. Despite the deep unpopularity of current U.S. policy, the United States remains the sole power capable of guaranteeing effective security arrangements. Its ability to offer credible guarantees has been compromised, yes, but no regional or external actor comes anywhere close to offering an alternative. Here, as elsewhere, unilateral U.S. policy will not suffice; the United States will have to engage others and genuinely consult them in the process. But the United States is the only power capable of mobilizing regional and international strategies for managing or resolving the existing crises.

In executing such policies, the United States must confront tough choices. If it wishes to avoid a crisis with Syria, it will have to evaluate whether there are sufficient carrots on the table—or sticks with enough credibility—to get Syria to accept the UN tribunal investigating the 2005 murder of Lebanese Prime Minister Rafiq Hariri. The UN Security Council established the tribunal at the request of the Lebanese government, and all signs suggest that the tribunal will point toward Syrian involvement. If it wishes to see a non-nuclear Tehran, the United States must offer the real possibility of establishing diplomatic relations with Iran at the end of the process, just as the Bush administration has done with North Korea. If it wishes to see a resolution to the Israeli-Palestinian crisis, and simply to ensure Israel's security, the United States will have to engage the Arab states in finding a credible mechanism to generate support for a deal among Palestinians who voted for Hamas.[22] And if it wishes to see success in Afghanistan—the real front line in the battle against al Qaeda—the United States and its allies will need to fully embrace the scale of the challenge and devote the resources to it that it demands. If it wishes to see a stable Iraq, the United States must invest in regional and international diplomacy, place it on par with military strategy, and make clear to the Iraqis that it cannot sustain an open-ended military presence if they are not willing to make peace among themselves.

THE ROLE OF MULTILATERAL INSTITUTIONS

As the United States grapples with insecurity in the region, it will find international help to be invaluable. Multilateral institutions have already performed credibly in several areas, including politics, peacekeeping, nuclear proliferation, and humanitarian assistance.

Politics

Efforts to resolve the region's conflicts frequently have been based on external political mechanisms, notably the United Nations. UN political engagement has taken on two dimensions, which have been most powerful when combined. First, the UN Security Council has often been used to codify progress in peacemaking or to set the terms for peace agreements—for example, in Afghanistan, in Lebanon, and on the Israeli-Palestinian front. Second, senior UN political envoys have directly assisted parties in negotiating agreements or in mobilizing international support for regime support or change. Among the more notable envoys were Lakhdar Brahimi in Afghanistan, Terje Roed-Larsen in Lebanon, and Sergio Vieira de Mello in Iraq (de Mello later fell victim to a terrorist attack in Baghdad). In both the Afghan and Lebanese cases, U.S. diplomats actively supported the UN initiatives, but the tactical decision to allow the United Nations to take the public lead helped generate regional and international buy-in.

The combination of on-the-ground diplomacy and UN Security Council codification can produce results. In Lebanon and Afghanistan, the dual approach forged political agreements (in Lebanon to bring an end to Syrian occupation and in Afghanistan to establish an interim administration after the Taliban was ousted). These political agreements became the cornerstones of international diplomacy. The combination has been absent in the Israeli-Palestinian case, in that the Security Council has not mandated a political role for the United Nations since 1948, when Ralph Bunche forged Arab-Israeli armistice agreements on the back of Security Council resolutions. The United Nations has also been absent in Iraq until very recently. In these two cases, though, UN Security Council resolutions remain the touchstone for regional and international diplomacy and conflict-management efforts.

The political contribution of the United Nations has thus been vital at times, modest at others—depending in part on the mandate and the personalities of key envoys and the Secretary General but more fundamentally on the question of whether the Security Council establishes a strong political role and marries it to on-the-ground diplomacy. We see prospects for more extensive use of UN political mechanisms in the region, including Iraq.

Peacekeeping

Peacekeeping has had a long and complex history in the region. Often it has been tarnished by failure and scandal, but at other times it has been a stabilizing influence, especially on the Israel-Syria border.[23] In Afghanistan, NATO's International Security Assistance Force, operating under a UN mandate, has been indispensable in containing the Taliban and creating the secure foundation that will allow Afghan politics and the economy to get established. However, it still falls far short (see chapter 6).[24] Although the government is unable to maintain security without NATO, NATO does not have the capacity to maintain security in all parts of the country. Even if the Taliban cannot seize control, it is able to create disorder, and international agencies cannot help the country rebuild as long as the Taliban can disrupt their efforts at will. Although Afghanistan would be worse off without NATO and the United Nations, the current mode of engagement is unsustainable.

In southern Lebanon, the United Nations once operated as little more than an impotent observer of violations. But an overhaul at the end of the war between Israel and Hezbollah in the summer of 2006 has left the UN's peacekeeping operation there far better equipped to provide security along the Israeli border. In the aftermath of the war, the United States had proposed a regional disarmament operation to be followed by a NATO stabilization presence; both were rejected by the Lebanese and the Arabs, who insisted on a UN presence. The United Nations fielded a large, robust presence with surprising speed, largely by bypassing its internal bureaucratic mechanisms and relying on troop contributors to deploy their own forces to the region. That mission has begun to restore Israeli confidence in multilateral peacekeeping, potentially removing a major obstacle to future peacekeeping options.[25]

Nuclear Proliferation

The role of the IAEA in monitoring and analyzing the nuclear situation in Iraq was muddied by the agency's failures in the late 1980s to accurately detect Iraq's emerging nuclear weapons program. The IAEA's later successes were largely obscured by political attention to the sanctions and the scandal-tainted Oil-for-Food Program. The fact is, however, that the UN-based inspection mechanism, combined with sanctions, actually succeeded in containing Iraq's weapons of mass destruction (WMD) program from 1992 to 2003, and it had correctly analyzed Saddam Hussein's nuclear program in the lead-up to the 2003 Iraq War.

In the case of Iran, the importance of the IAEA's monitoring role has been broadly recognized, although not always fully supported. Because the IAEA maintains inspections on the ground, we know a lot about Iran's nuclear capability that we did not know about Iraq's program at an equivalent point in time. The IAEA's diplomatic involvement in Iran has, however, sometimes complicated matters.

Humanitarian Assistance

Humanitarian operations are part of a broader set of conflict-management tools deployed to the region. Since 1946, the United Nations has maintained a massive humanitarian presence in the West Bank and Gaza as well as in surrounding countries in the form of the UN Relief and Works Agency (UNRWA). Although the UNRWA has at times been mired in controversy, its contribution to sustaining social conditions has been widely recognized, especially by Israel.[26] Since the outbreak of the Intifada in 2000, the United Nations has expanded its humanitarian support to the Palestinian population. More recently, the UN High Commissioner for Refugees (UNHCR) and other agencies have begun supporting a huge new population of about 2.5 million refugees from Iraq.

GAPS IN MULTILATERAL PERFORMANCE

On the issues of state building and terrorism, international mechanisms have been less relevant in the greater Middle East, reflecting the weakness of those mechanisms in the global context. No robust international mechanism is available to strengthen domestic capacities for combating terrorism. Similarly, no international mechanisms are especially salient when it comes to the management of turbulent political transitions, although lessons can be learned from the way the UN Security Council shaped the political transition in Lebanon. Had more effective mechanisms been available in Pakistan in 2007, they might have had substantial value; in any case, in 2008 members of the newly elected Pakistani Parliament were calling for a UN investigation into the assassination of Benazir Bhutto, a process which, if approved, would have to be designed ad hoc and from scratch.

Imagine a credible international mechanism—with the UN and NATO acting together—that could bring Pakistan and Afghanistan together to forge coordinated counterterrorism and state-consolidation strategies. In the absence of such a mechanism, Afghanistan may well end up a failed state or host to a protracted international presence that never addresses the core sources of unrest. Pakistan will grow increasingly dangerous, both in the region and within its own borders. And the United States has already found that it cannot succeed by acting alone in such complex contexts.

As outlined in chapter 7, the international machinery for postconflict reconstruction is flawed. Those flaws are on vivid display in the greater Middle East—perhaps most prominently in Afghanistan and Lebanon, where both state building and economic reconstruction have lagged dangerously, increasing the opportunities for opponents to challenge the central government. In the absence of stronger security in some parts of Afghanistan, it is unlikely that any reconstruction mission could have fully achieved the desired results. Certainly, though, a stronger, faster, and more skilled international response could have helped stabilize the country, reinforce and build on improved security in 2003 and 2004, and allow rebuilding to begin, particularly in Kabul. Now, with a regrouped Taliban acting in conjunction with drug lords, the job will be harder. In Lebanon, neither the international community nor the government had the capacity to rapidly deliver services in the south after the 2006 conflict with Israel, in effect surrendering to Hezbollah yet another perceived victory—not only in resisting Israel but also in leading the charge to rebuild after the war.

In Iran, more effective multilateral tools could help force the hand of the Iranian government regarding its intentions for its nuclear program. During the past five years, for example, having a multinational bank for nuclear fuel and consensus on enhanced IAEA inspections would have helped underscore that the international community's treatment of Iran was comparable to its treatment of other members of the NPT. Russia's 2005 proposal to enrich Iranian fuel on Iranian soil could have had greater traction if it had been part of an established mechanism. Under such a mechanism, the fuel bank would allow Iran to have a domestic enrichment program while leaving the most sensitive part of the fuel cycle in international hands. More robust inspections would help ensure that Iran does not cheat. The international character of the mechanism— it would not be aimed solely at Tehran, and it could not be dismissed as simply a Western ploy to weaken Iran—could ease domestic opposition in Iran. If Iran were still unwilling to go along, its intentions would be clear for all to see, increasing the likelihood of effective action by the UN Security Council.

The limits on international peacekeeping options also have constrained policy in the region. Still missing is a credible, pretrained, pre-equipped standby reserve of forces in addition to those that NATO provides. Right now, the options for Iraq are a sustained U.S. presence—with the local, regional, and U.S. domestic complications that it entails—or a U.S. drawdown that brings with it the risk of intervention by neighbors or further internal violence. Sending in NATO is unlikely to be a politically viable option, and sending in the United Nations is certainly not operationally viable.

THE CASE FOR A REGIONAL INITIATIVE

Given how critical Iraq is to regional security and how critical the region is to international security, U.S. efforts to stabilize the country are likely to have systemic effects. How well the United States engages with Iraq's neighbors and other powers can determine the basis for a lasting regional architecture.

There is merit, then, in exploring investment in a regional architecture capable of guaranteeing basic stability. Ultimately, any such structure should encompass even more: it should tackle underdevelopment in parts of the region as well as the thorny issue of political reform. Achieving a viable new set of political understandings and institutional arrangements in the Middle East, however, will require overcoming the political quagmire in which both the region and U.S. policy have become entangled.

To the extent to which the Bush administration has articulated a regional policy in the Middle East, that policy has been to drive the spread of democracy. The Middle East Partnership Initiative had democratization as its goal, as did U.S. support for elections in Iraq, Afghanistan, and the Palestinian territories.[27] But when confronted by complicated results—such as a strengthening of political Islamists through electoral means in Egypt and the electoral victory of Hamas in the Palestinian territories—combined with growing concern about terrorist networks across North Africa and the Middle East and rising energy prices, U.S. policy beat a retreat from reform as a top-tier objective. That has left reform advocates across the region stranded with little meaningful international diplomatic support. That in turn has made them even more cautious about trusting international democracy advocates in the future. Further, efforts to sow the seeds of democracy in Iran and Syria have had little impact, and any association with the United States is likely to discredit local organizations or shut them down completely.

George W. Bush leaves his successor the following dilemma: Although political freedom remains essential to long-term stability in the Middle East, the United States has discredited itself as an advocate of democracy. The use of torture in Iraq, Afghanistan, and Guantánamo, combined with the Abu Ghraib debacle, has made a farce of U.S. appeals to international norms. U.S. interventionism has soured receptivity to its promotion of democracy, which others may see as a self-serving attempt to impose external values. President Obama will have to take on such perceptions directly, standing up for democracy as a value to be nurtured, yet making clear that democracy's foundations must grow from within. Even as the United States pursues an inescapable agenda of counterterrorism, energy security, and prevention of proliferation and regional conflict, it will have to engage states in the region—working with others—to pursue their responsibilities to their own people, to their neighbors, and to the broader international community. Those responsibilities are well articulated in the UN's Arab Human Development Report.[28]

For Middle East leaders, the focus is on stability, not reform. To them, reform has come to suggest regime change, and they are likely to resist it or try to co-opt it as a way to control the space for and pace of political change.[29] The impetus to cooperate will be progress on issues that address the wider political imperatives of the region, most significantly creating a Palestinian state; curtailing transnational terrorist threats; settling destabilizing border disputes; and, especially for Arab leaders, reducing Iran's leverage through Hezbollah, Hamas, and Shiite allies in Iraq. No one in the Middle East wants to see a destabilizing nuclear arms race, but no leader wants to be at the tail end of such a race if the announced civilian nuclear ambitions of fourteen states in the broader Middle East go beyond producing nuclear energy for domestic use.

The challenge for a new regional initiative will be to bridge these multiple and at times clashing interests and realities. The United States cannot simply erase its negative image with reformers and leaders alike in the Middle East, but one way out is to heed the call to sustain its diplomatic engagement, starting with the issue of Arab-Israeli peace. Reform cannot be left off the agenda, or the shattered aspirations of millions of Muslims will inevitably find some form of expression that is likely to grow more radical and less tolerant over time. Settlements of the region's political conflicts are in the interest of Arab states, the United States, and Israel, but their demands diverge widely among the parties. There should be a common interest in the prevention of terrorism and nuclear proliferation.

All these factors point toward a two-track process. The first track is regional diplomacy to resolve crises: the Israeli-Palestinian question, the future of Iraq, conflicts in Lebanon and Afghanistan, and the crisis with Iran. The odds of all these processes succeeding or advancing would be enhanced if, on a second track, inclusive negotiations took place on the prospects for a regional mechanism that offers security guarantees to all. For several of the region's governments, such talks could create a stake in stability that right now is absent. The talks would have to include prospects for normalization of relations between the United States and Iran at the *end* of the process, with important progress toward that goal linked to progress on other fronts.

Track 1: Regional Diplomacy and Burden Sharing

The first track aims to calm the region and set the stage for enhanced cooperation on several fronts, including the Middle East peace process, and in especially troubled areas such as Afghanistan, Iraq, and Iran.

MIDDLE EAST PEACE PROCESS. The Bush administration's decision in November 2007 to convene a wide range of parties, including Syria, in Annapolis, helped breathe life into a moribund Middle East peace process. Keeping the process moving forward in the face of the constant temptation to abandon diplomacy in the face of renewed violence will be critical to stabilizing the region. The "Clinton parameters," which came close to securing the outlines of an agreement in the Taba negotiations in 2000, are reflected in the Arab Peace Initiative that underpinned Annapolis.[30] A bipartisan policy basis for sustained engagement on the Middle East peace process, then, does exist.

Support from a "group of friends" with key members of the G-16 at its core could help bring Middle East peace closer. Not only will the parties need encouragement, support, and occasionally pressure, they will need to know that there will be credible international commitments to sustain engagement and generate the troops and resources needed to implement peace. The Palestinians and the Arab states will seek that broader legitimacy as part of the process of accepting Israel; Israel will look for clear international guarantees, secured by the United States, that a settlement will remain viable. The Arab and Muslim majority members of the group of friends can ensure that Hamas accepts or does not obstruct negotiations or an agreement.

Moreover, if and when an Israeli-Palestinian agreement is reached, it will have to be implemented in the context of drastically weakened governing capacity on the Palestinian side and likely spoilers from both sides. Without the deployment of a credible multinational force with both peacekeeping and transitional administrative functions, the deal will likely be impossible to implement. Israel has long objected in principle to the notion of deploying an international force in the West Bank and Gaza, but the positive recent experience of the UN Interim Force in

Lebanon combined with EU operations on the Gaza border are starting to change that perspective. Our analysis suggests that the potential exists for deployment of a credible, international, transitional administrative and peacekeeping operation, mandated (though not necessarily commanded) by the United Nations, to help implement an Israeli-Palestinian peace agreement. The group of friends, perhaps under a Turkish lead, could begin developing operational plans for such a presence. The group could help ensure the necessary political authorization from the United Nations, as well as the support of the League of Arab States, and galvanize the necessary commitments of troops and financial resources. Finally, the group could serve as a political guarantor of the agreement.

AFGHANISTAN. The international stakes in the success of Afghanistan's recovery are enormous. The NATO mission in Afghanistan operates under a UN mandate and at the request of the government of Afghanistan. For the Afghan people, this is their chance to rebuild after almost thirty years of war. Failure would signal that the international community does not have the capacity to help a fledgling democracy overcome a legacy of poverty and terror. It would re-create a haven for the Taliban and al Qaeda, further erode stability in Pakistan, and generate a massive crisis in confidence in international security institutions.

As of mid-2008, NATO forces in Afghanistan needed to be strengthened to break the cycle of disruption and economic stagnation in the southern and eastern parts of the country. Even if the Taliban cannot hold areas against NATO, the combination of a weak Afghan military, a corrupt police force, and an inadequate NATO presence has limited the efforts at sustainable reconstruction. A first prerequisite will be adequate international and Afghan forces to control critical areas and give reconstruction a chance. A commitment to sustain those forces until local capacity is stronger also is crucial. To generate the necessary force levels, NATO and China should consider an unprecedented collaboration on security in Afghanistan. China already has shown itself capable of complicated operational roles in Haiti, and it arguably could make contributions in Afghanistan in such areas as border security. Because the political tensions between India and Pakistan would make Indian peacekeepers in Afghanistan a near-impossibility, involving China may be the most viable option to generate the scale of extra capacity needed to tackle the lack of security in the country.

The United Nations, with unequivocal backing from the United States, must engage Afghan leaders on corruption. It is estimated that 27 percent of Afghanistan's economy is now illicit, with narcotics the biggest driver.[31] U.S. pressure to eradicate heroin has proved unsustainable—producers return to poppies because they have no alternative livelihoods. With the United States discredited because it has been unable to eliminate narcotics, the United Nations and NATO must lead consensus on a new strategic approach. The secretaries general of the UN and NATO could together appoint an "eminent persons group" staffed by international security, governance, and development experts. The group's task would be to recommend a unified framework for Afghan and international efforts to tackle corruption and narcotics, while addressing the need for alternative livelihoods. Progress would be measured against specific benchmarks.

Civilian capacity to support Afghan government capacity building also needs to be radically increased. The dearth of human capacity in Afghan government institutions requires skilled international civilians to be deployed to train and support local administrators. The UN special representative of the secretary general could convene a national planning exercise in Kabul with key Afghan stakeholders and donors, who would need to fund a civilian planning team comparable to the kind of team that they would expect for a military operation.

IRAQ. Most nations want nothing to do with U.S. policy in Iraq, seeing it as an American quagmire. Yet the entire Middle East and much of the world would live with the consequences of a meltdown in Iraq that would spark a wider Sunni-Shiite struggle, entrench Iraq as a failed state and recruiting ground for terrorism, exacerbate the displacement of 4.5 million people, and further destabilize energy markets. U.S. and international concerns converge on the issue of regional stability, and here there is room for cooperation.

A starting point is to undertake a diplomatic surge with cooperation between the United Nations and the United States and with backing from the G-16. The goal of this surge would be to reach a political settlement in Iraq. The increased U.S. troop presence in 2007–08 contributed to a reduction in violence, but, more important, so have Sunni militias cooperating with U.S. forces. In addition, Shiite militias have called a cease-fire in their fight against the United States. U.S. forces are the stabilizing element between contradictory trends—stronger Sunni militias opposed to a Shiite-dominated state, and Shiite militias deferring to the U.S. forces that check Sunni aspirations. Remove U.S. forces and the chances for a conflagration are high. Keep U.S. forces without a political settlement and the chances for resentment and backlash against the United States are high. The emerging lesson has been documented repeatedly: eventually a political agreement that ends internal conflicts and provides a foundation for sustainable peace must be crafted.

The G-16 would support an invigorated peace process—if the United States engages regional actors and cooperates with the United Nations. The G-16 could exert its influence with Iraq's neighbors, encouraging them to support or at least not disrupt the search for a negotiated settlement. The United States would need to coordinate its bilateral military and diplomatic strategy to support a wider peace agenda. If, in exploring a deal among Iraqis, the United Nations were to call for a peace conference such as the Bonn negotiations for Afghanistan, the G-16 would need to commit to tangible support for a settlement.

The prospects for success may not be high; the parties involved may not have tired of fighting in Iraq. But even so, the effort to negotiate a political settlement will build a foundation for international engagement on Iraq, especially to address the needs of refugees and displaced persons and security spillovers in the region. If the G-16 members signal that a settlement in Iraq is a matter of international concern, not just a U.S. fixation, it will help create a better climate for compromise.

IRAN. G-16 support for regional diplomacy on Iraq would have an additional function—helping to create a more productive framework for negotiations with Iran. The prospect of inclusion in a regional security framework at the end of a negotiation process could create incentives for negotiation. The message sent to Iran's leaders and its people would be one of inclusion. That would promote a less inflammatory context for Iran's domestic politics, in effect taking a false card from President Ahmadinejad, who seeks to compensate for his economic mismanagement by stirring revolutionary fervor.

Iran could well determine the nature of the nuclear regime for the next fifty years. Fears of a nuclear Iran have already triggered a move toward nuclear programs across the broader Middle East, and Iran's development of nuclear weapons would surely launch a race to follow suit.[32] The

P5+1 members have told Iran that it can maintain a civilian nuclear energy program and have offered alternatives to enrichment. Iran's unwillingness to forsake an enrichment program perpetuates questions about the ultimate goals of its nuclear program.

To resolve the standoff between Iran and the UN Security Council, the United States will need to move from participating as a partner in the negotiations to using the P5+1 process as a foundation for bilateral discussions with Iran, much as it has used the Six-Party Talks as the basis for bilateral negotiations with North Korea. The G-16 states have the capacity to play a strong reinforcing role. G-16 backing for a proposal to Iran that includes civilian nuclear power, fuel guarantees, and reprocessing of spent fuel would underscore that such an alternative is credible, not just a Western ploy to deny Iran enrichment capacity, and that it reflects international consensus on a nuclear security strategy for a transnational world.

If Iran should continue to prove recalcitrant in the face of UN Security Council and G-16 efforts, the exercise of having worked diplomatically through those mechanisms would help to ensure a broad-based effort to contain Iranian ambitions and ensure no further proliferation of nuclear weapons in the Middle East. Some linkage between a G-16 and the Gulf Cooperation Council could add vigor to diplomacy, making it clear to Iran that if diplomacy should fail to resolve tensions over its nuclear program, in the medium term the use of force, through the Security Council, would remain an option.

Track 2: From Crisis Resolution to a Regional Security Mechanism

As the negotiations outlined in the first track move forward, they could be bolstered by a parallel track that begins to explore and set forth the parameters of a regional security mechanism. As others have argued, we believe that salient lessons for the greater Middle East can be learned from the process that led to the Conference on Security and Cooperation (CSCE) in Europe.[33] Launched at a time when U.S.-Soviet relations were at a nadir and both states had thousands of nuclear weapons trained on each other, the CSCE created a mechanism for the United States and the Soviet Union to lower tensions. At the same time, the CSCE process succeeded in opening an economic and human rights dialogue between the United States and the Soviet Union.

The CSCE had three categories of issues: border stability, economic cooperation, and human rights. It was no secret that at the time security was the primary focus of Henry Kissinger's diplomacy. Still, it was important that economic and human rights talks were part of the package, allowing the three elements to work together. After the Berlin Wall fell and the Soviet Union collapsed, it was the 1975 Helsinki Final Act, established through the CSCE, that created respect for existing borders and avoided the outbreak of wars over territorial disputes. That respect for territorial integrity gave states the political space to begin to address, even if imperfectly, their political and economic development. CSCE discussions on those topics went on to make major contributions to the development of a human rights and democratic agenda in eastern European countries. And that contributed to the foundation for their successful transition into the European Union.[34]

The parallels are not precise, but the basic elements of this approach could help maintain stability in the Middle East and create hope for economic and political reform. As was the case in Europe in the 1970s, issues of stability—specifically border stability—would need to take center stage. Ensuring border integrity is complicated by the fact that several Arab states continue not to recognize Israel's borders or even its right to exist. In addition, no agreed border exists between Israel and an eventual Palestinian state, although previous rounds of negotiations suggest that both Israelis and Palestinians would ultimately accept a modified version of the 1967 cease-fire line.[35] In Iraq, similarly, stable national borders are likely to be accepted by the country's neighbors after negotiations about internal arrangements, not as a precondition of those arrangements. These elements of the problem, in particular, illuminate the importance of a two-track approach. The contours of a regional mechanism, along with the benefits and advantages of participating in it, would be spelled out. At the same time, Middle East peace process negotiations would create incentives to pursue the second track and vice versa.

A Middle East security framework could comprise only a set of standards to be monitored and assessed, or it could become a regional organization. The outcome will depend on whether states in the region value its contributions to stability enough to create the institutional capacity to sustain it. The CSCE functioned as a set of meetings and conferences from 1975 until its formal creation as the Organization for Security and Cooperation in Europe (OSCE) in 1994. For the Middle East, the creation of a transparent framework that engenders respect for national borders is valuable in its own right and should not be undersold. Furthermore, a regional security framework would complement global efforts to halt nuclear proliferation in the region by reducing the demand for nuclear weapon acquisition.

The G-16, if managed strategically, could be used to ensure focused international engagement and to support the diplomacy required to move toward a regional security mechanism. Among the strengths of the G-16 is its diversity. A common effort to promote stability would reinforce that the initiative has international support from all major powers, including Muslim states. Some within the G-16 will be reluctant to help, given domestic resistance in the region to joining forces with the United States. There are divergent interests in the specifics of some of the region's crises, but all members of the G-16 plus others in the region share an overriding interest in avoiding a regional spiral into further chaos, curbing further proliferation, and preventing further violence and terrorism. Each member of the G-16, as well as much of the rest of the world, will be worse off if crises in the Middle East escalate, if terrorism spreads further, if energy supplies and prices swing out of control, if Iraq falls into permanent chaos, or if tensions between the Arab-Muslim world and the West are allowed to fester or escalate.

In the broader neighborhood, failed international efforts in Afghanistan would not only re-create a haven for al Qaeda and fuel a potential crisis in Pakistan but also shatter confidence in core international institutions and the very viability of cooperation against common threats. The G-16 and other states have frequently expressed an interest in having the United States involve them more actively in diplomacy in the region. And the United States has a deepening interest in finding partners to cooperate in stabilizing regional crises.

The potential benefit for ending tensions with Iran, which risk breaking into a more profound Arab-Iranian split in the Middle East, is also a major incentive. Critically, the G-16 could offer Tehran a credible prospect of inclusion—at the *completion* of a process—in a wider regional framework for stability. Economic incentives from the European Union and leading Gulf economies would increase the prospect of success.

Even if the regional arrangements first focus on security and stability, in the medium term they will need to address economic liberalization, energy security, and political reform—fostering conditions under which local catalysts for human rights and governance reform can prosper. That transition will not be easy. Indeed, a comparable set of challenges may undermine the viability of the OSCE as an organization. Russia, for example, has sought to undermine the OSCE's election-monitoring mechanisms, instead offering monitors from the Commonwealth of Independent States (CIS) that have interpreted election results to suit the interests of entrenched regional leaders and parties. We can only expect an even more complicated process in achieving consensus on the means to ensure political transparency in the Middle East. Initially a new regional arrangement might set standards drawing from the Universal Declaration of Human Rights and the experience of other regional bodies. Monitoring and upholding those standards will be an evolutionary process subject to intense negotiation.

To be effective, this effort would need to be supported by the UN Security Council, which could also task the secretary general with supporting it, either through an envoy or perhaps through a regional diplomatic office. Difficult questions will need to be addressed. For example, will the security framework be an alternative to the League of Arab States, the Organization of the Islamic Conference (OIC), and the Gulf Cooperation Council (GCC), or will those organizations be brought into the framework as entities with supporting functions? The OSCE, after all, made neither the European Union nor NATO irrelevant; instead, it complemented them by creating a mechanism to bring together states that did not have the shared goals, values, systems, and capacities to join those regional bodies. A similar approach will be needed in the Middle East: offering a mechanism to reinforce common principles that promote stability, using that mechanism to get states to establish a pattern of engagement, and building on that engagement to open up the prospect for stronger institutional arrangements. Although a sharper vision for a new organizational body would be desirable, it can succeed only if it develops through perceived self-interest, and that will take time.

In addition to tackling contemporary crises, the G-16 and other actors could help address broader tensions that have arisen between the West and the Muslim world (concentrating on the Middle East). Misunderstandings between Muslims and non-Muslims have already created a divide along religious and ethnic lines that could dangerously split parts of the world that desperately need to cooperate on issues ranging from economic stability to counterterrorism. The greater the misperceptions, the greater the distrust, particularly in a transnational environment in which ignorance breeds fear.

Consultations in the Middle East underscored that a change in the U.S. White House brings with it the potential to build bridges. Muslim-majority states increasingly see that they have an interest in a rule-based international system that restrains hegemons. One Islamic leader posed a challenge: "If autocratic rule is unacceptable nationally, we must expect the same internationally."[36] We believe that the United States should accept that challenge, act on it, and then turn it on its head, asking its allies in the Middle East how, if they insist on the rule of law in international relations, can they justify its absence at home?

It is slowly dawning on Western leaders that they must cooperate with the Muslim-majority states to achieve their goals on counterterrorism and regional security. Even with the U.S. military surge in Iraq, success has depended on the cooperation of local counterparts. Neither Muslims nor non-Muslims can afford the trend toward mutual antagonism. The G-16 could help create the impetus for dialogue and education that would build mutual respect and upend religious stereotypes.

In some cases simple vocabulary will make a difference. For example, phrases such as *Islamic terrorism* and *Islamofascism*, which make Muslims feel that the West sees their religion as driving violence, should be avoided. But it will be necessary to go further, into substance, including policies that are highlighted in this book—promoting peace in the Middle East, respect for international law, and a common understanding of responsible sovereignty. For Indonesia, Turkey, Egypt, and India, the countries with the largest Muslim populations, a dialogue of understanding with the G-16 leaders could set a new tone in the international arena. Part of the new tone would be an action agenda that leads to cooperation on counterterrorism, poverty eradication, and human rights.

MOVING FORWARD

To facilitate the two-track initiative, President Obama will need to rebuild bipartisan U.S. support for Mideast policy. U.S. policymakers have underestimated the negative impact of partisanship on foreign policy. Discontinuity in U.S. policy is emerging as a fundamental obstacle to effective policy by other states that would, in principle, be willing to be part of solutions in the region. The shifting policy line in Washington is driving states within the region toward self-help and self-reliance, including the pursuit of nuclear weapons. And those committed to frustrating any given U.S. objective have a viable option. They can simply wait out the policy of the moment.

Restoring bipartisan consensus on long-term policy would substantially bolster U.S. clout in the region. The substantive continuity between President Clinton and President Bush on the Middle East peace process is an asset to build on. Early engagement of the new administration in the peace process is necessary, and as along as it is sustained, it has the potential to reap substantial diplomatic gains. Using bipartisan mechanisms to manage this process—for example, appointing an envoy from the political party not in the White House or putting together a bipartisan advisory group—could be an important contribution to restoring consensus on regional policy.

CONCLUSION

The Middle East is a vital test case for the international order that we envisage. If current crises in the region are allowed to escalate, the consequences for global security will be grave. Tensions from the Middle East will reverberate in tensions among the major and rising powers, and the challenge of restoring credibility to the international regimes for nonproliferation and conflict management will be exponentially greater.

Yet progress is possible. A sea change in U.S. policy in the region is necessary, but the opportunity for such a shift is real. Concerted cooperation from the other major and rising powers will be needed, but the signs in Europe, the Middle East and elsewhere point to pent-up demand to respond positively to a shift in U.S. strategy. Between them, the powers can only enable responsible action by the regions' states, not guarantee it, but the gravitational pull on the region of joint action by the U.S. and the major powers would be substantial. And difficult though it will be for the states involved—including the United States and the G-16 but the regional actors foremost—common action to tackle crises in the Middle East not only is necessary to prevent future catastrophes, it also is in the medium- and long-term interests of all those states to help stabilize the region.

The two-track process that we envision here, which encompasses direct action on immediate crises and parallel negotiations on longer-term measures for stability, foreshadows our broader conclusions about the road map to a revitalized order to ensure international security. The gravity of the challenges in the broader Middle East serves only to underline the urgency with which that order is needed.

ELEVEN

URGENCY AND CHOICE

THE VISION PUT FORWARD in this book will be difficult to achieve, and the opportunity to build the kind of order we describe is narrow. America's scope for forging a world based on responsible sovereignty was greater in 2001 than now and greater still in 1993. But America's ability to lead is likely to be weaker in 2012 or 2016.

Rising tensions between major powers and the prospects for confrontation are palpable. The global economic crisis could lead to rising demands for protectionism and the resurgence of nationalism. Should protectionism and nationalism derail international trade talks and climate negotiations, the reverberations will be felt in other areas such as diminished commitment to fight terrorism or control the spread of nuclear weapons. Lack of credible response to the gross irresponsibility of states, whether it be Sudan's atrocities in Darfur, Myanmar and Zimbabwe's gross violations of human rights, or Iran's quest for a nuclear weapon, drains confidence in the ability of international cooperation to deliver in the hardest cases. In turn, the longer it takes for international action to address such cases, the greater the chance that governments will turn to ad hoc, even unilateral, action, further undermining international trust and confidence.

Nor can the impact of the global financial crisis be underestimated. As of fall 2008, it has cost trillions of dollars in equity value across the globe. Across nations tightened economic conditions may erode the political commitment and capacity to alleviate poverty and make the institutional investment to provide basic global public goods, let alone promote peace and stability. The fear of constraining growth will complicate negotiations on restricting greenhouse gases. To move ahead, leaders will need to focus on these measures as long-term investments and acknowledge that failure to make them will produce greater costs for everyone.

But all of this—tensions among major powers, the economic crisis, demands for protectionism, irresponsibility of states, and lack of coherent, unified action in the toughest cases—are symptoms of the underlying problem discussed in this book. They reflect the volatility and dangerous perturbations when there is a lack of fundamental international order. They are the signs of international entropy and are harbingers of a much more deadly world to come. Together they warn that the task of fixing today's transnational threats demands urgency.

This means that American foreign policy cannot be complacent in rebuilding international order. The challenge cannot be met through incremental, business-as-usual, approaches. Faced with the daunting agenda we describe in this book, it will be tempting for policymakers to deny both the breadth and the complexity of today's challenges, and hide behind dated mantras: "focus on one or two key issues," "we can't do it all," "some things will just have to wait." But take a look around: Iran, Afghanistan, Pakistan, North Korea, Israel and Palestine, Lebanon, Darfur, the global economic crisis, the rising influence of China, a reassertive Russia. Which one is supposed to wait on the back burner? And what about issues such as global warming, nuclear disarmament and nonproliferation, avian flu, catastrophic terrorism, and preventing state failure? This is the world's agenda, and it will come at policymakers with seeming lightning speed. The Obama administration must rapidly forge a negotiating position for the Conference of the Parties to the UN Framework Convention on Climate Change in Copenhagen in December 2009. It must have a position for the next Nuclear Non-Proliferation Treaty review conference in May 2010. A new administration's actions in its first year may well determine whether the Doha Round of the World Trade Organization or a successor arrangement can be concluded.

Moreover, American foreign policy must resist the temptation to over-simplify a complex agenda and seek solace in old certainties. For too long American foreign policy has seen the world in black and white and searched for enemies. After the Russian invasion of Georgia in 2008, it took minutes before some commentators hailed it as proof the world was dividing into democratic and authoritarian camps, and that conflict between the United States on the one hand and Russia and China on the other is inevitable. The prospect of international order based on major-power cooperation, they argued, is as illusory now as it was before and after the Second World War.[1]

The Russian invasion was not a sign that great-power rivalry was back, but rather profound evidence of the current void in international order. The invasion was sparked by Georgia's provocative military actions in South Ossetia, which should have been avoided through effective international conflict management. The Russia-Georgia crisis makes our earlier point. In the absence of global order and cooperative action to resolve thorny problems, great powers are tempted by unilateral actions. This does not excuse the invasion, but does provide insights for preventing this behavior in the future.

In a more fundamental sense, the worldview that sees an inevitable clash of democracies and authoritarians ignores the most fundamental sea change in international politics of the last century. Today's transnational threats have altered how states can make their citizens secure and protect them from harm's way. National security is now interdependent with global security. The worst threats to international peace and prosperity in the twenty-first century are shared. For the foreseeable future the survival of states, and indeed the state system, depends on governments protecting their citizens from nonstate actors and the existential threats of global warming and pandemic diseases.

This interdependence does not make great-power war inconceivable. Nor does it make cooperation inevitable. What is clear today is that in the absence of international order, our interdependence is producing conflict as the major powers bump against one another as they pursue their needs and grow frustrated when, in the face of common threats, they pull apart and not together.

But history is not fixed; leadership and effective policy matter. Our choices have consequences.

THE ALTERNATIVES

In this book we describe a vision of international order based on responsible sovereignty. To get there, the United States must again lend its power, leadership, and diplomacy to rebuild international order. The single most important innovation to build this order is institutionalized cooperation among the major and rising powers. The G-16 we propose can help energize negotiations of responsible sovereignty across the array of transnational threats to global security. In turn agreements on the content of responsible sovereignty will promote investments in the institutions that implement and monitor solutions to the threats. Confidence in threat-specific solutions will reinforce commitment to reform of the United Nations and how it relates to regional capabilities. The positive linkages are far from automatic. But to realize them, a cooperative relationship among major and rising powers is the essential foundation.

As we insist in chapter 1, the vision and proposals we put forward in this book have to be measured by today's status quo, and whether they make us safer and more prosperous than the current path of episodic cooperation and maximum freedom of action. But the international order that we advocate should also be compared to other proposed arrangements for global order: multilateralism à la carte or the establishment of a concert or league of democracies.

Multilateralism à la Carte

The very complexity that we describe in this book—diffusion of power by issues, a changing distribution of power, different configurations of stakeholders for different problems—leads some to advocate building international cooperation issue by issue, with no overarching steering mechanism or concept of order.[2]

We agree that international order today requires flexibility and creativity in bringing the right actors together to solve problems. But for all of the diffusion of power today, the major and rising powers continue to play an outsized role in most major issues. Sustained international action on climate, energy, peacekeeping, trade, economic stability, terrorism, and nonproliferation requires the participation of China and India. Brazil is on track to becoming a key actor on these issues. South Africa, because of its weight in Africa and among developing countries, has influence in many of these challenges. As we point out in chapter 3, the role of G-16 members may vary by issue area, but they usually turn up in the key cast of characters. As this is so, the G-16 actually lessens the transaction costs of finding cooperative solutions to different issues.

Moreover, the fact that the rising powers are demanding greater status and recognition commensurate with their growing influence requires something more than ad hoc, issue-by-issue partnerships. Not bringing these powers into the larger steering mechanisms of global governance is already reducing their cooperation in issue-based forums. Nor is their ad hoc participation a working alternative. On the global issues before us, these countries must be part of the solution: they have resources and capabilities that are needed to solve problems. And as we point out in chapter 2, the rising powers have blocking power on many issues; greater overall recognition and prestige reduce their incentive to use it.

Multilateralism à la carte also has real limits when interconnections among threats lead to policies on one issue that reverberate across others, often in harmful ways. There are issue-based solutions to energy, climate, nonproliferation, and economic stability, but in a world where policies toward climate change can adversely affect food security or increase the risks of nonproliferation, it is incumbent to bring actors together to address these connections. The G-16 will offer that service and help create new networks among the major and rising powers and across issue areas to promote cooperation. Networks matter in solving policy problems, but they are forged principally through the interactions over time of members of different institutions.

Finally, consider the issue of consistency across solutions to issue areas: what is expected of states, how to get them to comply, and how to sustain cooperation. Solutions to specific threats must be rule based, which means that they must be negotiated, predictable, and sustained. Making up rules as you go will ensure only inefficiency and illegitimacy. And rules without institutions to carry them out will be feckless: try to keep the peace without peacekeepers or the capacity to move them to conflict zones, or to monitor greenhouse gas emissions without a means to verify national reports. The results will be disastrous. Having an ordering principle across issues—responsible sovereignty—offers a source of predictability, which is a key component of order. Clear rules and viable institutions are the essential machinery to undergird international order.

For all of these reasons we ignore overarching institutions for international order at our peril.

An Alliance of Democracies

Members of both major political parties in the United States have advocated establishing a new international alliance: either a Concert or League of Democracies.[3] Such proposals derive from the assumption that the world would be much safer and prosperous if it consisted solely of liberal democracies. Undoubtedly this is so; democracies historically do not go to war with each other; their interests in free trade and economic growth foster easier economic cooperation; and shared values in promoting liberty, freedom, and human rights create greater amity and genuine friendships among people, all of which increase trust and confidence. This is a compelling, long-term ideal, one first espoused more than 200 years ago by the German philosopher Immanuel Kant.

It would be folly, however, to base American foreign policy and strategies for international order on this ideal, because just as Kant's ideal has not been realized in the last two centuries, we are unlikely to realize it in our lifetimes. Indeed, the attempt to pit democracies against nondemocracies will provoke conflict, mistrust, and hostility in the short term, and risk triggering a second cold war at a time when international cooperation is essential for mitigating transnational threats. Enhancing security, furthering prosperity, stopping deadly infectious disease, and solving global warming require cooperating with, to paraphrase the quote from Franklin Delano Roosevelt in chapter 1, nations that do not see and think exactly as we do.

Attempts to create a Concert or League of Democracies are misguided for several reasons. First, it is not clear what problems it is supposed to solve. Some believe that a concert or league would gain international legitimacy for using force, but we argue below that these proponents erroneously read recent history on the legitimacy of force. Others contend that international institutions are so broken that current arrangements have no value and we need a radical restructuring of international politics by democracies. But as this book makes clear, sweeping condemnations of the performance of international institutions drastically under-value the amount of international cooperation that exists today and that can be built upon for better global problem solving.

Advocates for both the Concert and League of Democracies contend that we need new rules on using force and how it is legitimated. Frustrated by the Security Council and its reluctance to authorize military force to address threats to international peace and security (for instance in Iraq in 2003) and to exercise the responsibility to protect from mass killing (Darfur), supporters of the league and concert imply that the bar to legitimate use of force is too high and set by those whose domestic legitimacy is inferior to that of the western democracies. They cite Kosovo as an example of the potential of the new alternative: faced with a sure Russian veto on the authorization of force against the former Yugoslavia, NATO, with agreement of all its members and the European Union (all democracies), intervened in contravention of the UN Charter, an intervention deemed by many to be legitimate.

But this misses the key point that we raise in chapter 3 about the legitimate use of force. The legitimacy of the Kosovo intervention came not from the fact that a group of democracies approved the intervention; it came from the fact that the relevant regional organization (the European Union) and its military alliance (NATO) approved the intervention. Second, the legitimacy bestowed by the European Union was supplemented by the legitimacy provided by key Muslim states such as Pakistan, Malaysia, Egypt, Kuwait, and the Gulf States and the Organization of the Islamic Conference (OIC), which supported intervention on behalf of a country that is overwhelmingly Muslim. (The chair of the Contact Group of the OIC who called then UN Secretary General Kofi Annan to relate OIC demands for strong humanitarian action, was none other than Iran's foreign minister.) By contrast, India, the world's largest democracy, broadly opposed the Kosovo action.

The combination of these two factors supplied overwhelming international legitimacy. A telling but little-known fact about the Security Council and the intervention: After NATO had intervened, Russia, wrongly believing that only a Security Council resolution can legitimate force, demanded a council vote to condemn NATO's use of force. The vote lost 12 to 3, with only China, Russia, and Namibia (a democracy) in favor of condemnation. The two Muslim-majority countries on the council, Malaysia and Gambia, voted against condemning the intervention.

A different case sometimes cited by proponents of the League is Iraq: they claim that a League of Democracies would have provided a different legitimating source than the Security Council for the U.S.-led invasion of 2003. This is hard to imagine given that two of the most outspoken opponents of that intervention were France and Germany, both democracies and long-standing allies of the United States. On the Security Council, Mexico and Chile, both democracies, opposed the intervention. In truth, the Iraq case shows that there is little reason to believe that democracies are any more likely than nondemocracies to agree to the use of force for difficult, risky military adventures.

Some proponents of the league or concert write off current international institutions, many of which function on the basis of universal membership. Given that international institutions are broken, they argue, there is little cost in trying to replace them with something radically different.

A closer look suggests the costs would be formidable. The United Nations is able to mount 18 peacekeeping operations with more than 100,000 soldiers. Many of those soldiers do not come from democracies. The missions and budgets are approved by the Security Council, which has two permanent members that are not democracies, and usually several nonpermanent members that are not democracies. Do we really expect this level of cooperation in a world explicitly organized into democratic and nondemocratic camps? In a new structured division of the world between democracies and nondemocracies, are the democracies going to make equal or better contributions to ensure the global public good of ending civil wars?

A key point that emerges from this book is that many governments are able to put aside differences to make progress in solving global transnational threats. The International Health Regulations, which mandate intrusive international inspection and place obligations on all governments in the case of deadly infectious disease, are universal. The Nuclear Non-Proliferation Treaty has 188 members. It is hard to see how structuring international cooperation by democracies is going to yield something dramatically better and not dramatically worse.

Another key question is whether most eligible members would want to join a club of democracies. Our consultations suggest not. To the extent that such an organization is created as an alternative to the United Nations or diminishes the legitimacy of the United Nations, most states will oppose it. Within Europe the proposal breeds much cynicism that this is but one more ruse for the United States to use in subverting the international rule of law.

Even if European democracies joined, the institution would need other democracies so that it did not look like NATO under a different name. In our consultations we found few takers. Policymakers in India, which is deepening its bilateral relations with Russia and China, argued that such a club would heighten, not reduce, international insecurity. Officials in Australia confided that they thought such an institution could usher in a second cold war at a time when integrating China into the international order is crucial.

Some proponents argue that their proposed alliance should not be seen as an alternative to the United Nations. But if a concert or league is not to be a rival to the United Nations, or an alternative court of legitimation for the use of force, then it already exists. As we discussed in chapter 9, a Community of Democracies was established during the Clinton years to bring democracies together to discuss common problems of democratic governance, to organize on key global policy issues, and to promote the spread of democracy through support of grassroots and civil society movements. The United Nations has a Democracy Caucus, where the ambassadors of the democracies, supposedly like-minded on the issues of the day, can gather and discuss common strategies. The fact that the community is at best an underachiever, and that the Democracy Caucus seldom meets at the United Nations, suggests that something is very wrong in the underlying assumption that democracy unites countries with different development levels, different histories, and different priorities.

Then there is China, whose cooperation and leadership will be necessary for addressing most of the transnational threats discussed in this book, certainly climate change, economic instability, and biosecurity. One of the most important stories in international relations of the last twenty years is not just China's rise in power, but China's increasing commitment to international institutions and its support for international order. An American initiative to establish an alternative organization to the United Nations with a mandate to use force will reinforce nationalist sentiments in China rather than encouraging the more open, cooperative policy strains that are emerging. A League or Concert of Democracies runs the risk of a self-fulfilling prophecy of those who see a future U.S.-China confrontation as inevitable.

The proposals for an alliance based on democracies border on escapism from the complexity of the global challenges discussed throughout this book and from a world that wants to see a United States commit itself to a rule-based international order. Today's problems cannot be resolved without systematically engaging nondemocratic states. Slowing climate change, tackling the problems associated with terrorism, and alleviating poverty cannot be managed without working with major powers that would be marginalized by a club of democracies. Difficult as it has been to forge effective joint diplomacy among the United States, China, and Russia over Iran and Darfur, it is hard to see how the United States and a like-minded grouping of democracies would have achieved more effective results faster. It is hard to see any prospect of walking back North Korea's nuclearization in a world divided between democracies and nondemocracies.

BUT HOW REALISTIC IS AN ORDER
BUILT ON RESPONSIBLE SOVEREIGNTY?

In response to a criticism of the Concert of Democracies, two of its proponents argued that whether or not democracies shared common positions and interests was largely irrelevant. Institutions, they answered, can construct common positions and shared interests.[4] We agree that institutions can have that effect, and we believe that it will be easier for 16 major powers to find common ground than 60 to 100 democracies.

And although we would acknowledge that it is easier for seven large industrial democracies to reach shared understandings of global problems than for sixteen major powers that include Russia and China, our threat analysis shows that even when the large industrial democracies may agree, it is not enough to solve today's problems. This is clearly evident with regard to the global economic crisis, nonproliferation and climate change, but it is also true of dealing with the hard cases, where one searches for enforcement of standards of responsibility.

Those who fear that including the rising powers in the decisionmaking of the IFIs or the G-8 will hamper reaching agreement on key issues miss the point. Excluding them from the decisionmaking chambers simply delays the point at which they must be brought on board, often with the additional hurdle that they will have a built-in resistance to any decision taken without consulting them. Reaching agreement on such issues as Myanmar, Iran, Zimbabwe, and Sudan would surely be easier among the United States, the European Union, and Japan. But in the absence of implementation of and compliance with decisions, such agreement would most likely have little effect.

As we have seen on various hard cases, decisions by global bodies like the UN Security Council largely depend on key regional actors to do some heavy lifting in eliciting compliance. Regional powers typically have economic and political ties to the ruling elites in recalcitrant states that the United States and the western powers do not. For example, South Africa accounts for 41.5 percent of Zimbabwe's exports compared to 17 percent for the twenty-seven EU states combined; Thailand is Burma's largest trading partner, with China a close second. These ties can protect or they can undermine, and in their absence there are few levers to pressure or persuade national elites to comply with international decisions or western policy. This was most importantly demonstrated in North Korea, where cooperation between the United States and China undergirded the Six-Party Process that by 2008 was making major progress in North Korea's denuclearization. Iran is more complex, but progress so far has required Chinese and Russian cooperation. And those who see in Iran less evidence of the merit of cooperation have as an alternative policy only military force, which, as we have seen, carries with it substantial costs.

Negative or mixed examples can illustrate the case as well. Myanmar is one, where what limited diplomatic progress has been made resulted in large part because China saw it as being in its interest to have a Security Council–approved envoy taking the lead in international diplomacy with Rangoon's junta rather than facing continued pressure about its bilateral relationship. Zimbabwe is another, where the absence of South African leadership meant that both international and regional initiatives to deal with President Mugabe foundered. South Africa's eventual mediation has at least provided a possible way forward, short of a bloody civil war.

If we evaluate international institutions through the lens of whether they are likely to produce agreements on hard cases, we might stick with the G-8, or even a G-7. But if we value compliance and effectiveness, we will surely need to build deeper patterns of cooperation with the rising powers. Decisions may be tougher to get, but they will be more likely to stick.

Creating the G-16 would be a starting point that recognizes shifts in global power and the corresponding need for the traditional and rising powers to make cooperation a central thrust, and not an occasional feint, of their foreign policies. The G-16 holds the promise for a deliberate reordering of relationships, built around the premises of responsible sovereignty and the need for cooperation to tackle transnational threats.

Each of the rising powers is currently caught between divergent policy beliefs about its position in the world. In each case, exclusion from the decisionmaking chambers of international politics reinforces factions who see national interest in traditional ways, to the detriment of factions who see cooperation as essential to national security and prosperity. This is true of China, where there is a struggle between policymakers who define the United States as an adversary and Asia as a sphere of potential dominance and those who believe that global economic instability and climate change are existential threats and want China to accept global responsibilities that accord with its rise in power. Similarly, India wavers between a foreign policy tradition of nonalignment and one that recognizes that India is a major power, has more shared values with the United States than with nonaligned states, and should have a foreign policy that reflects its changed status. Equally, South Africa is caught between an internationalist foreign policy and a resurgence of 1960s nonaligned solidarity, a resurgence fed by South African resentment in 2005 when South African support for several western positions on UN reform (on a strong human rights council, on management reform) was met with inaction on Security Council reform. In each case, exclusion from the core negotiating and decisionmaking structures of international politics reinforces those who resist taking on the responsibilities that are commensurate with their rising power.

In all of the above examples, the formation of a G-16 could shift internal politics toward global cooperation. Will this approach work with Russia? Certainly the evidence of 2007–08 suggests that the neoimperialist impulse in Russia has come back with a vengeance. The question then becomes, however, whether isolating or engaging Russia is more likely to lead to cooperation in some instances and containment of Russia's most aggressive instincts. Although there is no question that the international community had to condemn Russia's military invasion of Georgia, isolation will only spark Russian nationalism in the short run, when Russia is still heady from its resurgence during a period of high energy prices. Instead the goal should be to play to Russia's long-term interests. In the long run Russia will need technology and capital to sustain its energy sector and diversify its economy. It will need access to international markets. As the 60 percent decline in the value of the Russian stock market between May and September 2008 has shown, Russia must worry about scaring away international capital. And the wider financial crisis has even led to a Russian call for strengthened international oversight of financial markets. Bringing Russia into a wider grouping of major and emerging powers that emphasizes the need for and benefits of responsible sovereignty will better encourage restraint than trying to isolate Russia.

FINAL WORDS

We are realistic about the difficulty—substantively and especially politically—of our proposed road map to renewed order. Institutionalized cooperation between the major and rising powers will depend in substantial part on a new emphasis and style in American foreign policy, but also on whether Europe and Japan accept that their seats at the table will be adjusted to accommodate the rising powers. And it will depend very heavily on the willingness of the leadership of the rising powers to place long-term interests above short-term tactical advantage, to act with restraint rather than their own sense of hubris. Each rising power has a major stake in tackling shared threats and has everything to lose by actions that diminish the prospects for a stable international order.

We return to the opening paragraph of this book. We have ample fact finding and warning about today's threats. What we need now is fact facing and action. Cooperation on a grand scale is essential for tackling global warming, pandemics of deadly disease, and catastrophic terrorism, and for creating the economic prosperity and stability that is ultimately the best antidote to war.

Cooperation, of course, necessitates leadership. It requires leaders who will speak to their constituents about common global interests and the need for national interests to converge with a wider international agenda; leaders who will explain that nations are stronger, not weaker, when they act in partnership with others to achieve common goals; leaders who will state frankly that international law clearly respects the rights of nations to protect themselves, and that respect for international law advances and does not threaten national security. It requires leaders who are willing to work internationally to reach beyond established patterns of distrust; to listen to the perspectives of others and be willing to compromise not on values or goals but on tactics and methods; to see past differences in short-term national agendas to common interests in long-term solutions.

National leaders face a choice: they can either use this moment to help shape an international, rule-based order that will protect their global interests or resign themselves to an ad hoc international system where they are increasingly powerless to shape the course of international affairs. The agenda for action will not be completed in two years or ten. Yet we cannot wait to start. The longer the delay in new approaches and new cooperation against today's threats, the more difficult the challenges will become.

With power comes responsibility. We have a historic opportunity to build an international order for an era of transnational threats. It is incumbent on us to seize it before it slips away.

NOTES

CHAPTER ONE

1. Abraham D. Sofaer and Thomas C. Heller, "Sovereignty: The Practitioners' Perspective," in *Problematic Sovereignty: Contested Rules and Political Possibilities*, edited by Stephen D. Krasner (Columbia University Press, 2001), pp. 30–32.

2. Various international polls tell the same story. A 2006 poll in Israel, the United Kingdom, Canada, and Mexico found that respondents believed that George W. Bush was a greater danger to world peace than Kim Jong-il or Mahmoud Ahmadinejad. Sixty-nine percent of British surveyed believed that U.S. policy had made the world less safe since 2001; see "International Poll Ranks Bush a Threat to World Peace," *International Herald Tribune*, November 3, 2006. That same year, the Pew Research Center found that many respondents surveyed around the world felt that the U.S. presence in Iraq was a greater threat to international peace than Iran's nuclear ambitions. See the Pew Global Attitudes Project, "America's Image Slips, but Allies Share U.S. Concerns over Iran, Hamas" (PewResearchCenter, June 13, 2006), available at http://pewglobal.org/reports/display.php?ReportID=252.

3. Strobe Talbott, *The Great Experiment: The Story of Ancient Empires, Modern States, and the Quest for a Global Nation* (New York: Simon and Schuster, 2008), pp. 324–26.

4. James Goldgeier and Michael McFaul, "A Tale of Two Worlds: Core and Periphery in the Post–Cold War Era," *International Organization* 46 (Spring 1992): 467–91.

5. Robert Kaplan, "The Coming Anarchy," *Atlantic Monthly* (February 1994): 44–76.

6. David M. Malone, *The International Struggle over Iraq: Politics in the UN Security Council, 1980-2005* (Oxford University Press, 2006), pp. 84–113.

7. Ibid., pp. 121–22.

8. Speaking in Munich in February 2008, Secretary of Defense Robert Gates acknowledged that public opposition to the Iraq War hindered European governments from cooperating more intensively with the United States in Afghanistan. See Thom Shankar, "Gates Says Anger over Iraq Hurts Afghan Effort," *New York Times,* February 9, 2008.

9. Francis M. Deng and others, *Sovereignty as Responsibility: Conflict Management in Africa* (Brookings, 1996), p. 211.

10. Our formulation draws from Hedley Bull, *The Anarchical Society: A Study of Order in World Politics* (London: Macmillan, 1977), pp. 3–20.

11. Francis M. Deng, *Protecting the Dispossessed: A Challenge for the International Community* (Brookings, 1993), pp. 14–20.

12. Robert Jackson, *Quasi-States: Sovereignty, International Relations, and the Third World* (Cambridge University Press, 1990), p. 197.

13. For a history of the CSSDCA, see Francis M. Deng and I. William Zartman, *A Strategic Vision for Africa: The Kampala Movement* (Brookings, 2002).

14. *Report of the International Commission on Intervention and State Sovereignty, The Responsibility to Protect* (Ottawa, Canada: International Development Research Center, 2001). For the story behind the responsibility to protect, see Gareth Evans, *The Responsibility to Protect: Ending Mass Atrocity Once and for All* (Brookings, 2008).

15. *Report of the Secretary-General's High-Level Panel on Threats, Challenges, and Change, A More Secure World: Our Shared Responsibility* (New York: United Nations, 2003).

16. Human Security Center, *Human Security Report 2005* (New York: Oxford University Press, 2005), pp. 22–34.

17. See, for example, Stanley Hoffman, *Duties beyond Borders: On the Limits and Possibilities of Ethical International Politics* (Syracuse University Press, 1982).

18. Robert Axelrod, *The Evolution of Cooperation* (New York: Basic Books, 1984), and Robert Axelrod and Robert O. Keohane, "Achieving Cooperation under Anarchy: Strategies and Institutions," *World Politics,* 38, no. 1 (October 1985): pp. 226–54.

19. J. Samuel Barkin and Bruce Cronin, "The State and the Nation: Changing Norms and the Rules of Sovereignty in International Relations," *International Organization* 48, no. 1 (Winter 1994): 107–30; Stephen D. Krasner, "Sovereignty and Intervention," in *Beyond Westphalia? State Sovereignty and International Intervention,* edited by Gene M. Lyons and Michael Mastanduno (Johns Hopkins University Press, 1995); and Stephen D. Krasner, "Compromising Westphalia," *International Security* 20, no. 3 (Winter 1995/96): 115–51.

20. Our vision for a G-16 includes Canada, France, Germany, Italy, Japan, Russia, the United Kingdom, and the United States (the existing G-8), along with China, Mexico, India, Brazil, and South Africa (the existing "Outreach 5"), and Indonesia, Turkey, and a second African nation, most likely Egypt or Nigeria.

21. Franklin D. Roosevelt, State of the Union Address, January 6, 1945. Archived online at the American Presidency Project, www.presidency.ucsb.edu/ws/index.php?pid=16595.

CHAPTER TWO

1. See, for example, Fareed Zakaria, *The Post-American World* (New York: Norton, 2008), and Richard Haass, "The Age of Nonpolarity," *Foreign Affairs* 87, no. 3 (May-June 2008): 44–56.

2. Haass, "The Age of Nonpolarity."

3. Niall Ferguson, "The G-8 Aren't the Only Ones," *Los Angeles Times,* June 11, 2007.

4. The Pentagon is known for worst-case analysis of Chinese capabilities. Even so, its most recent report on the subject states that "China will take until the end of this decade or longer to produce a modern force capable of defeating a moderate-size adversary. China will not be able to project and sustain small military units far beyond China before 2015 and will not be able to project and sustain large forces in combat operations far from China well into the following decade." Office of the Secretary of Defense, *Annual Report to Congress: The Military Power of the People's Republic of China* (2008), p. 22.

5. Michael S. Chase, "Balancing China's Budgetary Priorities: Defense Spending and Domestic Challenges," *China Brief* 7, no. 20 (October 31, 2007): pp. 3–6.

6. *A More Secure World: Our Shared Responsibility. Report of the Secretary-General's High-level Panel on Threats, Challenges, and Change* (New York: United Nations, 2004), p. 23.

7. Steven Kosiak, "FY 2009 Request Would Bring DoD Budget to Record Levels," Center for Strategic and Budgetary Assessments, update, February 4, 2008 (www.CSBAonline.org).

8. China figures are from the Office of the Secretary of Defense, *Annual Report to Congress: The Military Power of the People's Republic of China* (2008). The $45 billion figure is China's stated budget. The Pentagon has a low estimate ($97 billion) and a high estimate ($139 billion). We have been unable to find any China watcher who finds the high estimate plausible.

9. The International Institute for Strategic Studies, *The Military Balance, 2005–2006* (New York: Taylor and Francis, 2005). For more information, see "The Military Balance" (www.iiss.org/publications/military-balance/ [October 16, 2008]).

10. BBC World Service Poll, 2007 (http://news.bbc.co.uk/1/shared/bsp/hi/pdfs/06_03_07_perceptions.pdf).

11. Pew Research Center, Pew Global Attitudes Project, "America's Image Slips, but Allies Share U.S. Concerns over Iran, Hamas" (Washington: Pew Research Center, 2006).

12. Pew Research Center, Pew Global Attitudes Project, *Global Unease with Major Powers* (Washington: Pew Research Center, 2007) (http://pewglobal.org/reports/pdf/256.pdf [October 16, 2008]).

13. Ibid.

14. See, for example, the discussion of "lawfare"—the beliefs of Donald Rumsfeld and other key Pentagon officials that international law is a tool of the weak to undermine the United States—in Jack Goldsmith, *The Terror Presidency: Law and Judgment inside the Bush Administration* (New York: W. W. Norton, 2007), pp. 58-63.

15. Gallup Poll News Service, "United Nations Ratings Remain at Lowest Ebb," February 8, 2007.

16. Ibid.

17. For more information, see "Weapons of Mass Destruction (WMD): Six-Party Talks" (www.globalsecurity.org/wmd/world/dprk/6-party.htm [October 16, 2008]).

18. Stephen C. Schlesinger, "Text of President Truman's Address, Bringing World Peace Parlay to an End," in *Act of Creation: The Founding of the United Nations* (Boulder, Colo.: Westview, 2003), p. 292.

19. Michael Mandelbaum, *The Case for Goliath: How America Acts as the World's Government in the 21st Century* (New York: PublicAffairs, 2005).

20. Zakaria, *The Post-American World*, pp. 182–91.

21. Mandelbaum, *The Case for Goliath*, pp. 90–95.

22. Nina Hachigian and Mona Sutphen, *The Next American Century: How the U.S. Can Thrive as Other Powers Rise* (New York: Simon and Schuster, 2008), p. 161.

23. Better World Campaign and United Nations Foundation, *The New American Consensus on International Cooperation: A Presentation of Key Findings from Focus Groups and a National Survey* (November 2007) (www.betterworldcampaign.org/resources/unf_national_survey2007.pdf [October 16, 2008]).

CHAPTER THREE

1. One of the first examinations of the issue was Helga Haftendorn, Robert O. Keohane, and Celleste Wallander, eds., *Imperfect Unions: Security Institutions over Time and Space* (Oxford University Press, 1999).

2. In parallel to this project, we engaged in an adjacent study of the evolution of multilateral security arrangements since the end of the cold war; see Bruce Jones, Shepard Forman and Richard Gowan, eds., *Cooperating for Peace and Security: The Evolution of International Security Institutions after the Cold War* (Cambridge University Press, forthcoming).

3. George F. Kennan, *Memoirs 1925–1950* (Boston: Little, Brown, 1967), p. 218.

4. Another example is U.S. and Chinese opposition to the International Criminal Court, which came into being nevertheless.

5. See Johannes F. Linn and Colin I. Bradford, "Pragmatic Reform of Global Governance: Creating an L-20 Summit Forum" (Brookings Policy Brief 152, April 2006), available at www.brookings.edu/~/media/Files/rc/papers/2006/04globalgovernance_linn/pb152.pdf; Alex Evans, "A New Global Leaders' Forum: Comparing and Analyzing Recent Proposals" (Center on International Cooperation [CIC] Policy Paper, February 2007), available at http://www.nyu.edu/pages/cic/internationalsecurity/docs/newgloballeadersforum.pdf; Peter I. Hajnal, "Summitry from G-5 to L-20: A Review of Reform Initiatives" (Center for International Governance Innovation [CIGI] Working Paper 20, March 2007) available at http://www.cigionline.org/community.igloo?r0=community&r0_script=/scripts/folder/view.script&r0_pathinfo=%2F%7B7caf3d23-023d-494b-865b-84d143de9968%7D%2FPublications%2Fworkingp%2Fsummitry&r0_output=xml&s=cc; John English, Ramesh Thakur, and Andrew F. Cooper, eds., *Reforming from the Top: A Leaders' 20 Summit* (United Nations University Press, 2005).

6. The secretariat arrangements on climate change may be altered as a result of negotiations on a new framework agreement on climate change.

7. See Anne-Marie Slaughter, *A New World Order* (Princeton University Press, 2004).

8. A similar grouping of fifteen countries was used by the president of the General Assembly in September 2005 to secure agreement on the most contentious issues eventually adopted by the World Summit 2005. The grouping was composed only days before the summit convened, however, and had no opportunity therefore for iterative negotiations with the broader General Assembly, generating resistance to its efforts to ram through agreements. A more structured interaction among G-15 ambassadors and the broader UN mechanisms might well have secured smoother passage for a better outcome document. Indeed, proposals to that effect were made early on in the negotiation process, notably by then Mexican Permanent Representative Barruga, but unfortunately ignored.

9. This point was noted and reinforced by the Princeton Project.

10. Here we are attempting to spare readers the minutiae of UN budgetary process, some of which can be hinted at by revealing that the name of the UN Secretariat's main budget committee is the UN Advisory Committee on Administrative and Budgetary Questions (ACABQ).

11. Progress has been made in establishing the Independent Audit Advisory Committee; creating a new UN ethics code and taking first steps toward its application to the whole UN system; and establishing a new framework for mandate review. Progress has been blocked in strengthening the Office of Internal Oversight: although the General Assembly approved additional posts, it still relies on funds from the office or program it is auditing and has yet to undergo significant improvements in professionalism. Other reforms have been implemented only in part, including transparency in procurement procedures and improved recruitment and mobility in human resources.

12. This was perfectly logical at the time. The United States found itself frequently outvoted in the budget committee under its prior voting rules, and thus paying the largest share of programs it did not support.

13. In substantial part, this is true because developing countries constitute the largest contributors of forces to UN peacekeeping operations and thus have strong domestic constituencies that support making sure that UN peacekeeping is credible and effective.

14. The Swedish, Thai, Chilean, and South African governments led a "Four Nations Initiative" to build support for management reform in 2005–07. Although progress from that initiative has been limited, the political support of that diverse set of states would help convince others that the U.S. interest in management reform was not purely political or U.S. interest based.

15. This would then cover the United Nations' peacekeeping operations, field-based political missions, humanitarian coordination operations—each managed from the secretariat—and the work of the World Food Program, the UN Development Program, the UN Children's Fund, the UN High Commissioner for Refugees, the UN Relief and Works Agency, the UN Food and Agricultural Organization, and the UN Environment Program—collectively, responsible for the lion's share of the UN's field-oriented spending. Each of these agencies' governing boards would have to vote on and approve adopting an accountability initiative and related reforms. Because the representatives to these boards report to different national departments (development, health, environment, and so on) the complexities in pushing this initiative are substan-

tial, but warranted if the United States truly believes that management reform of this type is a policy priority.

16. The panel of eminent persons that developed this idea agreed that if military force were essential to exercise that responsibility, the UN Security Council should do it. They argued further, however, that where the council was blocked, regional organizations could also authorize the use of force. In 2004, the High-Level Panel on Threats, Challenges, and Change was ambiguous on this point. It judged that the Security Council was the appropriate venue for decisions on whether to exercise the responsibility to protect; in a later discussion, it argued that regional organizations could authorize the use of force in situations of emergency and then seek council authorization after the fact. In 2005, when the UN General Assembly endorsed the responsibility to protect, it tied its exercise to the Security Council.

17. The Secretary General's High Level Panel on Threats, Challenges, and Change, *A More Secure World: Our Shared Responsibility* (New York: United Nations, 2004): paragraphs 190 and 191, available at www.un.org/secureworld/.

18. Ivo Daalder and Robert Kagan, "America and the Use of Force: Sources of Legitimacy," in *Bridging the Foreign Policy Divide,* edited by Derek Chollet, Tod Lindberg, and David Shorr (New York: Routledge, 2008).

19. Details on the Hoover Institution and Stanford Institute for International Studies Preventive Force Conference, Menlo Park, Calif., May 25–27, 2005, available at www.hoover.org/research/conferences/3022291.html.

CHAPTER FOUR

1. Kevin Watkins, *United Nations Human Development Report 2007–2008, Fighting Climate Change, Human Solidarity in a Changed World* (New York: UNDP, 2008): "Climate change will not announce itself as an apocalyptic event in the lives of the poor. Direct attribution of any specific event to climate change will remain impossible. However, climate change will steadily increase the exposure of poor and vulnerable households to climate-shocks and place increased pressure on coping strategies, which, over time, could stall and reverse human development" (p. 17). The report outlines how climate change will contribute, although direct causation may not always be evident, to increased deaths and poverty: (1) climate change will affect agricultural productivity, thereby threatening food security and sustenance of hundreds of millions (pp. 17–18); (2) rising sea levels and increased occurrence of climatic natural disasters will put millions living in coastal areas at risk (p. 17); (3) climatic changes will decrease water availability, driving 2.8 billion people to living in areas with water scarcity by 2080 (p. 18); (4) changes in ecosystems will threaten 30–40 percent of existing species (p. 19); and (5) climate changes will have health impacts in developing countries because of limited capacity of local health facilities (p. 19).

2. Ibid. "Some 262 million people were affected by climate disasters annually from 2000 to 2004, over 98 percent of them in the developing world" (p. 16). Based on this evidence, even the most conservative estimates accept the projection that 45–70 million people may pushed back into poverty in coming decades as a result of climate-related events. See also Intergovernmental Panel on Climate Change (IPCC), *Working*

Group I Contribution to the Fourth Assessment Report of the IPCC, Figure SPM 7 (IPCC, 2007), p. 10.

3. Jim Yardley, "Beneath Booming Cities, China's Future Is Drying Up," *New York Times*, September 28, 2007, p. 5; Jim Yardley and Joseph Kahn, "As China Roars, Pollution Reaches Deadly Extremes," *New York Times*, August 26, 2007, p. 3, available at www.nytimes.com/2007/08/26/world/asia/26china.html?pagewanted=3.

4. "Climate Change Front and Center at World Economic Forum," *Environment News Service,* January 29, 2007; particularly remarks by Montek Ahluwalia, deputy chairman of the Planning Commission of India, available at www.ens-newswire.com/ens/jan2007/2007-01-29-01.asp.

5. National Resources Defense Council (NRDC), "Consequences of Global Warming," NRDC, July 22, 2008, available at www.nrdc.org/globalWarming/fcons.asp: "The 2006 hurricane season was the most active on record, even apart from the Hurricane Katrina disaster. The number of Category 5 hurricanes has increased exponentially in the last 35 years" (pp. 2–3). We do not argue that climate change caused Katrina, but rather that climate change will increase the numbers and scale of such storms. NRDC demonstrates that this increase is already occurring. IPCC and UN reports (see notes 1 and 2) also establish how climatic changes will lead to increased frequency of severe weather occurrences.

6. Ibid. The 2006 wildfire season in the American Southwest and the Pacific Northwest was the worst on record, and rising costs of fighting fires in the area average more than $1 billion a year. In fact, temperatures across the United States have also risen considerably in the past decade, affecting both regional agricultural productivity and economic health.

7. National Oceanic and Atmospheric Administration (NOAA), "Observing Climate Variability and Change," June 17, 2008, available at www.oar.noaa.gov/climate/t_observing.html: "Every year from 1998 to 2006 ranks among the 25 warmest years on record for the United States, an unprecedented occurrence" (p. 1).

8. IPCC, *Working Group I Contribution to the Fourth Assessment Report of the IPCC*, Table SPM 6 (IPCC, November 12, 2007), p. 20. Note that global average sea level rise, the most potentially devastating impacts of a rise in global temperature, can be limited substantially if CO_2e is kept below 490 and temperature change does not exceed 2.4°C. See also Table SPM 6, note b, for estimated ppm in 2005.

9. Sir Nicholas Herbert Stern, *The Economics of Climate Change: The Stern Review* (Cambridge University Press, 2007): "The stock of greenhouse gases in the atmosphere is already estimated at 430 ppm, and currently rising at roughly 2.5 ppm each year"(p. 219). Estimates vary, but nearly all predict that 2008 levels are between 420 and 445 ppm CO_2e.

10. IPCC, *Working Group I Contribution to the Fourth Assessment Report of the IPCC*, Table SPM 6 (IPCC, November 12, 2007): "Percent change in global CO_2 emissions in 2050" (p. 20, column 4). See also Alex Evans, *The Post-Kyoto Bidding War: Bringing Developing Countries into the Fold* (New York: Center on International Cooperation, October 2007): "The IPCC Fourth Assessment Report (4AR) states that to limit warming to between 2.0°C and 2.4°C, the stabilization ceiling would be between 445 and 490 ppm. And while EU leaders acknowledge the need for global emissions to fall to 50 percent of 2000 levels by 2050, this is in fact the absolute best-

case scenario, according to the Fourth Assessment Report, which finds that the 2000–50 emissions cut needed for 2.0°–2.4° degrees would be between 50 and 85 percent," p. 4.

11. International Energy Agency (IEA), *World Energy Outlook 2007* (IEA, 2007), available for purchase at www.worldenergyoutlook.org/.

12. Ibid. "The world's primary energy needs are projected to grow by 55 percent between 2005 and 2030, at an average annual rate of 1.8 percent per year. Chinese and Indian crude oil imports will almost quadruple by 2030. . . . Fossil fuels will remain the dominant source of primary energy, accounting for 84 percent of the overall increase in demand between 2005 and 2030," pp. 42–43.

13. Ibid. See also Karen A. Harbert, assistant secretary, Office of Policy and International Affairs, U.S. Department of Energy, "China's Energy Consumption and Opportunities for U.S.–China Cooperation to Address the Effects of China's Energy Use," statement before the U.S.–China Economic and Security Review Commission, June 14, 2007, available at www.uscc.gov/hearings/2007hearings/written_testimonies/07_06_14_15wrts/07_06_14_harbert_statement.pdf.

14. IEA, "Projections of Chinese and World Energy Uses, 2025," *World Energy Outlook 2006* (IEA, 2007), available for purchase at www.worldenergyoutlook.org/: "China will have to add more than 1300 GW to its electricity generating capacity, which is more than the total installed capacity in the United States. China's per capita emissions reach European levels by 2030," p. 203. See also Harbert, "China's Energy Consumption," p. 2.

15. Ibid.

16. These percentages are not additive. For example, oil flowing through the Strait of Hormuz may also go through the Strait of Malacca. That said, it would be safe to estimate that at least 35 percent of global oil supplies go through these choke points.

17. Steven Mufson, "Oil Price Rise Causes Global Shift in Wealth; Iran, Russia and Venezuela Feel the Benefits," *Washington Post,* November 10, 2007, p. A.1.

18. Julian Borger, "U.S. Biofuel Subsidies under Attack at Food Summit," *Manchester Guardian,* June 3, 2008, pp. 1, 2, available at www.guardian.co.uk/environment/2008/jun/03/biofuels.energy.

19. Elizabeth Rosenthal, "U.N. Says Biofuel Subsidies Raise Food Bill and Hunger," *New York Times,* October 7, 2008, p. 1, available at www.nytimes.com/2008/10/08/world/europe/08italy.html?ref=world.

20. UN Framework Convention on Climate Change (UNFCCC), "Fact Sheet: Reducing Emissions from Deforestation in Developing Countries: Approaches to Stimulate Action," no date, available at unfccc.int/files/press/backgrounders/application/pdf/fact_sheet_reducing_emissions_from_deforestation.pdf.

21. Peter Brabeck-Letmathe, "The Water Crisis: Another Inconvenient Truth," *International Herald Tribune,* October 5, 2008, available at www.iht.com/articles/2008/10/05/opinion/ednestle.php.

22. UN Department of Economic and Social Affairs Population Division, "World Population Will Increase by 2.5 Billion by 2050," Press Release, March 2007, available at www.un.org/News/Press/docs//2007/pop952.doc.htm. According to the 2007 revision, the world population is likely to increase by 2.5 billion over the next 43 years, passing from the current 6.7 billion to 9.2 billion in 2050. This increase is equiv-

alent to the total size of the world population in 1950, and it will be absorbed mostly by the less developed regions, whose population is projected to rise from 5.4 billion in 2007 to 7.9 billion in 2050.

23. Parliamentary Office of Science and Technology (United Kingdom), "Access to Energy in Developing Countries," December 2002, p. 1, available at www.parliament.uk/post/pn191.pdf.

24. UN Department of Economic and Social Affairs Population Division, "World Population Will Increase by 2.5 Billion by 2050."

25. IPCC, "About the IPCC: Mandate, Who We Are," available at www.ippc.ch/about/index.htm.

26. UNFCCC, "Essential Background: United Nations Framework Convention on Climate Change" (United Nations, 1992), p. 5, available at http://unfccc.int/resource/docs/convkp/conveng.pdf.

27. Daniel Howden, "UN Calls for 40 Percent Cut in Emissions by Rich Countries," *The Independent*, December 11, 2007, p. 1.

28. United Nations, *United Nations Framework Convention on Climate Change* (1992), p. 1.

29. Ibid., p. 1.

30. Ibid., p. 3.

31. United Nations, *Kyoto Protocol to the United Nations Framework Convention on Climate Change*, Article 1 (1998), p. 4.

32. Ibid., Article 10, p. 10.

33. Joseph E. Aldy and Robert N. Stavins, eds., *Architectures for Agreement: Addressing Global Climate Change in the Post-Kyoto World* (Cambridge University Press, 2007), p. 11.

34. As cited in "Greenhouse gas emissions—perspectives on the top 20 emitters and developed versus developing nations," Climate Analysis Indicators Tool (CAIT) Version 4.0 (Washington, D.C.: World Resources Institute, 2007). See eoearth.org/article/Greenhouse Gas Emissions—perspectives on the top 20 emitters and developed versus developing nations.

35. "Rudd Acts to Ratify Kyoto Accord in Australia," *International Herald Tribune*, December 2, 2007.

36. "Carbon Emissions and Stocks, CO_2 Emissions per capita (tonnes)," *United Nations Human Development Report*, 2007/2008, available at hdrstats.undp.org/indicators/237.html. As of 2007, U.S. per capita carbon emissions in 2004 are estimated at 20.6 tonnes per year. China's estimated per capita carbon emissions in 2004 are estimated to be 3.8 tonnes, and India's 1.2 tonnes (all are projected to increase by 2008, but the latest reliable data come from 2004). By our calculations, even if the United States and other developing countries took drastic action to reduce their carbon and carbon equivalent emissions by more than 90 percent by 2050, China and India alone could still potentially produce emissions that would be more than four times the sustainable CO_2 target of 9 gigatons per year in 2050, as outlined by the IPCC and the 2007 *UNDP Human Development Report*. (The IPCC goal is to keep CO_2e concentrations below 535 ppm CO_2e by 2050; this will require at least a 50 percent reduction in GHG emissions levels in 1990 by 2050 or 62–67 percent reductions in 2007 levels by 2050. In other words, global GHG emissions will need to be reduced from 24–28 gigatons annually in 2004–07 to 9 gigatons in 2050.) China's projected popu-

lation in 2050 is 1.437 billion (see note 38). If China's per capita emissions reach those of the United States and other industrialized countries by this point, which is possible, China's GHG emissions alone would be 30 gigatons a year. India's projected population in 2050 is 1.747 billion; with U.S. per capita emissions levels, GHG emissions from India alone in 2050 would be 35.98 gigatons. This means that if either China's or India's per capita emissions rise near U.S. per capita emissions by 2050, which is possible given current increases, even if the rest of the international community slashes its emissions to near zero, global GHG emissions could still be anywhere from 30 to 70 gigatons a year; the safe level outlined by scientists is 9 gigatons a year in 2050.

37. *United Nations Human Development Report*, 2007/2008; Population Reference Bureau (PRB), 2008 World Population Data Sheet, "World Population Highlights, Population 2050 (Projected)," p. 3, August 18, 2008. Available at www.prb.org/pdf08/08WPDS_Eng.pdf.

38. "Climate Change: A Moment of Truth," *Economist*, May 15, 2008. "According to Mr. Wara, the riches on offer from the CDM are discouraging governments in the developing world from taking easy steps to reduce their countries' greenhouse-gas emissions. . . . He cites China, where partly state-owned power firms are applying for credits for building gas-fired power plants instead of dirtier ones run on coal. He argues that China, which is keen to improve air quality anyway, would probably be building such plants with or without the CDM. But the government might now hesitate to issue regulations to that effect, for fear of violating the 'additionality' rule, and so losing out on valuable credits"; Michael Wara, "Measuring the Clean Development Mechanism's Performance and Potential" (Program on Energy and Sustainable Development [PESD], Center for Environmental Science and Policy, Stanford University, July 2006), p. 8.

39. "A Fresh Start for GEF Reform and GEF NGO Revitalization," presented at the Global Environmental Facility (GEF) NGO Consultation and Council Meeting, Washington, D.C., December 4–8, 2006, available at www.gefweb.org/uploaded-Files/MB%20speech%20Council%20June. The GEF is the financial instrument and coordinating mechanism that supports the four UN conventions on the environment and provides resources to implementing agencies of the GEF (World Bank, UNEP, UNDP, and RMDB). The remarks of Monique Barbut, chief executive officer and chairperson of the GEF, highlight the need for reform of the GEF and of the broader web of agencies tasked with dealing with climate environment in some capacity.

40. Peter Haldis, "ConocoPhillips Announces Support Mandatory Greenhouse Gas Emissions Program; Joins USCAP," *Global Refining & Fuels Report*, April 2007, available at findarticles.com/p/articles/mi_hb5630/is_200704/ai_n23646654; Christopher Palmeri, "ConocoPhillips' Own Inconvenient Truth," *Business Week*, April 19, 2007, available at www.businessweek.com/bwdaily/dnflash/content/apr2007/db20070 419_165468.htm.

41. Jane Spencer, "Big Firms to Press Suppliers on Climate," *Wall Street Journal*, October 9, 2007, available at http://online.wsj.com/public/article/SB11918662 2895152448.html.

42. Moira Herbst, "Investors Call on Congress to Go Green," *Business Week*, online, March 20, 2007, available at www.businessweek.com/bwdaily/dnflash/content/mar2007/db20070320_535194.htm.

43. Ibid.

44. Dallas Burtraw and Raymond Kopp, "The European Union Emissions Trading Scheme (EU-ETS): A Brief Overview" (Washington: Resources for the Future, March 20, 2007). Burtraw and Kopp put the estimated value of the EU-ETS at $30 billion in 2006 but were unable to provide definitive figures for 2007 because of the crash in carbon prices in 2007. (At the time of their writing, the spot price in the EU-ETS was $1.33 but was predicted to rise to $20.65 in December 2008.) The $30 billion is a conservative figure; by the end of 2009 it may have more than doubled in value but it is hard to quantify given recent price volatility.

45. Warwick McKibbin and Peter Wilcoxen, *A Credible Foundation for Long-Term International Cooperation on Climate Change* (Brookings, 2006).

46. The Pew Center on Global Climate Change, "A Look at Emissions Targets and Regional Initiatives," available at www.pewclimate.org/what_s_being_done/in_the_states/regional_initiatives.cfm.

47. Fact Sheet, Energy Independence and Security Act of 2007, "President Bush Signs Energy Bill to Improve Fuel Economy and Reduce Oil Dependence," December 19, 2007, available at www.whitehouse.gov/news/releases/2007/12/20071219-1.html; Fred Sissine, "Energy Independence and Security Act of 2007: A Summary of Major Provisions," *CRS Report for Congress*, December 21, 2007, available at energy.senate.gov/public/_files/RL342941.pdf.

48. The Pew Center on Global Climate Change, "Learning from State Action on Climate Change," Figure 7 (May 2007 Update), p. 8. Some require as high as 25 percent renewable energy by 2050. A federal renewable portfolio standard (RPS) provision, originally part of the draft bill, was not included in the passed version of the Energy and Security Independence Act of December 2007. See www.pewclimate.org/docUploads/States%20Brief%20(May%202008).pdf.

49. Environmental Defense Fund, "Environmentalists Sue to Challenge EPA Ruling on Clean Cars," January 3, 2008, available at www1.environmentaldefense.org/pressrelease.cfm?contentID=7493.

50. Drake Bennett, "The New Dirty Energy," *Boston Globe*, August 19, 2007, available at pesd.stanford.edu/news/pesd_associate_reports_to_boston_globe_on_unclean_oil_alternatives_20070827.

51. Peter Gelling and Andrew Revkin, "Delegates in Bali for Talks on Climate," December 2, 2007, available at www.iht.com/articles/2007/12/02/asia/bali.php. Note, for example, the U.S. resistance at the Bali Conference of the Parties in December 2008, where the developing countries took the initiative and shamed the United States into consent.

52. Frank Biermann and Steffen Bauer, *A World Environment Organization: Solution or Threat for Effective International Environmental Governance?* (London: Ashgate Publishing Ltd., 2005), p. 2.

53. "Energy Supply and Economic Growth, Total Primary Energy Supply per Unit of GDP," *OECD Factbook 2008: Economic, Environmental and Social Statistics* (OECD, 2008), available at oecd.p4.siteinternet.com/publications/doifiles/05-01-02-t1.xls.

54. McKinsey & Company, "Reducing U.S. Greenhouse Emissions: How Much at What Cost?" *U.S. Greenhouse Gas Abatement Mapping Initiative, Executive Report* (McKinsey & Company, December 2007), p. ix, xii–xvii.

55. IEA, *World Energy Outlook* 2007, available for purchase at www.worldenergyoutlook.org/.

56. IEA, *World Energy Outlook* 2004, available for purchase at www.worldenergyoutlook.org/.

57. Agencies such as MIGA and OPIC were created to address political risk outside of one's borders. Investments in climate change are also needed within nation-states, yet for the most part no established mechanisms deal with risks within borders that have external impacts.

58. CCS has been called the most promising method to reduce carbon emissions from coal, but it is not a "miracle solution" nor is it close to commercialization. A comprehensive MIT study on carbon capture and sequestration concluded that the equivalent of a $30 per ton tax on carbon was needed to make the process economically feasible. (Other estimates put this price far higher when accounting for the cost of covering liability of demonstration projects.) It cannot be brought into wide commercial use without large-scale pilot projects run over a decade to determine the effect of injecting massive quantities of carbon into the earth. U.S. companies are not willing to take on the risk of piloting carbon sequestration without indemnity from legal liabilities and the U.S. Congress has not been willing to provide such indemnities. Currently, experts say that an infusion of $6.4 billion over ten years would be needed to make CCS at all commercially viable or investment neutral. Without this funding, technology development and transfer are frozen.

59. U.K. Department for International Development (DFID), "Europe for Development: Working with European Union," July 2008, available at www.dfid.gov.uk/pubs/files/eu-isp.pdf. At the spring 2007 European Council meeting, EU member states pledged to help share liability to build twelve to fifteen CCS demonstration plants by 2015, and all new fossil fuel plants are to be fitted with CCS by 2020. In the authors' consultations, we found that the French government has been particularly proactive in working toward this goal.

60. "World Bank Plans Clean Technology Fund for Poor," Reuters, February 9, 2008, p. 1, available at timesofindia.indiatimes.com/World_Bank_fund_to_help_poor_cut_pollution/articleshow/2769140.cms.

61. "U.N. Launches Program to Cut Deforestation Emissions," Reuters, September 28, 2008, available at www.reuters.com/article/environmentNews/idUSTRE48N91C20080924?feedType=RSS&feedName=environmentNews&pageNumber=1&virtualBrandChannel=0.

62. Jim Yardley and Andrew Revkin, "China Issues Plan on Global Warming, Rejecting Mandatory Caps on Greenhouse Gases," *New York Times,* June 5, 2007, p. 1, available at www.nytimes.com/2007/06/05/world/asia/05china.html.

63. Harbert, "China's Energy Consumption," p. 2; IEA, *World Energy Outlook 2007.*

64. Todd Stern and William Antholis, "A Changing Climate: The Road Ahead for the United States," *Washington Quarterly* 31 (Winter 2007–08): 184.

65. Ibid., p. 185.

66. Jason Bordoff, "International Trade Law and the Economics of Climate Policy: Evaluating the Legality and Effectiveness of Proposals to Address Competitiveness and Leakage Concerns" (Brookings, 2008), p. 4, available at www.brookings.edu/events/2008/~/media/Files/events/2008/0609_climate_trade/2008_bordoff.pdf; War-

wick J. McKibbin and Peter J. Wilcoxen, *The Economic and Environmental Effects of Border Adjustments for Carbon Taxes*, Brookings Policy Paper (October 2008).

67. Bordoff, p. 4.

68. Ibid., p. 5.

69. Ibid., p. 5, note 6: EPA analysis in Senate bill 2191, supra note 4, at 84.

70. "New ISO 14064 Standards provide tools for assessing and supporting greenhouse gas reduction and emissions trading," p. 1, press release, International Standards Organization, March 16, 2003. See quote from Dr. Chan Kook Weng, Convenor of ISO 14064 Working Group.

71. Ibid., p. 2.

72. According to IEA, *World Energy Outlook 2007*, emerging economies will account for 70 percent and statistics on the United States and the total percentage are forthcoming. Estimates project about 90 percent.

CHAPTER FIVE

1. This phrase was coined by Paul Bracken in "The Second Nuclear Age," *Foreign Affairs*, January/February 2000. For Bracken the second nuclear age is marked by the spread of ballistic missiles and weapons of mass destruction to countries in Asia. Our use of the term refers to more sweeping global changes in nuclear technology, demand for nuclear energy, norms of nuclear weapons use, and proliferation, including to and through nonstate actors.

2. "Fool's Gold," *Financial Times*, May 31, 2008.

3. *Doctrine for Joint Nuclear Operations, Final Coordination (2)*, Joint Publication 3-12, March 15, 2005, available at www.globalsecurity.org/wmd/library/policy/dod/jp3_12fc2.pdf. See also recent discussion on preemptive nuclear doctrine for the North Atlantic Treaty Organization (NATO) at www.guardian.co.uk/nato/story/0,,2244782,00.html.

4. See James Acton and George Perkovich, "Abolishing Nuclear Weapons," Adelphi paper 396 (London: International Institute for Strategic Studies, September 2008).

5. We (Jones and Stedman) heard all these sentiments in 2004 and 2005 when we worked for the United Nations and consulted with governments around the world on threat assessments. Two different Pakistani officials asserted that the United States had fabricated the threat of nuclear terrorism.

6. Even in the United States, where organizational control of the weapons is high, recent mistakes in handling of nuclear weapons led Secretary of Defense Robert Gates to fire high-ranking generals for their lack of attention to safety issues.

7. Among the entities still under the nuclear umbrella are NATO (with twenty-six members), Japan, South Korea, and Taiwan.

8. Chaim Braun and Christopher F. Chyba, "Proliferation Rings: New Challenges to the Nuclear Nonproliferation Regime," *International Security* 29, no. 2 (2004): 5–49.

9. Douglas Frantz and Catherine Collins, *The Nuclear Jihadist* (New York: Twelve, 2007).

10. Brazil, China, France, Germany, India, Iran, Japan, Netherlands, Pakistan, Russia, United Kingdom, United States.

11. The founding of the IAEA in 1957 predated the signing of the NPT, but the agency was given a central role in implementing the treaty's core provisions.

12. Henry D. Sokolski, ed., *Falling Behind: International Scrutiny of the Peaceful Atom* (Carlisle, Pa.: Strategic Studies Institute, U.S. Army War College, 2008), available at www.strategicstudiesinstitute.army.mil/pdffiles/PUB841.pdf. IAEA's inspection budget was raised from $89 million in 2003 to $102 million in 2004 and then to $108 million in 2007.

13. The Global Partnership's principles are to (1) promote multilateral treaties that help prevent the spread of weapons, materials, and know-how; (2) account for and secure those items; (3) promote physical protection of facilities; (4) help to detect, deter, and interdict illicit trafficking; (5) promote national export and transshipment controls; and (6) manage and dispose of nuclear, biological, and chemical weapons materials.

14. This section draws heavily from Robert Carlin and John W. Lewis, "Negotiating North Korea's Denuclearization: Defining and Using the Relevant Experience and Modalities," prepared for the Brookings Institution's Managing Global Insecurity (MGI) project, March 16, 2007.

15. Charles L. Pritchard, *Failed Diplomacy: The Tragic Story of How North Korea Got the Bomb* (Brookings, 2007).

16. Scott D. Sagan, "Failures of Regime Change: The United States, Iran, and the NPT," prepared for the MGI project (March 11, 2007).

17. IAEA, "Implementation of the NPT Safeguards Agreement in the Islamic Republic of Iran," GOV/2003/75 (November 10, 2003), p. 4.

18. Gareth Porter, "Burnt Offering," *American Prospect*, May 21, 2006.

19. National Intelligence Estimate, "Iran: Nuclear Intentions and Capabilities" (Office of the Director of National Intelligence, November 2007).

20. Karen DeYoung, "Gates: U.S. Should Engage Iran with Incentives, Pressure," *Washington Post*, May 15, 2008, p. 4.

21. Joby Warrick, "Spread of Nuclear Capability Is Feared," *Washington Post*, May 12, 2008, p. 1.

22. George P. Shultz and others, "A World Free of Nuclear Weapons," *Wall Street Journal*, January 4, 2007, and "Toward a Nuclear-Free World," *Wall Street Journal*, January 15, 2008.

23. Scott Sagan explores this key question in a research program at CISAC.

24. United Nations General Assembly, "General and Complete Disarmament," A/RES/48/75, December 16, 1993, available at www.un.org/documents/ga/res/48/a48r075.htm.

25. IAEA Press Release 2006/15, "IAEA Seeks Guarantees of Nuclear Fuel," September 15, 2006.

CHAPTER SIX

1. Mark Wheelis and Malcolm Dando, "Neurobiology: A Case Study of the Imminent Militarization of Biology," *International Review of the Red Cross* 87, no. 859 (September 2005): 566.

2. Michael T. Osterholm, "Preparing for the Next Pandemic," *Foreign Affairs* (July-August 2005): 24. "The reality of a coming pandemic, however, cannot be avoided. Only its impact can be lessened."

3. U.K. Cabinet Office, National Risk Register (London: 2008). The report suggests that an influenza pandemic could kill between 50,000 and 750,000 people in the United Kingdom and between 2 and 7.4 million people worldwide.

4. This paragraph draws on the following: Bernadette Tansey, "High School Biowizards Break New Ground in Winning Competition," *San Francisco Chronicle*, November 17, 2007, p. A-1; Jesse Lichtenstein, "Innocence and Syn: At This Science Fair, Students Are Creating New Forms of Life," *Slate*, November 30, 2007 (www.slate.com/id/2178897); and Alexis Madrigal, "Genetic-Engineering Competitors Create Modular DNA Dev Kit," *Wired*, November 13, 2007 (www.wired.com/science/discoveries/news/2007/11/igem_winner).

5. The BioBricks Foundation (http://bbf.openwetware.org/).

6. Freeman Dyson, "The Question of Global Warming," *New York Review of Books* 55, no. 10 (June 12, 2008).

7. Andrew Pollack, "The Race to Read Genomes on a Shoestring, Relatively Speaking," *New York Times*, February 9, 2008, p. B1.

8. Freeman Dyson, "Our Biotech Future," *New York Review of Books* 54, no. 12 (July 19, 2007).

9. Christopher Chyba, "Biotechnology and the Challenge to Arms Control," *Arms Control Today*, October 2006, p. 11.

10. Ibid.

11. Institute of Medicine and National Research Council of the National Academies, *Globalization, Biosecurity, and the Future of the Life Sciences* (Washington: National Academies Press, 2006), p. viii.

12. Ibid., pp. 4, 139–212.

13. Elizabeth Finkel, "Engineered Mouse Virus Spurs Bioweapons Fears," *Science* 291, no. 5504 (January 26, 2001): 585.

14. Mark Wheelis and Maaaki Sugishima, "Terrorist Use of Biological Weapons," in *Deadly Cultures: Biological Weapons since 1945*, edited by Mark Wheelis, Lajos Rozsa, and Malcolm Dando (Harvard University Press, 2006), pp. 284–303. See also Milton Leitenberg, "Evolution of the Current Threat," in *Bioterrorism: Confronting a Complex Threat*, edited by Andreas Wenger and Reto Wollenmann (Boulder, Colo.: Lynne Rienner, 2007), pp. 39–76.

15. Elizabeth Dowdeswell, Peter A. Singer, and Abdallah S. Daar, "Increasing Human Security through Biotechnology," *Biotechnology* 8, no. 1–2 (2006): 119–31.

16. David Morens, Gregory K. Folkers, and Anthony S. Fauci, "The Challenge of Emerging and Re-emerging Infectious Diseases," *Nature*, July 8, 2004, pp. 242–49.

17. Dowdeswell, Singer, and Daar, "Increasing Human Security through Biotechnology."

18. Peter A. Singer, "DNA for Peace," Director's Lecture to the Ford Dorsey Program in International Policy Studies, Stanford University, May 30, 2007.

19. Kate E. Jones and others, "Global Trends in Emerging Infectious Diseases," *Nature*, February 21, 2008, pp. 990–94.

20. Ibid.

21. Margaret E. Kruk, "Global Public Health and Biosecurity: Managing Twenty-First Century Risks," Coping with Crisis Working Paper Series (New York: International Peace Academy, July 2007), p. 8.

22. Ibid.

23. Ibid., p. 11.

24. International and domestic air passenger data come from IATA, "2007 Total Passenger Traffic Results" (www.iata.org/ps/publications/2007-results.htm). The figures on travel to and from the United States come from Secretary of State Condoleeza Rice, "Remarks," Global Travel and Tourism Summit Breakfast, April 12, 2006, Washington (http://news.findlaw.com/wash/s/20060412/20060412150501.html).

25. Kruk, "Global Public Health and Biosecurity," p. 9.

26. David Fidler, "Indonesia's Decision to Withhold Influenza Virus Samples from the World Health Organization: Implications for International Law," *ASIL Insights* 11, no. 4 (February 28, 2007).

27. Ruth R. Faden, Patrick S. Duggan, and Ruth Karron, "Who Pays to Stop a Pandemic?" *New York Times*, February 9, 2007.

28. James B. Petro and David A. Relman, "Understanding Threats to Scientific Openness," *Science* 302 (December 2003).

29. Leitenberg, "Evolution of the Current Threat."

30. Bruce Schneier, *Beyond Fear: Thinking Sensibly about Security in an Uncertain World* (New York: Copernicus Books, 2003), p. 275.

31. Mark Wheelis, Lajos Rozsa, and Malcolm Dando, *Deadly Cultures: Biological Weapons since 1945* (Harvard University Press, 2006).

32. M. Meselson and others, "The Sverdlovsk Anthrax Outbreak of 1979," *Science* 266, no. 5188 (November 18, 1994): 1202–08.

33. John Hart, "The Soviet Biological Weapons Program," in *Deadly Cultures*, edited by Wheelis, Rozsa, and Dando, p. 143.

34. "Note by the Secretary-General" (UN Security Council Document S/1995/864, October 11, 1995). The note transmits a report on the status of the implementation of the Special Commission's plan for the ongoing monitoring and verification of Iraq's compliance with relevant parts of section C of Security Council Resolution 687 (1991). The note and report can be found at www.un.org/Depts/unscom/sres95-864.htm.

35. Chandra Gould and Alastair Hay, "The South African Biological Program," in *Deadly Cultures*, edited by Wheelis, Rozsa, and Dando, p. 200.

36. Claire M. Fraser and Malcolm R. Dando, "Genomics and Future Biological Weapons: The Need for Preventive Action by the Biomedical Community," *Nature Genetics* 29 (2001): 254.

37. Ibid.

38. David P. Fidler, "Globalization, International Law, and Emerging Infectious Diseases," *Emerging Infectious Diseases* 2, no. 2 (April-June 1996): 80.

39. David P. Fidler and Lawrence O. Gostin, *Biosecurity in the Global Age* (Stanford University Press, 2008), pp. 154–55.

40. This paragraph draws from Fiona Godlee, "WHO in Retreat: Is It Losing Its Influence?" *British Medical Journal*, December 3, 1994, pp. 1491–95; Octavio Gomez-Dantes, "Health," in *Managing Global Issues: Lessons Learned*, edited by P. J. Simmons and Chantal de Jonge Oudraat (Washington: Carnegie Endowment,

2000), pp. 392–423; and Theodore M. Brown, Marcos Cueto, and Elizabeth Fee, "The World Health Organization and the Transition from International to Global Public Health," *American Journal of Public Health* 96, no. 1 (January 2006): 62–72.

41. To learn about Mann and his battles against HIV/AIDS and at WHO, see the PBS *Frontline* series, "The Age of AIDS," part 1, chapters 6 and 8.

42. Godlee, "WHO in Retreat."

43. The incident is vividly recounted in Laurie Garrett, *Betrayal of Trust: The Collapse of Global Public Health* (New York: Hyperion, 2000), pp. 15–49.

44. Stacey Knobler and others, *Learning from SARS: Preparing for the Next Disease Outbreak—Workshop Summary* (Washington: National Academies Press, 2004), p. 8.

45. Ibid., p. 14.

46. Ibid., p. 14.

47. Ibid., p. 2.

48. Jez Littlewood, "Back to Basics: Verification and the Biological Weapons Convention," in *Verification Yearbook 2003*, edited by Trevor Findley (London: Vertic, 2003), pp. 92–93.

49. World Health Organization, *The World Health Report 2007: A Safer Future* (Geneva: 2007), p. 66.

50. Ibid., p. 60.

51. Laurie Garrett, "The Challenge of Global Health," *Foreign Affairs* 86, no. 1 (January–February 2007): 14–38.

52. World Health Organization, *The World Health Report 2008: Primary Health Care, Now More than Ever* (Geneva: 2008).

53. EU–Latin America and Caribbean Summit, "Political Declaration: The Madrid Commitment," May 17, 2002 (www.bologna-berlin2003.de/pdf/Madrid_commitment.pdf).

54. Elizabeth Dowdeswell, Peter A. Singer, and Abdallah S. Daar, "Increasing Human Security through Biotechnology," *International Journal of Biotechnology* 8, no. 1–2 (2006): 122–23.

55. Ibid.

56. "DNA for Peace: Reconciling Biodevelopment and Biosecurity," McLaughlin Centre for Molecular Medicine, Canadian Program on Genomics and Global Health, University of Toronto Joint Centre for Bioethics (no date) (http://openwetware.org/images/d/d0/DNA_Peace.pdf).

CHAPTER SEVEN

1. Figures cited in this chapter, except where otherwise noted, are drawn from the Center on International Cooperation, *Annual Review of Global Peace Operations 2007* (Boulder, Colo.: Lynne Rienner Publishers, 2007).

2. Human Security Center, University of British Columbia, "Overview," in *Human Security Report 2005: War and Peace in the 21st Century* (Oxford University Press, 2005), pp. 1–11, available at www.humansecurityreport.info/HSR2005_PDF/Overview.pdf.

3. Ibid.

4. Ibid. The 2005 Uppsala/Human Security Center data set shows that the number of conflicts in Africa in which a government was one of the warring parties declined from fifteen to ten between 2002 and 2003. The number of cases of "one-sided" violence—defined as the slaughter of at least twenty-five civilians in the course of a year and called one-sided because the victims cannot fight back—declined from seventeen to eleven, a drop of 35 percent. Meanwhile, reported fatalities from all forms of political violence were down by more than 24 percent.

5. Bruce Riedel, "Troubled Pakistan: A Case Study in Modern American Diplomacy," unpublished paper commissioned by the Managing Global Insecurity (MGI) project (2006).

6. Peter Lewis, "State Weakness and International Engagement: Nigeria Agonistes," unpublished paper commissioned by the MGI project (2006).

7. Terje Roed-Larsen, speech delivered at the King Faisal Center for Research and Islamic Studies, Riyadh, Saudi Arabia, May 22, 2007.

8. Paul Collier and others, *Breaking the Conflict Trap: Civil War and Development Policy* (Washington, D.C.: World Bank and Oxford University Press, 2003), available at http://indh.pnud.org.co/files/rec/Conflictrap.pdf.

9. *The National Security Strategy of the United States of America* (The White House, 2002), p. 1, available at www.whitehouse.gov/nsc/nss/2002/nss.pdf.

10. For text of the document, see www.un.org/summit2005/documents.html.

11. Ibid.

12. Elizabeth Cousens, "The Security Council and Prevention," in *The UN Security Council from the Cold War to the 21st Century,* edited by David Malone (Boulder, Colo.: Lynne Rienner Publishers, 1995), pp. 101–17.

13. George W. Bush has used special envoys much less frequently than President Bill Clinton. Darfur is an exception.

14. Paul Collier, "Development and Conflict" (Center for the Study of African Economies, Department of Economics, Oxford University, 2004), available at www.un.org/esa/documents/Development.and.Conflict2.pdf.

15. Frances Stewart, "Crisis Prevention: Tackling Horizontal Inequalities," paper prepared for World Bank Conference on Evaluation and Poverty Reduction, June 14–15, 1999, available at www.rrojasdatabank.org/wpover/Frances_Stewart_Paper.pdf. For a dissenting view see Collier and others, "On the Duration of Civil War," World Bank Policy Research Paper 2681, available at http://papers.ssrn.com/sol3/papers.cfm?abstract_id=632749.

16. Paul Collier, "On Economic Causes of Civil War," *Oxford Economic Papers* 50 (1998): 563–73. An alternate perspective can be found in James Fearon and David Laitin, "Ethnicity, Insurgency, and Civil War," *American Political Science Review* 97, no. 1 (February 2003): 75–90.

17. Political Instability Task Force, "PITF Phase I-V Papers" (George Mason University Center for Global Policy, 2007), available at http://globalpolicy.gmu.edu/pitf/pitfdata.htm.

18. Ibid. See also Edward D. Mansfield and Jack Snyder, *Electing to Fight: Why Emerging Democracies Go to War* (MIT Press, 2005) and Jack Snyder, *From Voting to Violence: Democratization and Nationalist Conflict* (New York: Norton & Co., 2000).

19. Zalmay Khalilzad, speech delivered at New York University Wagner School of Public Service, April 16, 2008, and at the Doha Forum, February 18, 2008. For text of the speech, see www.thedohaforum.org/assets/speeches/khalilzad_speech.pdf. See also Ashraf Ghani and Clare Lockhart, *Fixing Failed States: A Framework for Rebuilding a Fractured World* (Oxford University Press, 2008).

20. A public version of this study is found in Barnett R. Rubin and Bruce D. Jones, "Prevention of Violent Conflict: Tasks and Challenges for the United Nations," *Global Governance* 13 (2007): 391–408.

21. Human Security Report Project, *Human Security Brief 2006,* Human Security Center at the University of British Columbia, available at www.humansecurity-brief.info/.

22. Thant Myint-U, "The UN as Conflict Mediator: First Amongst Equals or the Last Resort?" paper presented at the Oslo Forum of the HD Center, 2006, available at www.osloforum.org/datastore/Mediators%20Retreats/OSLO%20Forum%20Briefing%20Pack/TheUNasConflictMediator.pdf.

23. Bruce Jones, "Lebanon," unpublished paper commissioned by the MGI project (2006).

24. Chester A. Crocker, "Peacemaking and Mediation: Dynamics of a Changing Field," Coping with Crisis Working Paper Series (New York: International Peace Academy, 2007), available at www.ipacademy.org/asset/file/153/CWC_Working_Paper_PEACEMAKING_CC.pdf.

25. For accounts of the mediation process that led to the Dayton Accords, see Richard Holbrooke, *To End a War* (New York: Random House, 1998), and Ivo Daalder, *Getting to Dayton: The Making of America's Bosnia Policy* (Brookings, 2000).

26. Steven Lee Myers and Thom Shanker, "Pentagon Considers Adding Forces in Afghanistan," *New York Times,* May 3, 2008, available at www.nytimes.com/2008/05/03/world/asia/03military.html.

27. James Dobbins and others, *The UN's Role in Nation-Building: From Congo to Iraq* (Santa Monica, Calif.: RAND Corporation, 2005).

28. Data compiled from the Center on International Cooperation's *Annual Review of Global Peace Operations* (2007 and 2008) and from the UN Department of Peacekeeping Operations. See www.un.org/Depts/dpko/dpko/.

29. William J. Durch, *Twenty-First Century Peace Operations* (Washington: USIP Press, 2007), p. 576.

30. Dobbins and others, *The UN's Role in Nation-Building,* p. xxxvi. See also Paul Collier and Anke Hoeffler, "The Challenge of Reducing the Global Incidence of Civil War," Copenhagen Consensus Challenge Paper (Center for the Study of African Economies, Department of Economics, Oxford University, March 26, 2004), p. 22, available at www.copenhagenconsensus.com/Files/Filer/CC/Papers/Conflicts_230404.pdf.

31. See Collier and others, *Breaking the Conflict Trap.*

32. The misalignment of donor and host nation agendas often arises most poignantly in the security areas. International actors are generally under pressure to withdraw troops, and there is a massive shortage in internationally deployable police. Yet it will take a good five years to build a viable local military and police force, and even longer to revamp the justice system.

33. Information on the PBC can be found at www.un.org/peace/peacebuilding/. For the PBSO, see www.un.org/peace/peacebuilding/pbso.shtml.

34. See Center on International Cooperation, *Annual Review of Global Peace Operations 2007*.

35. Carlos Pascual and Kenneth Pollack, "The Critical Battles: Political Reconciliation and Reconstruction in Iraq," *Washington Quarterly* 30, no. 3 (2007): 7–19.

36. Ibid.

37. In 2008, a plan to this effect was blocked by the United States in the budget committee. In fairness to the United States, however, the plan was widely viewed among member states as poorly crafted and weakly justified, although many member states did see the merit in expanding the mediation and preventive diplomacy capacity of the United Nations. Failure in one effort at reform should not preclude putting forward a new, better-considered plan.

38. The U.S. Department of State's Office of the Coordinator for Reconstruction and Stabilization created such guidelines, which could serve as a base. See the *U.S. Government Draft Planning Framework for Reconstruction, Stabilization, and Conflict Transformation* at www.crs.state.gov/index.cfm?fuseaction=public.display&id=c065fc4e-065b-4c47-ab16-0acdd1807ede. *Postconflict Reconstruction: Essential Tasks* can be found at www.state.gov/documents/organization/53464.pdf. See also "Appendix 1: Joint CSIS/AUSA Postconflict Reconstruction Task Framework" in *Winning the Peace: An American Strategy for Postconflict Reconstruction*, edited by Robert C. Orr (Washington, D.C.: CSIS Press, 2004), pp. 305–27.

CHAPTER EIGHT

1. See www.state.gov/t/isn/rls/fs/46839.htm.

2. Recall that our vision of the G-16 includes the existing G-8 countries; the outreach five (Brazil, China, India, Mexico, and South Africa); and Indonesia, Turkey, and one additional African country.

3. This chapter owes an intellectual debt to our colleagues: Dan Benjamin, director of the Center on the United States and Europe at Brookings Institution; Sebastian von Einsiedel, currently serving with the United Nations in Nepal and a former colleague on the UN High-Level Panel on Threats, Challenges, and Change; and Eric Rosand, senior fellow of the Center on Global Counterterrorism Cooperation and visiting fellow at New York University's (NYU) Center on International Cooperation. It draws in part on a policy brief prepared by Benjamin and Rosand for the Brookings Managing Global Insecurity (MGI) project.

4. This is true even among U.S. data sets. Internationally, two additional controversies arise—many international studies do not count Palestinian attacks against Israeli soldiers as terrorist attacks, and similarly, many discount attacks against U.S. forces in Iraq.

5. Sebastian von Einsiedel, "Evaluating Responses to International Terrorism," High-Level Panel on Threats, Challenges, and Change Background Paper, unpublished, 2003.

6. Ibid.

7. International Crisis Group (ICG), "Nepal Backgrounder: Ceasefire—Soft Landing or Strategic Pause?" (ICG Asia Report No. 50, 2003), available at www.crisisgroup.org/home/index.cfm?id=1642&l=1.

8. John L. Esposito and Dalia Mogahed, "What Makes a Muslim Radical?" *Foreign Policy*, web exclusive, November 2006, available at www.foreignpolicy.com/story/cms.php?story_id=3637.

9. United Nations Development Program (UNDP), *2002 Arab Human Development Report* (New York: UNDP, 2002), pp. 25–28.

10. Robert A. Pape, "The Strategic Logic of Suicide Terrorism," *American Political Science Review* 97 (August 2003): 343–61.

11. The case of domestic terrorism in Pakistan is complicated in that several Pashtun groups based in and around Waziristan and the North-West Frontier Province (NWFP) have historically articulated the case for separation from the main body of Pakistan. In this regard, some part of the Taliban's and al Qaeda's support in that region can be seen as linked to a perception of occupation or a potential separatist struggle in Waziristan.

12. East Asia broadly comprises mainland China, Taiwan, Japan, North Korea, South Korea, Mongolia, Vietnam, Philippines, Thailand, Indonesia, Brunei, Cambodia, East Timor, Laos, Malaysia, Myanmar, and Singapore

13. See, among others, Alan Collison, "Inside al Qaeda's Hard Drive," *Atlantic Monthly* (September 2004): 55–70. For a fuller discussion of internal al Qaeda dynamics, see Jason Burke, *Al-Qaeda: Casting a Shadow of Terror* (London: I. B. Tauris, 2003).

14. See www.dni.gov/press_releases/20070717_release.pdf.

15. For definitions of the boundaries of West Asia, see chapter 10.

16. Bruce Riedel, "Troubled Pakistan: A Case Study in Modern American Diplomacy," unpublished paper commissioned by the MGI project, 2007.

17. Human Security Report Project, "Human Security Brief 2007," available at www.humansecuritybrief.info/access.html.

18. President Bush publicly discussed this strategy many times in 2007 and 2008. For example, see his speech from February 2007, in which he outlined strategy and progress in Afghanistan and the global war on terror, available at www.whitehouse.gov/news/releases/2007/02/20070215-1.html. For a more recent speech (January 2008), see www.whitehouse.gov/news/releases/2008/01/20080131 2.html.

19. Pew Global Attitudes Project, "Global Unease with Major World Powers: Rising Environmental Concern in 47-Nation Survey," June 2007, available at http://pewglobal.org/reports/display.php?ReportID=256.

20. Esposito and Mogahed, "What Makes a Muslim Radical?"

21. C. Christine Fair, Clay Ramsay, and Steven Kull, "Pakistani Public Opinion on Democracy, Islamic Militancy, and Relations with the United States," Joint Study of WorldPublicOpinion.org and the United States Institute of Peace, January 2008, available at www.worldpublicopinion.org/pipa/pdf/jan08/Pakistan_Jan08_rpt.pdf.

22. See www.un.org/Docs/scres/2001/sc2001.htm.

23. See www.un.org/Docs/sc/unsc_resolutions04.html.

24. See http://untreaty.un.org/English/Terrorism/English_18_15.pdf.

25. Report of the Secretary General, *Uniting against Terrorism: Recommendations for a Global Counterterrorism Strategy*, 2006, available at www.un.org/unitingagainstterrorism/sg-terrorism-2may06.pdf.

26. According to the information that member states reported to the al Qaeda and Taliban Sanctions Committee, as of late July 2006, $91.4 million, mainly in the form of bank accounts, had been frozen by thirty-five states under this sanctions regime. See UN Security Council al Qaeda and Taliban Sanctions Committee, *Fifth Report of the al Qaeda and Taliban Sanctions Monitoring Team*, S/2006/750 (New York, September 20, 2006), p. 21.

27. UN Security Council Resolution S/RES/1368 (New York, September 12, 2001), p. 1.

28. A minor exception is the expansive role of the UN humanitarian agencies in responding to the earthquake in 2005.

29. Riedel, "Troubled Pakistan."

30. International Task Force on Global Public Goods, *Meeting Global Challenges: International Cooperation in the National Interest*, final report (Stockholm: 2006), available at www.gpgtaskforce.org/uploads/files/169.pdf.

31. UNODC, "Legislative Guide to the Universal Antiterrorism Conventions and Protocols" (New York, 2003).

32. See the status of the two conventions under http://untreaty.un.org/english/Terrorism/Conv12.pdf and http://untreaty.un.org/English/Terrorism/Conv11.pdf.

33. Interpol Media Release, "Interpol Enhances Red Notice System for Terrorism Suspects; Widens Criteria for Alerting World to Suspected Terrorists," 2003, available at www.interpol.int/Public/ICPO/PressReleases/PR2003/PR200332.asp.

34. Mathieu Deflem and Lindsay Maybin, "Interpol and the Policing of International Terrorism: Developments and Dynamics since September 11," in *Terrorism: Research, Reading, & Realities*, edited by Lynne L. Snowden and Brad Whitsel (London: Prentice-Hall, forthcoming).

35. Eric Rosand, "The UN-Led Multilateral Response to Jihadist Terrorism: Is a Global Counterterrorism Body Needed?" *Journal of Conflict and Security* 11, no. 3: 399–427.

36. Ibid. See also "The Egmont Group: Financial Intelligence Units (FIUs)," April 18, 2007, available at www.egmontgroup.org/about_egmont.pdf.

37. Von Einsiedel, "Evaluating Responses to International Terrorism."

38. *The National Security Strategy of the United States of America* (The White House, 2002), available at www.whitehouse.gov/nsc/nss/2002/nss.pdf.

39. *A More Secure World: Our Shared Responsibility* (Report of the High-Level Panel on Threats, Challenges, and Change, 2004), paragraphs 190 and 191, available at www.un.org/secureworld/.

40. Ivo Daalder, *Beyond Preemption: Force and Legitimacy in a Changing World* (Brookings, 2007).

41. The Hoover Institution and Stanford Institute for International Studies, Preventive Force Conference, May 25–27, 2005, information available at www.hoover.org/research/conferences/3022291.html?show=agenda.

42. Sebastian von Einsiedel and Eric Rosand, "Counterterrorism Institutions," in *Cooperating for Peace and Security: The Evolution of Multilateral Security Institu-*

tions, edited by Shepard Forman and Bruce Jones (Cambridge University Press, forthcoming).

43. The most ample discussion to date of this issue is found in Alistair Millar and Eric Rosand, *Allied against Terrorism: What's Needed to Strengthen Worldwide Commitment* (New York: Century Foundation, 2006).

44. A new body could take over, focusing and building on the work of the existing council counterterrorism-related bodies (particularly the CTC), in addition to other relevant UN activities. Presumably, decisions of the Security Council and the General Assembly would be needed to transfer the work of their relevant bodies to a new dedicated counterterrorism body.

45. Millar and Rosand, *Allied against Terrorism,* especially pp. 35–56.

46. For a list of UN actions involved in counterterrorism, see Millar and Rosand, *Allied against Terrorism.*

CHAPTER NINE

1. Quoted in Robert A. Pollard, *Economic Security and the Origins of the Cold War, 1945–1950* (Columbia University Press, 1985), p. 8.

2. National Intelligence Council (NIC), *Mapping the Global Future,* report 2004-13 of the NIC 2020 Project (Pittsburgh: U.S. Government Printing Office, December 2004).

3. Brookings Global Economy and Development, *Top 10 Global Economic Challenges: An Assessment of Global Risks and Priorities* (February 2007), p. 24.

4. In an index recently released by the Center for Global Development (CGD) and the Brookings Institution, extreme poverty emerged as a predominant characteristic of the "critically weak" and "weak" states. See Susan Rice and Stewart Patrick, *Index of State Weakness in the Developing World* (Brookings, 2008). See also Bruce Jones and others, "From Fragility to Resilience: Concepts and Dilemmas of Statebuilding in Fragile States," research paper prepared for the OECD (Organization for Economic Cooperation and Development) Fragile States Group (Paris: OECD, August 2008).

5. World Economic Forum (WEF), *Global Risks 2008: A Global Risk Network Report* (January 2008), p. 20.

6. WEF Annual Meeting 2008, *The Power of Collaborative Innovation,* Davos, Switzerland, January 23–27, 2008. See www.weforum.org/pdf/summitreports/am2008/.

7. Ibid.

8. WEF, *Global Risks 2008,* pp. 7–11.

9. Lael Brainard, *Saving for the 21st Century: Is America Saving Enough to Be Competitive in the Global Marketplace?* Testimony before Senate Committee on Finance (Brookings, April 2006), available at www.brookings.edu/testimony/2006/0406macroeconomics_brainard.aspx.

10. Forbes.com, "Food Shortage Rises with Prices," April 15, 2008, available at www.forbes.com/business/2008/04/14/food-prices-china-biz-cx_0415oxford.html.

11. Reuters, compiled by Steve Slater, edited by Will Waterman, "The World's Biggest Banks," September 15, 2008.

12. IMF, *Making the Global Economy Work for All*, 2007, available at www.imf.org/external/pubs/ft/ar/2007/eng/pdf/ar07_eng.pdf.

13. *The Economist*, "So Near and Yet So Far: Trade Ministers Have Come Too Close to a Deal to Let the Doha Round Die," July 31, 2008, available at www.economist.com/opinion/displaystory.cfm?story_id=11848231.

14. Rice and Patrick, *Index of State Weakness*, p. 4.

15. Rice, "The Threat of Global Poverty," *The National Interest* (Spring 2006): 76–82.

16. Ibid.

17. United Nations, *United Nations Millennium Declaration*, A/RES/55/2, September 18, 2000, available at www.un.org/millennium/ and United Nations, *Monterrey Consensus of the International Conference on Financing for Development*, final text of agreements and commitments adopted at the International Conference on Financing for Development, Monterrey, Mexico, March 18–22, 2002, A/CONF.198/11, 2003, available at www.un.org/esa/ffd/monterrey/MonterreyConsensus.pdf.

18. *Monterrey Consensus*, p. 14.

19. The World Bank revised its estimates of the global poverty level in August 2008 from less than $1 a day to less than $1.25 a day. The new estimate reflects improvements in internationally comparable price data. The new estimates continue to assess world poverty by the standards of the poorest countries. The new line of $1.25 for 2005 is the average national poverty line for the poorest ten to twenty countries. She Shaohua Chen and Martin Ravallion, "The Developing World Is Poorer than We Thought, but No Less Successful in the Fight against Poverty," World Bank Policy Research Working Paper 4703 (World Bank Development Research Group, August 2008).

20. Brainard, *Saving for the 21st Century*, 2006.

21. NIC, *Mapping the Global Future*, pp. 47–51.

22. Dervis, *Perspectives on the New Structure of the World Economy*, On the Occasion of the Annual Commencement Day Lecture of the Export-Import Bank of India (Mumbai, India, March 18, 2008), p. 21 of transcript.

23. World Bank, "World Development Indicators 2008" (International Bank for Reconstruction and Development, 2008), p. 317, available at http://siteresources.worldbank.org/DATASTATISTICS/Resources/WDI08_section6_intro.pdf.

24. Lawrence Summers, "A Strategy to Promote Healthy Globalization," *Financial Times*, May 4, 2008, available at www.ft.com/cms/s/0/999160e6-1a03-11dd-ba02-0000779fd2ac.html.

25. Ibid.

26. *The Economist*, "World Risk: Alert—Global Downturn Will Test Asian Resilience," Country Briefing (London: Economist Intelligence Unit, Economist Group, March 28, 2008).

27. Arvind Panagariya, "India's Growing Economy: Song of the Crossroads," *Hindustan Times*, February 18, 2008, available at www.hindustantimes.com/StoryPage/Print.aspx?Id=898935f6-fbc8-4849-927a-c483c5c43a31Budget200809_Special.

28. IMF, *Regional Economic Outlook: Sub-Saharan Africa* (October 2007), p. 55.

29. "These days, industrialists in India mostly want protection against imports from China, not the United States. Perhaps the biggest loser from India's and China's resistance to lower farm tariffs was the agricultural powerhouse Brazil. The North-

South frame of the Doha negotiations ignored these cleavages," in "The Next Step for World Trade," *New York Times*, August 2, 2008, Opinion Section, available at www.nytimes.com/2008/08/02/opinion/02sat1.html.

30. Robert Zoellick, *A Challenge of Economic Statecraft*, speech at the CGD, April 2, 2008.

31. Under the most recent classification of MICs (as all countries eligible to borrow from the International Bank for Reconstruction and Development [IBRD], including India), nearly 70 percent of the world's poor live in MICs. See IBRD/The World Bank, *Development Results in Middle-Income Countries: An Evaluation of the World Bank's Support,* 2007, available at http://siteresources.worldbank.org/EXTMIDINCCOU/Resources/MIC_evaluation.pdf. Note that these figures were calculated before the World Bank released a new global poverty line. For middle income countries, though, the median poverty line of $2 per day is still suitable. See World Bank, "New Data Show 1.4 Billion Live on Less than U.S. $1.25 a Day, but Progress against Poverty Remains Strong," Press Release 2009/065/DEC, August 26, 2008.

32. Robin Broad and John Cavanagh, "The Hijacking of the Development Debate: How Friedman and Sachs Got It Wrong," *World Policy Journal* (Summer 2006): 21–30.

33. World Bank and IMF, *Global Monitoring Report, 2008* (April 2008), p. 11.

34. Jeffrey Sachs, "Hitting the Target," Words into Action, Development Agenda, UN Millennium Project, no date, available at www.unmillenniumproject.org/documents/Hitting-the-Target_IMF_WorldBank_Sep06.pdf.

35. Sachs, *The End of Poverty: Economic Possibilities for Our Time* (Penguin, 2005).

36. Homi Kharas, *Trends and Issues in Development Aid* (Wolfensohn Center for Development, Brookings, November 2007), p. 1.

37. Ibid.

38. Lael Brainard, ed., *Security by Other Means* (Brookings and Center for Strategic and International Studies, 2007).

39. Kharas, *Trends and Issues*, pp. 12–13.

40. Ibid., p. 11.

41. Commission for Africa, *Commission for Africa Report: Our Common Interest* (Commission for Africa, March 11, 2005), pp. 102–08.

42. Larry Diamond, "The Democratic Rollback: The Resurgence of the Predatory State," *Foreign Affairs,* March/April 2008, available at www.foreignaffairs.org/20080301faessay87204/larry-diamond/the-democratic-rollback.html.

43. Ibid.

44. See Department for International Development (DFID), *Why We Need to Work More Effectively in Fragile States* (London: DFID, January 2005), available at www.dfid.gov.uk/Pubs/files/fragilestates-paper.pdf.

45. Note these figures are likely to change based on the new global poverty line of less than $1.25 a day. The Institute for State Effectiveness, "Development Effectiveness in Situations of Fragility and Conflict," forthcoming.

46. Daniel Kaufmann, "10 Myths about Governance and Corruption," *Finance and Development,* September 2005, available at www.imf.org/external/pubs/ft/fandd/2005/09/basics.htm.

47. Ibid.

48. Robert Barro, *Determinants of Economics Growth: A Cross-Country Empirical Study* (MIT Press, 1997).

49. Daniel Kaufmann, Aart Kraay, and Massimo Mastruzzi, "Governance Matters VII: Aggregate and Individual Governance Indicators, 1996–2007," World Bank Policy Research Working Paper 4654, June 24, 2008, available at http://papers.ssrn.com/sol3/papers.cfm?abstract_id=1148386

50. Data found at www.freedomhouse.org and in Rice and Patrick, *Index of State Weakness,* p. 13.

51. Larry Diamond, *The Spirit of Democracy: The Struggle to Build Free Societies Throughout the World* (New York: Times Books, 2008).

52. The Community of Democracies, 2007 Bamako Ministerial Consensus, "Democracy, Development and Poverty Reduction," available at www.un.org/democracyfund/Docs/Bamako_consensus.pdf.

53. See www.mcc.gov.

54. Examples include the World Bank, the IMF, the WTO, the UNDP, the OECD, the Financing for Development Office on the Monterrey Consensus, the Millennium Project, the MDG Monitor created by UNDP and the UN Department of Economic and Social Affairs (DESA), and subelements of numerous agencies such as the UN Children's Fund (UNICEF), the UN Food and Agriculture Organization (FAO), the UN International Labor Organization (ILO), and the World Health Organization (WHO).

55. The idea of a poverty clock was first put forward by our colleague Homi Kharas, senior fellow in the Global Development Program at the Brookings Institution.

56. Colin Bradford and Johannes Linn, *Reform of Global Governance: Priorities for Action* (Brookings, October 2007).

57. Brett House, David Vines, and W. Max Corde, *The International Monetary Fund: Retrospect and Prospect in a Time of Reform* (February 6, 2008). An earlier version is forthcoming in *The New Palgrave Dictionary of Money and Finance.*

58. Lex Rieffel, "The IMF and the World Bank: It's Time to Separate the Conjoined Twins," Global Economy and Development Working Paper (Brookings, September 2008), available at www.brookings.edu/~/media/Files/rc/papers/2008/09_global_governance_rieffel/09_global_governance_rieffel.pdf.

59. Wing Thye Woo, "Understanding the Sources of Friction in U.S.-China Trade Relations: The Exchange Rate Debate Diverts Attention Away from Optimum Adjustment," *Asian Economic Papers* 7, no. 3 (Fall 2008).

60. "Freer Trade Is under Threat but Not for the Usual Reasons," *The Economist,* U.S. ed., October 9, 2008, available at www.economist.com/specialreports/displaystory.cfm?story_id=12373720.

61. These twenty trade areas were identified by *The Economist* in "So Near and Yet So Far: Trade Ministers Have Come Too Close to a Deal to Let the Doha Round Die," July 31, 2008.

62. John L. Thornton, "Presidential Candidates Should Address Globalization's Challenges," *Post and Courier Charleston,* January 14, 2008, Features Section, available at www.charleston.net/news/2008/jan/14/presidential_candidates_should_address_g27505/.

63. For U.S. TAA benefits, see www.doleta.gov/tradeact/benefits.cfm#2.

64. Lael Brainard, "New Economy Safety Net: A Proposal to Enhance Worker Adjustment Programs," *Democracy: A Journal of Ideas* 8 (Spring 2008), available at www.brookings.edu/articles/2008/spring_economic_security_program_brainard.aspx.

65. Kimberly Ann Elliott, "Trade Policy for Development: Reforming U.S. Trade Preferences," CGD Brief (Washington: CGD, August 2007).

66. Ibid.

67. World Bank and IMF, *Global Monitoring Report, 2008*, pp. 9–11.

68. Ibid.

69. Recommendations from the UN Millennium Project, "Investing in Development: A Practical Plan to Achieve the MDGs" (UNDP, 2005).

70. See www.whitehouse.gov/omb/budget/fy2009/.

71. Steven Kosiak, "FY 2009 Request Would Bring DoD Budget to Record (or Near-Record) Levels," Center for Strategic and Budgetary Assessments Update, February 4, 2008, available at www.csbaonline.org/4Publications/PubLibrary/U.20080204. FY_2009_Request/U.20080204.FY_2009_Request.pdf.

72. See www.oecd.org/dataoecd/27/34/40381949.xls.

73. In *The Spirit of Democracy* (p. 33), Diamond argues that no less than 80 percent of the public in every region of the world believes that democracy is the best political system.

74. United Nations, *Monterrey Consensus,* paragraph 4.

75. United Nations, *Millennium Declaration,* paragraph 5.

CHAPTER TEN

1. It is emblematic of the region that even its geographical designation is controversial. In the period following the Sykes-Picot Agreement in 1916, the term "Near East" was used for the desert region that stretched from the Persian Gulf to the Levant Coast. In post–World War II usage, the "Middle East" was used either to describe the same region or to refer only to those states that shared the Levant Coast, that is, Lebanon, Syria, Jordan, Egypt, and Israel. In official UN usage, "Western Asia" is the terminology of choice, a designation that encompasses not only the Levant and the Gulf states but also Pakistan and Afghanistan. In contemporary American usage, the term "greater Middle East" has the same connotation, minus Pakistan. In this book, we use "Middle East" to refer to the Levant states and the Gulf and use "broader Middle East" sparingly to encompass Afghanistan, where the conflict is tied in important ways to the broader region.

2. James A. Baker III and Lee H. Hamilton, *The Iraq Study Group Report: The Way Forward—A New Approach* (New York: Vintage, 2006). Baker and Hamilton were co-chairs of the Iraq Study Group.

3. See Department of State, "A Performance-Based Roadmap to a Permanent Two-State Solution to the Israeli-Palestinian Conflict," April 30, 2003 (www.state.gov/r/pa/prs/ps/2003/20062.htm [October 16, 2008]); UNSC Resolution 1397 can be accessed at www.state.gov/p/nea/rt/11134.htm and UNSC Resolution 1515 at www.state.gov/p/nea/rt/95541.htm.

4. Elaine Sciolino, "Nuclear Panel Votes to Report Tehran to U.N.," *New York Times,* February 5 2006, section 1, p. 1.

5. Mark Mazzetti and Thom Shanker, "Arming Hezbollah Reveals U.S. and Israeli Blind Spots," *New York Times*, July 19, 2006; Steven Erlanger, "Iran Pledges Money to Hamas-Led Palenstinian Authority," *New York Times*, February 22, 2006.

6. Vali Nasr argues this powerfully in *The Shia Revival: How Conflicts within Islam Will Shape the Future* (New York: Norton, 2006).

7. That was reflected most vividly at an international diplomatic conference hosted by Italy and held in Rome in June 2006, against the backdrop of the outbreak of open war between Hezbollah and Israel (and simultaneously the kidnapping of an Israeli soldier in Gaza, apparently by a terrorist group backed by Syria and Iran). During the conference, Arab governments forcefully called for an immediate end to hostilities, most blaming Israel—although Saudi Arabia broke with tradition and publicly fingered Hezbollah as having caused the crisis. Every single Arab government at the Rome conference, however, used its private meetings with U.S. Secretary of State Condoleezza Rice and UN Secretary General Kofi Annan to stress that Israel should not be stopped until Hezbollah had been destroyed or at least until its infrastructure was dismantled. This is based on Bruce Jones's confidential interviews of members of Annan's and Rice's delegations in Rome.

8. This is based on Jones's confidential interviews of members of Annan's and Rice's delegations in Rome.

9. National Intelligence Council, "Iran: Nuclear Intentions and Capabilities," November 2007 (www.dni.gov/press_releases/20071203_release.pdf).

10. Associated Press, "Jordan's King Abdullah II Wants His Own Nuclear Program," *USA Today*, January 19, 2007 (www.usatoday.com/news/world/2007-01-19-jordan-nukes_x.htm [October 23, 2008]); Michael Slackman and Mona El-Naggar, "Mubarak's Son Proposes Nuclear Program," *New York Times*, September 19, 2006, section A, p. 14; William J. Broad and David E. Sanger, "With Eye on Iran, Rivals Also Want Nuclear Power," *New York Times*, April 15, 2007, section 1, p. 1.

11. World Nuclear Association, "Emerging Nuclear Energy Countries," July 2008 (www.world-nuclear.org/info/inf102.html).

12. Helene Cooper, "Rice under Pressure in Trip to Turkey," *New York Times*, November 3, 2007 (www.nytimes.com/2007/11/03/world/europe/03Turkey.html?scp=1&sq=Rice%20Under%20Pressure%20in%20Trip%20to%20Turkey&st=cse [October 23, 2008]).

13. Pew Global Attitudes Project, "Global Unease with Major World Powers: Rising Environmental Concern in 47-Nation Survey," June 27, 2007 (http://pewglobal.org/reports/display.php?ReportID=256 [October 23, 2008]).

14. For a full discussion of the impact of wealth and inequality in the Middle East on political tensions, see Tamara Cofman Wittes, *Freedom's Unsteady March: America's Role in Building Arab Democracy* (Brookings, 2008).

15. IMF data are available at www.imfstatistics.org/imf; Nimrod Raphaeli and Bianca Gersten, "Sovereign Wealth Funds: Investment Vehicles for the Persian Gulf Countries," *Middle East Quarterly* 15, no. 2 (Spring 2008): 45–53.

16. For a discussion of the political and security implications of economic inequality and political constraints in the Middle East, see Kenneth Pollack, *A Path out of the Desert: A Grand Strategy for America in the Middle East* (Brookings, 2008).

17. Wittes, *Freedom's Unsteady March*.

18. Ibid.

19. Navtej Dhillon, "Boosting Smart Power: The Role of the United States in the Middle East" (Brookings, February 22, 2008).

20. Ibid.

21. Pew Global Attitudes Project, "Global Unease with Major World Powers."

22. Not, it should be recalled, a majority; a majority of the population voted for Fatah and formerly affiliated parties that had split from the main body of Fatah before the election. By running multiple candidates in several voting districts, Fatah split its own vote, leading to electoral victory for Hamas.

23. Virginia Page Fortna, "Does Peacekeeping Keep Peace? International Intervention and the Duration of Peace after Civil War," *International Studies Quarterly* 48, no. 2 (June 2004): 269–92.

24. The European Union—an emerging peacekeeper—has also deployed civilian monitors in Gaza, including along the Israel-Gaza-Egypt border. EU Border Assistance Mission Rafah is perhaps more significant as an expression of the perennial EU search for relevance in the region than it is in operational terms. Nonetheless, the mission reflects the broadening menu of operational capabilities that may be relevant in future conflict management efforts in the region.

25. Yakov Katz, "Deployment Diplomacy," *Jerusalem Post*, February 22, 2008, p. 13.

26. Controversy has arisen around two issues. First, some UNRWA employees (there are almost 20,000 Palestinian employees in the West Bank and Gaza alone) have been affiliated with political parties that are in turn affiliated with terrorist organizations. Second, UNRWA employees have on occasion been accused—but not successfully prosecuted—for collaboration with such groups as Fatah. By and large, however, Israel has maintained that the UNRWA's operations are humanitarian in nature and function not only in the Palestinian interest but in the Israeli interest as well. The United States and the UNRWA's major donors have generally supported that position.

27. See U.S. Department of State, "Middle East Partnership Initiative" (http://mepi.state.gov/ [October 3, 2008]).

28. UNDP, *Arab Human Development Report* (Oxford University Press, 2002).

29. Steve Heydemann, "Upgrading Authoritarianism in the Arab World," Saban Center, Brookings Institution, October 2007 (www.brookings.edu/papers/2007/10arabworld.aspx [October 23, 2008]).

30. The text of the Clinton parameters can be found at www.peacelobby.org/clinton_parameters.htm; see also Rob Malley and Hussein Agha, "The Road from Mecca," *New York Review of Books* 54, no. 8, May 10, 2007; Dennis Ross, *The Missing Peace: The Inside Story of the Fight for Middle East Peace* (New York: Farrar, Straus and Giroux, 2005); and Martin Indyk, *Innocent Abroad: An Intimate History of American Peace Diplomacy in the Middle East* (New York: Simon and Schuster, forthcoming 2009).

31. Doris Buddenberg and William Byrd, *Afghanistan's Drug Industry: Structure, Functioning, Dynamics, and Implications for Counter-Narcotics Policy* (UNODC and the World Bank, 2006) (www.unodc.org/pdf/afg/publications/afghanistan_drug_industry.pdf [October 23, 2008]).

32. See note 10.

33. For the evolution of the debate over this proposal, see Martin Indyk, "The Post-War Balance of Power in the Middle East," in *After the Storm: Lessons from the*

Gulf War, edited by J. S. Nye and R. K. Smith (Lanham, Md.: Madison Books, 1992); Ronald D. Asmus and others, "A Transatlantic Strategy to Promote Democratic Development in the Broader Middle East," *Washington Quarterly* 28, no. 2 (Spring 2005): 7–21; G. John Ikenberry and Anne-Marie Slaughter, "Forging a World of Liberty under Law: U.S. National Security in the 21st Century," Final Report of the Princeton Project on National Security, September 27, 2006 (www.princeton.edu/~ppns/report/FinalReport.pdf [October 23, 2008]); and Marc Grossman, "A Middle East Final Act?" Opinion, German Marshall Fund, June 2008.

34. In 1994, the CSCE became the Organization for Security and Cooperation in Europe (OSCE).

35. Although the fact has received little attention, both sides presented draft maps of their proposals for a territorial settlement during the Taba negotiations in December 2000 and January 2001. The Israeli map showed 97.1 percent of the current territory of the West Bank and Gaza remaining in Palestinian hands; the Palestinian map showed 97.8 percent remaining in their hands. The main difference in the maps was the question of Israeli sovereignty in the lands surrounding roads that link Ma'aleh Adumim, a major settlement, to Jerusalem. From field notes of Bruce Jones, 2000 and 2001.

36. Sheikh Hamid bin Jassim of Qatar, speaking at the U.S.-Islamic World Forum, February 16, 2008.

CHAPTER ELEVEN

1. Robert Kagan, "History's Back: Ambitious Autocracies, Hesitant Democracies," *Weekly Standard* 13, no. 26 (August 25, 2008).

2. Richard N. Haass, "The Age of Nonpolarity: What Will Follow U.S. Dominance," *Foreign Affairs* 87, no. 3 (May/June 2008): 56, and Fareed Zakaria, *The Post-American World* (New York: W. W. Norton, 2008), pp. 242–44.

3. A League of Democracies was proposed by John McCain, "Senator McCain Addresses the Hoover Institution," May 1, 2007, and can be downloaded at www.cfr.org/publication/13252/. A Concert of Democracies was proposed by G. John Ikenberry and Anne-Marie Slaughter, co-directors, *Forging A World of Liberty under Law: U.S. National Security in the 21st Century: Final Report of the Princeton Project on National Security* (Princeton: Woodrow Wilson School of Public and International Affairs, September 27, 2006), and Ivo Daalder and James Lindsay, "Democracies of the World, Unite," *The American Interest,* January/February 2007.

4. Ivo Daalder and James Lindsey, "The Debate Continues," *The American Interest,* March/April 2007, p. 138.

INDEX